ESCAPE TO FREEDOM

ESCAPE TO FREEDOM

The Real-Life Events of One Man's
Relentless Pursuit for Freedom

Generations Strong Book 1

ALOIS HUF
and CRISTIE JO HUF JOHNSTON

Library of Congress Catalog-in-Publication data available upon request.

ISBN 978-1-952257-00-1 (paperback)
ISBN 978-1-952257-01-8 (ePub)
ISBN 978-1-495620-46-1 (Kindle)
ISBN 978-1-952257-02-5 (audio)

Manufactured in the United States of America.

The late Mr. and Mrs. Charles and Lillie Edna Lukesh

We are eternally grateful for the compassion and commitment of two selfless, caring people who shared Jesus with us, so we continue the legacy of Generations Strong in Christ. You both will shine in our hearts and the heavens forever.

Those who are wise will shine as bright as the sky, and those who lead many to righteousness will shine like the stars forever.

—Daniel 12:3 (NLT)

Alois and Poldie Huf's eighteen years of volunteer service to men and women incarcerated in the Ottawa County Jail in West Olive, Michigan, inspired their six children to donate the first one thousand copies of *Escape to Freedom: The Real-Life Events of One Man's Relentless Pursuit for Freedom* free of charge to the inmates in thirty-four different Michigan county jails upon its release in 2020. The distribution was done via Forgotten Man Ministries and their dedicated, faithful chaplains (www.forgottenman.org).

If you would like to provide *Escape to Freedom* to the men and women incarcerated in your county, state, nation, or country, your tax-deductible gift will be designated in its entirety for the same purpose.

For more information, contact the following:

Intentional God Ministries
1708 Spring Green Blvd.
Ste. 120 #25
Katy, TX 77494

Phone: 713-487-6511
escapetofreedombook.com

Also, if you are interested in Alois and Poldie's CD, *Glorious Old Hymns*, you can listen to or download all twelve songs for free on the escapetofreedombook.com website.

CONTENTS

Map 1. The town of Cheb, where Alois escaped into Germany. Source: Lencer
/ CC-BY-SA-3.0, https://commons.wikimedia.org/wiki/File:Czech_Republic
_location_map.svg.

Acknowledgments

Blessed be the God and Father of our Lord Jesus Christ, who according to His abundant mercy has begotten us again to a living hope through the resurrection of Jesus Christ from the dead, to an inheritance incorruptible and undefiled and that does not fade away, reserved in heaven for you.

—1 Peter 1:3, 4

Thank you . . .

To the lovely Lord Jesus Christ, who is our eternal hope.

To our children, grandchildren, and great-grandchildren, who inspire us to raise a family Generations Strong for God.

To our son-in-law Jerry Johnston, who gave us multiple opportunities to share our story on platforms across America and planned and produced our *Glorious Old Hymns* recording.

To our daughter Cristie Jo, who, sparked by the curiosity of our life story, inspired the dream for us to put pen to paper and write so that subsequent generations will become strong. Throughout the twenty-year project, she turned the dream into reality with constant encouragement and a relentless game plan that produced this book. We thank Cristie Jo for her painstaking research to tell our story in vivid detail.

To our grandchildren, Betsy VanderBrink and Josh Kramer, for collating the original handwritten notes to document form.

To Elizabeth York, who provided helpful submissions.

To Danny Constantino at Scribe Inc., for utilizing his editing skills to further enhance the manuscript. The professionalism he displayed and his attention to detail are unmatched.

To Steve Ushioda, special projects manager at Scribe Inc., who promptly communicated with Cristie Jo, researched some unknowns, and facilitated the process to see this project through to the end.

Alois and Leopoldine Huf

PREFACE

---◆---

Each generation goes further than the generation preceding it because it stands on the shoulders of that generation. You will have opportunities beyond anything we've ever known.

—Ronald Reagan

I believe this quote by Ronald Reagan, the fortieth president of the United States, is one of the most profound and discerning statements ever made. How much influence and inspiration does one generation exert on the next? Are there lessons to learn, wisdom to gain, experiences to engage in, laughter to share, and opportunities to seize? Is it possible for the trials and triumphs of one generation to so immensely impact the next generation, rousing them to take advantage of every opportunity, risky or safe, and see it as a gift beyond anything ever imagined? I believe so, and here's why.

The story you are about to read is true. The principal characters depicted in this narrative endured shattered childhoods and, amazingly, survived evil injustices and post–World War II brutalities. They belong to the Silent Generation, and they were young enough to experience the unforgettable atrocities of the largest and deadliest war in human history. Uncertain what characterized this demographic as "silent," we can only imagine that the preceding generation felt it was best for children to be seen and not heard, or perhaps because of the volatile wartime conflict, it was considered dangerous to speak out, and it would be safer to remain silent.

In this book, they are silent no longer! The main characters are my parents, Alois and Leopoldine Huf, and they speak freely in *Escape to Freedom*, book 1 of a trilogy called Generations Strong. I am honored to stand on the strong shoulders of this distinct generation, allowing the lessons learned to shape me into the person I am today and what I hope to become moving forward. My father and mother inspire me to see the landscape of life through a different lens, a world torn up by terror and trauma but rebuilt by redemption and restoration.

As a young child, I was frequently in earshot of stories rehearsed about their turbulent childhoods. After my husband and I married, we moved away and had three children. My parents often traveled to cities across North America to spend quality time with us. One of my favorite memories was hiding in the hallway adjacent to my kid's bedrooms at bedtime during Dad and Mom's visits to catch a glimpse of them kneeling beside the kids' beds, retelling stories of when they were young. I loved watching my children engage and interact. It seemed natural for Dad and Mom to write a book, so I encouraged them to do so and fill its pages will their epic stories. The idea was first introduced twenty years ago, but the writing did not commence immediately. Honestly, it took root after my husband, Jerry, scheduled studio time for Dad and Mom to record a CD of their music. Yes, my parents sing and harmonize beautifully together. Once the recording was complete, I sat with them at the breakfast table and pushed play on a handheld Sony microcassette recorder. At first, recalling the painful experiences of their early years was difficult and distressing for my parents to speak about. They simply did not know how to express the sacrifices made and the depths of despair they suffered. It was then I realized that this was going to be more difficult than I ever imagined—prompting the silent ones to finally speak up and share openly. The stop button on the recorder was pressed repeatedly, always giving them time to recover after each attempt to formulate their tender, heartfelt emotions. At one point, I remember reaching across the table, taking my father's hand while he wept, and asking compassionately, "Dad, were you suicidal while in the refugee camps?" The look in his aging blue eyes, wet with tears as he responded affirmatively, is unforgettable to me. I'm not sure I had ever seen my father cry like this. While the recordings continued, we pressed pause repeatedly to pray for strength. I sensed my mother was holding back from being totally vulnerable about a traumatic event she encountered at the age of eleven. What was she afraid of? This was unlike the woman that raised me. I experienced my mother's strength on multiple occasions, as she was the rock in our family. At times when Dad was being taken advantage of in business, it was Mom's discernment that uncovered deceitful plans from disingenuous people. Where was that rock now? What about the strength she displayed that I had always been accustomed to? As I probed deeper, her voice became innocently childlike, and her hands began to shake. Within seconds, the tears began to roll down her cheeks. Admittedly, I think this was the first time I paused, taking time to acknowledge that my parents were human. For years, even though I viewed them as strong and steadfast, they were just like the rest of us—dealing with or attempting to make peace with life events that rocked their world.

As the silent ones persisted in speaking up, giving daunting details, I was able to experience an entirely hidden side of my parents' lives that I innocently or carelessly ignored while growing up. Drawing out specifics on what they lived through gripped me. I silently confronted myself with questions like "What in the world was so important or more literally so inconsequential in adolescence that kept you from treasuring the gift of these strong shoulders?" Again, I queried, "Cristie Jo, did you truly learn from them and cherish and love them more every waking moment while they were raising you?" I never recall disrespecting my parents or causing them grief, but looking back, I believe experiences were lost in a relationship that could have been richer earlier on. This was truthfully one of the most tender and emotive times I have ever experienced—reliving my parent's past alongside them.

Within days, there were multiple microcassettes filled with riveting accounts of their shredded beginnings that ultimately transitioned to strong and stable journeys. As the years passed, life interrupted and stalled our efforts to finish writing the book. Frustrated with my busy lifestyle and not having the time to work on the narrative with Dad, I convinced him to continue making notes. He took me literally as he and my mother vacationed in Florida for a month during the cold winter in Michigan, where they live. Dad sat under the awning of their camper the entire month, handwriting his thoughts for the book. When he returned home, he hired a couple of his grandchildren to come to his home and type as he sat beside them, reading his notes. Over the years, I traveled to Michigan on several occasions to assist in fleshing out more of the noteworthy details.

As we raced toward the finish line, the final months consisted of multiple calls and daily FaceTime chats to delve deeper. My parents are new to smartphones and mostly focused their cell phone camera on the top portion of their heads the entire time we chatted. At first, I didn't say anything. In my mind, Dad and Mom had already earned the title of "champions" for withstanding the constant barrage of my daily calls asking permission to rehearse the personal details of the story one more time. It was essential to get the facts accurate, and I did not want to add to the list of concerns by educating them on new technology. I give my parents credit for always attempting to learn, but I sensed the frustration when we were meeting deadlines and emails with document attachments went missing or smartphones were too advanced for them to use properly. Mom always says, "This cell phone doesn't obey me when I touch the buttons on the screen! Help me, what shall I do?" After days of seeing their upper foreheads, I snuck a few screenshots for remembrance and finally mentioned how great it would be to see their faces. We chuckled and decided that FaceTime should be renamed "TempleTime," because only the sides of their foreheads were exposed as we video chatted.

The phone calls were mingled with laughter and tears but always concluded in prayer. Conversations were often monotonous as we repeatedly reviewed timelines, names, and dates. Finally, as a reprieve to bring some happiness into the mix, I requested they speak only German with me on our calls. My father is pentalingual (speaks five languages), and my mother is bilingual. Together, we hooted and howled while I attempted to pronounce unfamiliar German words.

Dad is relatively proficient on a computer, so each new chapter I wrote and rewrote was sent to him by email. He edited every single word. At eighty-nine years of age, he can give the most skillful editor a run for his or her money. One day, Dad left me a voice mail and very seriously said, "Yah, Cristie Jo, you have one big mistake in this section. Call me when you can." Naturally, I was concerned when I heard that stern voice, which I recall hearing as a child whenever I did wrong and was about to be disciplined. When I returned the call, he asked me to hold while he put the call on speaker so Mom could hear. Now I was trepidatious. I questioned myself: "Girl, what did you write?" Dad began reading what I penned about his later years, when he was about to have major surgery: "Dad was scheduled for surgery to remove the goofball-sized tumor from his brain." The three of us immediately burst into uncontrollable laughter. What I meant to write was that my father was having surgery to remove the golf-ball-sized tumor from his brain, but it came out "goofball!" My parents are not easily offended and have always been quick to see the humor in things, making laughter part of every sweet memory.

In spite of the countless comedic distractions along the way, we were finally able to capture the essence of their stories and deliver a rough manuscript to the publisher for copyediting. Since that day, my parents and I miss our daily calls and FaceTime sessions. We still talk most days, but mostly health updates have once again replaced the tender interactions and cozy conversations we experienced.

In the quiet moments since coauthoring this book with my parents, I have had significant time to reflect. It's interesting how my relationship with my parents—especially my father—has come full circle. My father is a parent, but he also included me in the business. That began early on for me; on many weekends during my junior and senior years in high school, my mother woke me early in the morning so that I could be my dad's business partner for the day. When I say early, I mean 4:00 a.m. I'm not going to lie—I grumbled and offered a few choice words under my breath. As a teenager, I had better things to do with my time, like sleeping in, spending hours on the phone chatting with friends, or lounging around for the day. That would not be the case for me; Dad had other plans. He worked flea markets and state fairs around Michigan and Indiana, selling the all-purpose cleaner from his company as well as other choice items. He utilized his time well, and that meant waking early and driving two or more hours so that we could be the first to set up and be ready to sell. After a hard day's work, we packed up the van and drove off, and on the way home, Dad had me count up all the day's earnings. When I gave him the total, he always had me set aside a larger amount than what I deserved and said, "Cristie Jo, here is your cut for the day. Thanks for going with your dad today." Now to be partnering with him in this book is how it has come full circle for me.

My parents' experiences were traumatic, and I cannot imagine what it must have been like for them to go without food for days or to encounter fear so daunting during childhoods. I've forgiven myself for not engaging with them more while still living at home under their roof. And I have also come to appreciate something vital to my own journey. For all the years that I believed were lost for failing to interact with them, I now know that even though I may not have realized it, all along, I truly have stood on the shoulders of my parents—the ones who showed me, mostly without ever uttering a word, that there is a beautiful and yet sometimes desperate world waiting for me to leave worthy evidence of my presence.

I want to invite you to consider your own life as you read their stories. I hope you were raised by parents who loved you and shaped your life. If so, hopefully, you engaged with them more than I did. If not, you can rekindle that relationship. Perhaps reading this book will prompt you to reevaluate how strong your parents' shoulders truly are and forgive them for any shortcomings that stood in the way during your childhood or even carried into your adult life. See them and all of their "silent" experiences through another lens. Helping my parents recount their journey in this project has given me the opportunity to cherish the heritage I have. While not perfect, the atmosphere I was raised in created an environment for me to thrive beyond anything I could have ever imagined if I would but take the risk. My parents never once discouraged me from any crazy ideas I had and always gave their consent for me to at least give it a shot, whatever that was. The one significant value I will always appreciate is that they always played down compliments, hoping to inspire humility, and they played up the dangers of pride and its destructive consequences.

I feel so privileged to have participated with my parents in their book. Every attempt was made to respect my parents' voices throughout the narrative, inviting you in to experience events from their viewpoint. Some of the names were changed when fitting. Dad and Mom are ethical, hardworking, mostly self-taught individuals who possess entrepreneurial skills that allowed them to become successful business owners—thrice. I will always cherish the special memories that are now part of our

Generations Strong story. Dad and Mom taught me that strong people endure challenges, survive, and thrive. Strong people also pass endurance on to others. I learned strength from my father and mother, and I hope to make the moments count within my own family to add to our legacy. I hope that one day, my children will also choose to stand on the shoulders of their parents and view the landscape of their world through the lens of the incredible lesson learned.

As a gift to my parents for Christmas 2019, Jerry and I purchased a place on the American Immigrant Wall of Honor at Ellis Island, where their names will be inscribed and memorialized, honoring them for their journeys to immigrate to the land of the free. I hope that all forthcoming generations of our family line will make the journey to Ellis Island and learn to treasure the gift of Alois's and Leopoldine's strength.

Please join me in anticipating books 2 and 3 as the saga of Generations Strong continues. The second book in the nonfiction trilogy reveals an unexpected twist of fate in the lives of two nineteen-year-olds, sparking a love so powerful, no obstacle could stand in the couple's way as they pursue a dream that takes them places they could never have imagined. The narrative is packed with romance, drama, conflict, heartbreak, and lightheartedness. It is honest and raw. I have anxiously awaited telling our stories. It is a tender account of how my husband and I met and the experiences we weathered to build another Generations Strong heritage.

Jerry and I are delighted that our daughter, Jenilee Johnston Mullikin, is currently formulating years of journal notes and thoughts to bring you book 3. Get ready for a touching and transparent account of love, loss, heartache, and redemption. This is truly a Cinderella story.

A final note of thanks to you for picking up this book and being a part of our story. We hope that in reading about our backstory, you might find some unexpected treasures in your own. Perhaps the vulnerability of our family story will compel you to investigate your own Generations Strong inheritance.

"Let each generation tell its children of your mighty acts; let them proclaim your power" (Psalm 145:4, NLT).

Thank you.

Cristie Jo Huf Johnston

CHAPTER ONE

POSTWAR BEGINNINGS

I n the Austro-Hungarian Empire of the early twentieth century, the land nestled between Western and Eastern Europe stood somewhere between the present and the past, amid a future only the rest of the world seemed to control. Utilitarian wooden farmhouses dotted the countryside, littered with livestock like cattle, pigs, and chickens. Ancient cathedrals and stacked apartments filled the cities, their spires and mansard roofs beckoning the eye to the heavens. Between villages, rolling green hills and forested mountains were lined with a few quiet paths, which were conducive to travelers when the snow melted in the spring. People did things the way they had for centuries—making a modest living, following the Catholic faith, and being loyal to their own.

From 1914 to 1918, everyone felt the rumblings of the First World War. It swept across the Eastern Front (Russia) and the Western Front (France and Belgium). An estimated sixteen million people were killed in the war. The casualties included military personnel and civilians who died directly from war-related injuries, disease, and famine. The future of Central Europe was uncertain. The Czechs, Moravians, and Slovaks were among those placed under the dictatorship of the Habsburg Empire.

At the war's inception in 1914 and continuing throughout, Tomas Garrigue Masaryk, a Czechoslovak politician, sociologist, and philosopher, gained influence among Western allies as a resistance leader advocating for the independence of the Czechs and Slovaks from the Austro-Hungarian Empire. Earlier, while studying in Leipzig, Germany, Masaryk met Charlotte Garrigue, a fellow student who was from Brooklyn, New York. They fell in love and married in the United States in March 1878. Masaryk took his wife's maiden name as his middle name. They traveled back to Europe, where Masaryk taught philosophy at the University of Vienna. Shortly after that, the couple and their children moved to Prague, where Masaryk accepted a position teaching philosophy at Charles-Ferdinand University. There he met one of his students, Milan Rastislav Stefanik, who along with Edvard Benes later collaborated with him to establish the new and independent state of Czechoslovakia.

During the war, Masaryk went into exile, hiding out in many Western European locations as well as the Russian Empire, the United States, and Japan. He began organizing and establishing contacts while campaigning relentlessly for the freedom of his people. In 1918, while visiting Chicago, the epicenter of Czechoslovak immigration to the United States, Masaryk witnessed his influence throughout the city. Chicagoans who were sympathetic to his cause lined the streets to welcome him. They shared affinities with him because of his marriage to an American woman and other significant connections to the US. Masaryk gained an audience with US president Woodrow Wilson. As a result of the critical intervention of Wilson and others, in October of that same year, Czechoslovakia was officially established, and Masaryk was recognized as its first president.

The war years left their ruthless mark on the people. Hardships lingered even after democracy paved the way for a more prosperous Czechoslovakia. Most citizens were still quite poverty stricken and struggling to make a basic living. The country, composed of Czech-speaking Bohemia, Moravia, and the Slovak Republic, lived in peace with its neighbors. From as far back as the 1300s, German settlers and their descendants lived in border regions along Czech lands, numbering about 3.5 million during the interwar period. These sections of land of northern and western Bohemia and northern Moravia became known as Sudetenland in the early part of the twentieth century, and German-speaking people made their homes there. The Sudetenland would later become the basis for embroiled conflict between Germany and Czechoslovakia.

In an eastern Czech village called Drozdov, a young man named Josef Huf met Marie Joklikova. Young Josef was a skilled rough carpenter, but since most people could not afford to build new homes or make use of his woodworking talents, he secured a job working primarily as a lumberjack. Marie's family made their home in Crhov, only a few miles away. Like many girls, at the age of seventeen, Marie left her family to be employed as a maid on a farm, where she cooked, cleaned, and did other similar farm work. While Marie diligently performed her duties on the farm, Josef and other loggers from the small village would hike deep into the dense forest surrounding Drozdov, disappearing from sunup until sundown.

The couple married in 1926, when Josef was twenty-three and Marie was twenty-one. There was no festive celebration or fanfare at weddings. It was merely like the changing of a season; the first one would go quietly so that the next one could begin. The newlyweds moved into a one-room house. Like most families, they were able to obtain a lease to purchase a parcel of land. This property was situated one and a half miles away from the house, and Marie then cultivated the land for food. She had left her position working as a maid because of the demanding hours required to plant and harvest the young couple's property. They planted potatoes and rye, from which Marie made the family meals. From that time on, she would only be available when the local farmers needed extra help with temporary duties.

The Hufs welcomed their first child in 1927, a baby girl named Marie, whom they affectionately called "Maruska." Little Josef, nick-named "Pepa," arrived next. Josef and Marie were elated when another baby girl, Zdenicka, came into the world. She was beautiful and full of life and energy. However, at only six months old, she unexpectedly passed away from supposed crib death. The Hufs were heartbroken at the loss of their precious baby; however, struggling to survive the poverty-stricken existence meant there was little time to grieve. Life had to move on. Shortly thereafter, on March 14, 1931, the couple rejoiced at the birth of their second son, Alois. They celebrated his arrival especially after experiencing so much anguish from losing their precious little girl.

Josef designated an adjoining room in the house for his mother, Grandmother Huf. The children loved having Grandmother so near. She was gentler than their strict parents and had a lovely twinkle in her eye. In earlier years, Grandfather and Grandmother Huf had owned a small village market, selling groceries and alcohol. The children never met Grandfather Huf, as he passed away before their births.

Life progressed routinely for the Huf family until a cold and unsuspecting night in January 1933. Tragedy struck when their home caught fire and began to burn rapidly. While flames raged and smoke swiftly filled the house, Josef grabbed his toddler sons, Alois and Pepa, and carried them out of the burning house. After he set them on the icy ground, scantly clothed and a safe distance away, he jetted back into the blazing inferno to locate his wife. Marie was in shock. Josef carried her to safety while she screamed in a panic, "Maruska!" Where was their little daughter? Hastily, Josef ran back into the burning house and found the child with Grandmother Huf. During the night, she had crawled into Grandmother's bed to snuggle with her. He carried them both out to safety. The family watched helplessly as their home crackled and dissolved into ashes. Josef was grateful his family was saved, but the emotion of the experience got the best of him, and he wept profusely. The local fire department, operated only from manual water pumps, arrived too late. The house and everything they owned was incinerated.

The family smelled of smoke and stood in the cold for what seemed like an eternity. In the early morning hours, Marie's employer, the farmer, arrived with a horse-drawn wagon and offered to transport them to Marie's family in the village of Crhov, eight miles away. The elements took their toll on tiny Alois; he contracted pneumonia, pleurisy, and a high fever. The nearest city was six miles away from Crhov, and the road was filled with almost impassible snowbanks. Still, a doctor made his way in a horse-drawn sled and did his best for little Alois. After treating him with meager remedies, the physician's departing words did not console the Hufs or leave them with much hope about the boy's recovery.

Soon after, the local police made an unexpected visit and took Josef away. The family was shocked and begged for the authorities to reconsider. The neighbors had rumored that he was guilty of setting a match to his own house. The police detained him for three weeks and questioned him repeatedly. Finally, they concluded Josef would have no reason to burn down his house, since there was no fire insurance in place. By the time he returned to his family, Alois was healing. For that miracle, Josef and Marie were grateful.

The Hufs were eager to begin rebuilding and indebted to Marie's employer for inviting them to stay in a room at his farm in the meantime.

Their neighbors protested and said, "What if there is another fire, and it catches our homes as well?" The mayor of Drozdov gathered the neighbors and suggested they cast their vote on whether or not to allow the Hufs to rebuild their house. Josef begged them to be gracious and consent; "Where will my family go?" he asked. "Where will we live?" After some intense negotiating, the neighbors finally agreed to let them rebuild. Josef and Marie took to the task with swift determination. During the day, Josef spent long hours in the forest working while Marie cultivated the land. Evenings presented no time for rest. Together, they labored on rebuilding their home until its completion.

Once again, Joseph created a space for Grandmother. The Huf family continued to grow with the addition of another son, Hynek, and two girls, Ludmilla and Anicka (Anna). Anna was a beautiful little baby, but right from birth, she did not seem at peace. She experienced periods of significant distress and cried almost continually. Alois wondered why his newborn sister fussed so often and seemed to be terribly uncomfortable. Marie struggled with how to calm her precious newborn. When Anicka turned two weeks old, Josef arrived home from work and took the little infant into his arms to console her. She stopped crying immediately, and within moments, the baby gasped and took her last breath. The Huf family was devastated. They had lost another baby girl. It was determined that the cause of her death was neonatal sepsis, a condition where bacteria can enter through the newly cut umbilical cord and cause sepsis or death. Utterly distraught, the family began making preparations for the infant's burial. Alois watched as his father and other family members took the little coffin and walked to the cemetery in Jedli. Marie's heart was once again broken from the loss of another baby girl, and only time would heal it.

That sorrow soon turned to gladness when shortly thereafter, Marie gave birth to their last child, a son named Frantisek. The Huf family was now complete with six children.

As the family grew, so did the homestead. They built a stall on one side of their dwelling in which a milk cow, a few goats, and several rabbits lived. A small barn for straw and hay was attached to the other end of the house. Marie worked extra hours during the summer months to bring in the necessary food for the animals. She and other women from the village ventured into the forest, where, in open spaces, new trees were planted, and grass grew in between the new saplings. They cut down the tall grass with a sickle and then placed it into burlap bags. This allowed for the new plantlets to grow unhindered. The fresh grass provided food for the cow and goats and dried as hay for feed in the winter months. The cow not only supplied milk for the family but also pulled the plow to till the fields. Pepa and Alois, being the two oldest sons, would help their mother guide the heifer and plow as it furrowed the mountainside fields. The task was daunting, as the terrain was littered with buried rocks, making it difficult to till. They worked together as a team; the boys led the cow in a straight furrow while Marie guided the plow. As the animal took periodic rest breaks, the two boys dug up the partially buried rocks from the ground, either tossing them into the grassy knolls nearby or gathering them in baskets.

Inside their one-room house, the humble family cooked, dined, and slept. A metal stove served as both a heater and an oven, allowing Marie to make potato soup, rye bread, and on rare occasions, roasted rabbit meat. After hours of preparation, a meal of cabbage and potatoes, mixed with salt and milk, tasted like the soup of heaven. The cow's and goats' milk contributed significantly to the family's subsistence, and Marie used it to add richness to each meal of washed vegetables. The cream provided nutritious fat essential to their diet.

When Alois turned five, his parents attempted to enroll him in school a year earlier than was accustomed. It seemed to them he was noticeably perceptive. They scheduled a time for Alois to interview with the teacher, who asked him a few test questions. "How many legs does a horse have?" she asked. "Three," Alois quickly replied. The teacher chuckled and sent the family home with instructions to come back in a year. Alois's parents and siblings and even Grandmother Huf teased him for a long time about that three-legged horse.

The children were never allowed much time to play, except for brief rounds of soccer. Each of them completed chores, which felt more like ensuring their survival than merely doing their part. Pepa and Alois were in charge of gathering wood for the family, so the boys would rove into the nearby woods and collect the scattered cuttings left behind by the lumberjacks. One handled the saw and the other an ax. After cutting through several inches of wood, they assembled them into bundles and carried the load back to the woodshed at their home and stacked them securely. Sometimes Alois would play a game to pass the time during his chores; he would count the branches and sticks and imagine that they were unique treasures. This game helped remind him that he was still a child. It was important for the family to have plenty of wood to last through the winter. The wood kept a fire burning in the stove, allowing Marie to provide hot meals cooked from vegetables they harvested and also keeping the family members warm through the night.

Like other youngsters in the village, the Huf children never celebrated birthdays. Instead, on his birthday, Alois was warned by his father not to misbehave so that he would not have to take disciplinary action with his belt. Besides, there was no exceptional food around, and there were no extra funds with which to buy gifts for a celebration. A cake with icing or a toy would have been an extravagance. Having something to eat and a roof over one's head were accepted as gifts enough. Parents were not given to express words of love and affirmation to their children. Children were expected to behave and follow stringent rules and received no pampering or special treatment on their birthdays.

After all, feelings held little value. Parental affection and affirmation did not make food magically appear on a table or keep feet automatically warm in the winter; sensations like hunger and melancholy were best ignored. Children's cheerful sentiments were fleeting; airing feelings was just another luxury no one could afford. Still, when Alois's father taught him skills or when his mother prepared and served a meal, he felt his parents cared and that they were glad he was around.

Every Saturday, the children would help carry a wooden bathtub into the house, and Marie would fill it with several pots of hot water, heated from the woodstove. Each family member would take turns having a bath, from youngest to oldest. It was important for everyone to be tidy and clean for Mass on Sundays. In the neighboring village, the church offered two morning Masses, which proved very convenient for the Hufs because the boys shared shoes. The family trekked to the church in two separate groups. Pepa headed out for the first Mass, and after it concluded, he made his way back on the two-mile walk in time to meet up with Alois, who was part of the second group. Pepa removed his shoes and gave them to Alois. After the switch, Pepa headed home, most times barefoot, and Alois continued to the church. During the summer months, Alois went barefoot. In the winter, he wore foot wraps his father fashioned out of straw.

The Catholic chapel was rustic and cold. The Masses were uneventful and mostly boring for young Alois. In the ice-cold wintertime months, the chilly air circulating inside the unheated chapel would occupy Alois's time during the dull liturgy. He inhaled the frigid air and then exhaled warm puffs back out into the room, watching the disappearing vapor glisten in the sun's rays, which streaked down into the chapel through the colorful stained-glass windows. Most times, Alois sat subserviently during Sunday Mass and watched everything with his azure eyes. Anyone who sat several rows behind them could see tufts of his blond wavy hair. It was often difficult for Alois to focus since he understood little of the Latin liturgy. He often tried to keep his legs from playfully swinging as he looked on from the hard, nippy pew. As the priest would say, "Ad te levávi ánimam meam: Deus meus, in te confído, non erubéscam: neque irrídeant me inimíci mei: étenim univérsi, qui te exspéctant, non confundéntur," he held everyone's attention, his eyes stoically straight, his voice rising and falling with the readings and recitations. It mattered little that no one understood Latin; it was the holy language. This is from the first Advent Sunday as a responsive reading taken from a compilation of Old Testament scriptures from Psalms and Jeremiah. It translates as "To thee have I lifted up my God, my God, in you I trust; let me not be ashamed: neither let my enemies laugh at me: for none of them that wait on Thee shall not be confounded."

--------------------------------◆--------------------------------

Along the southern region of Czechoslovakia, near the city of Znojmo in the Sudetenland village of Gross Grilowitz, lived two families of German descent, and their paths would soon cross. They lived modestly and eventually came together when Johann Kellner and Anna Gehbauer married in 1930. Each of the two families had a long lineage of ancestors going back generations who settled in the Sudetenland reasonably uninterrupted. Johann was an only child for most of his adolescence. When his father passed away, his mother remarried and then gave birth to a baby girl. Anna, on the other hand, grappled with the joys and struggles of being part of an extensive family. In 1929, when Johann turned twenty-four, he asked the twenty-three-year-old Anna to marry him. Their family multiplied quickly with the addition of several children. Little Johann was their firstborn, and shortly after that, they had another son, Anton. The Kellners were ecstatic when their first daughter arrived as the third child in 1934. The couple chose to name her after Johann's half sister, Leopoldine, who held the baby at the christening. The couple later shortened their baby girl's name to "Poldie." In the following years, the family continued to grow with the arrival of Josef "Sepp," little Anna and Erna, and three more boys—Walter, Karl, and Willi.

After the births of the first three children, Johann secured a job working for the railroad company in the nearby Czechoslovakian town of Hodonice, about ninety-one kilometers (around fifty-six miles) north of Vienna, Austria. The railroad provided much-needed housing for the growing family. The house was called the Wachterhaus and sat only about twenty-five feet from the railroad tracks. It had two rooms as living space and a basement for storing coal, which was used for heating the stove. At nighttime, the two living spaces transitioned into bedrooms to accommodate the large crew. And the babies kept coming. When Anna would go into labor with each new child, Johann sent all the children to Frau Mülhausen's house a half mile down the street. The children loved her and called her Gödel, which meant "Godmother" in German. Poldie spent the nights quite often with her. When the new Kellner baby arrived, the children ran home to find Anna in bed with a swaddling baby at her side. Johann and Anna announced to the children, "Look over here! We have a new baby that the stork brought down the chimney." The youngsters gathered around in amazement, wondering about the specifics of how this event happened. Since the house was tiny, most of the children slept in one of the rooms that served as a bedroom. Anna hung portraits of Poldie and her two older brothers above the small wooden beds. Poldie exuded childlike innocence in her framed school picture, revealing a sweet-looking girl with thick, brown braids and curious hazel eyes. Johann, Anna, and Poldie slept in the kitchen. The married couple snuggled together on a single bed and tucked Poldie in on a small cot nearby. A delicate crib sat beneath the kitchen window to cradle each new baby born into the family.

Johann's responsibilities at the railroad were to provide safe passage to trains and act as a coupler. He stood between the boxcars, and as they came together, he guided the link into the coupler pocket. At the crossings during sunset and at night, Johann brought a lantern and ensured the tracks were clear. He had to be available at any moment of the day or night.

Johann worked many long hours at the railroad while Anna tended to the children, prepared family meals, and managed other household duties. Johann's intense work schedule would not detour him from delighting in a particular hobby. He kept a colony of honeybees, which provided a steady supply of rich honey. Poldie and her siblings loved watching as their father worked with the mostly docile bees. One of Poldie's favorite memories was when her father encouraged the children to suck honey directly from the honeycombs taken from the hives. It tasted sweet like candy, and the children devoured it like a dessert. The feisty little insects sometimes retaliated and bit Johann, but he never incurred an allergic reaction from his attackers. Johann fished in the Taja River, a couple of miles from the house, and was also a skilled marksman. The boys liked to fish and hunt as much as their father, making the most of the abundant resources the verdant countryside provided. Each fall, the region's hunters gathered to select a parcel of woods about two to three hundred acres vast. They and their hunting dogs encircled the land and, at the sound of a horn, moved methodically toward the center. As the startled jackrabbits, pheasants, and foxes came into view, the hunters took aim and shot. The dogs bolted to retrieve the downed game and carry it to their masters. Johann's retriever, Tref, was the best-trained dog among the pack.

One day, when Tref was still in training, Poldie accompanied her father as they made their way quite a distance from the house into a wheat field. Poldie was a petite little girl and was always up for an adventure. Her father sent her out a few hundred yards away in the field and instructed her to hide, keep still, and utter not even a sound. She agreed and looked angelic in her dress, nestled in the grain. Johann waited and then turned to the dog. "Tref, die Poldie ist niht do. Geh find sie." (Tref, Poldie isn't here. Go find her.) In a flash and without hesitation, Tref submitted and was immediately at Poldie's side. When she did not move, he began barking to announce to Johann that he had found her. Poldie sat up in the golden grain, waving in the sun at her father while tenderly petting and praising the dog. Tref accepted the affection with many wet licks to Poldie's cheeks. She stood up and ran with Tref back to her father.

In another instance, Johann went on an extended hunt with men from the village. He stopped at the local pub afterward before heading home with his hunting bag full of game. When finally arriving home, he wanted to show Anna the giant jackrabbit he shot that day, but he realized it must have fallen out of his bag. He called Tref: "Tref, ich hob dem hase verloren. Geh hols ihm." (Tref, I lost the rabbit. Find him and bring him back.) After only a few minutes, Tref reappeared at the door with the rabbit in his teeth.

The Kellners could not afford toys for their children; however, once, Poldie's mother fashioned a rag doll from an old sock and some yarn and gave it to her, which was a welcomed companion. The children's playground was often the railroad tracks. Sometimes the boys would lie down on the tracks and pretend they were waiting for a train to barrel down, almost daring the locomotive to test their patience. It made Poldie incredibly uneasy because she did not want anyone to get hurt, and so she refused to play.

The liveliest times at home were when the family played a popular board game called *Mensch Ärgere Dich Nicht* (Do not get angry). Family members would gather around a wooden board and take turns throwing the dice. Each player had a colored peg, and the goal was to move clockwise around the wooden cross-shaped board. If a player overtook another player's peg, then the first player's peg would be sent back to the starting position. Their mother, Anna, was extremely competitive and hated to lose. She would get delightfully indignant, and the children thought it was especially funny to displace one of her pegs.

The family frequently traveled to Vienna to visit Anna's many relatives. The cosmopolitan city seemed to go on forever; in Poldie's eyes, the centuries-old structures of the city were each castles unto themselves. Relatives' homes were the sites for family camaraderie; Poldie's cousins loved having the extra playmates. Once, when the children were in the middle of a game of hide-and-seek, Poldie jumped down from a picket fence, and her foot got lodged within the boards. Her body swung to the ground, and her head hit the concrete violently. Sepp attempted to wake her, but she was unresponsive. After several tries, Poldie regained consciousness and began convulsing. Hastily, her mother and aunt tucked her in a baby buggy and wheeled her to the local doctor. Poldie suffered from a serious concussion. It took some time before Poldie was well enough to walk again. The family continued to keep a close eye on her, monitoring her progress. She suffered from headaches and poor balance and coordination for a time and ongoing headaches for her entire life.

As the oldest daughter, Poldie was required to take on extra responsibilities for the family. Every Saturday, she swept the dirt yard outside with a special rake-like broom her father made from thin tree limbs. Poldie deeply desired to please her parents and make them proud. It thrilled her when her mother was delightfully contented with her attempts at the housework. She would clean the dirty floors, which was quite the task for a young girl, but the anticipation of satisfying her mother made the work tolerable. Before mealtimes, Poldie helped with the cooking. She took the wooden cutting board and pounded veal or pork with a particular mallet to tenderize the meat. She marinated it with special seasoning and added oil to a pan for frying.

Poldie learned to make homemade noodles, kneading the ingredients together and then rolling out the dough into a flat circle. Then she placed a towel across the makeshift clothesline in the bathroom and laid the dough over it to dry. When the dough dried, she cut it into long strips, making noodles for various kinds of noodle soup.

A family favorite was Anna's German potato salad. After peeling a pile of boiled potatoes, Poldie and Anna sliced them delicately, added them to a large bowl, and then mixed in cucumber, diced onion, salt, pepper, vinegar, broth, and parsley. As involved as Anna was with other domestic responsibilities, Poldie was grateful her mother invested the time to teach her how to prepare and cook family recipes.

The Kellners attended Mass only at Easter and Christmas. Poldie understood that she and her family were Catholic, but thoughts about

God or church were fleeting. The occasional Mass was akin to paying one's respects to the dead at a gravesite; it was the proper thing to do.

One day, Johann's mother, Grandmother Kellner, came to live with them. Since he was her eldest child and only son and her health was waning, she knew she needed his assistance. By the time she arrived at their home, Grandmother Kellner was barely able to move about and was very feeble. Tenderhearted Poldie was saddened when she watched her grandmother struggle to pace across the room or when she tried to cut a piece of meat small enough to digest. Anna remained occupied with Poldie's younger siblings, so Poldie became her grandmother's primary caregiver. She bathed and dressed her, walked her to the outhouse, and did whatever errand the elder adult needed. Grandmother would smile at Poldie and sometimes told her stories about her father and his life. When Poldie brushed her grandmother's silver hair and wrapped it into a bun, she joyfully exclaimed, "Oma Kellner, you are so beautiful." She came to love her grandmother so very much.

One unsuspecting afternoon, as Poldie and her brothers walked home from school, a friend met them to deliver the message that their grandmother had died. Heartbroken, the children hurried the remaining distance home, arriving breathless. As they approached the house, they saw the silhouette of Grandmother Kellner through the window. Her body already washed, she was dressed in black clothes and was lying on a board stretched between two chairs. Shortly thereafter, the local mortician arrived to transport Grandmother's remains to the cemetery, where she lay in a cabin-like shed for the customary three-day mourning period. During the funeral procession with her family, Poldie's grief became almost unbearable, as she felt that part of her life was passing away too. Losing her grandmother was, for Poldie, like losing a dear friend.

◆

People in the countryside had vague ideas about the world beyond their region. Having electricity was rare, and there was only one radio in the village of Drozdov. Alois began school in 1937, at the age of six. Alois should have been filled with excitement about school, but instead, he was terrified by the bomb drills amid the German air attacks before World War II began. All anticipation of attending school by the Czechoslovakian children was soon overshadowed by terror. Petrified, the young students were instructed to leave the classroom and quickly huddle around a tree outside the school. They hoped to go undetected and appear like stones instead of people from the view high above.

When the German annexation of Austria occurred in 1938, a leader named Konrad Henlein represented Nazi Party leaders among the Sudeten Germans, who were Czech citizens. He seemed to believe that those of German descent and those of Czech origin could not live among one another harmoniously. He was a Judas of his time; though he kissed the cheeks of his countrymen, he secretly met with German chancellor Adolf Hitler and turned them over to their enemies. Nationalsozialismus (Nazism) spread like a virus into Sudetenland.

Czechoslovakia had a layer of protection; England and France were to defend her in case of an outside attack. But Hitler continued to spread his influence far beyond the borders of his country unchecked. In the end, England and France broke their promises. English prime minister Neville Chamberlain and French prime minister Edouard Daladier permitted Hitler to take the defenseless land of Czechoslovakia. Appeasement would lead to peace, many outsiders hoped.

In 1938, Edvard Benes, the successor to President Masaryk, heard of the leaders' meeting in Munich. He called for the mobilization of all able-bodied men to defend Czechoslovakia. All European men were required to train for military service for two years after their schooling was complete. Alois's father, Josef, was prepared, and like other peers waiting for the day, he would be called on for service. Soon, Josef and the other men in the village would report for military duty. Josef was assigned to a machine-gun position in a unit near the northern border between Czechoslovakia and Germany, about twenty-five miles from home. Marie and the other women from the village visited their husbands when they could, taking them meals and bread.

Sadly, President Benes learned that the English and French reneged on their support for his country. The unexpected and disappointing events after the Munich summit essentially gave the Nazis Sudetenland, but even Benes knew that would not be the end of the take-over. While the countrymen had been prepared to defend their land, Benes sent them home. Their friends had betrayed the Czechs; they were alone. There was no viable choice but to surrender in protest.

Alois stood with the people of Drozdov to welcome his father and the other men back home. It was not a happy homecoming. Many of the soldiers wept in a rare show of emotion when they met their loved ones. The men were helpless to defend their country and their families. Immediately after the Munich Agreement, the German army invaded Sudetenland. Soon, the Nazis broke the terms of the contract and began pouring into Bohemia and Moravia. The Slovaks took a different approach; they announced their independence and asked Hitler to take over the protection of the new state. Since the Slovaks were willing to fight alongside the Germans, Hitler agreed.

At school, a stately portrait of the Czech president was destroyed and replaced with a jade-tinted image of Adolf Hitler, whose eerie eyes seemed to perpetually watch Alois and the other children in the classroom. Even more frightening for Alois and his classmates was when the German authorities arrived at the country school. Their intention was clear: they came to deliver a threat. After isolating the two teachers, they ordered them to warn their students that if any of them heard their parents, neighbors, or anyone else uttering derogatory statements against the German occupation or against Hitler, they were to immediately report them to the teachers, who in turn would notify the Gestapo.

As the secret state police of Germany, even the name "Gestapo" instilled terror and distrust in the adults and children.

Alois found it difficult to understand why the Germans wanted their mountainous land. No one he knew seemed to have much of anything worth any value for the taking. When the children arrived home from school and delivered the alarming message, fear gripped the village. Josef and Marie gathered the youngsters and warned them, "Do not say anything and don't listen to anything. If you hear something, just run away and come home. We must all stay out of trouble."

Once a week, a leader whom the village appointed walked down the main street and beat on his drum. He gave people time to gather and then pulled out a document and would start with "Zprávy jsou . . ." (The news is . . .) He updated the villagers on what was happening in the region and with the Germans. The news updates were always very positive about Germany—how the Nazis were winning and how they were going to make things better in the world. This was because the news that reached the communities was only what the occupiers wanted people to hear. No one dared to make an adverse remark about the occupation outside of the confines of his or her home's four walls.

After the German occupation began, Marie was no longer allowed to keep the supply of all their cow's milk for her family. She could only retain about one quart per day. The rest was confiscated and turned over to the local creamery. In late spring, when the grass and weeds grew faster than the potatoes, farmers needed to cultivate their fields by hand to prepare for a potato crop. Marie needed help, so Josef took two days off from working as a lumberjack to toil in the field. Since the Nazis seized the best resources, they had a vested interest in productivity. When the Gestapo learned Josef had missed work for two days to tend to his crops, officers came and arrested him. They transported Josef to jail and imprisoned him for several weeks, giving him only bread on three occasions. Marie and the children were terrified. They prayed and prayed for Josef's safety and return. The days turned to weeks, and when he was finally released, the family was thrilled.

For meals, Marie rationed their supplies to keep up with the family's needs, as she had done before. She diluted the cow's milk with three parts of water to each part of milk. Alois noticed that the formerly creamy potato mixture was now runny and his mother looked unusually tired.

She would tell the children at mealtimes, "Eat up."

"But, Mother, where is your soup?" one of the children asked.

"Don't worry about me," she said. "I have already eaten, and I'm not hungry. Eat up."

Alois scooped up every drop and morsel from his bowl. He knew his mother was suffering, and he felt very sorry for her. However, he had no idea she had divided her meal portion among the children. To make matters worse, Marie struggled to deal with the extra stress of Josef's and Grandmother Huf's drinking.

After long days of cutting down colossal trees in the forest, Josef wanted to escape from his responsibilities and the occupation. He took much of his earnings and used it to purchase liquor at the store or drank it away with his companions at the pub. He came home intoxicated and belligerent; there was nowhere for him and Marie to go for some privacy from the children during their volatile arguments. Grandmother didn't interfere; grown men were to be left alone. And every few months, she would go on a drinking binge too. Her struggle with alcohol went back to the days when she and Grandfather Huf owned the village market. They were able to keep inexpensive liquor on hand at the store. Grandmother gave in to the temptation far too often. She became a spectacle; people around the village thought it humorous to watch an older woman lose all her dignity, and they laughed at her.

Marie provided meals with whatever ingredients she could muster. She continued to pretend she had already eaten as the children ate their meager portions, but they too were still hungry. Tension filled the atmosphere of the Huf home, and it became a battle zone of conflict. Josef and Marie would not talk with one another for weeks after one of their arguments. But they would carry on as usual, Josef leaving every morning with most of the bread in the house for his daily sustenance. During the war years, families had to survive on minimal rations, and the daily allowance of bread was meager.

Alois struggled with the strain that had entered into their lives. The family could certainly not control the outside world, but couldn't they have a place of peace within their home? In his heart, Alois prayed, "Dear God, if not for this miserable alcohol, my mother's tears would cease. There would be no more fights, and our family would not have to go hungry." He asked, in prayer beyond his years, "God, give me a distaste for alcohol so that I will not be a slave to it, like my father and so many in our village are."

During Sunday Mass, Alois looked around at all those he knew. Forgiveness and avoiding temptation seemed like impossible tasks as they prayed, "And forgive us our trespasses, as we forgive those who trespass against us. And lead us not into temptation but deliver us from evil. For thine is the Kingdom, the power, and the glory, forever and ever. Amen."

One Sunday, when Alois and his mother were returning home from Mass, just the two of them walking hand in hand, Marie breathed in deeply and sighed. "Promise me, lad, that you will not drink." He tried his best to comfort her. "I will not, Mother," he vowed. Alois squeezed his mother's hand, signifying his firm commitment.

Life for the Kellners remained quite the same after the German troops entered the Sudetenland. Most of the Sudeten people welcomed them with open arms; they were all German people, after all. While Johann and Anna did not support the Nazi regime, they, like many, hoped to go unnoticed and to keep living as usual until the world came to its senses again.

The men of military age were drafted into the German Wehrmacht (unified armed forces). But Johann was exempt and spared from duty because by 1941, there were six children in the Kellner brood. Germans called families like his a *kinderreiche familie* (family rich with children).

While the Germans took control of area resources in their methodic pattern of domination, the Kellners fared well partly because Johann was a skilled hunter and Tref was an expert companion. As long as Johann retained a rifle or fishing gear, there was never any shortage of meat or fish. It didn't matter if the Reich claimed the land now; it was Johann's home first, he felt.

Poldie's older brothers, Johann and Anton, were expected to join the Hitler-Jugend (Hitler Youth), but only Johann began the training. He was ultimately spared from full recruitment because the war soon ended. The male youths who were recruited were taught Nazi ideology and taken on scouting expeditions, but soon thereafter, they were trained for the military. Leaders instilled pride in one's health, academic performance, and race, always with an unwavering allegiance to Germany. The group's tan collared shirts were emblazoned on the left sleeve with the same strange, black, interlocking bars, known as the swastika. Their uniform shorts were reminders that the boys still held the lingering innocence of childhood.

One day, when young Johann and Anton were walking together, they passed the mayor of Hodonice. The boys did not salute him by holding their right arms out straight or give him the customary "Heil Hitler." The man summoned their father in a froth of anger. If the boys did not greet him with devotion to the führer the next time he saw them, they would be shot, the mayor warned.

Echoes of the effects of the Nazi regime reached into the Sudeten-land. There were whispers of what was happening elsewhere, but no one knew the extent of it. It wouldn't be until much later that Poldie and others learned of the hundreds of camps and even more subcamps operated by the regime and the millions of people slaughtered. The Jews and Gypsies were taken to concentration camps or killed. Political opponents who crossed ways with Nazi ideology didn't stand a chance in custody. They were incarcerated, treated with extreme cruelty, and never given a trial. The German citizens who publicly disagreed with the Nazi beliefs were removed. Christian clergy members taking their stand against the German rulers were made examples. Most people taken away were never heard from again. Many of the Germans were taught that the camps were simply "work camps." Laborers there were serving to further the cause of the homeland in the war—or so people were told.

CHAPTER TWO

ARDUOUS CHILDHOODS
WHILE COMING OF AGE

The village of Drozdov was like a nest at the top of a mountain spruce. About one hundred modest, single-dwelling homes encircled its center. The road to reach the village was steep, and before World War II, it was rare to see a car or truck making the trek. But after the occupation, the sighting of a vehicle was almost always a harbinger of bad news. At times, Alois and the other children watched the road below from a rocky perch. From as far as half a mile away, whenever a mysterious black car came into view and slowly began scaling the road, the children would run in all directions and yell, "The Gestapo is coming!"

News in the village traveled fast. If anyone dared utter a word of dissatisfaction or spoke out against the Germans or Hitler, he or she was apprehended and taken away. The villagers all nervously wondered, "Whom would they target next?" The black car would then stop in front of a house, and that was the beginning of the end. There was no recourse.

Two miles away from Drozdov lay the village Jedli, which was much like Drozdov. Drivers had to carefully navigate a treacherous climb on a winding road to reach it. However, it seemed as though a Gestapo vehicle managed to scale this terrain to capture its prey before the village inhabitants could scatter. One terrifying week, officials forcibly escorted three men away, the youngest of whom was not yet eighteen. The Schutzstaffel (SS) took them to prison and interrogated them, using a combination of torture and starvation. Within two months of their detainment, the officials brought the haggard men back to Jedli. The soldiers took a small beam and placed it between two trees. Officers forced the men's families and all the inhabitants of the village to gather and watch the men as they hanged them.

News of the murders spread throughout the region. Intimidation seeped into every community, tamping down courage and strangling independence. The Nazis intended to make fighting back more terrifying than living under oppression. Many Czechs did not submit to the cruelty; they joined the underground movement, passing forbidden information, hiding weapons, and looking for ways to undermine the rule of the Nazi overtakers.

On a late May morning in 1942, when the winter had given way to a warm sun, Reinhard Heydrich, who ruled over Bohemia and Moravia as the chief of the police and the deputy chief of the Gestapo, was being driven in his Mercedes convertible with the top down. He was one of the main fiends behind the "Final Solution to the Jewish Question," the plan put together by Nazi leadership in 1942 to intentionally exterminate all Jews, beginning with German-occupied Europe. Even Hitler called him the "Man with the Iron Heart." His cruelty and malevolence were known far and wide. When he spoke, it was as if his soul had departed his body and only a distant record was playing. To the Nazi Party, he was a giant—a tall god who never let his emotions get in the way of the mission.

On that fateful day, as he traveled from his country villa to Prague, someone hurled a British-made bomb at his vehicle. It shattered the car and morbidly injured him; he died several days later. The two Czech defectors responsible for this successful assassination, which was called Operation Anthropoid, were Jan Kubis and Josef Gabeik of the Free Czechoslovak Army in England. They parachuted from a Royal Air Force plane and then hid, with the help of a priest, at the Karl Borromaeus Church in Prague.

The Nazis were enraged at Heydrich's killing and retaliated. They immediately had more than thirteen hundred Czechs executed. The two assailants were discovered hiding in the church, along with more than one hundred members of the resistance, and the SS killed all of them. Then about three thousand Jews were removed from the ghetto of Theresienstadt and shipped for extermination. Joseph Goebbels, Reich minister of propaganda, had five hundred of the few remaining Jews in Berlin arrested. On June 4, the day Heydrich died, 152 of them were executed in a vengeful wrath.

The Nazis were determined to squash anyone who might be sympathetic toward the rebellion. The village of Lidice, not far from Prague, bore one of the most ruthless acts of retribution over Heydrich's death. The SS surrounded the village and began arresting its citizens. The men and older teenagers were taken to a farm at the village's edge. Male residents working in the Kladno mines nearby were also arrested. A firing squad shot the men in groups until more than 170 were dead.

The ladies of the village fared no better; they were taken to Ravensbruck, a notoriously cruel concentration camp for women in northern Germany. Pregnant women underwent forced abortions, other women were gassed, and many more perished by alternate means. The children who remained were confined in a concentration camp in Gneisenau. A handful of babies, approved under Heinrich Himmler's racial guidelines, were sent to Germany to be raised with new names and identities.

When the job was complete, cruel soldiers decimated the remnants of Lidice with dynamite and fire. The same pattern of desolation was repeated in the village of Lezaky and later in Javoricko and elsewhere. Some people were being executed because they shared the same surname as one of the two parachutists. Thousands more people met their deaths at the hands of these executioners.

In the rubble of the settlements, the people who survived this cruelty were in a daze. Where there used to be the sound of activity—laborers working hard, men and women talking, and children playing—there was only the echo of a few birds singing a lonesome chorus in the forest. It was beyond understanding; such hideous things happened in such a beautiful place.

Alois heard rumors of the carnage in the surrounding villages. He wondered what they would do if the Gestapo came for his own family. Maybe each of them could climb high into the dense trees or hide in a ravine. But daily, people continued to live life as ordinarily as possible.

Even amid the poverty, Marie would not allow her children to attend church or school with rips and holes in their clothing. She stayed up late to sew so the youngsters looked presentable. In school, Alois tried to comprehend subjects in a world that confused him. He learned some of the German language and spoke it in halting phrases in class. When school was canceled for various wartime reasons, the children would help at home.

In late 1944, the youngest of the Huf family was born. Josef and Marie named him Frank, and he entered the world suffering from severe asthma. Like those around him, his tiny body was struggling for life against the suffocation of a confounding evil, and the health aliment added to his struggles. The nearest physician was in Zabreh, about six miles away from Drozdov. People took their horse-drawn wagon or sled between the two communities, but the Hufs did not own any means of transportation. Marie wrapped Frank in a tight roll of blankets and made the journey on foot. The doctor utilized a bronchodilator and helped little Frank breathe normally. He instructed Marie to return twice per week until the young boy recovered.

Pepa and Alois took turns accompanying their mother on each trip to Zabreh. They dressed as warmly as possible, and Marie carried Frank for a while before passing him to her companion for a break. When Alois's turn came to hold his ill brother, he looked down at the little bundle wheezing in the cold air and wiggling weakly. Frank squinted up at him, and Alois wished so desperately that he could help his little brother.

Although the doctor continued to treat Frank faithfully, he cautioned Marie for two months that the infant would not survive. After the physician repeated the warning on one of those visits, Marie vehemently replied, "I pray day and night for this child, and somehow I feel that God will heal him." The doctor raised his eyebrows in doubt and spoke again firmly: "This child is not going to make it."

Marie lifted her chin and said with conviction, "Doctor, you do your part, and I will help by doing mine." At that moment, Alois understood fully Marie's love for her children and her devotion to prayer. Even the doctor was surprised by her dedication. She would have done anything for her offspring.

As they left the clinic, Marie and Alois were startled to see a caravan on the road before them. The German troops were marching an endless string of prisoners of war through Zabreh. There were stooped bodies walking as far as the eye could see—thousands of weary people traveling sluggishly. The Germans gave no supplies or provisions to the Russian soldiers they had taken prisoner, and many of them were barefoot. Locals gave them burlap bags in compassion, and the travelers took a fleeting moment to wrap their feet and then kept walking. Some of their extremities were grotesquely frostbitten; many of the walkers hobbled on crutches, while prisoners in better condition would help the others move along. Alois felt as though he was witnessing a horrible dream—some terrible mistake that could not possibly be real. The Germans soldiers did not give them food, but they didn't stop people who lived along the road from sharing it with them. While the villagers had very little for themselves, they still managed to give potato soup and bread to as many of the prisoners as possible. The Russian soldiers were in the worst condition. They were no longer seen to be of use to Russia and were the enemies of Germany. The defeated soldiers were all but lost to the world. If only for a moment, they enjoyed a warm gesture of humanity.

Visibly shaken, Marie and Alois walked the rest of the way home. "Now I will no longer cry to God for Frank to be healed," she said quietly. "If the Lord takes him now, at least I know where he would be. Then Frank would not grow up and be taken as a prisoner of war in some strange land and be treated as badly as these pitiful soldiers."

Alois thought, "Where would I go if I died? Surely I would be guaranteed at least purgatory."

Somehow, after that, Frank improved. Soon, he was able to experience unlabored breathing, and the wheezing subsided. The family was thankful for this small spark of life. Marie called him the "miracle child."

At the start of 1945, signs that the tide of the war was turning came into view in Hodonice. Its proximity to the Austrian border gave residents an even closer look at the goings-on than rural dwellers had. Every week, Poldie and the other children saw trains packed with wounded German soldiers traveling from the Eastern Front on their way to Vienna. She caught a glimpse of those with missing limbs, lacerations, and infections. By the end of February, all the schools were closed and transformed into field hospitals. Poldie felt sorry for those suffering; she wondered when life would return back to normal.

Because the train system was utilized as Nazi infrastructure, it became an Allied target, and German troops began building foxholes near it in case of a sudden onslaught. One day, Poldie was playing by the tracks with her brothers. Since schools were closed and there was no school-work, playing outside was the best diversion for kids upon completion of their daily chores. Then the screams of swooping planes sounded sharply, and several nearby German soldiers grabbed Poldie and her brothers and ducked into the trenches. Poldie and the others could hear bullets pounding the concrete and structures and splitting the ground around them.

The Kellners stopped using lamplights after dark to be as undetectable as possible. Bomber planes were flying by more often as they completed missions around Znojmo. Once, an American or Russian plane dropped a phosphorous bomb close to the Kellners' house. The phosphorous substance would burn the skin and make it difficult to breathe for anyone who was near it. Curious, Poldie and her siblings ventured into the crater left by the massive bomb. They discovered leftover shrapnel and other elements. It proved to be too tempting for the youngsters to walk away, so investigating became a playful activity.

Since the Kellners were a German family, they had access to flour and baking supplies. Anna made plenty of baked goods for her family and for others who needed it. At times, when the trains of wounded soldiers stopped near their house, Anna carried strudels and kuchen (sweet cake) outside to give to them. The recipients were always grateful; the men were pitifully weak and depleted. As Poldie looked out from her house one day, she noticed a train with wounded infantrymen sitting on tracks at the side of the thoroughfare, waiting for an oncoming train to pass. Fighter-bomber planes flew in seemingly out of nowhere and sprayed the train with a barrage of bullets. Soldiers emerged from the train cars, limping and hopping, bleeding and dying. Poldie gasped; life ended so quickly.

It was no longer safe for the family to live close to the tracks, so the Kellners secured temporary housing in an underground root cellar dug out into the side of a hill about a mile away. Two large trees flanked the shelter's entrance; a large dark-brown cross with a crucifix stood between the trees, making a Golgotha-like image. To the family, the image of Jesus outside of the cellar door felt like a sentinel—a symbol of peace and protection in a harsh world. Poldie and her siblings descended into the nippy and damp cellar, where odors of potatoes and ground vegetables used as feed for cows still lingered. The children adjusted to sleeping in the wet and frigid space and cooking meals outside. Word began to spread among the Sudeten people that Russian soldiers were approaching their region on foot. While they worried less about bullets raining from the sky, this new threat was just as terrifying. Some of Poldie's friends repeated alleged stories of Russian soldiers who nailed people's tongues to tables out of pure spite. Others feared these deserted men would resort to criminal and immoral ways and force themselves on the women sexually.

As was predicted, after the Germans had moved on, the Russian soldiers marched into their region. Unlike the Germans, who initially had well-nourished bodies in pressed uniforms, the Russian soldiers were famished and filthy. The Russian military did not have the equipment and supplies of its rivals. No one knew how long the men had marched on foot in their own massive country before reaching their destination. After traveling with few reserves, they were as hungry and thirsty as stranded animals. The troops pressed out any remnants of the German rule. Soldiers moved into the schools and buildings and took over houses that had been abandoned by frightened locals. The Russians broke into stashes of anything they could find, and not even underground root cellars were safe places anymore.

Anna instructed her children to hug her tight at all times. If she stepped out of the cellar, she hoped that having up to seven children at a time at her heels would keep the soldiers' darker urges at bay. It seemed to be what kept the invaders away. Poldie was blessed to appear very young, with a small and undeveloped stature and youthful braids; the men did not pursue her.

Johann and Anna hoped that the Russian occupiers would soon move on and the family would be able to leave the cellar and return to live in the Wachterhaus once again. Anna sent Poldie periodically to check on the home. Poldie and her friend, Anna Pfeiffer, would make the trek together and investigate to see that their house was still in good condition.

One day, the Kellners walked together as a family to check on the Wachterhaus. As they approached the partially open front door, Johann and Anna knew something was wrong. Like they had done throughout Hodonice, a group of Russian soldiers had claimed the Kellners' temporarily abandoned home. When the family walked inside, they found the house in complete disrepair. The squatters had left, but the damage they did made them seem cruel and inhuman. The precious photos of the children that Anna had lovingly framed and hung on the walls were smashed and torn in meaningless waste. Anna walked over to the ripped school portrait of Poldie and touched it gently. She began to cry.

There were only a few ripped pieces left of their sheets and blankets. The soldiers cut them in strips and used them to replace their worn-out socks. Other items in the home were senselessly smashed. It appeared the only thing the squatters had not destroyed were the beds in which they slept.

Poldie looked up at her mother, who was still weeping. She felt numb; she could not understand why their home and memories were demolished so carelessly. Johann looked dejected. Everything they had worked for had fallen into the hands of cruel, uncaring men. The family stood silently for a moment to pay homage to the life they used to know and then walked out together slowly and sadly. The war was not yet over, and the Kellners had suffered their own personal defeat.

It seemed there was not an area of life that the war did not touch. Work on the railroad was scarce for Johann during this time, so he was eager when Mr. Gloetzel, a friend of his, asked him to move in with the family and manage his grocery store. The Gloetzel family was especially anxious about the Russian occupation. Their fears were founded; Mrs. Gloetzel and their three teenage daughters were the kind of targets the unrestrained occupiers looked for. Within the store, the Gloetzels had built a hideaway—a room that escaped detection from outside or inside. It abutted a workshop room and was accessible through a small crawl space. That is where they hid during tenuous times. After the

Kellners moved in, Anna would secretly pass food and supplies to the frightened young women when they were in hiding.

The Kellner took over the Gloetzels' living quarters, and the Russians assumed they had been the storeowners all along. During terrifying streaks, when the Russians frequently came around, the four Gloetzel women stayed in hiding for days. Different soldiers appeared asking Johann if any young women were around. They demanded to see everyone in the house. Johann called his small children, and they assembled around him and Anna like frightened little ducklings clinging to the comfort of their parents. Frustrated, the brutes left.

Among the town's intruders, Slovaks and Czechs arrived too and moved into the German houses as opportunities allowed. They regarded the German Sudeten as traitors and Nazi sympathizers, even though the Germans had forcibly entered their land also. Within weeks, a Czech friend of Johann warned him outright. "Hans," he said, "your family needs to leave the Sudetenland soon and go to Austria. Things are going to get bad here."

The Czechoslovakian government, they discovered, had plans to confiscate the belongings of those of German heritage and sell the properties for low prices to other Czechs who were willing to relocate there. The border country was called Grenzgebiet territory. The sins of the Germans would fall on all of German heritage. One more time, Johann's friend, a Czech farmer, strongly advised that the Kellners leave as soon as possible—that way they could avert any potential harm of being forcibly removed, he said.

Johann was devastated, but he realized they had already lost their home. First, the Germans had invaded them, then the Russian assailed them, and now their own Czech countrymen were stripping them of their rights and rejecting them. Johann had made a good life and home for his family, but it was no longer possible or even safe to live there. He arranged for his friend to take his family to the border of Austria, about six miles away. Hastily, the Kellners gathered the few belongings that remained along with their beloved hunting dog, Tref. Each person took only a small bundle of mostly clothing and bedding. Anna prepared loaves of bread for their journey. As they piled into the horse-drawn wagon, they whistled for Tref to hop in.

The August warmth spread over the green land and offered a hint of hope as they traveled south. Poldie peered out from the wagon. She fondly remembered times not long ago as she ran and played outside before the bomber planes circled and the Russians arrived. The caring farmer took them from Hodonice, through Jaroslavice, and then to the Austrian border. Poldie remembered in earlier days going across the border many times to visit family in Vienna. Formerly, border officials treated visitors as casual guests, but now the guards demanded the Kellners turn over their small bundles. As the guards searched for valuables, the family watched in fear. One fear mounted the next, and for Poldie, a group of teenage Czech girls was even more terrifying than the guards. They stood at the border crossing like vultures ready to feed on the leftover carcasses from the war, harassing all wanting to escape into Austria. Poldie watched as they assailed other women and girls and pulled at their hair, necks, clothing, and wrists, looking for anything of value. The soldiers ignored them as they ripped earrings out of crying girls' ears. Poldie was horrified and wondered if she would be their next victim. As her family approached the teens, the girls quickly saw that the Kellners were poor. They had nothing worth stealing.

Eventually, the Kellners were released to travel on foot a bit farther. The family was relieved to be past the border, and although they had very little in possessions, they felt as though their destinies remained narrowly in their hands. Carrying only remnants of their old lives, the Kellners walked a little farther. Johann and Anna spotted a ditch not far from the road that would provide privacy from passersby and a semblance of shelter for the family. They stopped there for the night and opened their bedrolls. Anna pulled out the bread she had baked before leaving and divided it among the children.

That night, Poldie looked up at the sparkling stars peering out between floating nighttime clouds. Was her family homeless now? Would more of the threatening planes come and pellet the ground with bullets and bombs? She looked over at her brothers and sisters sleeping. Her younger siblings would look to her for support and would follow her lead. She knew she needed to be strong for them. At least in the ditch, her family had one another.

———————————————◆———————————————

Marie's brother, the children's uncle Jenda, came to visit the Hufs on occasion. The gregarious man brought with him a spirit of laughter and celebration. He seemed to have an indomitable faith that the world could be at peace. He brought an old silver trumpet when visiting and liked to sing and play traditional songs in Czech and Slovak: "Tecie voda, tecie cez Velecky majír . . ." (The flowing water flows through the Veleckys' land . . .) Alois loved to join in and sing along. It was good medicine for the weary family. Uncle Jenda discerned that Alois liked the jovial and heartfelt stirrings of the trumpet songs. Music was a welcomed outlet for emotion, and its beauty could be created and enjoyed at any time. He showed Alois exactly how to position his lips on the mouthpiece and how to blow through nearly closed lips. Then he demonstrated where to place his fingers on the buttons. Alois quickly adapted to the instructions and played melodious music with the trumpet his uncle gifted him. Alois practiced and played as much as he could, emoting all his thoughts and fears through the brass pistons.

Each week, the war front was getting closer to Drozdov. Alois heard artillery exploding in the distance. From the peak of the village, Alois and other young men gathered to look down into the valley between Zabreh and Olomouc. It was hard to decipher what was happening; there were spouts of dust and smoke from explosions and sightings of bomber planes in the distance. They were uncertain if these were Russian or German planes, and no one was sure of the planes' destinations. Once, as the group talked and observed, they heard cannons being fired and shells landing near a house in the village, killing the occupant. Alois and his companions ran for shelter, praying the trees and the rocks would shield and hide them.

News arrived that the German army was retreating. The military traveled only along the main roads and thoroughfares while bypassing the mountain village of Drozdov. Soon after, the Russians followed on foot and in horse-drawn wagons. A few of the Russian soldiers stopped in Drozdov and asked for alcohol and something to eat. Then they were off again, pursuing the Nazi soldiers.

It was as if the whole region breathed a collective sigh of relief. The Germans were gone. The occupation, the stealing of goods, and the terrorization of residents were over, they hoped. The people were cautiously thrilled. Children had not attended school for many days as the war was ending, but now it was time to return to regular routines. In May of 1945, Pepa and Alois were old enough to attend the high school in Zabreh, six miles away.

The boys remembered Zabreh well because of the days of carrying their younger sibling Frank to the doctor over the steep terrain. It took them two hours each way to walk the distance. When the brothers were finally able to make the trip on a bicycle, they were thrilled. One would sit in front, steering and pedaling, and the other would sit behind, holding on. The last stretch of the road to Zabreh was steep. The pair would push the bike up the hill for about three-quarters of a mile. The country road converged onto the main street of Zabreh.

One day, Russian troops were moving in caravans of trucks past them. One of the vehicles stopped abruptly, and a soldier jumped out in front of Pepa and Alois. The boys looked up at his olive-green uniform and stern countenance. "Davaj samochod! Davaj casy!" (Give me your bike! Give me your watches!), he commanded. Of course, neither of them had a watch. The boys witnessed helplessly as the soldier loaded their bicycle onto the back of the truck and drove away. Afraid, disappointed, and left wondering what would be next, it was back to walking for the brothers.

That August, the Hufs moved from Drozdov to Vikyrovice, about thirty miles away. Josef purchased a government property there that became available after the Germans vacated. Families would make monthly payments to the Czech government for these properties, and the Hufs were thankful for an opportunity to live on the fertile land. Josef was even able to acquire a few horses, which he treasured. They all hoped they could put the pain of the past horrible season behind them.

Alois joined a local marching band that played for festivals and funerals. Shortly thereafter, he and two other members decided to establish their own band. They invited a twenty-three-year-old accordion player to join them. With four instrumentalists, the band was complete, and soon they were accepting invitations to play for various events. Alois, the youngest, was sixteen and played the trumpet. The other two from the marching band were eighteen. One of them played the trumpet, like Alois, and the other played the clarinet. They were offered many gigs because their fee was significantly less than other bands. They relished playing songs like those his uncle Jenda played. Soon Alois purchased another trumpet from a member in the band. He paid the musician five hundred Czech crowns for the instrument. On Saturday evenings, the group members dressed in traditional Czech wide-sleeved blouses and vests and gathered to entertain the locals. Several hundred townspeople came together for dance nights; the ladies stood on one side, and the young men on the other. Slowly, the fellows crossed the dance floor, and each boldly asked a girl, "May I have this dance?" The band played love songs, patriotic songs, and all the local favorites. As a musician, Alois never danced; he was happy to play so he could earn an income to help his family.

After their second day of huddling together in the ditch, the reality of the Kellners' situation became even direr. Anna had already reached out to her relatives in Austria, but they had declined to accept them into their home. "There are too many children," they complained. Poldie thought of the image of Jesus that had stood outside of their former root cellar home; she wished the family had something like that to bring them luck in Austria.

A farmer on his way to work in the fields came by and noticed the group looking lost. He asked what they were doing there. Johann answered the man that they had left Czechoslovakia and had nowhere to go. The farmer looked at the seven children and thought it over in his head. "My wife and I don't have any children," he started. "We do not have much room; we just have a small farm." He continued, "What I do have is an empty horse stable, and it's clean. You could use it if you like."

A horse stable sounded a world better than a ditch. The children and their parents, along with Tref, climbed into the farmer's wagon. They rode with the man south to Guntersdorf, Austria. Just as he promised, they arrived at a clean horse stable. The Good Samaritan put fresh straw on the floor, and they placed their blankets on top of the straw.

Johann searched for odd jobs to provide food for the Kellners. He met the owner of a flour mill and was hired on to clean out ditches surrounding the property. They were large ravines that were catchalls for the Russian soldiers who disposed of every item they felt was waste. Johann worked for the owner for a few weeks and took Tref with him. The flour mill owner was intrigued by Tref's abilities and obedience toward his master and kept a close eye on him. As time drew near for Johann's work to end, the Kellner family still struggled to find enough food. The mill owner had a plan. He asked Johann if he would be willing to trade Tref in return for flour, wood, and a few more days' work on his farm. At first, the offer seemed ludicrous to Johann; it was as if he would be giving up a child. But upon further thought of his family's circumstances, Johann reluctantly made the trade. When Johann arrived home from work without their Tref and the entire family learned of the trade and Tref's new home, they wept, but they came to understand their state of desperation for food. About two weeks after the trade, Tref escaped and returned to the Kellners, wagging his tail and jumping up and down as he excitedly licked every family member's face. He had run away and found his beloved family again. The children were thrilled at the reunion; they hugged Tref tightly, hoping they never had to let him go back. In a short time, however, Tref's new owner came to reclaim the dog. He tied Tref to his carriage and began to pull away. Poldie watched in anguish as their family dog was led away, his tail hanging low in bitter despair. The tears persisted for days, and the Kellners quietly continued to hope Tref would again journey back to them; however, that was the last time they ever saw him.

One afternoon, Anna told Poldie and Sepp to go to their aunt's house in Immendorf, about three miles away. They were to take some of their flour and ask for lard in exchange. The children set out on the country road. They made the exchange with their aunt and began the journey home. Poldie noticed a man following closely behind them, who seemed to be watching them intently. It was a Russian soldier—one of many in Guntersdorf who occupied Austria.

The young man got closer and started speaking. Poldie, barely twelve, looked back. He seemed to be around eighteen years of age. He spoke in Russian, but Poldie knew exactly what he wanted. His intentions were clear. He wanted to rape her. He continued making a strong case and gesturing for her to come to him. Poldie's heart began beating rapidly; she understood the danger. She picked up the pace and walked faster and faster, holding her nine-year-old brother's hand. Poldie replied over her shoulder in rapid succession, "Nichts verstehen. Nichts verstehen." (Don't understand. Don't understand.)

Still, the man followed. Up ahead in the distance was a hill, and the two children saw a horse and wagon at the edge of a field and a farmer working nearby. Poldie whispered to her brother, "Hold my hand tightly; we're going to run up and ask the farmer for help!" Sepp did as she asked, and the man quickly ordered them to jump into his wagon. They could wait there until the soldier left. As the children hunkered down inside the wagon, the soldier persisted in advancing, pulling out his gun and firing two shots in their direction. The farmer stood his ground. In irritation, the soldier finally left.

The children were not sure how long they hid in the wagon. When their guardian was finished working in the field, he drove them back into town. Poldie and Sepp jumped out of the wagon and walked home from there, clinging to the lard while surveying the surroundings at all times for any Russians. By the time they arrived back at the stable, it was quite late. Anna was panicked when she learned what happened yet grateful to be reunited, and they felt safe together again.

As winter came, the stable was no longer warm enough. Their kind host offered the *Wäschekammer* (laundry room). Anna was pregnant with their eighth child, and Johann headed out every day to find work projects where he could. Karl was born in February of 1946. When the whole brood came to the Hollabrunn hospital, they were found out. They were the *ausgewiesene*—the refugees. Immediately, they were ordered by authorities to be transported from Guntersdorf to Vienna by train. The family once again uprooted. From Vienna, a truck driver agreed to take the family to Bad Voslau, Austria, in exchange for Anna's wedding band, which Johann gently slid off her finger and gave to the man.

There, Johann found work on the nearby railroad. The Kellners lived in a house previously owned by a Jewish family. They felt like a wandering pack that had found an empty den. The children could not go to school as refugees in Austria, so they spent much of their days in the city watching the activities of the local people and the Russian soldiers.

The derision they all felt was tangible; they were outsiders. The Austrians rejected the Germans in Austria. News spread throughout the world of the atrocities of the Nazi regime. Although Austria was complicit in many ways, its people wanted to disassociate from the Germans. In about six months, officials told the Kellners they must head to Germany; they could no longer remain in Austria. Escorted by the authorities, the family of ten were corralled and herded into groups with other refugees and ordered to climb into one of a line of cattle cars waiting on train tracks. They felt like they were livestock heading for their slaughter.

Poldie missed home; it had been so long since leaving, and she felt displaced. She pictured what their house initially looked like in Hodonice. She imagined the pretty portraits on the wall before the Russian soldiers destroyed them; she thought of beloved Tref wagging his tail. Her memories were interrupted as the train jolted to a start and began rolling down the tracks. There were many families, including the Brunners, who made the lengthy journey with the Kellners, stuffed into the compartments and processed in and out of many camps along the way.

In the evening, the train made stops, allowing the families to disembark, stretch their cramped legs, and relieve themselves. While the train was in transit, family members ask for loved ones to block others' view while relieving themselves between the battered and stained boards of the cars.

As the train moved slowly from Vienna to Germany, the conductor called for periodic stops to wait along the side rail tracks for other trains to pass. After one of those stops, the train did not move; it remained stationed there for three full days. During that period, the passengers would leave the cars for fresh air but would return periodically for shelter from the elements. The livestock cars had no facilities, and passengers were weak from hunger and the lack of water. Sadly, these dire circumstances took their toll on Anna. Her breast milk dried up, and she could no longer nurse tiny Karl. Several of the families gathered to talk; it was no good to stay on the tracks, hoping they would leave soon. Together, they surveyed the surrounding countryside and decided to set out to see what, if anything, could provide nutrition. Nearby, they discovered a field recently harvested for potatoes. There were a few remnants of the crop remaining. Overjoyed, Poldie and her family gathered what they could find and cooked the vegetables over an open fire. Poldie and her siblings experienced hunger before, but they could not remember getting to the point of such weakness that they felt that faint.

It was time for the train to set out again, and the locomotive traveled a short distance before halting for another extended stop. The children in the cars were continually crying from hunger. Anna caught sight of a steeple some distance away. She and a group of women convened and set out together, journeying toward the marker of hope. Finally, they arrived at the edifice and knocked on the door. A quizzical priest opened the rickety door. Anna explained their predicament and that there was a trainload of families who were hungry and thirsty. In her arms, Karl was weak from crying and had become quiet and still.

The man observed the haggard group with compassion. "When you get back to the train," he said, "the supplies will be there." The women walked back, clinging to every hope that the priest was telling the truth. By the time the halted train came back in view, the women saw Red Cross vehicles parked nearby. They all rejoiced. The famished travelers were refreshed with water, milk, bread, cheese, salami, and fruit. The passengers ate more than they had in a very long time. Anna finally told her children they had eaten enough, worrying they might get ill from the abundance.

Soon the train was off again, rolling westward toward Germany. When the metal wheels screeched to a halt, they looked outside. There were soldiers at the German border, but they were not the Nazis or even the Russians, with their turtle-shell helmets. It was the Americans stationed there who escorted everyone off the train. These soldiers seemed like a force for good, but the amount of help they could give was unknown. Each person received a generous spray of the insecticide DDT to kill their lice. The Kellner kids were petrified and afraid of what the residual white dusting would do to them. The older siblings understood it was for their own good, but the younger ones remained terrified and untrusting.

From there, German authorities took them to a refugee camp in Marbach, deep into Germany. With survival on their minds, the Kellners didn't have time to experience the town's picturesque center, the several cathedrals that surrounded it, and the historic houses that populated the city. One such home dated back 186 years and was where the famous classical poet and dramatist Friedrich Schiller was born. Schiller's close friend was Johann Wolfgang von Goethe, the poet, novelist, and playwright who acquired literary celebrity in his early twenties. But the struggles of postwar Germany would take priority as the Kellners attempted to make some semblance of a home in the camp.

The rooms were like large dormitories. Several families stayed together in a room, each staking out a small space as their own. If someone needed to change clothes, family members used a blanket to provide them some privacy. At night, there were unfamiliar snores of other bunkmates. Mercifully, the Red Cross organization came again with food. The refugees stayed there for several weeks, always wondering what the future held for them.

After about a month, the Kellner family and the others loaded another train, this time arriving at Bietigheim. Now their temporary housing consisted of wooden barracks built by the Germans for their soldiers during the war. The shantytown was outside of the city. Local people were wary of these *flüchtlings* (refugees), who had become accidental outcasts. The travelers looked less and less like themselves as the weeks passed. It was hard to be well kept without proper resources. At home, they had clean bedding, maintained clothes, something to occupy their time, and a school for the children to attend.

It was so ironic to the former Sudeten Germans, who were German by ancestry and language but had lived peacefully inside Czechoslovakia. When the Nazis invaded the Sudetenland, the citizens there were effectually considered Germans. The men were drafted and fought and died alongside their German comrades, as did Austrians and others from the territories nearby. After the war, the rest of the world appeared unforgiving toward the Sudeten Germans. All countries that cooperated with the Nazis or were under their jurisdiction were eager to be rid of any remnants of the Reich. For people from the Sudetenland, former countrymen saw them as traitors for merely being of German descent. For Germans, the temporary countrymen went back to being foreigners. And many of the Germans were full of poison for the outsiders. It was confusing for Poldie to comprehend. Why did her family and others like them have to carry the guilt of the Nazis?

As refugees, the Kellners became accustomed to being moved every few weeks and enduring the scorn of others in the camps where they were detained. Throughout this burdensome ordeal, they reminded themselves that they were the lucky ones. From camp to camp, they made do with what little they possessed and, in the evenings, joined along with other families singing and dancing to pass the time. Poldie loved watching her father dance. He was quite the dancer and often took Poldie and her siblings in his arms for a spin or two, performing the waltz, the tango, and the polka. Laughter filled the air like a sweet fragrance. Poldie loved to dance, twirling and giggling until it was finally time to turn in for the night.

As the atrocities of the war were revealed, everyone learned that masses of people had perished in appalling conditions. After briefly staying in several refugee camps, the Kellners finally found something of a home in Ludwigsburg, Germany. They enjoyed, at last, a small barrack of their own. The family spread their blankets and pillows on the floor and slept in the security of one another's presence.

Nights were not peaceful for long. As soon as the lights went out, the elusive *Bettwanzen* (bedbugs) appeared from out of their cracks in the walls and bit any soft flesh they could find. Startled, Johann jumped up and, in the dim light, took a needle and punctured as many of the bugs as he could and then struck a match to incinerate the invaders. The residents wished for some of the DDT the Americans had used on them as they entered Germany. People adjusted apprehensively to the bugs. They called the place "wanzen konzentrationslager" (bugs concentration camp).

Three times a day, families lined up at the central kitchen for meals. Again, they tried to remind themselves of their blessings—not too long ago, they were on train cars with no food, water, or toilets. Once again, for reasons unknown, the refugees were transferred to a new location, an abandoned school building nearby. The families all crowded inside, but at least there, the bugs had not taken over. There was no school for the children, and there were no jobs for workers. In about six months, they were again relocated. Everyone felt powerless; they wondered when they could be in control of their own lives once again.

♦

CHAPTER THREE

ESCAPE TO FREEDOM

I n the fall of 1945, Alois attended school in Petrovice. This one year of higher education was similar to high school or college. Alois began thinking more seriously about his future. He had always worked in the fields and at home to help his family. He used his earnings from playing in the band to support his family. It was different to think about what he would do as an adult. In recent years, his future had been about survival and lying low while the Germans and subsequently the Russians were in charge. It was a new thing to think about normal life and being a grown-up.

Alois enjoyed a photography course he took in school. He imagined capturing images of life in a peaceful world. Near the end of the school year in 1946, one of the teachers encouraged every student to write what he or she planned to do for a career after graduation. Alois remembered the many times he had gone hungry. He often daydreamed about eating tasty meat—the kind they rarely ate. Like many other families, the Hufs grew accustomed to their food being regulated with ration cards. And even if they could have obtained more legally, meat was costly and unaffordable to their kind. Consequently, Alois wrote "butcher" on his paper to specify his desired occupation. In this way, he imagined, he would be able to eat plenty of the delicacy.

Ms. Minarikova, the teacher, collected the papers. She looked at Alois's wish and then glanced back at him, saying, "Hufe, ty reznik? Ja jsem si tebe nepredstavovala za reznika." (Huf, you a butcher? I didn't think of you as a butcher.) It was customary for teachers to call the students by their last names.

She was probably right, Alois realized. Maybe that would not be the best vocation for the young man. He needed to settle on doing something that would pay him enough so he could afford to buy food. One of Alois's friends served as a forester and told him there was an opening for three young men. Alois's father worked in the forests at one time and earned a modestly sustainable living. It seemed like a good idea. Alois applied for a position, grateful to be hired as a forester *praktikant* (intern). In this role, he was able to complete three years of work as an intern and then proceed to finish two to four years of forestry school.

He and the other practicants wore vivid green uniform jackets with high collars and leaf patterns around the cuffs. They could walk on the roads, no longer afraid of any foreign soldiers. This was their country again. Part of the young men's job was scaling trees and gathering seeds. The young foresters inventoried, dried, and stored the seeds. In springtime, they planted the seeds in nurseries with high fences to guard against animals. When the trees were about two years old, they transferred the saplings with the help of students from the agricultural school. Each student took a hoe and dug a new spot for a tree and planted it, replenishing the forest.

At other times, the interns searched for trees suitable for harvesting by the lumberjacks. The young men measured the trunks and the branches. They numbered each chosen tree with a tag, which they attached to its trunk with a small hammer. Alois and his coworkers also learned how to gather information about the deer population. Alois often led hunters to the choicest locations where the deer gathered. Most of the hunters were prominent people who could afford a hunting license. During the winter, the interns placed hay along with salt blocks into feeders for the deer. It was a sight to see the deer prance slowly through freshly fallen snow and graze. Alois took great pleasure in his chosen occupation. Spending hours planting saplings, which would become towering trees, he was involved in the rebuilding of a war-torn, fractured country. Being outside among the trees and forest animals was itself life giving.

In his third year of training, Alois was given permanent employment at the forestry headquarters office in Sumperk, the city called the "Gate to the Jeseniky Mountains," which is considered the second-highest mountain range in Czechoslovakia. He was well liked and efficient. He applied to the forestry school, confident in his ability to do well.

It was also in early 1948 that the Communist Party took over Czechoslovakia. After World War II, the Russians were viewed positively by Czechoslovakia because the people credited Russia for liberating them. These sentiments dated back to the 1920s, and the postwar president, Eduard Benes, authorized a friendship treaty, during his exile, with the Soviets in 1943. Even though the Russians had vacated by 1946, somehow they had made their way back, and the country faced an impending dictatorial rule. In its most vulnerable state after the brutal war, the country fell into yet another peril. By July 1947, things in Czechoslovakia appeared to be functioning efficiently, but the following year, at the disapproval of the Soviets, it sought help from the Marshall Plan. The United States passed an initiative to aid Western Europe, giving more than $12 billion to rebuild the economy. The Soviets retaliated and prevented the Czechs from receiving assistance. The people were distraught and began viewing the Communist Party in a new light.

One of the required documents Alois needed to be accepted into the forestry school was a statement from the local city administration on whether or not Alois's father, Josef Huf, belonged to the Communist Party. He had not been. After being jailed twice—once by his countrymen after the house fire and another time by the Gestapo for taking time off to work on his land—Josef was certainly no pushover. He did not like the smell of what was spreading over his homeland; it had the faint odor of bombs and gunpowder that infected the region during the German occupation.

Shockingly, Alois's application for forestry school was denied. He attempted again to apply six months later. After all, he proved that he could do the work. Astonishingly, his application was returned with "Rejected" stamped on it. Nearly eighteen years old, Alois was disappointed and contemplated what his future might now be. He earned his driver's and chauffeur's licenses in another attempt at autonomy. He felt there was little freedom to determine his course. Once eighteen, he would be eligible for the draft, and if called on, he would have to serve in the military for two years. It was only a matter of time before his older brother, Pepa, was called to serve. Alois was not opposed to fighting for a just cause, but his mistrust in the new communist regime was heightened. There was no determining what they might have the soldiers participate in.

With the forestry school rejections fresh on his mind and the draft imminent, Alois felt trapped. He hoped to shape his own destiny, but that seemed impossible in Czechoslovakia. The time to find an alternative solution was running out. He was offered office work in the forestry headquarters in Sumperk, which gave him a temporary sense of purpose, but his heart kept tugging him toward a brighter future. Was that even possible now in a land where dictatorship ruled? In January of 1949, on the train to Sumperk, he crossed paths with a former schoolmate, Mirek Stransky, who was attending a business academy there. The two exchanged greetings, and Alois congratulated his friend on his placement in the academy. When Mirek inquired what Alois planned to do, he hesitated and could not hide his disappointment. He went on to explain he was denied entry into forestry school because his father was not part of the Communist Party. "I feel so disgusted about it," Alois confided. "I prefer to just disappear."

Mirek leaned in closer and asked quietly, "Across the border?" Alois nodded. Mirek commiserated. He said that even though he gained admission into business school, his ultimate concern about being able to obtain a job after he graduated was ubiquitous. His father was not part of the Communist Party either, so what did that mean for his future?

Alois shared more details, giving a voice for the first time to his intentions: "If I have the chance, I will try to escape." These thoughts had been percolating since his childhood, when he first heard of the Gestapo's brutality toward his people. He remembered how during those gruesome times, he would imagine climbing up a very tall tree in the forest or diving into a deep ravine to hide from the tyrants.

Mirek's response was barely above a whisper: "If you go, I want to come with you."

The two felt a special bond after that. All the young people in Czechoslovakia understood what it was like to face adulthood with a new and very strict parent—the communist government. It could be a cruel and unpredictable authority, and it had already shown them that it would rule over each aspect of their futures.

The one thing that gave Alois the most happiness and fulfillment was being part of the band. As previously discussed, every other week, the group performed for a community dance. They also played for different occasions like funerals. Being a musician was a rewarding gig for Alois; he earned more in one night than he took in during one month of his forestry work. Alois always gave his earnings to his mother because the family was consistently short on money.

Each workday morning, Mirek, Alois, and Pepa rode the train together. After disembarking, Pepa walked a few minutes with the two before splitting off and heading to his job as a chauffeur and truck driver. Then for the remaining ten minutes, Mirek and Alois discussed their plan of escape until it was time for them to part ways and go to their respective jobs. Alois loved Pepa passionately, but he could never tell him that they wanted to escape. His parents would certainly want to stop Alois, and telling them too much might put them in danger.

Later that same month, Alois began having sharp pains in his chest and difficulty breathing. A doctor told his parents that it could be a severe illness and ordered bed rest for several weeks. It was similar to the asthmatic issues that little Frank had experienced years before. The suffocation Alois felt about his circumstances was just as real as the painful breaths he took. He longed to speak openly with his parents, but he knew they would never support his decision—it was a life-threatening risk. By early March, the chest pains mostly subsided but left Alois extremely weak. As soon as he was able to return to a regular work schedule, Alois was reunited with Mirek on the train heading to Sumperk. His friend was thrilled to see Alois again, and after catching up, Mirek asked, "Is the escape still on?" Alois confirmed.

On Friday, March 11, 1949, Mirek invited Alois to visit him at his home in Wiesenberg that weekend, about twenty-five miles away from Alois's home. They needed to finalize their escape.

That Saturday, Alois was scheduled to play the trumpet with the band. When his mother learned that he planned to play even though he was still recovering from the illness, she strongly objected. Alois argued and told her he was going to do what he wanted. Sensing she was facing a lost cause with his disobedient and rebellious attitude, Marie slapped Alois twice on his face. She wanted what was best for him, even when she did not know precisely how to show it. Alois performed anyway, and when he arrived home at 2:30 a.m., he laid his earnings on the kitchen table.

Alois slept for only a few hours; his mind raced with potential scenarios as he attempted to make his way through an unknown future. As he usually did on Sundays, he rose early to attend Mass with his family. At church, Alois couldn't focus on anything the priest said; his mind continued racing, coming up with possible complications in his escape and then finding their solutions. His first concern was creating a believable reason to tell his parents why he would be gone that afternoon; they were extremely overprotective since his sickness. The family returned home and ate a meal Marie prepared. Once finished, Alois turned to his father since his mother was offended by his disobedience the night before. Using a bit of teenage manipulation, he explained as calmly as possible that he had a meeting with three of his forester friends in the village of Wiesenberg.

Josef inquired how he would get there. "I'll ride my bicycle. That is faster. It will take too long to walk to and from the train," Alois said. His father looked displeased and suspicious. The ride will be too strenuous, he protested. Alois replied in a more firm and loud voice: "I will go slowly." To get his persistent son off his back, Josef reluctantly accepted the idea. Alois hurried to leave before his mother could say anything adverse.

Alois hopped on the bike and took off, pedaling quickly. His body was exhausted from the recent illness and the lack of proper sleep, but he was fueled with adrenaline. After arriving at Mirek's house and greeting Mirek's parents, he met a new acquaintance there, Jindra Chalupa, who was renting a room from the family. The three of them secluded themselves in a room for a meeting that felt part business and part devious. The young men leaned in to communicate in more of a whisper, feeling the nervous energy swirling around them. Alois was tense but instinctively knew that he could trust these two companions. Each of them witnessed and heard of the atrocities the Germans and Russians committed during the war, and now they could not rely on their own country's leaders. However, they could depend on one other.

Mirek's first point of business was to inform Alois that a fourth man was joining them in their escape. His name was Bohus Trouba.

He was twenty-three years old, had served for two years in the military, and was working in Prague as a driver for a supply company. Bohus was unable to attend this first meeting because Prague was 250 miles away. The three of them were pleased he was coming. Bohus was five years older and had more experience, which they counted as a great blessing. Crossing the border was going to be rife with potential detriments, and they would be treated like criminals or worse if found out or apprehended. By the end of the meeting, they decided that Wednesday, March 16, was the day to leave home and escape. Knowing he had companions made the journey much more acceptable for Alois. "I'll see you Wednesday at the train," he said.

Alois took longer on the way home, giving himself time to digest the impact of all that was about to happen. He began processing the details of what his new reality might look like. Doubts and hopes competed for prominence in his mind. He took in deep breaths and realized the deep, sharp pains from his illness were softening. When Alois finally arrived home, Josef confronted him and asked why he was gone longer than anticipated. Alois covered for the delay by giving the most natural and unsuspecting response possible—that he had wanted to be cautious because of his recent illness and thus had taken extra time returning. That evening, when the family gathered to eat leftovers from the midday meal, Alois purposely paused and looked into the faces of each of his family members. He studied the soft lines on his parents' faces and the smiles of his siblings. Alois committed their visages to his memory. He resisted the urge to hug each of them firmly and to tell them he sincerely loved them. That would have tipped them off that something unusual was happening. His emotions wanted to take control, but he kept his feelings to himself.

On Monday, March 14, 1949, Alois woke to his eighteenth birthday. Not one member of his family wished him a happy birthday; however, this was nothing out of the ordinary for most European families. He dressed and went to work as usual, put in the required hours, and then returned home. The crossover into adulthood meant that his autonomy would soon be ending—he would now be eligible for the military draft. On Tuesday, March 15, he and Mirek met to gather information. As they parted ways, they told one another, "Tomorrow is *the day!*"

At work, Alois willed himself to focus on his tasks, realizing this was his last day there. On his forestry office desk, there was a nice compass. Alois eyed it; compasses were difficult to come by and were only sold at specialty stores. He reasoned that if he borrowed it for a good cause and found a way to give it back someday, his supervisors would understand. Making certain that no one noticed, he slipped the compass quietly into his pocket. Every thought was now focused on making it across the border, and the compass would be critical for determining their direction. Once free, his group could join forces with the Americans and British and fight with their armies to overthrow the communist government. They would be freedom fighters, and then all would return to normalcy, he hoped.

One other essential matter Alois needed to address would be to obtain advance pay. He asked for a one-time advancement and hoped his employer would grant the request. He stated the advancement was to purchase a pair of ski boots. At about 4:00 in the afternoon, it was granted, and he received his pay. Alois sighed with deep relief; the money was necessary for the costly train ticket the following day. It was not in Alois's character to be untruthful, but he rationalized the lies he had to tell over the past week for his plan to be a success. On the way home in the train later that day, Alois slipped his hands into his pant pockets occasionally and ran his fingers across the compass and the money, reassuring himself. He was overcome with a mix of guilt, fear, and excitement. Everything appeared to be coming together.

When he arrived home, Alois wanted to rest, but Tuesday nights were reserved for band practice. If he missed, his parents would realize something was amiss. Alois took his trumpet and rode his bike to play. That evening, his mind was somewhere else as he played his old horn. At one moment, he felt sure that he should let his parents know he was going away. But he reasoned that his father would likely report his escape to the police; Josef and Marie would probably rather see their son in jail than lose him. However, it also seemed cruel not to inform his family of any of his plans. They would be extremely concerned if he simply vanished.

After midnight, when everyone in the house was fast asleep, Alois returned home from practice. He quietly tiptoed into the kitchen, being careful not to wake his parents, who slept in another part of the room. He shuffled over to the small wooden dining table, turned on a dim light to illuminate just enough for him to be able to jot down a farewell missive, but he hesitated when contemplating where he should leave it. It would have to be in a place that could stay hidden until he crossed the border. He studied his surroundings in the faint light—he was saying good-bye to everything, he realized. Alois's gaze stopped at the tall kitchen cabinet. At the top was Josef's special shaving dish, filled with lathering soap and a shaving knife. That was it, he told himself. Josef shaved every Sunday morning. During the week, his father never reached for the dish, and no one in the family ever touched it either. Alois calculated it in his mind: it would be four full days until his father used the shaving dish. By then, Alois and his companions would be safe across the border, and it would only be just a few days that his family would have to suffer not knowing what happened to him before learning his plans.

Alois glanced over at the unlit part of the kitchen to make certain his parents were still sleeping. He saw their silhouettes side by side in a deep sleep. He reached up carefully for the dish. The razor blade was rolled up in a napkin. Alois quickly found a piece of scratch paper and swiftly scribbled these words in pencil: "Dear Father, I am escaping from Czechoslovakia. I do not know how long I will be gone, but I hope not very long. I hid my shotgun and pistol inside the chicken coop for you. The two trumpets, atop the wardrobe, are paid off; you can do what you want with them. I leave my forestry uniform for brother Pepa." There was no time to pen his true intentions. He needed to turn the light out before his parents woke, and he also wanted to protect his family members from knowing too much. As a forester, Alois was permitted to carry firearms, and he didn't want the police to search the house for them. With his hands shaking, he hastily unrolled the napkin that contained his father's razor and placed the note inside. He carefully rolled it up again, put it in the kit, and replaced the dish on the high shelf. He silently made his way outside with his shotgun and pistol and then hid them behind boards in the chicken coup.

Exhausted but unable to rest, Alois lay awake in bed for hours. He tried to keep from stirring, lest Pepa, sleeping beside him, might wake.

Alois quietly prayed to Mother Mary and asked her to help him and his friends escape and to keep them from being apprehended. Even though he'd been planning to flee for months, the reality was sinking in. Alois scanned the ceiling in the dim light and examined it from corner to corner. He could almost hear his inner voice ask, "Am I doing the right thing? What if we get caught? What if guards shoot and kill us? What will become of my parents? What will they think? What will I put my family through?" Alois willed his heart to beat more slowly. He had no idea where he and his companions would be in a week. Weary, he finally realized that he would have to settle with these unanswered questions for a time. With his fatigue overtaking him, he finally closed his eyes and drifted off to sleep.

The next morning, Wednesday, March 16, Alois intentionally lingered longer than usual at the house. He picked up four-year-old Frank, tossed him in the air, and caught him to his brother's delighted squeals. Of all the brothers, little Frank possessed similar facial features as those of Alois. He was just a toddler; would he ever remember who his older brother was? Alois proceeded to give high-fives to ten-year-old Ludmilla and sixteen-year-old Hynek. He wore his favorite sweater, which his older sister, Marie, knitted for him from wool spun by their father. The turtleneck had three buttons on the shoulder. Alois found his mother and sister tending to the animals in the stall. "Maruska," Alois began, "will you button the sweater for me?"

His sister gave him a questioning look. "You always button your sweater yourself. Why not today?"

Alois hesitated to think of a good response while Maruska patiently fastened the buttons. He wanted desperately to say good-bye to his sister and mother, realizing they might never see one another again. Alois desired to speak to his mother, but his eyes teared at the sight of her. His spirit screamed, "I love you, and I wish I could embrace each of you!" Instead, he thanked his sister and turned to leave. As he walked away, Alois tried desperately to memorize their delicate faces so that he could forever remember them.

Pepa and Alois kept their normal routine and walked to the station together. They sat in the first train car, while Mirek and Jindra sat in the last car. When they arrived at Sumperk, Pepa walked with his brother, as they normally did every day. When they reached the point where they typically separated, Alois turned to his brother, looked in his eyes for a moment, and then patted him on the shoulder. "Pepa, I'll see you later," he managed. Alois walked a bit farther until he was sure Pepa was out of sight. He spun around and backtracked toward the train station. Mirek and Jindra were waiting. Each of them approached the ticket booth individually to avoid the appearance of traveling together.

Once they secured tickets, each of them boarded a train to the city of Zabreh. Upon arrival, they caught another train to Prague. That train ride was three and a half hours but seemed to take a lot longer. Alois took comfort in knowing that his family would not yet know he was missing. When they arrived in Prague, the men took a streetcar to the predetermined spot to meet up with Bohus, the fourth member of their company. The friends waited there until Bohus returned from his deliveries. Mirek introduced him to Alois and Jindra, and the four of them were eager to carry out their mission.

Bohus lived in a dormitory along with sixty other men with whom he worked. Alois, Mirek, and Jindra joined Bohus and ate dinner with the other workers and slept in the dorm that night. The four of them would have to wait until the end of the workweek to escape; they would arouse suspicion and a potential chase if they left in the middle of the week.

The next day, the three visitors contemplated what to do with their time. They took the streetcar to a home show, an exhibition of furniture and other house products. The young men bought baked rolls and soda to eat and drink. As Alois walked around the home show complex, someone tapped him on his shoulder. He turned around anxiously. "Alois, what are you doing here?" he heard. The inquiring voice came from Mr. Hanzal, a neighbor and fellow band member.

Alois scrambled to hide his terror. He introduced Mirek and Jindra, who were standing next to him, and told Mr. Hanzal that they had made plans to attend the home show for the next three days. He and Mr. Hanzal said good-bye, and Alois felt sick to his stomach. By now, his family knew he was missing, and Mr. Hanzal would surely tell them he saw Alois in Prague. He hoped, however, that telling Mr. Hanzal that he was staying for three days in Prague would satisfy his family. From that moment on, Alois cautiously scrutinized each place he went during his short stay, careful not to be spotted by any other acquaintance or friend.

On Friday afternoon, Bohus returned from work promptly at 5:00 p.m. The four young men flagged a ride to the train station and, once inside, studied the departure times to the border town of Cheb the following day. This was where they would make their escape. After making a plan, they ate baked rolls and drank soda pop again and headed back to the dorms. Bohus told his coworkers that the visitors would only be there for a few days, so no one seemed to mind. Everyone gathered around Ping-Pong tables and played. It seemed like a typical Friday night. The young men went to bed early that evening, and Alois again had to put the questions plaguing his conscience aside: "Is this right? How much is my family suffering?"

In the morning, the team of four gathered for a quick meeting. Between the four, they had acquired two compasses, and Bohus had a map of Cheb and the surrounding areas. The boys went out for a last-minute stroll in Prague. The city had minimal damage during the war, since it had submitted to the Nazi regime and was not a target to the Allies. The four men purchased as many packs of cigarettes as possible, filling their pants pockets to the brim. Alois shifted his small leather pocket calendar to the corner of his pants pocket to fit more of the cartons inside. He knew his parents disapproved of his smoking, but he picked up the habit at sixteen and was addicted to it. Alois also fell back on his promise not to drink since he had been in the band, but at least he did not get drunk, he reasoned. The young men made their way to the Wilson Rail Station in the late afternoon. Each traveler went to a different ticket window to avoid raising suspicion.

Alois reached in his pocket and counted the money he had left—about two hundred crowns. He went to the post office by the rail station, purchased an envelope, placed two bills inside, and wrote his mother's name and address on the front. Alois had given his earnings to his mother for a long time. He worried about how his family would fare without him, and he felt tinges of guilt. It seemed impossible to write anything at that moment to his greatly loved parents; hopefully, the gesture would be enough to say "I love you," he thought.

After another meager meal, the four travelers boarded the train. Many of the passengers were coal miners who worked in Kladno. Once the train began to move, Alois sat stone-faced as he looked out the window and watched the ground move past. It was hard to stop thinking about his precious family, so he tried not to think at all. Jindra turned to Alois; they both liked to sing folk songs. "We should sing and cheer everyone up," Jindra suggested. Alois obliged, and the two started a simple harmony. Before long, the whole train full of passengers joined in to sing the Czech songs. Many of the young workers missed their families and appreciated the melodic reminder of home.

A voice interrupted the chorus as they neared their stop: "This is the final destination: Cheb." After the four young men disembarked, Bohus spoke with conviction, and Mirek, Jindra, and Alois gave him deference: "We shouldn't try to cross the border at night," he said. "We will go to a hotel and register and do as all the normal Czech citizens would do. We can cross the border tomorrow during the day, when it is daylight. On Sunday, the border guards will be somewhat relaxed, so this will be to our advantage." He reassured the others and reiterated that, as a former soldier, he was assigned for a few weeks to patrol the borders.

Alois could barely remember ever being so nervous. His insides felt like cords of rope twisting and turning. He looked at his other companions and tried to gauge their reaction. Alois was uneasy. For one, he knew his father might have already reported him missing to the police. Hotels were in the practice of bringing registration forms of all their guests to the police station. And worse, Alois had spent all his money and mailed the last few crowns to his mother. He reasoned that after they crossed the border and joined with the foreign armies, he would not have need of Czech funds anymore.

Bohus eased at least one of these concerns. He offered to pay for the hotel. It was about 11:30 p.m. when the group arrived at the very modest accommodations. The clerk asked each of them to show photo identification. Mirek, Alois, and Bohus pulled out their IDs, but Jindra looked stunned. He suddenly realized he had forgotten his ID at home. The others glanced at Jindra horrified. The hotel manager ordered Jindra to go to the police station. Perhaps the authorities would issue him a two-day pass to stay in the border town, the manager said. Jindra quickly headed off to the station by himself, and the three others went to their rooms without a single word. Alois and Mirek were to share one room, and Bohus and Jindra another.

Bohus joined Alois and Mirek in their room. He whispered, "If I had known that Jindra forgot his ID, we would not have come to this hotel!" They all felt the gravity of the situation. They felt as if the police would show up at any moment and arrest them all. "There is nothing we can do except wait and hope for the best," Bohus said. With those parting words, he departed to his room.

Is this where their plans would end—in Cheb? Alois was frightened. His concern for Jindra overshadowed his dread for himself. Mirek had been in the same religion classes at school, and Alois suggested they do the only thing they could do—pray. They knelt beside their beds and began to whisper their prayers to Mary and the saints, as the Roman Catholic Church had taught. Alois had never heard the verse "Come to me, all who labor and are heavy laden, and I will give you rest" (Matthew 11:28, ESV). Oh, how they needed their burdens lifted. The two continued praying softly, asking for the intermediaries to take their requests to Jesus. Their petition was interrupted by footsteps in the hallway. Alois and Mirek knelt motionless when a knock came at the neighboring door. They waited silently, afraid to peek into the hall or guess what might be happening. Then there was a knock at their door. They steadied themselves and apprehensively cracked the door. It was Jindra and Bohus, and by the smile on Jindra's face, it appeared all was well.

Jindra explained his ordeal at the police station. First, the police had forced him to pay five hundred crowns, a hefty fine for not carrying his ID. Then they asked him to explain why it was that he was in Cheb, so far from home. Jindra fabricated a story about working for a company called Velamos. The enterprise produced bicycles. Jindra told the police that in the factory back home, an appeal was made for young workers to move to the border town of Cheb, where Velamos had a factory and needed workers. The story proved convincing enough, and although the loss of so much money was a travesty, it could have been much worse. Jindra showed the other three his two-day pass, permitting him to wait until Monday morning to apply for the factory job.

All four men still felt concerned about the police. Not only did the hotel have records of them, but their friend was tied to the police station now as well. Still, as Bohus observed, if the hotel clerk had sent them all to the police station to accompany Jindra, they would almost certainly have been found out. They were thankful that things were okay for the time being. They headed to their respective rooms, wished each other a good night, and went to sleep.

On Sunday morning, March 20, 1949, Bohus and Jindra came to Alois and Mirek's room. Bohus opened up the map of Cheb. Again, Bohus asserted his know-how. They should not travel in a group together, he said. Four men would stir suspicion. Instead, they must split up two by two. He pointed to a place on the map near a railroad track bridge. There was a plan in place—at least the best one they could come up with for now. Bohus and Jindra left the hotel first at around 9:00 a.m., and Mirek and Alois followed closely behind. They walked about an hour to reach their destination at the back of a building. When Alois and Mirek arrived, Bohus and Jindra were nowhere to be found. After waiting some time, Alois and Mirek thought the police must have caught the other pair. They had already agreed, whatever happened, each one would carry on the mission to get across the border.

"We better try to cross the border on our own," Alois finally told Mirek. They were worried about their friends, and only Bohus had the map, but it was dangerous to stay there for too long. Alois and Mirek spotted a ravine nearby, gray with snow, and the two darted into it to avoid anyone seeing them from the road. They hiked along the ravine in a crouched position in an attempt to keep hidden. At one point, Alois straightened up and noticed a humble house with smoke softly emanating from the chimney. For some reason, he felt they should approach the home and ask for directions from whoever answered the door.

"Alois, are you crazy? The people will call the police on us!" Mirek exclaimed.

"Mirek," Alois replied convincingly, "we don't have a choice. We don't know the shortest way to the border. Besides, if they go for the police, we will just run for our lives." They glanced at the compass to determine their best route if they needed to run. Mirek conceded that Alois should try his luck. Alois climbed out from his cover in the ravine and approached the house. There was no one around, but the smoke assured him there must be people inside. He knocked and waited, turning to look behind him. He heard a voice coming from inside, inviting him to enter. Alois knew he recognized that particular accent before.

Alois stepped past the threshold and into the house and was greeted by a man standing near the door. "I need some information if you could help me," Alois began. "But—are you by chance a Volin soldier from Ukraine?"

The man studied Alois briefly. "Yes, I am. Who are you?"

Alois confessed he was from Vikyrovice by Sumperk and that many of his friends were Volin soldiers. Czech by heritage and residing in Ukraine, the men were recruited by Russians to fight against German occupiers. The group was called the Svoboda Army, after their leader, Ludvik Svoboda, and fought alongside the Russians against the Nazis.

"Who of the soldiers lived in your village?" the man asked.

Alois mentioned several names, including Vlada Bartos.

The man's countenance warmed. "I served with Bartos in the same military unit in signal corps!" he exclaimed. He reached for a bottle of whiskey and offered a drink of solidarity to Alois. This was like a dream. Alois was astonished at his fortune—he found an ally. Alois wasted no time. He explained he was seeking to escape and needed to find the shortest way to the border. He was looking for a place where minimal border guards might be posted.

The man was older than Alois, and he looked at him with both intrigue and concern. He seemed gratified with Alois's explanations. He watched Alois, who had fear in his eyes, and knew he was telling the truth. The man suggested the best route for Alois to make his escape and warned him to stay in the deep ravine until he crossed the highway. There was a bridge where the railroad crossed the ravine, he explained. Border guards slowly patrolled the path, but if Alois could reach the woods, he would be fine. Alois thanked the man and hugged him before stepping back outside to reunite with Mirek.

As the two departed and walked onward, they wondered what had become of Bohus and Jindra. Just a short time into their journey, they saw two figures in the distance ahead. It was Bohus and Jindra! The two in the rear quickly advanced and hugged their companions. The team felt as if it had been two years rather than two hours since they had seen one another. Mutually, the four decided, safety concerns aside, they would not separate from one another again. Bohus took the lead, and they moved methodically, keeping their steps and any sounds as muted as possible. One wrong move or loud noise could mean death for them all.

The ravine hid them well, but it hindered them from anticipating what was ahead. The four hardly looked up in trepidation of what each might witness. For the last half mile, the young escapees crawled on their bellies through the frozen snow. They were shivering but pushed onward. Alois's hands and feet were numb, but he knew he was alive by the small puffs of air he saw escaping from between his frozen lips. As he continued to slither through the slushy ravine, he felt the items inside his pockets rubbing against his body. He hoped that the elements did not dampen or damage the only possessions he took with him.

As they came in sight of what they hoped was the border, the group members came upon a narrow trail used by the border guards. About every fifty feet, a white square stone post stood about one foot high. One side of the post read "CSR" (Czechoslovak Republic) and the other side "Bavaria" (Germany). In their state of fright, chill, and hunger, they were confused about which side of the border was which. The younger travelers looked to Bohus, but he was puzzled too. As they glanced around at the snow-covered evergreens surrounding them, the young men gasped at the sudden sight of a soldier taking a rifle from his shoulder and lowering it. Bohus said quickly, "Put your hands in the air and walk toward the soldier!"

So they did. Alois was unsure if he even saw clearly; running now would be more dangerous. They had to plead for mercy. As they neared the soldier, the characteristics of the green German uniform came into view. The young men started to run toward him. They were on the right side of the border after all! When they neared the soldier, the four friends heard dogs barking. The guard looked at them as if he had seen many escapees before them. As the dogs' barks echoed, the soldier pointed to some underbrush and said, "Mach schnell!" They all understood enough German to know he was telling them to hurry up and get there fast. They hid until a Czech border guard passed.

When it was all clear, the German soldier walked them to a police station. He reminded them of how lucky they were. Others who tried to escape were shot, or shot at, by Czechoslovak authorities, even after crossing the border. The soldier escorted them to the German village of Waldsassen, where they were turned over to the police department. Each one endured the evidential interrogation. In school, they took German classes but had hardly rehearsed the language enough to totally understand. Not one of them purposely spoke German during or after the war. Still, they were glad they retained some of the language, allowing them to communicate.

Their reason for leaving their home country was the tyranny of the communist regime, each of them explained. The police interrogator wrote on a sheet of paper that they were "anticommunist." Police officers confiscated their compasses, Alois's map, and their remaining cash. The only possession they were allowed to retain was their precious cigarettes and the damp and soiled clothing on their person. Finally, the men had to confirm that they knew each other and that Jindra belonged to their group, since he did not have a photo ID.

It was almost dark when they were led to a jail cell, where they were incarcerated with German inmates. An officer told the group they would talk to them again in the morning. Alois, Mirek, Jindra, and Bohus sat on cots and pulled out a few cigarettes. Smoking helped dull the hunger. Their fellow inmates piped up when they saw the generous stash of cigarettes. They told them that the next day, the American soldiers would pick the refugees up. The Americans would give them all the American cigarettes they wanted. After several iterations of the story, the four friends were convinced that the US soldiers would take care of them the next day.

When the jail lights were turned out, Alois lay in bed. He was far from the final destination he hoped for, but he felt so grateful to have made it across the treacherous border. He prayed his thanks to God through the saints for getting them through. Today was Sunday—Josef would have shaved that morning. His father must have seen the note by now. "What are they thinking? How is Mother doing? Have they been worrying about me the past few days?" Alois thought. He grieved when he thought of his family and imagined the pain they had likely experienced. "Will they ever forgive me?" he wondered.

But Alois comforted himself with thoughts of uniting with the Americans the next day. The officers would pick them up and give them good food and cigarettes, and then, along with the US soldiers, he and his friends would return to Czechoslovakia and free their country from the communist oppressors. It would all be worth it in the end.

CHAPTER FOUR

THE REALITY OF REFUGEE STATUS

At the Huf household, the days after March 16 were excruciatingly painful. When Alois did not return from work on the 6:30 p.m. train, his family decided he must have missed it. But there was no sign of him on the later trains either. The following three days were almost unbearable, consisting of sleepless nights and anxious days. Saturday, March 19 was Saint Joseph's Day, a holiday celebrated by many Europeans, especially Czechs, that honored those named "Joseph" and any variant spelling thereof. The Hufs were particularly reverent toward this custom, being such devoted Catholics. The feast of Saint Joseph pays tribute to Joseph, the husband of Mary and stepfather of Jesus. Alois was scheduled to travel from house to house with the band and play for boys named "Joseph." Josef and Marie saw Alois's trumpets still resting on top of the wardrobe cabinet in the bedroom. "What could have happened?" they wondered.

The family was in a dilemma—should they report Alois's disappearance to the authorities, whom they did not trust, or remain quiet? Any family member not accounted for should by law be declared missing within two days. Failing to do so could result in stiff consequences, but they waited and hoped Alois would return and life would return to normal. Josef remembered his conversation with Alois a few days before his disappearance, when he asked his permission to travel to see his friend Mirek. Perhaps that was a clue to uncovering any information to help him locate Alois. Josef hopped on a bike and peddled quickly to Wiesenberg to ask if anyone knew an eighteen-year-old named Mirek who took the train each day to Sumperk. He reasoned that maybe the post office was the best place to find details about residents.

Josef entered the post office and stated his inquiry to the postal worker, Mr. Stransky. The postman was astonished. "Mirek is my son, and he's been missing for three days," he said. The two fathers expressed individual concerns for the boys, exchanged personal information, and began putting pieces of the puzzle together. Mirek's father had already reported his son's absence to the police. Josef knew he could not hold out any longer. He headed straight for the police station and followed suit. Their worry for their sons had not yet given way to the grief of their possible loss.

By Sunday morning, the Hufs were wracked with anxiety. Fear conquered every hopeful thought. In their hearts, they imagined Alois might walk through the front door at any moment, and the nightmare would cease. In their optimistic scenario, he took a trip with the band or worked extended hours and would be returning soon. In an attempt to calm their nerves, Josef and Marie tried throughout the day to continue with daily routines. Josef stroked his chin, and the stubble reminded him that he had not shaved. He meandered over toward the tall cabinet, reached for the shaving kit, and prepared for his weekly shave. He slowly unrolled the napkin with the razor inside, and the blood rushed from his face upon discovering the letter his son left behind. Josef's hands began to shake uncontrollably while reading the pointed and final message from his missing child. Unable to process it, Josef stumbled toward Marie and handed her the note. He found it almost impossible to console her as the tears flowed and she realized the finality of life without their boy. Josef joined her in crying like a child in agony. Alois was gone. The thought that he may never see him again paralyzed him.

From that moment on, the family prayed that God would grace them and bring Alois home. Out of desperation, they even begged God to allow the border patrol to apprehend him, regardless of the mandatory two years of imprisonment or a sentence of hard labor in the uranium mines; that seemed preferable to losing Alois to an unknown fate. At church, Josef lingered behind at the close of Mass while the other family members gathered outside. Shortly after that, Marie asked, "Where is our father?" Concerned, they reentered the chapel and found Josef at the pew where they left him, slumped over on his knees and crying out to God through tears. Marie peered off into the distance in a blank stare, her eyes swollen and red from tears, and she wondered, "Has my son eaten? Are his clothes warm enough? Where will he sleep? Is he well?" Not long after, the local police pressed the Huf family for information, but there was none to be shared. They wished they had any idea where Alois was.

On Monday morning, March 21, Alois and his three companions awoke in Waldsassen in their jail cell; the guards acted as their early wake-up call. They began the day with a slice of bread and German coffee. It was a scant breakfast, but anything was appreciated and tasted good. Besides, the men told themselves it was only a matter of time before they would be eating like kings alongside the American soldiers. Their jail mates once again reminded them that the best cigarettes, of much better quality than what they currently possessed, would soon be theirs as a gift from the Americans. "Why don't you give those poor-quality cigarettes to us, since you're going to receive better ones?" someone in the cell suggested. The four agreed, handing over their stashes and wishing the German inmates well.

The German police checked the young men out of jail and gave them each a paper stating their status as Czechoslovakian escapees. Their group had grown to nine people; five other escapees had joined them. The next steps were for them to report to the American Central Intelligence Agency (CIA) office in the city of Tirschenreuth. The guards pointed the men in a specific direction, along with the instruction to follow the road signs, and then sent them on their way. The wanderers began traveling the road on foot. Where were the Americans, the Jeeps, the food, and those special cigarettes? They all speculated how long it would be before the big welcoming party would find them. Arriving at the city limits of Waldsassen, they encountered a sign that read "Tirschenreuth: 18 km." They looked at each other. It would be a twelve-mile walk from there.

It was only then that they realized the other captives had lied to them. The American group waiting to shower them with goodies was not coming. The other German inmates duped them. Intense hunger and thirst made the journey in the chilly air seem even longer. By midday, one of the new men in their group had an idea to ease their pangs. His nickname was "Gypsy," and he had a dark complexion. He spoke German very well. He thought he might walk to a nearby farmhouse to see if he could trade his winter coat for food for everyone. The others wished him well and waited as he went to a dwelling. A few minutes later, Gypsy returned coatless—but with a loaf of rye bread. He divided it into nine pieces. They were humbled and grateful for this good-hearted friend. It was just enough to give them the strength to keep going.

By the time they reached Tirschenreuth, they were quite fatigued and hungry. They searched for the CIA barracks, formerly belonging to the German military. Finally finding it, they entered. Promptly, each of the men was assigned a cot to sleep on, but they were not initially allowed to rest. Instead, they were ordered to report for interrogation immediately. Alois entered the room alone and took a seat at the table. A very strict American military officer began hurling questions at him for hours. One by one, each of the escapees withstood intense cross-examining sessions lasting two days. Similar questions were posed over and over again, and never with the same interrogator. It appeared the Americans knew more about Czechoslovakia than the young men did. As the rounds of questions continued, Alois became more and more irritated. He was oblivious to any of the derogatory information the American officer had on his homeland. The examinations continued, and it soon became apparent that the escapees were viewed as traitors or spies and were being vetted. Once they were satisfied, the American soldiers sorted out escapees from the others and sent them to domestic refugee camps or camps run by an international refugee organization.

When not being subjected to fierce questioning, they were crammed in a room with twenty other people. Three times per day, they received two thin slices of dark bread and coffee that tasted like warm water that was tinted brown. Alois used one handkerchief as a washcloth and one as a towel; soap and other essential toiletries were hopefully forthcoming. He wondered how long it would take before they could join the military. As time passed, more and more escapees joined them.

Two days later on Thursday, March 24, an announcement alerted the detainees they were moving. Military trucks took the two hundred refugees to the train station in Tirschenreuth, and from there, they would head south for the city of Amberg. There were many more escapees there from Eastern European countries. Like Alois and his friends, those refugees were fleeing a life under communism as well. Again, at Amberg, Alois was assigned a military cot, and the same meal plan of two slices of bread and coffee began. There was no soap, no towels, and no toothbrushes.

Once again, they went through extensive rounds of interrogation. Alois sometimes thought of the Germans in the surrounding communities. Most residents would undoubtedly want to help them if they could, but they hardly had food for themselves; others disliked the refugees. Alois started thinking more longingly of home. Back at home with his family, he had a place to belong and regular meals. "Why did I do this?" he asked himself. He dreamed of sitting around the table with his family. The hunger he felt was a constant reminder of the decision he had made. But even when homesick and daydreaming of going home, he knew that it was no longer a possibility. For a crime like escaping, Alois faced years of labor in the mines. Many captured men died before their sentence was complete—those who did survive suffered from significant health problems. No, there was no life back home.

The escapees soon learned that the Amberg camp was operated by the International Refugee Organization (IRO). It was a sorting center to determine which of them qualified as political refugees and would then be granted asylum. If not, they were assigned to a camp operated by the Germans.

The interrogations were unreasonable to Alois and the others. The uncertainty of the future and the pain of the present grew exceedingly tiresome. Multiple times, Alois assured the interrogators that he was not a member of the Communist Party. He pointed out his birthdate on his identification and explained that he had just turned eighteen. The interrogators then inquired if he was part of a communist youth movement, which was a mystery to Alois. He had never heard of such an organization. The detainees learned that several escapees were sent to Germany from communist strongholds as spies. The CIA officers counted everyone as a suspect.

Alois and the eight other men with whom he had journeyed stayed together. They found a kind of family in one another. After a day's interrogation, which ended around 5:00 p.m., they ate their food rations and were then free to move around the city of Amberg. During the evening hours, they went to the city park and joined the Germans, many of whom spent that time in recreation there. Jindra and Alois were nominated to sing the beloved love songs they knew. As Alois sang, a longing sadness came out of his voice; he was incredibly homesick and hungry. The German people appreciated the young men's traditional songs and emotive delivery. The park goers gathered around and asked them to continue singing. Some of the onlookers gave them German pennies and cigarettes as gestures of admiration for their talents.

The nine refugees found ways to pass the time in the barracks. Gypsy knew a man among the refugees who claimed to be a hypnotist. The two of them arranged a trick that Gypsy learned while working in the circus. The hypnotist told Gypsy that he would cast a spell on him, saying, "Gypsy, you are getting tired. You will not be able to move any parts of your body, and your body will become stiff like a log." Gypsy then became perfectly still. The other men set up two chairs and lay Gypsy out with his head on one chair and feet on another. Another collaborator in the trick proceeded to sit on Gypsy's torso, and still, Gypsy's body remained as flat as a board. The group then stood Gypsy upright, and the hypnotist snapped his fingers. In an instant, Gypsy returned to his usual self again.

Escapees in neighboring buildings managed to retain the money and cigarettes they brought with them from their journeys. One in Alois's group suggested they perform for their comrades in exchange for some cigarettes. Once again, Gypsy performed his logic-defying stunt. When the hypnotist snapped his fingers, Gypsy looked around and asked, "What happened?" In awe, those in the other group appreciated the entertainment and shared a few packs of cigarettes with their new friends.

Upon returning to their barracks, one among the company asked, "Gypsy, how do you make your muscles do that, going so solid?"

Gypsy responded with a hint of a grin: "I don't know what you're talking about."

At the close of two weeks, the refugees were issued a DP (displaced person) card stamped with the arrival date of March 24, 1949. From then on, the officers frequently referred to the refugees as "DPs." They heard rumblings that the DPs would soon be moving to a more permanent refugee camp somewhere near Stuttgart, Germany. Shortly after that, several hundred people climbed aboard a packed train. Younger ones like Alois stood the entire trip; there was no room to sit. As the transit rolled on, Alois stared out the window at the vivid, blue sky. There was no turning back now, so he and the others continued wondering how soon it would be before the US Army would allow them to help free their beloved nation of Czechoslovakia from the communists. The train stopped between cities on sidetracks to allow other trains to pass. By evening, they arrived in Ludwigsburg, about fourteen miles from Stuttgart.

Upon disembarkment, passengers were grateful to step out and away from the stuffy confines of the packed train. While most were taking in the clean, fresh air, Alois noticed the train unloaded all refugees in a freight terminal as opposed to the main passenger terminal. It seemed fitting. The group consisted of a jumble of nationless, homeless vagabonds that no one knew where to place. The men climbed into military trucks, their next stop, "Krabenloch Kasserne" (crab-hole barracks), which consisted of four separate, four-story buildings. The new tenants soon learned these buildings had previously held Polish, Latvian, and Ukrainian refugees. This time, the tenants were Czechoslovakian.

Upon arrival, Alois and the others felt their first sense of belonging when they were presented with blankets, military cots, and utensils. Next, they lined up for an individual dose of DDT spray to combat the lice and bedbugs many carried. It was appreciated and considered a gift at this point in their journey. Each received a generous spritz on their heads and under their clothes; the white-colored residue settled into their hair and clothing and dissipated after a short period. It was now time to line up for supper. Other Czech refugees operated the military kitchen in the barracks. The first evening's menu consisted of boiled potatoes and white pickle gravy. Portions were scarce, but Alois treasured anything with a touch of flavor after the diet of bread and weak coffee he became accustomed to. It was his first experience eating pickle gravy, and it proved quite tasty compared to the meager offerings since his escape.

All young men ages eighteen to twenty were housed together, with about thirty per room. The unit operated like a stringent military operation. One man, a refugee himself with previous military training, was assigned as the group's leader. Each morning, they awoke at 6:30 a.m. The day commenced with an hour of exercise. The leader utilized his creativity and taught them some moves in karate, which they thought might come in handy when they were able to join the army. During minimal daytime breaks, their leader gathered the men around and took out his guitar. He taught them notes and lyrics for military songs. One song in particular was a very sad Czech song. These tunes reminded the men of home. Feeling discouraged and lonely, Alois reached into his pocket and pulled out his pocket calendar to jot down the lyrics to the song in Czech.

> *Everything around me is dying. A dying grove. It is so strange.*
> *A long way off the sun's glare is disappearing.*
> *Good times have flown away from us.*
> *The faded blossom is behind.*
> *Sorrow and freezing frost linger behind.*
> *Your palm so soft and tender,*
> *Your hand so soft and tender,*
> *Longing for you, my beautiful lady.*
> *With my own eyes, I visualize kissing your soft hand,*
> *Which chases away the frost and sorrow and sleepless nights.*

When sung in the Czech language, the song reflected a sort of reality Alois was now living in. He sang it one more time quietly to himself and then closed the pages of his pocket calendar to keep the song tucked away for safekeeping.

Every resident took turns cleaning the barracks, mopping the hallways and stairs, and scrubbing the washrooms. Twice per week, Alois had kitchen duties. One of his responsibilities was peeling a mountain of potatoes. In the basement of each building were the bathing facilities. Refugees were permitted one warm shower per week. Since towels were unavailable, Alois continued using his handkerchief to dry his five-foot, eight-inch, ever-thinning body. The only shirt and sweater he owned, the ones he wore during his escape, were showing signs of wear and tear. He was able to wash them interchangeably each week while he showered, but with only water and no soap. While the shirt dried, he wore his sweater.

Finally, one day, the occupants received toothbrushes, toothpaste, and soap. Shower time now meant they could lather up their fragile bodies. Alois was thankful to feel a sense of cleanliness finally. After about six months, each man received a new shirt and a pair of trousers. Alois was especially grateful for these items, since his clothes were falling apart. His pants had become too large for his shrinking frame, and it was now time to part with the sweater his beloved sister, Maruska, made him.

Twice per week, a new transport of escapees from Czechoslovakia arrived at the camp. It became an event; all of the several thousand inhabitants would crowd around the newcomers to see if, by chance, there was someone familiar. The onlookers determined if the arrivals had mutual friends or acquaintances. Heartbreaking homesickness infiltrated the surroundings. Each of them had sacrificed much and gone to great lengths to leave their homes, yet they longed for it. Alois never missed an opportunity to carefully survey the crowds each week. Perhaps his brother Pepa might attempt to follow in Alois's footsteps. Week after week, there was no sign of Pepa. Alois consoled himself with silent prayers: "God, please keep Pepa from escaping home." Alois's concerns for Pepa were founded. He doubted Pepa would fare well in the extreme, arduous conditions.

Hunger was the worst part of this ordeal for these young men. Dealing with constant pangs of a gnawing stomach became a daily challenge. For breakfast, each inhabitant would receive a piece of rye bread and coffee. The food was edible, but there was never enough of it. At noon, potato soup, and at suppertime, boiled potatoes and white pickle gravy. The Germans called the dish *Sauergurkensauce* (sour cucumber sauce). On weekends, the refugees received only two slices of bread at breakfast, with which they initially experienced jubilation. Disappointment followed as they were urged to eat only one slice and save the other for lunch or supper so that no one had to work in the kitchen those afternoons and evenings. Like many there, Alois found it an impossible task. The two pieces of bread disappeared within seconds after distribution, which meant hunger pangs manifested themselves the remainder of the day and night.

Some nights, when the lights were turned out, Alois mourned as he heard the muffled cries of several of the men. They were all famished. Many regretted leaving their countries, families, and lives back home. Feelings of despair intensified as the weeks continued. Alois became acquainted with two brothers who resided in his quarters—one was eighteen, and the other was twenty. The older one became extremely unsettled, and his emotions gave way as the hunger and homesickness became too much to bear. He rushed into the basement of the building, turned on one of the gas valves, and killed himself. The surviving brother was devastated. By this time, the young men in the camp bonded and felt like some semblance of a family. Heartbroken, they all attended his funeral and laid his body to rest in the city cemetery of Ludwigsburg. As several men lowered the coffin into the ground, Alois's thoughts once again slipped back to his brother Pepa. He missed his family so much, but he did not want any of them to escape to this fate.

After many transitions from camp to camp, the Kellner family finally found a more permanent home—an apartment in Ludwigsburg. The family lived in a small section of a building the length of one-fourth of a block; they called it the "Karlstrasse apartment." The family occupied two rooms on the third floor, along with nine other families who shared the remaining spaces on that level. Not long after moving in, Anna went into labor with the youngest child, Willy. It was a difficult birth for Anna; a doctor had to perform a specialized procedure after they removed the placenta from her uterus. During Anna's long recovery, Leopoldine, only fifteen years old, took on all the mothering duties for the six younger siblings. Earlier, Anna birthed two other children who did not survive. One of the babies, a girl, died from an infection after the midwife cut the unbiblical cord too short. The entire family showed considerable sensitivity to Anna as she healed. It was soon time to begin rebuilding the lives they had left behind in the Sudetenland before being forced to evacuate. Johann, always resourceful, acquired a secondhand stove, which they placed in the corner of the main room. It served as both a cooking stove and a heater. The stovetop was large enough to fit five pots for cooking, so they thought it was especially unique.

The ten families who lived in the upper level shared only one water faucet and two toilets. The water faucet was located in a smaller room all on its own, separated from the occupants. Poldie tried to avoid that room because of what happened there. She could not forget the small coffin with the remains of a baby boy that was held in that room some time ago. The baby belonged to the Brunners, another Sudetenland refugee family who traveled most of the journey with the Kellners. They were a lovely couple that had two healthy daughters, Marie and Anna. Upon arriving at the camp in Ludwigsburg, the mother, Frau Brunner, who was pregnant during much of their refuge travels, delivered another baby, and this time it was a boy. However, the baby did not utter a cry. He entered the world stillborn, and the Brunners were devastated. They could not find comfort in the midst of their heartache. The sorrow of their loss reverberated throughout the third-floor dwelling. The baby's lifeless body lay in that small coffin for the customary three days of mourning in that isolated faucet room. It was a sorrowful time, and all the families bereaved this loss.

The shared toilets consisted of a high tank system with a pull chain. The Kellners were impressed and thankful for these toilets, considering that they had to use outhouses in previous locations or had to urinate and defecate through the cracks in the floorboards on the cattle cars. It felt like a little piece of heaven. At bath time on Saturdays, Anna filled a small wooden tub with hot water. Then each family member bathed—from youngest to oldest. A special treat for anyone who could afford to do so was to rent a small room called a stat bath by the half hour or hour to take a lengthier private bath on weekends.

The first floor contained more quality housing for some German families while the second level provided a specialized school for those desiring to learn a particular trade. By age fourteen, most youths in the building sought jobs working in factories if they could secure positions.

In the years following World War II, life in areas in and around Stutt-gart limped along despite the damaged infrastructure. Bombs destroyed about 80 percent of the area—the train station suffered damage, and many roads were impassable. Johann searched desperately for work, but there was nothing available to him. The Kellners relied on ration cards for food. The family ate mostly bread some days and potatoes on other days. Having meat was rare. Anna often traded meat and butter ration cards with neighbors for bread ration cards, because the inex-pensive carbohydrates went a lot further for a family of eleven. Once, Anna woke Poldie at 5:00 a.m. and asked her to stand in line at the butcher shop. Two hours later, after Anna got the younger children off to school, she took Poldie's place in line so that Poldie could head to school. The butcher sold horsemeat, and it was available without ration cards.

Anna did all she could to find food for her family. She trekked to local fields and orchards to collect apples and pears that fell from trees. Times were so burdensome, she found herself often humbly begging farmers for food and other necessities for her children. Weekly, Johann walked to the employment office, attempting to find work. Finally, one day, he was hired for a job that would take a few weeks, but it was different than what he ever would have imagined. So desperate to provide for his family, Johann agreed and took the job immediately. After working the first day, he came home, washed thoroughly, and then went to bed without eating or speaking. The next day, Johann revealed to Anna the details of the job. He and a group of men were responsible for digging up the remains of fallen French. The Germans had taken the people from France to work in Germany during the war. The French who died were buried. After the war, the remains were to be sent back to their loved ones in France.

Poldie, from the time she was only thirteen, was expected to take on the responsibilities of an adult in the household. On laundry days or whenever Anna needed extra help, she ordered Poldie to skip school to assist her. Tears would stream down Poldie's face during these times; she dearly loved school. At school, Poldie could be a child, free from her adult responsibilities, and she could learn about the world. One school day, Poldie was forced to skip and was on an errand to the local bakery.

She caught sight of the school superintendent; it looked as though he was headed straight for her apartment. Poldie hurried home and told her mother the school leader was coming. Anna ordered her daughter to jump in bed and covered Poldie with a blanket.

Poldie heard a knock on the door and then his voice as her mother invited him inside. He asked Anna why Poldie was missing so much school. Anna explained that Poldie would continually complain that she was ill. The leader appeared to take her words at face value, but days later, the Kellners received a letter from the Ludwigsburg Health Department summoning Poldie to come in for a checkup. Poldie nervously walked to the health department alone and underwent a blood test and X-rays. When it appeared that nothing was wrong, the doctor scolded Poldie, saying she was just too lazy to attend to school.

Poldie felt defenseless and left in shame, crying the entire way home. Once inside her apartment, she cried out, "Mother, you know that I love school very much, and I don't want to miss! You always make me stay home."

Anna replied, "What shall I do? We have so many children. You are the oldest girl, and I need your help."

Sometimes, Poldie stayed home to attend to her siblings while Anna went to the farmers in the villages surrounding Ludwigsburg to beg for food. The farmers had at least some food and would sometimes help. Anna knew a kind friend who would go with her.

In Ludwigsburg, just north of where they lived, was a prison surrounded by an apple orchard. When the apples ripened, some of the children would set out before dawn, crawl over the fence, and pick the apples that had fallen. If the children got caught, it meant sure punishment, as it was considered a crime. Nothing went to waste in Germany; even the correctional officers gathered the fallen apples to make apple cider. The excursion was a risk, but the hot applesauce Anna made from them was worth it.

One day, Poldie's friend Emma said she would accompany her to search the farmers' fields for potatoes. Emma was an only child and well provided for, and she truly wanted to help Poldie. The two girls walked for three miles to Kornwestheim. When they came upon a potato field, they scouted the area to see if anyone was watching. There were *Feldpolizei* (field policemen) in Germany who patrolled the fields with binoculars for hungry thieves. When the girls saw no one, they began digging the tubers out of the ground with their hands and filling Poldie's bag. The friends kept digging until their bag was full.

Poldie looked up at Emma. "Oh, my goodness!" she said. "We can't walk home like this. Others will see the potatoes, and we will be found out." The girls decided to take their under slips off to wrap and conceal the potato bag, though it didn't hide the thin layer of dirt that coated their hands and arms. They prayed that they would not get caught and took turns carrying the heavy bag.

After walking for a while, they reached a water tower, and a semitruck stopped alongside them. Out of it jumped a field policeman. He walked toward the girls quickly. "What do you have in your bag?" he asked.

"Potatoes," they both replied.

"Where did you get them?"

The girls both scrambled to tell a lie, saying the produce was from a farmer in Kornwestheim. Emma, although the same age as Poldie, was taller and more outspoken. She appeared to be older and the one in charge of the mission. The man slapped Emma hard on the cheek. Her short, blonde hair fell around her face.

"Do you know why I slapped you?" the man challenged. "Because you lied to me. That's why."

Unsure what to do, Poldie offered to give the man the potatoes. The policeman told them they could keep their loot but warned them never to let him catch them stealing again. The girls parted from the scary confrontation and kept walking. Emma's brown stockings, held in place with rubber bands, were streaked with urine. The encounter was so frightening, Emma could not keep her bladder from unloading. As the friends walked back to town, Emma, showing signs of embarrassment, said to Poldie, "I'll carry the bag low in front of me, and you walk behind me, so others won't see my wet stockings."

A few of the fellows in Alois's barracks were fortunate to get jobs in Stuttgart as construction workers. The city was rebuilding after the war, and to secure employment, the men were required to present proper ID cards—not the DP card they were issued—which required them to travel to an office in the city of Nellingen. A specific truck would pick up those wanting to obtain an ID. Alois, Mirek, Jindra, and Bohus learned of this arrangement on a day the vehicle had already departed. They wasted no time, and at about 6:00 a.m. the next day, the four of them set out on foot to Nellingen, about eighteen miles away. They secured their picture ID and then found a ride part of the way back to the camp. As they trekked the rest of the way by foot, US military officers stopped their Jeep and questioned them. The men showed their IDs and were free to go on their way. There was no room in the vehicle for the four friends to ride back.

It was after dark when the men finally arrived back to their cots, but the mission was accomplished. Their bunkmates offered to save their daily food rations for them, and they ate their bread, soup, and potatoes before falling asleep.

With new waves of refugees coming in, the buildings were becoming severely overcrowded. Camp authorities announced there were opportunities for escapees to immigrate to receiving countries. First, they appealed to those with specialized skills. Alois offered his services as a forester, but that didn't seem to be what anyone was looking for. Mirek had training as a student, but "student" was not appealing either. Alois, Mirek, Jindra, and Bohus all decided they should try for jobs as construction workers in Stuttgart. They were optimistic when they were offered work digging building foundations by hand. However, when the areas were dug out, their jobs were terminated.

They combined the several German marks they earned and located a bakery. Each bought a loaf of bread, then they pooled more money and purchased a pound of lard from the grocery store. The bread smothered with the thick fat was more filling than anything they had enjoyed in recent memory.

The Czechs continued their quest for work, finding it as area project superintendents allowed. Alois landed a job on a project laying tracks for streetcars between the German cities of Zuffenhausen and Stammheim. With a pick and a shovel, Alois dug trenches that were four feet wide and two feet deep. The workers then filled them with stones before placing ties. Next, they laid tracks down on the ties. Finally, they placed stones between them. Alois had worked hard at home, but this kind of heavy labor and strenuous lifting proved to be more arduous. He looked down at his throbbing hands. There were no gloves, and his palms were bleeding and blistered. He remembered how he used to make money using his hands to play the trumpet, and sadness crept over him. After about a week, Alois contracted blood poisoning, so his boss sent him home. When he felt better, Alois went back to the construction site to work again. The boss refused him entrance, thinking Alois was too frail for the intense labor.

Each of the other young men did all they could to earn money, using their wages to purchase bread at every opportunity. On one occasion, an agent with the French Foreign Legion came to the camp to recruit. The agent promised the prospects ten German marks if they followed him to the train station. Several of the refugees complied, boarded the train, and collected the cash. When the train began to move, the recruits made a mad rush, jumped out, and dashed instead to buy food. Some of the men stayed, and many of those eventually died fighting in the First Indochina War, which lasted a grueling eight years.

One of the men in their building, Juraj, was in his thirties and had been a newspaper reporter in Prague. He began working for the American and English intelligence-gathering agencies. He knew his young comrades still longed to join the liberation army. Juraj shared with Alois and the others that the US and British armies were looking for a few young men to be trained to work in their organizations. Volunteers were compensated several marks for participating. Alois signed up for the training and completed basic requirements. The work seemed very simple; it involved more observation than hard labor.

Following the training, Alois and two other volunteers were given an assignment. They were told to meet at a place called Jagerhof's Kasserne in Ludwigsburg. From there, they would be picked up by a vehicle and given the necessary documents and further details. The small group waited for three hours, but the car never arrived. A messenger let them know that the mission was postponed due to complications with something in Hungary. The three were told to return to the camp and await the next order.

During the next several days, no further orders came. Something did not seem right. Alois had time to think about potential scenarios. He did not know where he was going or any details of the assignment. He might find himself in a worse fate than the one he already found himself in. Alois approached Juraj and withdrew his intentions for the mission and began rethinking what he wanted to do with his life. Sadly, about a month later, Juraj went missing, and no one knew what became of him.

Alois finally accepted what he had been denying: The western nations were not going to eliminate the communist oppression, at least as far as he could tell. Furthermore, the idea of joining their army units was just a fantasy. With no purpose, Alois felt despondent and began sinking into a deep hopelessness. He had escaped his country with the firm intention of serving in liberation efforts. Now what would he do? As he lay on his cot one night, his stomach churning and his mind whirling, he pictured his mother, father, and siblings. He watched the community dances in his mind's eye and saw himself playing the trumpet. Then his thoughts took him into the dark uranium mines, and he watched himself falling under a weight too great to bear. Somehow, he already felt spent and old, with nothing to look forward to. On a few occasions, as more and more desperation set in, Alois contemplated ending it all via the gas pipes in the basement, but he quickly pulled himself back from the brink.

One day, Alois strolled over to the camp bulletin board and saw a new advertisement posted. It was an announcement for a mass immigration to Australia. This time, the receiving country was not specifying unique skills; anyone could apply. Mirek, Jindra, and Bohus registered. They knew nothing much about the country, but they figured that they would be free and that they could find work and hopefully have a future, one that looked brighter than the one they knew now. Something stopped Alois from applying; he had already made a significant, irreversible life decision once, and he had to think hard about doing it again.

For the next several weeks, Bohus, Jindra, and Mirek reported to immigration officials and were examined by a doctor. The young men were eager to go, and those who operated the camp were glad to free more bed space. Finally, the three went to the Australian consulate. If they were accepted, they would work as shepherds for two years somewhere in Australia. Alois tried to picture himself among sheep. He didn't care as much about the type of work as the steady food supply. Shepherding sounded better than the lifting and hard labor, which had worn his hands raw. Still, Alois was not ready to leave the only world he knew.

◆

Despite missing so many days of school, Poldie was allowed to graduate from the eighth grade at fourteen. She began looking for work right away and found a position in Kornwestheim at Salamander Shoe Factory. Her job was to fasten laces into shoes, then polish them on a wheel before placing them in shoeboxes. She worked there forty hours a week, earning thirty-five marks per week. She kept enough money to pay for a train ticket—three and a half marks. The rest of the money was given to her mother.

The most fun diversion for Poldie was going dancing on Saturdays. Poldie remembered those lessons her father gave her on how to dance back in the refugee camps. Now she and her older brother Tony would go dancing on the weekends. In the absence of other partners, they practiced their skills as a pair. The brother and sister were so good at waltzing, all the other dancers stopped to watch them glide gracefully to the sound of the accordion.

On Sunday afternoons, Poldie and her friends enjoyed attending the movies. It was a nice reprieve from working all week and cleaning the kitchen on Sunday. One particular Saturday, the girls missed the 4:00 p.m. show by a few minutes and were told that they must wait until the 6:00 p.m. showing to get in. By the time Leopoldine returned to the apartment, it was dark outside. She had planned to sneak up to her family's apartment, but when she entered the building, her mother was waiting for her on the first floor with a *kochlöffel* (wooden spoon) in hand and began striking Poldie with it.

"Mom, don't hit me! I didn't do anything wrong," Poldie protested.

"Where have you been so long?" Anna demanded.

"We had to wait for the second movie. That's why I'm late."

Anna didn't care about Poldie's excuse. She told her daughter she must be home on time from now on. Poldie didn't think her mother was being cruel; it seemed more to her that life itself was harsh, and they all had to adjust to it.

Alois's three companions were accepted to go to Australia, and they congratulated one another. Within two weeks, the camp bulletin board informed everyone that the volunteers would be leaving in two days. On the morning of the departure, the three men turned in their cots, blankets, camp photo IDs, and food cards. Alois accompanied them to the freight station in Ludwigsburg. He said a sad good-bye to his dear friends. Mirek, Jindra, and Bohus promised they would write Alois when they arrived in Australia. It was the first time the refugees separated since escaping together earlier that year. In spite of an unknown future, they were full of hope. Alois suggested he might go on the next transport ship if possible and that they would see each other again on the Australian continent—maybe even later on in the year.

When Alois returned to the camp, he felt a lonely emptiness. He had parted from his family, and now he was separated from this band of brothers. The following weeks alone proved difficult, but within days, Alois deepened friendships with some of his other bunkmates. They all had similar hopes and sorrows. Three of them—Tomas, Jarek, and Vasek—became close friends and eased the absence that Mirek, Jindra, and Bohus left. After several months, Alois had still received no word from his departed friends. He wondered daily about their well-being.

Everyone hoped, as more time passed, that things would get better, opportunities would come, and more food would be available. If a change was happening, no one in the camp witnessed it. Hunger was a constant, unwelcome companion. The landscape around them was still severely damaged from the bombings, and the native Germans competed for food and jobs. Many of them despised these foreigners in their land. They called them *verflucht ausländers* (cursed foreigners).

Observing the rubble of his adopted country, Alois began to think seriously about leaving. Other than occasional odd jobs, there were few opportunities. Tomas, Jarek, and Vasek agreed. Immigration to yet another location seemed to be the only way out. Alois tried processing this new reality. Each day, the friends would glance at the camp bulletin board and study the advertisements. There was always a need for doctors, nurses, and experts or specialists, but not for young men who had no training or qualifications.

About a month after they began seriously investigating the chance of becoming Australians, the four men saw another announcement on the board. Australia still opened its arms to them, and no special skills were required. This time, Alois went with his three friends to register. They submitted their paperwork and a month later were called to the Australian consulate. All four were accepted and given entry visas for Australia. As Alois prepared to make the transition, he envisioned reuniting with his old friends and starting a new, useful life there. Sometimes he and his companions talked about what it would be like to be in a new land, to experience total freedom, and how it would feel to have plenty of food.

The morning of departure arrived. Alois said good-bye to many of the men he grew close to at the camp. He returned his cot, blanket, camp ID, and food card. Those accepted to Australia walked out together, feeling like strange international travelers with no bags and a minuscule amount of money. The camp authorities drove them to the Ludwigsburg train station. They boarded the train, and each took their assigned seat. When the train began rolling, Alois felt glad to be leaving Germany. He wanted to go somewhere he belonged. The train moved along to the northern city of Aurich, where the group stayed for several days. At that location, the men had much more food than they were used to eating. They also received medical exams and were given the necessary shots. Eventually, they were taken to the embarkation center at Emden, Germany. The ship to their future would depart in two days.

In all the time he had been a refugee, Alois never sent a letter to his family. Contacting the families back home was dangerous and would expose escapees' families to persecution by the communist regime. It was permissible for family members living in England or the United States to send letters back home for them, but Alois and his friends had no loved ones in these countries. Leaving Germany made them feel like they had a sense of freedom. They decided to use their money to buy postcards. They would write on the cards, "We are sending you final greetings from Europe." As they mailed the cards, they hoped the message was vague enough so that it would not arouse too much suspicion. The young men walked back from the post office to the barracks, and all felt a sense of buoyancy. Finally, they were going to start a new life with the dawn of the very next day.

CHAPTER FIVE

REJECTION, HOPELESSNESS, AND A WELCOME REPRIEVE

When the four men returned to the barracks, they heard an announcement coming through the loudspeakers, which were located at the four corners of the building. The announcement said a name, but Alois could not make it out. He listened again. "Alois Huf," the voice repeated, was to report to the camp office. Curious, Alois instantly headed to the office and identified himself. A camp authority handed him a piece of paper with simple instructions. Alois was to go back to Ludwigsburg. A train ticket was provided; he would be leaving that afternoon.

Alois found it impossible to contain the shock and disappointment that suddenly swallowed him up. He grappled to understand how such a weighty message could be delivered with such ease. "Why? What did I do wrong?" he asked. He explained to a camp leader that he came with three of his friends from Czechoslovakia. He had no one in Germany to return to.

The authorities seemed somewhat sympathetic but unhelpful. "We don't know why. We received orders to send you back to Ludwigsburg," one of them said. Arguing with them was useless; they were following orders. There was no appeals process.

The walk back to his bunk felt dizzying; Alois found it impossible to think coherently. The one who could sing like a bird suddenly was virtually mute. He handed the sheet of paper to his companions. They were stunned. "This cannot be happening. There must be something we can do!" one of them said. Together, they marched back to the camp office and asked if there was some mistake. The camp authority explained that the order was clear: Alois Huf must return to Ludwigsburg. No one knew the reason.

Tomas, Jarek, and Vasek escorted Alois to the train station. When they arrived, Alois wept bitterly, and his buddies could not hold back. The band of new brothers was a sobbing mess. Never before had Alois experienced so many conflicting emotions at one time. Having to leave his family back in Czechoslovakia in secret robbed him of his right to say the proper good-byes. This time, he pulled himself together enough to exchange a tender farewell. He climbed the steps to the train, unable to stop crying. When the train began to move, he waved at his friends. This was undoubtedly the last time he would see them, just like Mirek, Jindra, and Bohus, he thought. The train might as well have been careening toward the center of the earth. It felt like the world beneath him had crashed. The rhythmic sound of the steam engine seemed to beat against his consciousness. Since leaving home, Alois lost everything: his forestry job, his place in the band, and most importantly, his dear family. Now he lost two sets of close friends. The loneliness overwhelmed him and rushed in like a violent storm, enveloping him with darkness and gloom. There was nothing left to live for. Suicidal thoughts began tempting him to end it all.

Alois peered outside the lightly clouded window. He wished for a steep cliff with rocks below to throw himself into, but he only saw flat land for miles to come. Maybe if he jumped out of the train the right way, it would be just as effective. Tears continued rolling down his cheeks as he closed his eyes and imagined ending his life. As Alois reasoned with the finality of his premeditations, the train's whistle began to blow. Alois opened his eyes, his thoughts interrupted. Something about the whistle was cheerful, telling him that this was not the end and that God was still there. The steam whistle blew repetitively, as if to say, "Listen again."

He closed his eyes. All the hardships made him wonder if God cared about him at all. He prayed silently, "God, if you are really up there, look at what is happening to me. My three friends—they are going on to their new lives, and I'm going back to nothing! I don't have anyone in Germany, and I'm at the end of my strength." But there appeared to be a deafening silence.

The train ride took twelve hours from Emden back to Ludwigsburg, Germany. Alois was returning empty-handed—he didn't even have money to purchase a meager meal. That day, he ignored the hunger pangs and remained contemplative. At one point, he reached into his pocket and took out his calendar, where he had written the lyrics to the sad song taught to him by the Czech leader in the barracks. In his loneliness, Alois sang the lyrics over and over again while allowing profound sorrow to overwhelm his being.

On one of the many stops along the way, a German-speaking American doctor from New York boarded the overcrowded train and took one of the only vacant seats near Alois. As the train rolled on and a brief period of time passed by, the man noticed that Alois was sad. "Why are you so sad?" the doctor queried. The truth came spilling out. Alois held nothing back from this stranger. Anyway, he figured he had nothing to lose. After recounting his struggles, Alois finished by confessing, "I feel I have nothing left to live for." The doctor consoled Alois and offered to help. He invited Alois to look him up in New York if he ever had the chance and then asked for a paper so he could leave his New York address. Alois handed the cordial doctor his little green pocket calendar along with a pencil and watched as the man turned to a blank page near the back and penned, "Dr. R. Conraut, 142 Calton Road, New Rochelle, New York, United States." His cursive penmanship was neat and legible. Alois stared at it for what seemed like an eternity. He sensed it was a sort of lifeline pulling him up out of the water. They said their farewells and parted ways.

When Alois finally staggered back into the refugee camp in Ludwigsburg, he felt as if he were in an altered state of consciousness. Reality was too stark to accept. He handed camp authorities the sheet of paper that ordered him back, along with his DP card from Amberg. He asked why he had been sent back. The camp officials told him it could take a few days to learn why and that they would issue a new ID card. Alois departed for the dining hall and waited to see if there were any leftovers, since he had previously forfeited his food card.

The next few days were miserable. A deep heaviness set in, and the air around Alois seemed thick and tentative, like walking through a fog.

Life at the camp was even more difficult after being denied the prospect of leaving. Was he that powerless over his destiny?

Alois reached into his pocket and pulled out his small worn pocket calendar. Paging through it, Alois came upon the New York doctor's information. A tiny bit of hope surfaced. Alois took a chance and penned a short note to the doctor and mailed it to his home in the United States. Shortly thereafter, an airmail envelope arrived addressed to Alois from the doctor. Alois ripped it open, and inside was a short response with five American dollars inside. Alois was elated that the respectable doctor kept his promise to stay in touch and grateful for the unexpected gift enclosed. He wrote him back to thank him for the kindness he showed Alois. Keeping in contact with anyone outside the refugee camp seemed like a move in the right direction.

Alois considered ways in which he might change his situation. In his building, the residents turned a vacant room into a makeshift chapel. He attended Mass there on Sundays and listened to the priest, who was also a Czech escapee. Alois remembered the times he walked to Sunday Mass with his mother and the special conversations the two shared. He wondered, "Was Mother in church today back in Czecho-slovakia?" The more he pondered memories of his family, the more the loneliness continued. Sitting in the chapel, Alois looked around. There was no one whom he recognized anymore, since so many had departed for Australia, and newcomers had replaced them. He was alone once again.

The priest began administering the Mass, but Alois felt spiritually empty and was only physically present. His mind and heart were else-where. He retraced his steps since arriving in Germany. Self-pity and pain commingled in a hopeless web. His homesickness had reached an overwhelming level. There was seemingly no promise of divine involvement for Alois, as suggested in the scripture: "Now no chastening seems to be joyful for the present, but painful; nevertheless, afterward it yields the peaceable fruit of righteousness to those who have been trained by it. Therefore strengthen the hands which hang down, and the feeble knees" (Hebrews 12:11–12). During the month of May, Catholics gathered every evening in the chapel to pay homage to Mary. Alois considered what the summer might hold for him.

After the service, he went outside and wandered into neighboring gardens. Sometimes there were tomatoes and apples available. Any time he saw a piece of fruit, he ate it immediately. That was one of the reasons the Germans disliked the foreigners. The displaced persons looked like invading birds of prey; they consumed scraps before they were shooed away.

Alois remembered a day when Jindra, Mirek, and Bohus were still at the camp. In the building adjacent to theirs, they spotted four sticks of salami hanging tantalizingly on ropes outside of a high window. "I know how we could get the salami down," Jindra said. He took a knife and fastened it to the end of a broomstick, then went to the attic of the building that night. A coconspirator held his feet while two others watched from below. Jindra stretched his thin body and cut the ropes. On the last rope, he slipped and accidentally hit the windowpane. In a few seconds, the lights in the building turned on, but Jindra and the others had disappeared out of sight with the meat in tow.

The team met up and ate the best salami they had ever tasted. The salami belonged to a man who operated a small canteen at the camp. At night, he kept the salami cool by hanging it outside. But to the hunger-ravaged residents, civility would not keep them away. The canteen owner never left food out again. The humor of the memory made Alois realize just how dire his situation was. Back home, although they had little, Alois and his family never had to steal food. "Oh God, what has become of me?" Alois prayed. "I'm so lonely and in need. If you can hear me, God, I need you right now. I don't have strength anymore." Inadvertently, Alois went straight to God in prayer, bypassing Mary and the saints, to lament his dire situation. Alois felt that God heard him.

It took a few weeks, but Alois was given a new camp photo ID. He took it with him and, with a fresh resolve, began looking for work again. He landed a position as a construction helper near the Stuttgart main rail station. The project was rebuilding a hotel named Zeppelinbau. Each morning, Alois took the twenty-minute train from Ludwigsburg to Stuttgart. From there, he walked about two minutes to the work site. This was a reasonable and welcomed commute for someone in the camp. Others who found work had to travel up to two hours each way to and from their places of employment. Alois liked his new job, and he learned more of the German language each day. His confidence grew as he felt useful and made income. After six weeks, the job ended. On his way back to the camp, he thought of his dream to join the US Army. That dream was still in view.

Alois continued to check the camp bulletin board. It was like a window of hope to a future life. Seeing announcements of opportunities caused people to dream again. One day, Alois read about an opportunity requiring no special skills. Canada needed men to work in silver mines. He believed the conditions would be better than those in the uranium mines back home, and it was better than wasting away at the camp. Alois registered for the opening and submitted his documents eagerly. Two weeks later, he went through the same procedures he had completed for the Australian assignment. The Canadian doctor gave him a clean bill of health, and he went to the Canadian consulate. He was accepted, and once again, Alois turned in his camp paperwork and required items and boarded a truck with other men to the freight train station in Ludwigsburg. He wished he could make the journey across the world with close friends, but he was still thankful for this chance.

From Ludwigsburg, the train was scheduled to take the group to Bremerhaven. While they waited for the train to leave Ludwigsburg, US military police came into their car, and Alois was shocked to hear his name: "Alois Huf, take your belongings and follow us to the Jeep. We must take you back to camp." Alois was dumbfounded. "This cannot be happening again," he said to himself. He followed the officers. As they drove back to the camp, he asked, "Why are you taking me back? What terrible thing have I done to deserve this?" Alois felt like he was reliving the same nightmare over and over again.

The soldiers had no idea. "It was our orders to bring you back," one of them said.

When he arrived at the camp, Alois went directly to the camp office, feeling a combination of anger and betrayal. "What have I done? Please tell me! Why was I sent back a second time? You promised me after I was sent back the first time that you would find out why this was done. Why am I hindered from leaving Germany?"

None of the camp officials were able or willing to tell him why. Instead, they looked at him with mistrust, as if he was a felon. It was such a hard blow to absorb. "I escaped the injustice in Czechoslovakia, and I put my life on the line when I crossed the border. Now I am asking for justice. Why won't somebody say what I've done?" The more he talked, the quieter the officials became. Alois's continued probing was not helping his cause.

When he left the camp office that day, his suicidal thoughts returned. It was embarrassing to go yet again to the camp supply room and ask for a blanket, cot, and utensils. The supply room manager looked surprised to see Alois. "Weren't you here this morning to turn all this in?" he asked. Alois could not muster the necessary energy to tell him what happened; it was too painful. He took the supplies in his arms and began walking away. As he climbed the three flights of stairs to his room, he wondered why he was alive if all he could do was merely exist.

When he set his belongings down, the men whom he had left a short time before peppered him with questions. "You must have done something bad!" they concluded with a combination of curiosity and shock. There would be no defending himself; Alois's patience had been worn thin, and he carried a heavy heart. For the next mealtimes, he was forced to wait in the dining room for leftovers until the office issued him a new ID card. He wished there was an alternative to suicide, and he could just cease to exist.

On Sunday, Alois returned to the chapel and just watched as the priest led his fellow Catholics in Mass. Alois had no prayer left. He had never heard promises like "Trust in the LORD with all your heart, and lean not on your own understanding; in all your ways acknowledge Him, And He shall direct your paths" (Proverbs 3:5-6). Or "Fear not, for I am with you; Be not dismayed, for I am your God. I will strengthen you, Yes, I will help you, I will uphold you with My righteous right hand" (Isaiah 41:10). As the Mass dismissed, Alois slowly walked out, feeling empty. The future had never looked bleaker.

By the late fall of 1949, Alois adjusted to the routine of camp life again. One day, he heard loud screams coming from outside. He looked out his window to see where the commotion was coming from. All he could distinguish were people gathered in a circle. He hurried downstairs and was surprised to witness the Czechs and Slovaks quarreling. The Slovak separatists were arguing for an independent state, and a fistfight broke out. In a few minutes, a number of American military police vehicles drove in, and soldiers began to subdue and question the fighters. A man among the group who spoke English translated.

The explanation did not calm tempers, and the police arrested several of them, reiterating to them that rioting was not permitted. Alois thought about how Czechoslovakia was under the iron grip of communism and how the people in the camp had all escaped from there. But instead of sticking together, they clashed, even with fists, over who would rule Czechoslovakia in the future. Alois heard more discussions about the Slovak separatist movement, but that was the end of the political fighting.

Since the colder weather necessitated firewood for the boiler room, part of Alois's work detail was splitting wood with an ax. There were no work gloves, and before long, a sharp splinter penetrated one of his fingers, causing sharp pain. Alois finally visited the camp first aid station, where a doctor attempted to dig the intruder out. In spite of the physician's efforts, the splinter stayed lodged in Alois's finger. The doctor sprayed some rubbing alcohol on the area, rolled some gauze around the finger, and told Alois it was all taken care of. Alois knew it wasn't—it hurt more as time went by. Three days later, on a Sunday, he went back to the first aid station, explaining that, by now, the pain was excruciating. The doctor unrolled the bandage, looked at the finger, and rolled it up again. He told Alois to go immediately to the hospital in Ludwigsburg. He notified the hospital by telephone and informed the staff to care for Alois.

Alois set off for the hospital and arrived in about twenty minutes. The nurse on duty uncaringly tugged to remove the gauze. Alois asked her to please take it off gently because his hand was painfully tender. She was a hardened army nurse and told Alois to be as strong as a soldier. Thankfully, a surgeon was present who was from Sudetenland. He spoke some Czech and told Alois he would take the wrapping off himself. After a look at the finger, the doctor told Alois he needed to operate right away. "You have blood poisoning," he said. "Whatever is in there needs to come out."

When he awoke from the anesthetics, the surgeon was at Alois's bedside and revealed that he had to cut out some of the infected tissue and left a surgical drain made of soft rubber in the wound for draining pus, blood, and fluids so his hand would hurt for a while. He also instructed him to keep the hand level with the shoulder. Alois walked back to the barracks, dizzy from the drugs and without any pain medicine. The stinging over the next few days was agonizing.

When he lay on his cot, Alois thought of home. It would be so nice to hear comforting words from his mother. She would have brought him soup and would know how to relieve the pain that drove him to tears. When his hand throbbed with pain, he would recall each day beginning with the escape. He could not remember one day in which he experienced happiness—he knew only disappointment. He pulled out his pocket calendar and studied it. He had jotted notes in it since March, marking his experiences and hoping that soon he could write down happy memories. He wished for relief so badly to numb more than just his physical pain.

One day, walking along the outskirts of the barracks, he prayed, "God, if You are really up there, You must see that I am religious. I go to the chapel and do all that our religion calls for. God, can't You take the pain from me?" The silence was palpable; there was no one to comfort him.

The fourth day after the surgery, Alois made a trip back to the hospital for a follow-up. When the surgeon asked how he was doing, Alois said, "I feel terrible; the pain is killing me."

The surgeon said, "It's most likely because of the drainage rubber that had to stay in to get rid of the infection. Today we can remove the rubber, and I'm sure that it will begin to feel much better." It was just as the doctor said. After the drain was removed and the wound cleansed, Alois began to heal.

On the way back to his barracks, the world looked friendlier. Alois even said in his heart, "God, I should not have argued with You the other day. Thank You that I feel so much better. Forgive me for foolishly doubting You." It was about a month before Alois regained the use of his hand. The cold air and snow of December reminded him that Christmas was coming soon. What a strange Christmas season it was, he thought.

There was a husband and wife in the camp whom Alois became acquainted with. They opened a basic canteen for camp residents. They prepared hot, home-cooked meals for the people who worked and could afford the modest sum to purchase them. The couple inquired if Alois was willing to walk each afternoon to the town's grocery store and pick up what they needed for the business. In return, they would treat Alois to a hot meal; they were not able to pay him. Remuneration in meals sounded like a good deal to Alois. Besides, it was challenging to find work while he waited for his hand to fully heal.

Every afternoon, they sent Alois off with a backpack, money, and a shopping list. Once Alois arrived at the store, he searched for and gathered specific items, practicing his German often. On his way back, Alois thought of what he had to look forward to. A traditional Czech dinner of dumplings, cabbage, and pork was such a welcome addition to the usual sparse pickle gravy and boiled potatoes.

Christmas 1949 was in view, and Alois was especially appreciative of his job as an errand runner. It kept him from thinking only of home. He imagined spending Christmas in a house—what a wild dream that seemed. Leading up to the holiday, Alois took two or three trips in a day to compensate for the extra business.

On Christmas Eve, Saturday, December 24, 1949, Alois leaned back on his cot in the camp and closed his eyes. Two hundred eighty-four days had passed since he left his family back in Czechoslovakia. He lovingly thought of his siblings, Frank, age five; Liduska, eleven; Hynek, seventeen; Pepa, twenty; and Maruska, twenty-two. Then he envisioned his dear mother and father gathered with his brothers and sisters around the Christmas tree. He hoped they were all well. Alois wondered if they missed him as much as he missed them. He knew the ache of his absence would be difficult for each of them. The fact that he could not even write to his family felt like a punishment.

"God, is this fair?" he cried in his mind. Alois opened his eyes, wondering if he had screamed aloud. But seeing the sad faces of the other men on their cots, he knew he did not—they were in their own lonely recollections. Alois gained a sense of solace from the group's shared sorrow. There were about two thousand men in the camp who were dreaming of homes and families in Czechoslovakia too. The midnight hour ushered in the very first Christmas Alois ever spent without family.

The holidays passed, and with a new year before him, Alois resolved that, after two rejections, he should simply forget about immigrating. Obtaining supplies for the canteen had given him more nutrition but no income. He needed better and warmer clothes and an improved life that only a steady job could provide. Alois went into the bombed city of Stuttgart and asked for a job working again as a construction helper near the main rail station. A manager agreed to hire him. He could start the following Monday. Alois returned to the camp to meet with the canteen owners to turn in an unofficial resignation notice because of his new job. He would only be able to help them through Saturday. They were happy for Alois and loaned him three and a half marks for the weekly train ticket from Ludwigsburg to Stuttgart.

During the first week of employment, Alois gained physical and emotional strength. The regular canteen meals had begun to nourish his thin body and enliven his mind. It was difficult throughout the day because he did not yet have money to purchase food. Alois asked his bunkmate if he was willing to collect his allotted food from the camp kitchen and keep it for him. When Alois arrived at the camp in the evenings, he ate the lunch and supper portions. Fridays were paydays, and things were beginning to improve. He trusted the job would last longer this time.

Over the next few weeks, with a modest but steady income, Alois purchased several necessary items—after filling his stomach first. He was proud to obtain a white dress shirt and a tie. The tie might have seemed an extravagant purchase to some, but it gave him dignity after so much loss. He could now go to chapel on Sundays and feel like he belonged. At night, Alois no longer felt famished while resting on his cot. He often thought of his six companions who immigrated to Australia. He wondered how they were doing and if they would ever write to him.

By April, the construction job was finished, and Alois was terminated again. It was back to camp life, and his meager savings slowly disappeared. Just a little over one year passed since escaping his invaded homeland and leaving his family. It seemed that 1950 was not to be any different than the year before.

◆

In July, a man by the name of Vlada who lived at the camp in the same room as Alois began a job as a driver for the US Army. He told Alois that they were searching for more drivers. Alois eagerly listened. Vlada said, "All you need is your driver's license from Czechoslovakia. When you show it to the German transportation department, they will issue a German driver's license to you. After that, you present yourself to the Americans and take their driving test, and that's it."

Alois immediately felt a knot in his stomach. Only six months prior to his escape, he and his brother Pepa completed driving school. They went after work each day from 6:00 p.m. to 8:00 p.m. to the Hanak Driver's School in Sumperk. At the end of three weeks, Alois and Pepa took written tests. Both brothers went a step further, taking a more rigorous exam in order to obtain a chauffeur's license. They were educated about diesel engines and air brakes. The brothers passed the driving test as well. Obtaining the license came at a cost however; each of them paid about two months' wages. The total for each boy was three thousand Czech crowns.

Since Alois normally took the train and rode his bike at home, he did not carry the specialized license on him. Amid the stress of leaving Czechoslovakia, Alois had inadvertently left his driver's license behind.

Alois remained hopeful; he had the skills, after all. He asked Vlada, "What could I do to get a German driver's license?"

Vlada often called Alois "Tkanicko" (shoestring) because Alois was so skinny. He repeated, "Tkanicko, either present your Czech license or you need to go to German driver education school."

Alois carried his disappointment like a heavy burden for several days. Being a driver wouldn't be the kind of injurious, physical labor that had caused him to contract blood poisoning; it would also be a position that could provide stability. That Sunday in the chapel, he prayed, "God, You know I need this driver's license to get the job." He would have given anything to have that license in his hand. Alois silently conversed with God about how great it would be if he could get the job driving for the US Army. It wasn't his original goal of joining the liberation army, but at this point, it would be his first dream to come true since leaving home. Alois wondered if such a prayer request was too difficult for God. He had never heard the verse "Behold, I am the LORD, the God of all flesh. Is there anything too hard for Me?" (Jeremiah 32:27). As he left the chapel in the morning, Alois determined to get the job.

When he returned to the barracks, Alois mentioned to Vlada his plan for obtaining the license he needed. "That is crazy," his friend replied. "It will never work. If it did, it would be a miracle." Alois thought that Vlada was probably right, but still he felt a flicker of hope.

The next morning, Monday, July 10, 1950, Alois ate his breakfast and then set out on foot to the Ludwigsburg Ladratsamt on Stuttgarterstrasse. This was an administrative district office that included the courthouse and police station. The driver's license offices were located on the first floor. During the half-hour walk, angst set in, and Alois began to fret whether or not his plan could work. Would they even speak to him since his German was lacking? Would they scorn his request? Yet if he did not try, he would never know. By the time Alois reached the massive door of the building, he noticed that his hand was shaking as he turned the doorknob. Once inside, he found the directory on a wall nearby, which listed the department and floor he needed. After locating the office, he braced himself as he knocked on the door.

A voice responded, "Herein" (Come in). Alois walked in and said, "Guten morgen" (Good morning) as cheerfully as he could muster. He took special care to comb his hair and smooth the wrinkles out of his clothes. He hoped his appearance and jovial attitude would gain a fair hearing.

It was an older woman he presented himself to. She stared at Alois and asked, "Was kann ich fuer sie tun?" (What can I do for you?)

Alois began conversing in his best German: "Ma'am, I wonder if you would be so kind as to help me. I think you are the only one who would be able to do this for me." He noticed his hands were shaking again, and he hoped the saliva would return to his mouth once he felt a bit more comfortable.

"Go on," she said.

Alois moved closer to her desk, attempting to pray silently and talk at the same time. "A year ago, in March, I escaped from communist Czechoslovakia." Her face appeared kind. "Since April of 1949, I have been living in a refugee camp in Krabenloch Kasserne. Life in the camp is not pleasant. I wanted to immigrate to other countries, but I was refused twice. I have gotten work now and then but am unable to keep a steady job. Now I learned I could have a chance to secure a job as a driver for the US Army. The Americans require a German driver's license. I completed all the training back home and even earned my chauffeur's license. It was issued by the Czechoslovakian Transportation Department. Ma'am, would you be able to please write a letter to the International Red Cross and see if perhaps they would ask the Czechoslovakian Transportation Department to send the driver's license to you? Or maybe could you write the transportation department directly? This is my only chance to obtain a steady job."

The woman looked at Alois and seemed attentive but firm. "You ask an impossible thing. The communist government of Czechoslovakia would most likely ignore your request," she said. "You would have to take the driver's school course in Germany. Then we could issue a driver's license to you."

There it was again—Fahrschule (German driver's school). Alois decided to press further, even as he felt the flicker of hope fade. "Ma'am, I do not have the four hundred marks to pay for driver's school," he admitted.

The woman looked at him for a few seconds and then said, "Augenblick bitte warten Sie mal." (Please wait a few moments.) She rose and went to the next room. Alois sat in a chair, and angst filled his body. Was he in trouble? He kept waiting in the hope that something good would happen. She returned after twenty minutes. Alois stood at attention.

"I would need two pictures of you, then come back again," she said simply.

Alois excitedly said, "Ma'am, I do have two pictures of me, but I don't know if they're good enough."

She said, "Let me see them."

With trembling fingers, Alois reached into his jacket pocket. He kept the photos he had needed for Canadian immigration, along with his photo ID. He questioned if they were adequate as he handed them to her.

"Let's try it. Maybe they will work," she said and left the room again. Alois had been through so many almosts, maybes, and not-quites. Yet he dared himself to hope again.

A few minutes later, the woman reappeared and handed Alois two documents to sign. He held his hand steady enough to scribble his signature. The employee retained one of the documents and folded the other in half. "Mr. Huf, here is your driver's license. I wish you luck," she said. She handed him the official Fuhrerschein, and he accepted it with awe.

"Many, many thanks," Alois said. "You will never know what this means to me!"

When Alois was back outside, he was sure it was Christmas in July. There was no doubt he had just received a miracle. He looked to the sky and prayed, "Thank You, God, a thousand times. I thought it would have been a miracle if they checked with Czechoslovakia, and yet You gave me even more than I dared to ask—and free of charge!" Alois didn't know the scripture "Bless the LORD, o my soul; and all that is within me, bless His holy name" (Psalm 103:1), but his heart was singing it. He wondered if this woman had been an angel, sent to help him on his way.

That evening, when Vlada returned to the barracks from work, Alois asked him, "Could you please tell me again what I would need in order to apply for the chauffeur job with the US Army?"

Vlada said, "You would need the German driver's license."

Alois said nonchalantly, "I already have that."

Vlada looked skeptical. "Yeah, right. That sure would be nice."

"I'm serious," Alois said. "I really have the driver's license!" He reached into his coat pocket and pulled out the new treasure. Vlada took the light-gray bifold document, opened to the inside page, and studied it with conviction. Everything appeared to be in order. It contained all pertinent and official information, was stamped and signed by the proper authority, and pictured Alois.

Vlada gasped. Didn't they just discuss that Alois would have to pay and go through training again? "How did you do that? This is impossible! It would be like a miracle."

"I think it was one!" Alois exclaimed.

Vlada shared in Alois's joy and congratulated him. "Now," he said, "you need to take their test. The test is administered only in English.

First, there is the written test and then the driving test. It's supervised by the army sergeant, and he does not speak any German."

That was Alois's second big obstacle. "I don't know any English," he said.

"That's no problem," Vlada said encouragingly. "I will write down what I remember the written questions were. They were mostly about traffic signs. When you take the driving test, you need to know instructions like 'Go on,' 'Stop,' 'Turn left,' 'Turn right,' and 'Shift in higher gear and in lower gear.'" Vlada continued, "There is somebody here in our building who has a Czech-English dictionary. That is what I did—just study it. It worked for me." Vlada was about twice Alois's age, so he said, "You are much younger than me, so you can memorize a lot faster."

Alois immediately asked to borrow the Czech-English dictionary. All evening, he practiced the words and the pronunciations with Vlada. He wrote down questions from Vlada on a sheet of paper and rehearsed them over and over in his mind. Alois copied many of the words from the dictionary before returning the book. He studied earnestly throughout the next several days.

Alois enrolled for the driver's test with the US Army. When the test day came, he prayed fervently, "God, could this be the beginning of a new life for me—a different life? Please help me pass the test. This would mean so much to me." Alois had not been taught the verse "Ask, and it will be given to you; seek, and you will find; knock, and it will be opened to you" (Matthew 7:7). But still he asked with all his heart. As he walked in to the take the written test, Alois pleaded again, "Please, God, don't forget me!"

The test was not difficult; it contained information about traffic signs and the new words Alois learned. Afterward, the supervising sergeant took Alois for a road test. Alois tried not to speak much, lest he give away his limited English vocabulary. But he listened attentively, heeding every instruction given by the test administrator. When they returned and Alois parked the car, he was told he passed. The instructor felt he had a good handle on everything. Alois was given instructions on when and where to report to work. Once again, he prayed in his heart, "Thank You, God, for remembering me."

CHAPTER SIX

NEW START
AND NEW SWEETHEARTS

This job was Alois's golden ticket; he would be a working professional now with a steady job. The US Army motor pool was located in Stuttgart-Moehringen, in the Kelly Barracks. It was about thirty miles from Ludwigsburg. Alois and Vlada went to work together. They woke up at 4:45 a.m., left the camp by 5:00, and walked twenty minutes to the railroad station. Then they took the train from Ludwigsburg to Stuttgart. The final connection was a thirty-minute electric streetcar ride to Moehringen, leaving them with a fifteen-minute walk to Kelly Barracks. Alois and Vlada arrived in plenty of time to start work at 7:00 a.m.

The American military trucks were not automatic transmission vehicles. Alois had no idea how to use a stick shift. Again, Vlada proved to be an enormous support. He took Alois's pocket calendar and opened it to the inside page. He drew two diagrams, one for a Volkswagen and the other for a Dodge. Alois rehearsed the two manual gearshift drawings and felt confident that he would be able to master the military vehicles.

The motor pool dispatcher gave the drivers trip tickets, indicating their day's assignments. From the motor pool, Alois was given a three-quarter-ton Dodge truck to drive. It was an open-frame vehicle with no side doors. On the first day, Alois was sent to the Signal Corps in Kelly Barracks. The sergeant in charge was named Bryan. He was easygoing and not like the callous military men Alois had known the Russians to be. When Alois arrived at Signal Corps, the sergeant brought him to a room with a cot in the corner. He told Alois, "Go and rest there. When we need you, we will come for you."

It seemed very unusual to Alois. He had never heard of anyone getting paid to sleep. Alois decided to take a look around. There was a larger room where six soldiers were sitting. Some were working on repairing phones, and others were awaiting service calls from the surrounding areas. Alois introduced himself to the young GIs. Alois was eager to learn English and made it a point to converse with them. He asked, "What is this? How do you say that?" The Americans were willing to teach Alois, and in the repair shop, they even showed him how to restore broken telephones. Alois preferred utilizing his time like this instead of napping on the cot. Alois's personality exuded with friendliness, and he was happy to call himself one of the guys.

When a request came in for maintenance, two American GIs were sent to conduct the repairs. Alois hurried to join right in. The GIs eventually invited him to join them in the mess hall. While the Americans thought the food was nothing special, Alois thought the meals were delicious. When the GIs were working outside, they sent Alois to the local stores to buy dinner rolls, salami, and beer. The group took such a liking to Alois that they requested to Sgt. Bryan that he be their permanent Signal Corps driver. Without hesitation, Alois gladly accepted. There were multiple repairs to complete; the Echterdingen Military Airfield sustained significant damage. The Americans installed new telephone lines from the tower to all the hangars. When a new helicopter airfield was built in Nellingen, the Signal Corps connected new telephone lines.

Alois valued his job and the camaraderie a great deal. The GIs taught Alois all about telephones and the English language—even if their version of English was a little coarse. He picked up slang and foul language, and he started smoking a lot more, since everyone smoked on breaks. Cigarettes were about $1.50 per carton of two hundred for the soldiers.

When the GIs went around on business, Alois served as a translator, since not many Americans knew German. It was ironic to him that he was translating in two languages that, just a few years earlier, he hardly knew. Translating was even more essential than his driving job. Even the Germans who knew English would sometimes avoid speaking it out of pride or spite. The Americans were on German soil, after all.

When the weather turned cold and snow started to fall, the GIs donned their all-weather coats, which protected them from the chill and moisture. They noticed Alois did not have a jacket, so the soldiers gave him one. It was helpful for Alois, especially since the precipitation came into the cab while driving. The men also offered him a pair of military boots and a hat for protection from the elements. When Alois zipped up the jacket to just under his chin, no one noticed his civilian clothing underneath. When he put on the boots and hat, he was just like one of the GIs, except for his strong foreign accent.

One morning, the group left for Echterdingen Airfield to conduct telephone repairs. Alois walked among the GIs with a pipe hanging from his mouth. When the men crossed paths with an officer, the GIs saluted their superior. The officer barked, "Soldier, take that pipe out of your mouth when saluting an officer!"

Alois removed the pipe quickly. "Yes, sir!" he replied. The GIs enjoyed a good laugh about that for weeks to come. It felt like Alois had come back to life again. He loved his new brothers so much, he would have joined the US Army if he could have.

The refugee camp barracks continued to fill up, and Vlada suggested he and Alois rent a room in town. Together, they found a room at a place called "Fremdenheim-Zimmer" on Stuttgarterstrasse in Ludwigsburg. From their new location, getting to the train station was much faster. The next six months passed by quickly, and the two looked for an alternate place to live. After World War II ended, the mandatory German ID cards (Kennkarte) were replaced with new ones that no longer indicated the owner's ethnic designation. During the war, these IDs indicated the person's ethnicity by their color: yellow for the Jews, blue for Russians and Ukrainians, and gray for Poles. After 1951, all identity cards became gray. On June 2, 1951, the Ludwigsburg office issued Alois a new photo ID card. Vlada and Alois transitioned to a very modest apartment building in Seestrasse, also located in Ludwigsburg. Six rooms were available for rent in the complex, and the men were able to have their own private spaces. Vlada got a place on the second floor and Alois one on the third floor. Vlada's room faced the street, and Alois's looked out over the backyard, with other buildings in view. Alois's six-by-twelve-foot room had a bed with a table and chair. There was no running water, but the side table had a porcelain pitcher and washbasin, which an attendant refilled daily with fresh water. A chamber pot served as the bathroom. Alois took sponge baths during the week and went to the city bath on the weekends for a warm shower.

Having a room to himself was a strange sensation—it was both liberating and lonely. Alois looked into the bedroom mirror and studied himself for the first time in a long time. His shoulders looked like they had pulled forward into a slouch. All the hunger and the mental burdens he'd carried had changed his appearance, he thought. Alois consciously pulled his shoulders up and back. He lifted his chin. His straight nose was still distinguished, and his bright-blue eyes were pensive and kind. His thick blond hair was straight, and he always combed it neatly. Alois had his place now and felt proud of how far he had come.

The motor pool where Alois worked moved its location from Moehringen to downtown Stuttgart. In the late fall of 1951, the US Army began accepting volunteers from among the Czechoslovakian refugees. A dream come true for many of them. Five of Alois's closest friends from the refugee camp signed up, including Rudolf, who had helped fill the gap that Alois's friends left when they departed. Alois signed up enthusiastically. Soon, the volunteers were called in and began basic training. Alois was anxiously waiting to receive word on his acceptance.

Finally, a letter arrived from the US Army stating that Alois's application to join the military was rejected. This could not be happening. How many refusals could one man take? Rejection and disappointment hovered over him like a chronic disease. But he became accustomed to expecting both refusals and setbacks. How was it that he alone of his many friends was singled out and turned away for immigration to Australia and Canada? Alois was determined to find answers and knew a confrontation of sorts was looming. He was young, fit, smart, and willing to be a good citizen like the others. The refusals did not make sense. He again turned to prayer as he had many other times: "God, will I be forced to stay in Germany, where I've faced so much sorrow and dejection?" Alois wished he knew some answer that would comfort him, like the scripture verse "Trust in the LORD with all your heart, and lean not on your own understanding . . . and He shall direct your paths" (Proverbs 3:5–6). Alois reminded God that he was a religious person and should be remembered when it was time to pass out answered prayers.

Alois's rejection and dismay this time were short-lived. Before, Alois had no job and was alone. This time was different. When he had had moments of quiet on his train ride to work, Alois prayed, "God, I just want to say 'Thank You' for the excellent job that I have. Please help me keep it."

For the first time, it seemed as though Alois might be seeing with more clarity: Was it possible that these refusals had happened for a reason? Was there some higher plan behind it all? How was Alois to know what that plan was? Spiritual guidance was nowhere in sight, and it now appeared that someone else was controlling his destiny. Slowly, optimism began to replace the sadness. Was something better coming into view? Alois felt he was getting closer to some bright star and something good was on the horizon.

◆

When Poldie's oldest brother, Johnny, got married, he and his wife, Rosa, moved in with the Kellner family. A dozen people lived together in two rooms. Nobody seemed to be bothered by the crowded dwelling. For several years, the best they had was refugee camp life, and at least now, the family had their own place. After the young couple's first child was born, Johnny's family moved to Stuttgart. Poldie found another job in Stuttgart making umbrellas in a factory. She and her brother Tony took the train and worked together. Poldie always worked hard to help her mother, and she continued to be a caretaker in the home. She worked her full shift each day, and some days she also worked at a restaurant as a dish maid for two hours. When she arrived home, Poldie assisted in the kitchen, swept floors, washed dishes, and tucked the younger siblings in bed.

The autumn season was ushered in with fresh, crisp air, and Europeans made a habit of opening windows in the apartments to allow the air to circulate. One Sunday, Poldie and her friend Margret were leaning out of an open window from her family's second-story dwelling, watching the passing crowds below. Among the pedestrians walked a group of eligible young men. Alois and three of his friends took customary strolls on Sundays and made Karlstrasse part of their weekend route. He lived

just around the corner in Die Neue Sonne on Seestrasse. It was the
first time Poldie captured a glimpse of the young Czech boy. From the
moment she laid eyes on him, she was smitten. Like most starry-eyed
teenage girls, she and Margaret teased one another and coyly made
their selections from among the potential suitors. "I'll take that one,"
Poldie said as she pointed directly at the only dapper blond wearing a
dark suit. She already had a boyfriend named Manfred. His trade was
barbering, and his presence pleased Poldie's father because he gave him
and all his sons free haircuts. The gesture made no difference to Poldie.
She didn't fancy him, but she was not accustomed to making her own
decisions and went along with the courtship. Once she laid eyes on the
handsome blond among the lot that day, she imagined he would fly up
to her, and together they would ride away into the sunset just like in the
movies. The girls giggled and brushed off the conversation as a simple
joke, but Poldie was lovestruck from that moment on.

Every morning and afternoon, Poldie rode the train to and from
work. Local residents filed in, and for the time the train rolled, no one
had to labor. Poldie stood most times because there was simply no
room to sit. She spent her time on the short journey studying people,
wondering where they were going and what their lives involved. One
day on the overcrowded train, she paused in delightful amazement when
she caught a glimpse of that same handsome man she saw from her family's apartment window. His features stood out in the crowd with bold
blue eyes; neatly combed, copious blond hair; and a strong jawline. He
appeared to be in deep thought until she caught his eye. When their
eyes locked for the very first time, Poldie flashed a coy smile, and Alois
returned the gesture with a deliberate wink. Poldie had never looked
at men that way before, but this guy was so striking, she felt transfixed.

From that day on, Poldie intentionally searched for the man each
day on the train ride to work. The cars on the train were congested, but
still, Poldie intentionally moved just enough to catch his eye through the
crowd. On another occasion, after she and her brother Tony stepped
off the train, she noticed that the striking young fellow walked in their
same direction. Next to the Schlossplatz, where she and Tony worked,
was a large area where bombs had destroyed homes. The Americans had
cleared the area and set up their motor pool for the military vehicles.

Poldie then realized that this must be where the young man works. She continued to watch more carefully for glimpses of him. Whenever she saw him on the train, she would send a delicate smile his way. Sometimes, if she didn't see the stranger on the train, she would notice him driving a military vehicle wearing an army jacket.

One day, Poldie and her mother were walking to the bakery. Poldie caught sight of the man from the train again. He walked a few feet in front of them and turned into the Neue Sonne Guesthaus building.

She could not contain her infatuation with the stranger any longer. If Poldie didn't tell someone, she would just burst.

"I sure like that handsome young man, even though I don't know his name!" Poldie confided to her mother.

As she and her mother stepped into the bakery, Anna said, "He is probably an auslander [foreigner], because only auslanders live there. Besides, you already have a boyfriend! He is a barber; he is making good money."

"Mother, I don't care for him," Poldie declared.

Although it appeared to be a lost cause with her mother, Poldie was satisfied at least that she knew where this interesting yet mysterious gentleman lived.

Poldie's father was stricter than her mother. In an attempt to work a plan to meet this newfound love, Poldie knew she needed to convince her mother first. She persuaded Anna to walk around the corner with her to where the man lived. The main level of the Neue Sonne Guesthaus was where the men from the apartment met to enjoy a beer and socialize. Certainly out of character for Poldie, she and her mother entered the building and took a seat at a small table in the tiny cramped room. There he was—her blond beau. Poldie's heart fluttered. She and her mother felt out of place but ordered a popular nonalcoholic sparkling water drink called Sprudel. Poldie lost no time in clarifying her desires: "Mutter, schua da drüben. Siehst du den Blondem? Er ist der neue Typ, den ich wirklich mag!" (Mother, look over there. See the blond? He is the new guy I really like!) Anna glanced over and delightfully responded, "Er sieht so gut aus!" (He is so good looking!) Alois was more reserved than usual because of the many rejections he experienced after escaping. He had noticed Poldie too but remained a bit guarded.

Poldie wanted to get his attention, but how? She went with her heart and uncharacteristically began flirting creatively. She took the *bierdeckel* (beer coaster) from under her perspiring glass and tore very small pieces of the dampened paper. Then, rolling them up into tiny balls, she put them between her thumb and forefinger and flicked them in Alois's direction. Poldie felt a mixture of both embarrassment and confidence in stepping over typical boundaries to show how interested she was in Alois. He would have to make the next move.

That summer, Poldie's father was able to find a steady job for the first time in a long time. He worked at the Autobahn Strassen-Meisterei, a road commission for the German highway located in the suburbs of Ludwigsburg near Eglosheim. It was about two miles from the city limits. On the site stood a large building where all the trucks, snowplows, and tools were kept for road repairs. Vast piles of salt and sand were also stored there for the winter months.

As part of the job, workers would be on call during the day and night to respond to traffic accidents and to remove oil from the highways. During the winter months, they plowed snow and sprayed sand and salt on the icy roadways. The road commission wanted employees like Johann to live on-site so they would be able to respond to any highway-related needs quickly. Since relocating to Germany from Sudetenland, this was the most significant opportunity the Kellner family had received. One of sixteen living quarters was provided for them at the Strassen-Meisterei. The family was also allowed to rent a piece of land on which they could grow potatoes, plant a garden, and even raise livestock like chickens, rabbits, goats, and pigs. Unlike in the urban setting, grass would be plentiful, and they could dry it as hay.

Poldie's sister-in-law, Rosa, secured a job in Stuttgart with a paper recycling company named Pfleiderer Alt-papir. Poldie asked Rosa to keep her in mind if the company needed more workers; she was eager to earn more than her job provided. Soon, a position became available, and Poldie applied. The boss thought Poldie was small and not very strong, but he offered to give her a try. Poldie accepted the job enthusiastically and worked diligently sorting the used paper by color. The boss appreciated her thoroughness. Poldie was paid twice as much as she earned in her previous position. There was just one thing she did not like, however: Poldie's train route stopped just shy of her typical destination, and she got off before the handsome blond man exited the train. Poldie contemplated how she could get his attention.

One morning upon boarding the standing-room-only train in Ludwigsburg, Poldie saw him about twenty feet away and smiled. He winked back. From Ludwigsburg, the train stopped at Kornwestheim, Zuffenhausen, Feuerbach, and then Poldie's stop, Stuttgart-Nord, before it stopped at his station, Stuttgart-Haupt-Bahnhof. As people disembarked at the first three stops, Poldie tried to get a better look at the man who had captivated her. The thrill of him looking back at her was breathtaking, and the wink he gave in return for her smiles made her more confident. After the announcer proclaimed her stop, Poldie slowly strolled off the train.

At work that day, she couldn't stop thinking about the passenger in his military jacket. The next week, Poldie boarded the train feeling like they might finally meet, but to her displeasure, she did not see the man on the train. Day after day, evening after evening, not even a glimpse of him. Had she missed her opportunity to engage with this beautiful man? Even though she didn't know him, she missed him. About two weeks later, while waiting for the morning train in Ludwigsburg, Poldie reached into her pocket for her weekly train ticket and realized her pocket was empty. With no money to buy a ticket, her mind immediately raced. She could not miss work—the boss might be upset, and her parents depended on the money she earned. Horrified, Poldie knew she must hurry back home to pick up her ticket. If she went as quickly as possible, maybe she could still make the train.

As Poldie ran at full speed toward the apartment, she was surprised to see the young blond man walking toward her on the same side of the road. As she sprinted toward him, the man asked, "Fraulien, wohin laufen sie so schnell?" (Young lady, where are you running to so fast?) Poldie, so lost in her thoughts, kept racing past him without saying a word. When she arrived home, she quickly retrieved her train ticket and ran back to the station. When she passed the location where the man had attempted to converse with her, she thought to herself, "I've been waiting all this time for him to talk to me, and today it finally happened, but I did not even say one word. What a stupid mistake." Poldie felt tortured. "What will he think of me now?"

As she approached the station, Poldie saw the rear lights of the train disappear toward Kornwestheim. The train and the young man were gone. Poldie felt desolate. He would probably never want to speak to her again, she thought. Poldie took the next train to work. During the entire day at the factory, she kept thinking about the hopeless interaction. Maybe that evening, she would see him on the train. If so, she decided that she would approach him and explain why she was so rude, but to her dismay, he was not onboard. Sadly, she did not see him for the rest of the week. Poldie thought, "Will I ever see him again?" She could tell by his accent that he was a foreigner. Many of the Germans shunned the auslanders, and maybe he thought she was rejecting him. "He probably thought I was a snob," Poldie concluded and felt even worse.

The next week, to Poldie's utter glee, she saw the young man board her train car; they were both on their way home from work. Poldie kept looking his way, desperate for him to turn toward her. He never did. His pride was probably hurt, she realized. During the remainder of the train ride, Poldie got resourceful and began strategizing how she could undo the damage. When the train arrived in Ludwigsburg, Poldie disembarked with the other passengers. She was one of the first to get off and looked back to see if the man was walking behind her on the same side of the street. As Poldie walked past the large windows of the stores that lined the sidewalk, she got an idea. She would pretend to window-shop and study the items in the picture windows while she waited for the gentleman to approach. Poldie glanced back to ensure he was still headed in her direction. This time, they were going to talk to each other one way or another, she decided.

Poldie selected a store that showcased fine chocolates and candies. She faced the window, pretending to select her choices of the excellent treats, but instead, she intently concentrated on the reflections of the people who were approaching behind her, making their way home. She took in a breath—it was him! He was almost to her. Poldie stepped back and extended one leg behind her into the man's path, exposing her brown stockings and low heel. His foot caught on hers, and she quickly retracted it. She spun around to see him trip and watched as he regained his composure. The blond man looked at her with astonishment. Alois pulled his shoulders back and for a brief second paused to take in the girl before him. She looked startled too. She had a sweet, round face, framed with wavy brown hair and lit with coy blue eyes.

"I'm sorry," Poldie started, clearing her throat. "I wanted to explain why I didn't have time to talk the other morning. I realized that I left my train pass at home, and I had to run back and get it."

Alois responded, "It's all right! Well, if I had known, I would have bought a one-day train ticket for you, and you would not have had to run all the way home." He continued, "We could have walked together to the station and could have been friends ever since."

Poldie smiled, and Alois thought it felt like heaven to have a young lady like her smile at him. So many of the Germans did not want to talk to him; they never smiled when he spoke.

"My feelings were hurt," Alois admitted. "I saw you on the train, but I thought you changed your mind about me when you heard me speak with a foreign accent. I am from Czechoslovakia, and my German is not very good. I have a hard time understanding the dialect of the people in Ludwigsburg and Stuttgart—the Schwabisch dialect."

Poldie started laughing. "I also have a hard time understanding the Schwabisch dialect, because my family came from Czechoslovakia too!" she said. "We are Sudeten Germans." Poldie noticed his face dropped in disappointment when she relayed this.

"Miss," Alois began, "now you are for sure going to hate me because I am Czechoslovakian, and the Czechs chased your people out of your homeland."

Poldie dismissed his concern. "No, I don't hate you. You and I were young at the end of the war. We were not responsible for what the politicians decided about the Sudeten Germans," she said.

As their conversation continued, most of the people walked past, and it became quiet around them. The light emanating from the store windows seemed softer to Alois. In fact, the whole world seemed kinder. Alois's face showed his satisfaction. "Forgive me, miss," he said. "I didn't introduce myself. My name is Alois Huf."

"That sounds like a German name," Poldie observed, shaking his hand. "My name is Leopoldine Kellner—Poldie."

They turned and began strolling down the sidewalk together. Alois remembered seeing Leopoldine with a young man before. He wondered if she had only been flirting with him on the train. "You do have a boyfriend, don't you?" Alois asked.

"Oh, Manfred? You could say that. He comes around, but I'm not serious about him at all," Poldie said emphatically. "My father likes him because he's a barber and gives haircuts to my dad and brothers free of charge." Poldie hoped that was enough to make Alois realize she was, indeed, interested in him.

They talked a little more about their lives and families. As they prepared to part ways, Alois turned to his petite companion. "May I see you again?" he asked.

"When?" Poldie replied.

"Well, I would like to see you today again—if you can," Alois said.

Poldie answered, "Yes, let me go home to help my mother get the children in bed, and then maybe I can come out for a while." They both understood that her "maybe" was a reflection not of her sentiments but instead of her responsibilities.

Alois walked Poldie to her apartment building. "I will wait for you on the corner in one hour," he told her. "But if you cannot come, I understand."

They both said their good-byes, and Poldie disappeared into the stairwell of her building.

Typically, Poldie came home tired, but after meeting this friend, she felt happiness in her heart. "Alois," she repeated in her mind several times. "Alois Huf." She continued smiling as she made her way to the door.

———————————◆———————————

CHAPTER SEVEN

THE DAWN OF LOVE, MARRIAGE, AND A NEW FAMILY

Alois walked back to his apartment with extra energy in his steps. He lived only two blocks from Leopoldine. He stopped in the building's Neue Sonne restaurant for a meal and then went back up to his apartment. He looked at himself in the mirror and thought he better look a little sharper. There was only one bathroom in his building, but the maid brought a fresh pitcher of water to his room earlier, as usual. He poured some of the cold water in the washbasin and then washed his hands and face and shaved. His hair was a bit disheveled from work so he combed it. He removed his work clothing and changed into a crisp white shirt, tie, and royal-blue suit jacket. Then he added some aftershave, and he was ready to head out.

Alois walked to the agreed-upon corner ten minutes early to be sure he was there when Poldie came to meet him. He looked in all directions and then glanced at his watch again. He paced back and forth for ten minutes, then for another fifteen minutes. "Her parents probably prevented her from coming," he thought. Disappointment sank in. He officially met the pretty girl from on the train, and they had finally talked. Within just one afternoon, he felt carried by the greatest hope he had ever felt. Alois smiled as he remembered how she had tripped him. This little lady was a princess to him; he didn't even mind falling. As he looked for Poldie down the sidewalk, he wondered if this budding relationship was just an illusion.

After another twenty minutes, Alois decided that she was not going to come. He walked one more time to the door of Poldie's apartment building, but she was nowhere in sight. He hung his head low and smelled his enticing aftershave. It would be an evening filled with self-pity. Just then, he heard a voice behind him saying softly, "Hier bin ich." (Here I am.)

Alois turned around and saw her. Poldie had changed into a beautiful white blouse. The finger waves in her hair looked lovely. As she walked toward him, Alois wanted to run for her. Instead, he smiled. "You are as pretty as a kocicka," he said, using his native tongue to describe a kitten.

Poldie smiled that coy little smile again. She was glad he waited for her to arrive. "I'm sorry that I came so late," she said. "First I needed to send my mom and dad somewhere so we could secretly meet. I reminded my father that *The Mark of Zorro* is playing at the theaters. He likes those movies so much. The American actor, Errol Flynn, is my dad's favorite. He loves all the heroic characters he plays in the westerns. I suggested, 'Dad, here is some money. Take Mom and enjoy a movie!' He was all for it." Poldie continued by sharing that she had several younger siblings that she typically put to bed. "And to my mom, I said, 'I will tuck the children in and clean up. Just go and don't worry about anything.' It took me a little longer than I anticipated, but I did my best."

Alois stared at her face with such delight. It was like meeting someone he had always known. "It's all right! I'm so glad you came," he said.

They talked about their lives and how similar they were to one other. Both of them were away from home, having relocated from Czechoslovakia. During the quick conversation, they discovered they had both been sent from camp to camp. How was it that they had ended up in the same neighborhood in Ludwigsburg? Poldie thought of the children upstairs, but her whole being, charmed with this new acquaintance, stood paralyzed. He wanted to get to know her, and he listened when she spoke. Poldie's feelings toward him were mutual.

Alois felt embarrassed that his German was not adequate enough to express what he intended to say. "I'm delighted I met you," he said. "You must promise that you will teach me how to speak better German."

Poldie readily agreed, and they continued talking and walking down the sidewalk. After a time, Poldie said, "I should get home and make sure the children are okay and still sleeping."

They made their way back to Poldie's building, and Alois turned to her. "I will walk with you to the train in the morning." Alois embraced Poldie and kissed her on the cheek. "Kocicka, I will see you tomorrow."

Alois watched as Poldie's figure disappeared into the apartment hallway. He walked to his apartment leisurely, holding his head a bit higher and replaying the day's events in his mind. When he got back to his apartment, he prayed, "God, I still can't believe this is real. If it was only a dream, then let me dream a little longer."

Although he didn't know the scripture "Be anxious for nothing, but in everything by prayer and supplication, with thanksgiving, let your requests be made known to God" (Philippians 4:6), Alois prayed about what was on his mind. God was a presence he knew was there.

Before he went to lie down in bed, Alois prayed again, "God, I think I already love this girl. Could she be the one You have prepared for me? If she is, let me dream about her some more. And—one more thing—today was the nicest day I have had since I arrived in Germany. Thank You, God, for that."

The next morning, Alois waited for Poldie at the corner again. She smiled when they saw one another. "Now that we know each other, we can stand close together on the train and talk," Alois suggested.

Poldie agreed. That would be so much better than looking at the blond man from across the train, she thought. Poldie wished she owned better clothes or that she had more time to spend ensuring the waves she had pinned up overnight were still neat. A few times at night, she woke up when her younger siblings were crying. She wondered if she looked unattractive or haggard at all. But like Alois, cleanliness was a high priority for her, and her grace and politeness gave her a presence that money could not buy. The way Alois looked at her and treated her made her feel pretty. She put her threadbare stockings out of her mind. The two of them understood each other, and they were rich in one another's company.

The following Sunday afternoon, they went together to the Kaffee House Haree, and Alois treated Poldie and himself to a piece of Black Forest cake. The two of them sat at a corner table. While Alois was still acquiring fluency in German, his kind and alluring eyes told Poldie everything she needed to know. They took bites of the cake slowly. If only time stood still, they could stretch the pleasure of being together in the café as long as possible. Alois began teaching Poldie some Czech words—he had a few pet names for her that she didn't understand. Time floated by; the world was right again.

In the café, the young lovers held hands, and they continued their subdued chatter. Every few minutes, their laughter echoed from the walls. Mrs. Haree, the restaurant owner, marched over to the young couple's table. She looked to be in her sixties and had an expression of displeasure on her face. "You can't hold hands here; you can't do it here," she told them sternly.

The two lovebirds looked bewildered. "Ma'am," Alois said, "we love each other, and that is why we hold each other's hand. That shouldn't displease anyone." Alois surmised it was his accent that was so offensive.

"Oh, it displeases me," the woman retorted. "I will not allow a boy to hold a girl's hand in this place."

Alois and Poldie looked at one another and rose from their chairs. They each kindly thanked her and left the restaurant.

The two of them continued to spend as much time together as possible, walking together, talking on the train, and meeting for brief moments when time allowed. A deep bond of love was growing. Poldie had yet to break the news to her family that she had a new boyfriend.

One Sunday afternoon, Poldie and Alois met to spend time together. Alois watched Poldie as she approached and immediately noticed something was wrong. Poldie's polished finger waves were slightly out of place, and she looked ready to cry.

"What's wrong?" Alois asked, taking Poldie's hands.

Poldie squeezed his hands and then put her arms down. "You remember Manfred, my ex-boyfriend?" Alois nodded. "He has seen us together and went to my father. He told him, 'Your daughter is going out with a foreigner from Czechoslovakia.' When I came home, my father was terribly angry. He said, 'First, the Czech people chased us out of our homes, and now my daughter is dating a foreigner?' My father said if he sees me once with 'that Czech,' he would kill us both!"

Poldie lowered her head and whimpered, and Alois took her in his arms, hugging her close to him for several moments. Alois cupped her face. Poldie noticed that Alois did not seem frightened. "Do you love me so much that you would be willing to die for this love?" Alois asked.

Poldie nodded. "Yes, I do already love you that much."

"Okay," Alois said. "Then let's go. You can introduce me to your father."

Poldie looked alarmed. "Are you not frightened to approach him?"

Alois shook his head. "If you love me that much, then I am not scared," he said. "Come and introduce me to your family."

Alois remembered from Poldie's descriptions of her family that her father was a heavy smoker. Alois recalled how, in American movies, when the US Army and the Native Americans stopped fighting and negotiated peace, they would smoke a peace pipe together. He stopped and picked up two shiny packs of American cigarettes and slipped them into his pocket. American cigarettes were a luxury for Germans, and most men, Alois reasoned, would be quite pleased to receive them.

As they walked toward the apartment, Poldie moved slowly. She seemed to hesitate with each step. Abruptly, she stopped and turned. "Do we want to think this over? Shouldn't we wait for a few more days until my father calms down a little bit?"

Alois replied, "Did you say that your father would kill both of us if he sees you with me?"

"Yes," Poldie said. "That is what he told me."

"If you go with me, then I am not scared," Alois said, smiling at her reassuringly. "If he is going to kill both of us, then at least we would be buried on the same day. That wouldn't be so bad after all, would it?"

Poldie smirked. He was too cavalier, but she adored him. "No, that would not be so bad. The only thing is that I don't want to die young," Poldie said, lightening up a little bit. "But there is one thing we have going for us: my mother defended me. When I talk to her about you, I think she likes you. I think she would speak up for us."

The young couple walked the rest of the way quietly for the fateful meeting with the Kellner family. While Alois kept a strong front for Poldie, he felt incredibly nervous. His heart beat more rapidly with every step he took as he ascended the apartment building's stairs. Together, they reached the Kellners' doorstep and stood for a moment. Alois softly knocked on the door. From the other side, they heard a voice: "Herein."

Alois and Poldie walked in, and the room froze for a moment. Everyone in the apartment became silent and still, staring at the stranger. "Guten tag," Alois began, surveying the room, then focusing on Mr. Kellner. "My name is Alois Huf."

Poldie stood close by Alois's side. "This is my friend, whom I met on the train," she said nervously. "He drives for the Americans, and he brought you a pack of American cigarettes."

Johann looked at Alois, then at Poldie, then back at Alois. He unfroze his face. "Sure, it would be nice to smoke some American cigarettes," he said.

Alois pulled a fresh pack out of his pocket and handed it to Mr. Kellner, who grunted a thank-you. Alois asked if he could join him for a smoke. When Poldie's father granted permission, Alois pulled out the other pack. "Please save the pack I gave you for later," Alois said. "We can open this one."

Poldie watched incredulously as Alois greeted her other family members, sat down next to her father, and helped light Mr. Kellner's cigarette. She looked over at her mother, who appeared pleased. Alois certainly had a persuasive way with people. Within minutes, Alois and Mr. Kellner were talking together like old buddies. Johann told Alois that he had served in the Czech army before the war in the city of Brno, as all the young men used to do. He even told Alois that he still remembered some words in the Czech language. In a few minutes, Johann determined that Alois and his family were not the types of people who would have kicked his family out of the country. He eyed Alois and took puffs from his cigarette. From that day on, Johann approved of Alois Huf. As the weeks went by, Mr. Kellner greeted Alois like a dear friend and loved him like a son.

Alois felt his heart rise higher and higher in the joy he'd found with Poldie. His desires and hopes, which had been suppressed beneath a heavy weight of sorrow, were now coming back to life. Alois continued to pursue Poldie, and together they talked about the future. He was delighted that they had found such unmistakable, unplanned love. As Alois contemplated marriage, the idea of raising a family in Germany seemed unfavorable. Never mind the steady job driving for the US Army, which he was grateful for; the infrastructure was primitive due to the war. Many families in Germany were on long waiting lists for apartments; it could take years to obtain a simple dwelling. The social stigma of being a foreigner meant that Alois would have an even more difficult time finding an apartment.

Thoughts of leaving Germany resurfaced again, this time to the United States. After working for the US Army, Alois felt part American already. If only the couple were allowed to immigrate to the US, he thought. But Alois vividly remembered the terrible disappointments of his three previous attempts to leave Germany. He had promised himself that he would resolve the mystery of why he was rejected all those times. He was no longer self-absorbed about his future and well-being; he was in love with Leopoldine now, and he wanted to take her to the land of opportunity, the US.

Alois was unsure how to determine why three different countries turned him away. Was the problem with Australia, Canada, and the United States, or was it with the Germans? Had the Czech government issued some international security restriction on Alois Huf? He did not know where the issue lay. The idea that the countries themselves could have turned him away seemed unlikely because his friends made the transition without any complications. Alois remembered how the fellows in his barracks concluded he must have committed a terrible crime. Although he had not, Alois felt strangely guilty.

With tinges of apprehension, Alois went to Robinson Barracks at the Stuttgart US military base. He hoped to get information from the American officials. The United States military had entrusted him with a job on the military base, so surely they would be of assistance, he conjectured. The receptionist was friendly but told him that, because part of Germany was under the US occupation, his best chance of discovering information would be to report directly to the headquarters of the CIA, located in Heidelberg.

Rarely did Alois miss work; however, he arranged to take a day off. On that day, he set out on an early, northbound train to arrive in Heidelberg before 9:00 a.m. The journey would take just short of two hours, so Alois had time to prepare the best method to find answers to the questions that had plagued him for months. At the CIA headquarters, a police escort accompanied him around. Alois was sent from department to department, with each person saying that no one at the agency would likely know why the rejections took place but each one suggesting someone else who might be able to find out why.

Alois remained patient in his desperation to find answers. Finally, he told a representative that he wanted to speak to someone at a high level of authority. He courteously stated he would not leave until someone with a higher rank spoke to him. Alois took the nearest seat and waited for two hours. Finally, they escorted him to the office of a high-ranking officer. Alois introduced himself, and the officer immediately asked him what he wanted from the CIA.

Alois briefly gave the officer a summary of his escape from Czechoslovakia until the current time. He explained how he was sent back from the ship departing for Australia, how he was ordered to disembark the train heading to Canada, and how the US Army also rejected him from joining the military. He emphasized that his friends were all accepted and given the green light to go in each instance.

The officer seemed especially intrigued when Alois said the military police had picked him up from the train on his second immigration attempt. When Alois's story concluded, the officer excused himself, indicating he would return in a few minutes. He reappeared at the door a short while later and asked Alois for his identification. Alois gave it to him and waited.

About thirty minutes later, the man came back to the office, handed Alois his ID, and sat down.

The officer wasted no time. "Did you once sign up for espionage?" he asked.

Alois's surprise showed on his face. "Yes, I did. That was a little over two years ago when I was living in a refugee camp shortly after my escape over the border. My other refugee friends and I were constantly hungry, and we went for every opportunity to better our lives," Alois said. "I did the training for a few days and then was supposed to go on a mission. Later, when I thought it over and considered what it might be like, I told the man who recruited me that I was no longer interested."

The officer was blunt: "That is the reason you cannot leave Germany."

Everything became apparent, and Alois began to finally understand. He was not in trouble for signing up to serve the CIA; he was considered a suspect for completing the brief training and then dropping out. Alois's countenance dropped as he felt the overall consequences. "Thank you for letting me know. I am so disappointed," Alois uttered in a shallow voice. "How long will the CIA keep ruining my future life?" The officer looked at him with an unmoved expression. "I would like to marry the girl I love and attempt immigration to the US. I can't see any future in Germany for my future family and me." Alois paused and waited for a response. "Is there any way you could give me assurance that the CIA will no longer hinder me in the future?"

The officer looked at Alois with a hint of care. "I cannot give you that assurance," he said. "But one thing I can tell you is that once you are married and have children, the CIA will lose interest in you. But there is no guarantee."

Slowly, Alois absorbed the message. There was nothing else he could do. Now he understood what caused all the rejection and confusion. Alois stood and thanked the officer, and someone escorted him to the exit. As he sat on the train for the two-hour return to Ludwigsburg, Alois thought about the last couple of years. In some ways, it seemed that each year had been a decade—they had brought so much challenge and change. He wondered how he would plan for his future with such an unknown factor. "Will the CIA stop me again? Who can give me advice?" he contemplated.

Alois prayed, but he was not sure that even God could get him out of this problem or solve the riddle of his future. He had never been taught the guarantee "Call to me and I will answer you and tell you great and unsearchable things you do not know" (Jeremiah 33:3, NIV).

◆

Within a short time, the streets were covered in frost. Alois looked forward each day to seeing Poldie, tendrils of her hair coming out from the scarf she wrapped snuggly around her head and neck. Alois decided he would not burden Poldie with the knowledge of the CIA incident. She might think that Alois was in trouble and worry, and worse, she might decide to leave him. He knew he was not in danger; he was just not sure if he was free yet.

For Christmas in 1951, the Kellners invited Alois to spend the holiday with them. Poldie was delighted to have her new beau right at her side. That was destined to be so much better than the two previous Christmases, when Alois was alone and miserable. This time he had a song in his heart and felt happy again.

On that Monday, Christmas Eve, he joined the Kellners for dinner. Spending time with Poldie's family took him back to the Christmases he spent with his own family in Czechoslovakia. Alois felt the closeness and familial love he had been longing for. The family enjoyed a simple meal that Anna prepared and then gathered to sing Christmas songs like "Silent Night." Alois looked over at his sweet Poldie; he knew he had found the treasure of a lifetime. In his heart, Alois prayed, "God, it feels so wonderful to be loved and to love someone so much. Please, God, let nothing come between us to destroy our happiness."

Amid his joy with the Kellners, Alois thought about his own family in Czechoslovakia. It was their third Christmas without him. "Are they all still okay? Are they all still alive?" he wondered. He wished he could write to them or, better yet, visit them. Crossing the border back into Czechoslovakia would be the end of Alois's freedom, and his family would be in trouble if he returned. "Why would a country limit a family's ability to at least visit one other? How could a nation censor personal mail?" he questioned. He uttered a prayer that his family members were well and that somehow, he would be able to communicate with them again soon.

As the young couple's love continued to blossom, Alois decided that he wanted to ask for Poldie's hand in marriage. His love for her was absolute, and there was no one else with whom he would rather spend his life. One afternoon, as they walked on the wintry street, Alois turned to Poldie and studied her sweet eyes and soft cheeks. "I do not have anything, but Poldie, would you marry me?"

Poldie answered in her quiet but sure way. "I do not have anything either, and yes, I will marry you," she said, looking deeply into Alois's bright eyes. "We will start our lives not having any of this world's goods, but we will be rich in the love we have for each other."

In January of 1952, the young lovers went to the city office to inquire about the required documents needed for marriage. They were told they needed blood tests and birth certificates. Neither Alois nor Leopoldine had birth certificates. Alois was twenty, and Poldie was only seventeen until her approaching birthday in May, which was four months away. Her parents would have to sign for her to be able to marry Alois. The German clerk seemed impatient with both of them; he made the process more complicated than it needed to be over the next six months. Alois felt sure the reason was that the clerk was a Sudeten German and he harbored a marked bitterness toward any Czechs.

It was also in early 1952 when Johann was approved to move his family from Karlstrasse to his place of employment in Eglosheim-Alatch, where they would live with sixteen other families. The Kellners once again had a house and land to cultivate. There was a large kitchen with two sizable bedrooms and another small room.

The move meant that Poldie had to get up an hour earlier each morning to catch a bus from Altach to Ludwigsburg. The new living arrangements also meant that Alois and Poldie had less time to spend with one another. Poldie continued her long work hours and her chores at home, doing dishes, sweeping, and putting the younger children to bed each evening. Alois and Poldie longed to be with each other always, as any young lovers would. Their desire for intimacy heightened, and they found it challenging to be apart. They wanted to be married right then and there, but the clerk kept postponing approval of their papers so the marriage could not take place.

By May, Poldie began missing a few days of work. She was pregnant and experiencing morning sickness. Her father inquired, "Why are you home from work and what's wrong with you? You should be at work!" Anna hastily scolded him and confessed, "Leave her alone, okay? She is pregnant." Johann was not immediately happy about Poldie's pregnancy; however, after two days, he put his contempt aside and accepted that he was going to be a grandfather again. During wartime, it was not uncommon at all for young lovers to get pregnant prior to marriage.

Poldie and her mother were best friends. They confided in one another about most of life's issues, and this gave Poldie such comfort. Since Poldie was now with child, her parents agreed to allow her to move in with Alois back in Ludwigsburg because she would be closer to work and could sidestep unnecessary bus rides and the long train commute from their home.

In midsummer, Poldie and Alois finally received word that their birth certificate documents were ready and approved. The clerk asked Johann and Anna to come to the city office to sign for their approval for Leopoldine to be wed. It was a mandated law for any child under the age of twenty-one desiring marriage. The clerk asked Mr. Kellner where the couple planned to live. Johann confirmed that once Poldie went into labor, the newlyweds would live with the family in Altach. With everything now finalized, the wedding date was set for October 4.

Poldie was now convinced dreams did come true. She had known poverty, hardship, and toil, and now she knew real love. There were only minimal preparations for the wedding. The Kellners were not able to assist their daughter and future son-in-law, as they could hardly afford to feed their nine children. Poldie worked extra hours to set aside a small amount of money each month to purchase a black taffeta dress she wanted to wear for her special day. She also saved up some cash and went to the local jewelry store to purchase two basic yellow-gold bands for herself and Alois to wear. It was the same store where Poldie had her ears pierced at fourteen.

On the morning of their wedding day, Alois and Poldie walked to the local justice of the peace. Alois's friend Vlada and another buddy from the refugee camp agreed to serve as witnesses for the couple's nuptials. Alois looked sharp in his suit. Poldie's skin was rosy and radiated with that fresh pregnancy glow. Alois, smitten with his bride, thought she looked exceptionally beautiful in her one-piece black velvet sequin-embellished top with a taffeta skirt. The cap sleeves rested delicately midway down her upper arm. Poldie was six months pregnant by now, and even though she was petite, she had a noticeable baby bump peeking through her dress, but on this day of celebration, no one seemed to judge. A single string of inexpensive pearls encircled Poldie's slender neck, and she wore a matching pair of pearl studs for earrings. Alois tenderly wrapped his arm around Poldie as they stood before the judge. The couple held hands and pledged vows to one another in the sight of God and celebrated their love. When the ceremony concluded, the group of four walked down the street to the photographer's studio and had only a few pictures taken to commemorate the special day. Poldie held a beautiful bouquet of white calla lilies with leatherleaf filler that the photographer provided for her. Afterward, the newlyweds said good-bye to their friends and returned to the Kellners' home for a celebration lunch. Anna bought extra food on credit and prepared Wiener schnitzel and German potato salad.

There was no honeymoon, just the accommodation of the six-by-twelve-foot room that Alois rented. It mattered little though because the love that brought them together would be the love that held them together for better or worse. The young newlyweds were happy and giddy to finally be together as man and wife. In the tiny dwelling, the couple established their own household. There was a bed, a small table with a pitcher and basin for washing, and a chair. They had an electric plate and a two-quart pot, along with two cups, two plates, and two sets of cutleries.

Since there was no refrigeration, Alois and Poldie purchased a pint of milk daily and placed the bottle in water to keep it fresh. Heated milk and rye bread for breakfast was all they could afford. For lunch, they purchased a meal at the work canteen. In the evenings, Poldie prepared soup and bread.

Alois's job moved from downtown Stuttgart to Bad Cannstatt. He and his sweet pregnant Poldie traveled on the train together, and both exited at Stuttgart-Nord. Poldie's workplace was nearby, and Alois walked an additional twenty minutes. US Army personnel replaced his prior driving responsibilities. However, Alois was given a two-and-a-half-ton GMC truck to drive. He conducted errands including taking garbage to the dump.

When they gave him scraps of wood to dispose of, Alois asked the officer in charge if he would be allowed to take them to his father-in-law for kindling wood. The officer agreed, and the Kellners were pleased. It was surprising to Alois and the others how the Americans discarded so many items. Alois had been accustomed, from an early age, not to waste anything. Being resourceful was part of subsistence.

Poldie continued to give a fair amount of her paycheck to her family, even after she married Alois. Her younger brother Sepp made the weekly trips to her apartment to pick up the money and bring it back to their parents. Poldie's small stature made her pregnancy enlarge her body even more. Her employee health care provider promised her that if she worked until two weeks before the baby's due date and then breastfed the baby, she would receive additional money. Poldie resumed her regular work hours until the beginning of January. A midwife named Frau Batz came each week to check on her. Poldie was determined not to go to the hospital so they could save money that would have been spent on a doctor and medical facility. The health care provider would give Poldie a stipend for having the child at home. Poldie would also use the extra money to buy a baby carriage, clothes, and blankets in preparation for their tiny little bundle, who was due to arrive anytime soon.

In the early morning hours of Wednesday, January 21, 1953, Poldie woke to labor pains. Alois wasted no time in calling for a taxi so he could accompany his wife to her parent's home in Eglosheim-Altach. When the expectant couple arrived at the door before dawn, Anna was unaware Poldie had gone into labor and quickly ushered them in. Anna immediately went to the office on the main level of their housing development to place a call to the midwife. Anna hurried to the stove to start a fire and put on pots for boiling water. After arriving, the midwife checked Leopoldine and told her the baby might come quickly. When Alois left for work, he asked Poldie if maybe she could wait to have the baby until he came home from work. Her young, excited husband wanted to be present when the baby arrived. Poldie labored for twelve hours, as is typical with most first-time pregnancies. However, her back pain was almost unbearable. All day long, Anna walked Poldie back and forth across their tiny dwelling, rubbing her backside gently while blurting out, "Oh, girl, how I wish I could take this pain from you and carry it myself!" Throughout his errands that day, Alois stopped by four times to check on his wife. By 4:00 p.m., at his last check-in, Poldie was well into the stages of intense labor. Surely he would get home in time to be with her when the baby came, he thought.

Soon after he departed for the last time, Poldie knew she must begin pushing. She transitioned to the bed, and with Anna at her side and the midwife at her legs, she started panting and pushing. After several good pushes, the midwife proclaimed, "It's a girl!" Together, Anna and Poldie hugged and wept and rejoiced at the arrival of this precious little one. The midwife laid the babe on Poldie's bosom so she could inspect her new darling daughter. She had loads of black hair and appeared to be just perfect. It was time for the first bath. The midwife took the newborn and gently put her into a tub of warm water to thoroughly cleanse her. Then she wrapped her up in swaddling blankets. Poldie's father arrived home from work first to his newborn baby granddaughter. He already had two grandsons, so this was a welcomed joy.

When Alois returned at 7:00 p.m., the family told him that his beautiful baby girl had been born one hour before. They handed Alois the tiny bundle. Poldie glanced to see what Alois's reaction might be. Alois stared for a bit at all that black hair. Poldie wondered if perhaps Alois was disappointed because he wished for the baby to resemble him. Alois quickly rejoiced. He thought the baby looked just like Poldie, with her dark hair and round face. Poldie had fared well during labor, but she was exhausted and recovering from the pain. Alois remembered the experience when his little brother, Frank, was an infant and was sickly. Poldie had memories of the death of two of her young siblings. Alois and Poldie were delighted that their little girl was healthy.

That evening, they both thanked God for their gorgeous daughter and prayed for His blessing. Neither of them knew that God had spoken His blessing over them in scripture: "Children are a heritage from the LORD, offspring a reward from Him. Like arrows in the hands of a warrior are children born in one's youth. Blessed is the man whose quiver is full of them. They will not be put to shame" (Psalm 127:3-5, NIV).

From that moment on, Alois and Poldie lived with the Kellners. They had a separate room so they could be a family. There was no crib for their newborn, only two twin iron beds that Alois and Poldie pushed together where the three of them could cuddle together. That night, Alois let Poldie sleep undisturbed, and he put the baby beside him. Many nights since escaping, Alois had slept fitfully, having nightmares and then dreams of Czechoslovakia and letting his mind race about his failed tries at leaving Germany. That night, however, Alois slept as peacefully as his baby beside him. Poldie awakened in the middle of the night and realized the space beside her on the bed was empty. She turned on the lamp to see her husband and new baby sleeping soundly. Smiling, she went back to sleep.

A few days later, on Sunday, the couple took their baby in a carriage to the Catholic church in Eglosheim and had her christened. Looking up from the carriage, the baby appeared as a tightly wrapped doll, swaddled in blankets to protect her from the cold. Poldie's younger sister Anna went along and served as the baby's godmother. The priest baptized the infant, and the parents named her Jana Gabriela. Alois chose the Czech first name, and Poldie chose the German middle name.

While there was no baby shower or gifts for babies, Poldie's family welcomed the baby girl. The Hufs set up a homey room within their apartment. Since the Kellner family had mostly boys, they delighted in another girl. Poldie used the money she received from the health care company to purchase clothing for her. Everyone in Altach was taken with her thick black hair and thought she was adorable, and they affectionately called her "Januli."

Since Alois had taken a photography course during the last year of his schooling, he decided to purchase a camera shortly before Jana's birth. It was a quality camera, and along with it, he purchased the film, paper, and supplies he needed for developing his photos. When the baby was one week old, he asked Poldie to put her in a pretty dress and fix her hair nicely. Poldie dressed Jana in one of the precious ensembles she had purchased and combed the infant's hair forward and into a curl. They placed the baby tummy-down, with her chest propped up by a pillow. Alois snapped all thirty-six photos in a film roll, including pictures of the entire Kellner family.

The following evening, when Alois came home from work, he processed the photos. First, he placed the film in a projector, then determined the desired size of the picture. At his cue, Poldie turned the lights off, and then Alois turned on his red flash. He placed one paper at a time under the projector. Next, Poldie turned the projector light on for eight to ten seconds. Then she switched the light off. Alois took the paper and placed it in a developing solution. Under the glow of the red lamplight, the family watched. Within seconds, images began to emerge. The Kellner children spoke in awe as they recognized their faces. It was like magic.

Alois and Poldie especially cherished the images of their little Jana. She was so full of life and lovely. About a week after the first photo shoot, Alois came up with an ingenious idea about how to reach out to his family back in Czechoslovakia. He asked Poldie for a favor: "I will write a few sentences in Czech. Will you copy them in your handwriting and sign your name as Mrs. Leopoldine Hufova? I think that will work."

Poldie was happy to reach out to Alois's family. She knew if they were anything like him, she loved them already. While the communist government would suspect anything that came from Alois, a letter from a female might not arouse much suspicion if they inspected it. Poldie wrote, "I would like to send you greetings and a picture of your grand-daughter. With all my love, Leopoldine Hufova." (The suffix *-ova* is added to the surnames of Czech women.) They enclosed one photo of their precious little one and mailed it to Alois's family in communist Czechoslovakia. After these four long years, Alois was finally able to reach out to his parents and siblings through his wife, and they would be reminded how much he loved them.

CHAPTER EIGHT

RECONNECTING WITH CZECH FAMILY

After Alois left his country, the Hufs back in Czechoslovakia grieved continually. While the rawness of his absence lessened, the worry of what became of their son and brother was ubiquitous. When the Huf family received the postcard Alois sent six months after his escape, the one that read "We are sending you final greetings from Europe," they had some relief, but the questions still nagged in their minds, and they wondered where he might be and if he was still alive.

The post office was under orders to report suspicious items to the police. The same day the postcard arrived, two police officers appeared at the Hufs' door asking if the family had received any mail from outside of the country. Josef and Marie knew the officers already had their answer. They watched as the officers scrutinized the postcard. They even removed the stamp to see if there was anything hidden behind it. The family was bewildered; for them, news from their son was welcomed. But for the police, he was considered a fugitive and a criminal.

Alois's sister Marie began nursing school, and more than once, authority figures came to the school and demanded to the superintendent that she not be allowed in school because her brother had escaped Czechoslovakia. Pepa cherished the forestry uniform that Alois had left behind. Sometimes Pepa put it on and immediately missed his brother. Pepa was drafted into the army and several times called before the officers for questioning. He was denied any promotions due to Alois's escape.

News circulated in the state-run media that many young men who had escaped Czechoslovakia were brought into refugee camps in Germany and were recruited by the French Foreign Legion to fight in Indochina. The media reports made fellow countrymen angry to think that their own neighbors' children might be fighting for a foreign army. Josef and Marie felt social isolation and received the cold shoulder from others in their community.

About four and a half years after the last time Josef and Marie saw their son, a special letter came to the village of Vikyrovice, Czechoslovakia. The letter was sent from Germany and had in the return address the name Leopoldine Hufova. Maruska, Alois's sister, was home when the letter arrived, and when she read "Hufova," she began to tremble. "Was this from a Mrs. Huf?" she wondered. Maruska opened the letter with unsteady hands. She was amazed to see a photo image of a newborn baby girl. The letter said, "I would like to send you greetings and a picture of your granddaughter. With all my love, Leopoldine Hufova."

Tears began falling down Maruska's cheeks. She wiped them and kissed the image, wishing these beloved family members were there in person. She had a niece named Janicka, and she immediately loved her and Leopoldine as if she knew them. Alois was alive, and not only was he alive, but he was also doing well! Maruska looked up. Joy had filled her heart.

This news had to be shared. She put the photo and letter back into the envelope and ran outside. Her mother was working in the fields about half a mile away. Maruska yelled, "Mother!" as she approached, and her mother turned, wondering what was wrong. "I have good news!" Maruska yelled, knowing instinctively that her worried mother would fear the worst.

Alois's mother watched her daughter approach expectantly and then grabbed her arm affectionately. "Hurry, tell me the good news!" she said.

First, Maruska pulled out the adorable baby photo. "You are a grandmother!" Marie laughed and cried simultaneously and kissed the image of the baby. It was all that Marie could do to keep her legs from collapsing beneath her as she read the letter. She stopped to thank God for answering her many desperate prayers for her son's safety. "Let's go home and celebrate the rest of the day," Marie said.

When Josef came home, his wife was still crying. "What happened?" he asked.

Maruska said, "She is crying because she is a grandmother, and you are a grandfather." She handed Josef the photo and letter. He was elated to read the letter, but he wished that his son had written also. When all the children came home—Pepa and Hynek from work and Liduska and Frank from school—the family members could not get enough of seeing Jana's picture.

Finally, the entire Huf family reached the conclusion that Alois was not uncaring by not writing. He knew that penning anything himself might bring hardship on his family. The family gave thanks to God through Mary and the saints for the joyous news they received that day. The laughter finally had a place in the Huf home again.

In Eglosheim-Altach, Germany, the multiple families who lived in the work housing complex interacted with one another regularly. The small community all considered little Jana as their own. Each day they would inquire about "Januli." When Mr. Kellner came home, he would take the girl's small hand and say, "This is my little girl." Alois wondered if his own family in Czechoslovakia had gotten to see his daughter's photo and if they had received the letter.

Two weeks after mailing the photo, Alois received a letter from his parents and family. They expressed how thrilled they were to receive the message and their pleasure in seeing their granddaughter. Then they welcomed their daughter-in-law and said they loved them both already. Josef and Marie and Alois's siblings wrote how happy they were to know he was alive and loved. Alois was so relieved to receive their letter! It was the very first communication he had from them in all those years. Many times, he wondered about his family's well-being. It gave him such joy to know they were in good health.

The mail exchange continued from that point on, with Alois taking new photos of Jana frequently. In their letters, the families kept personal details to a minimum, knowing that if the communists saw baby photos and talk of family, they would not be overly interested. Poldie continued writing for the couple, and while she only spoke of herself and the baby, the Hufs understood when she often subtly referenced Alois.

It did not take long for Marie to include a veiled admonition that Alois take his family to church. Growing up, Alois never would have imagined missing Mass. The Kellners were also Catholic, but they were not devout like the Hufs. Johann and Anna attended church only on special occasions, like Easter and Christmas. However, they often sent their children by themselves to the nearest Catholic church for Sunday Mass.

Alois and Poldie attended church faithfully from the time they were married. It was a foreign concept for Poldie to attend every single week. Her family did not see the need for a weekly religious routine. Poldie gladly went when Alois explained to her that it was the duty of every Catholic to go to Sunday Mass. Poldie could now write and tell her mother-in-law that they did, indeed, attend church regularly. Privately, Poldie felt that she did not get much out of the church service, but she wanted to please Alois. The newlyweds didn't talk about God or religion during the week, but on Sunday mornings, faith was at the forefront.

Alois cared about living a good life and pleasing God. But even after all he experienced, he did not feel God was involved in his day-to-day life. He had not heard the scripture "Love the Lord your God with all your heart and with all your soul and with all your strength and with all your mind" (Luke 10:27, NIV). Mentally, Alois assured himself that although he had not been perfect, he was a good man. He was not only going to Mass each week but also taking his family, and he had convinced his wife of the importance of being religiously devout.

◆

In late May, Jana was scheduled to receive a required vaccination. Poldie took her to the clinic, and the mother and child waited in a room full of other mothers and babies. A number of the infants were coughing incessantly. While Poldie was a new mother, she was an experienced caretaker. "This is not a good place for the baby," she feared. Nevertheless, there was nothing she could do but wait. Poldie sat with Jana until a nurse called them in for the baby's shot.

A few days later, Jana began to cough. The coughing bouts increased in intensity until it seemed the baby was choking. Poldie called the doctor from the phone on the main-level office in their building. He ordered her to take Jana to the hospital without delay. Poldie bundled Jana in heavy blankets, put her in the carriage, and scurried along the uneven sidewalk for five miles to the hospital. The doctor immediately diagnosed Jana with whooping cough. He admitted Jana and instantly placed her in a glass-enclosed room with other babies who also had that same dangerous illness.

Poldie felt anxious. It was insufferable for her to watch her daughter through a window as she gasped for air.

Poldie left the hospital brokenhearted over having to leave her very ill baby behind. By the time Alois arrived home from work, Leopoldine was in a state of panic. Sobbing uncontrollably, she showed Alois Jana's empty crib and explained through tears that their daughter was very ill. Poldie collapsed in his arms while relaying the sad news. Alois tried to comfort Poldie, but she would not be consoled. He remembered that the month of May was set aside for the exclusive worship of Mary. Alois encouraged Poldie to pray with him to Mary and ask the mother of Jesus to implore her son to intervene. After all, who could reject the request of his mother? Neither of them knew the verses "Come to me, all you who are weary and burdened, and I will give you rest. Take my yoke upon you and learn from me, for I am gentle and humble in heart, and you will find rest for your souls" (Matthew 11:28–30, NIV).

Poldie made the trek to the hospital daily to be close to Jana. Visiting hours were only from 2:00 p.m. to 4:00 p.m. On one occasion, it appeared that Jana was turning blue. Poldie knocked on the glass to get the attention of the nurse in the room. She pointed to her precious child, and with the other hand, she gestured for help. The nurse lifted Jana and drained the fluid that was choking her. She gave the baby oxygen and put her back in the crib. On another occasion, Poldie spotted a large fly in the room that landed several times on Jana's face and mouth. With no nurse in sight, Poldie burst through the door and chased the fly away. A nurse came in and reprimanded Poldie; she was too involved for their liking. She gave Poldie another scolding, telling her that she must leave the hospital at once. Leaving the hospital was painful for Poldie. She felt as if half of her heart was still there in the pediatric ward, lying in that little hospital bed. Tears began to flow as Poldie walked back home to Altach. If only she could be there to comfort her child. It could not be good for the baby to be alone all day and all night. Poldie did not know the verse "Do not fear, for I am with you; do not be dismayed, for I am your God" (Isaiah 41:10, NIV). She had no comfort.

Although the nurse had strictly enforced the visiting hours, the doctor allowed Poldie to come to the hospital at 10:00 each morning to take the baby out for fresh air. Poldie had pleaded with the doctor, arguing that a baby needed to be held and not left in the hospital bed all day. Poldie waited outside the hospital for a nurse to bring Jana to her. She was wrapped up tightly in warm clothing and blankets. The hospital had several baby carriages parked under an awning, but Poldie brought Jana's carriage from home, laid her in it, and off the two of them went for daily strolls to the nearby park called Schloss-Garten. The most difficult moments for Poldie were when Jana started coughing and could not catch her breath. Poldie would turn the baby face down and help her clear out the phlegm that was choking her.

Many Ludwigsburg residents visited the park for daily walks. One afternoon, Frau Brunner, who lived in the same apartment building as the Kellner family before their move to Altach, was walking by when she spotted Poldie. She greeted Poldie enthusiastically and sat to talk with her. Leopoldine told her how sick little Januli had been. As they spoke, Jana's face turned blue, and Poldie had to clear the little girl's airways. Frau Brunner was not optimistic about the baby's ability to survive and later told Poldie's mother so.

Poldie, however, was tireless in her care of Jana. On Sundays, Alois and Poldie walked to the hospital and spent the day at the park together with Jana. They continued to pray that Jana's health would improve. After returning Jana to the hospital on Sunday, the couple watched through the nursery's glass window.

After four weeks, the doctor told Poldie that Jana would finally be released from the hospital the following day. The next day, Poldie took the baby home, but she would not keep food down, and she cried incessantly. Jana continued to vomit throughout the night. In the morning, Poldie was exhausted and worried. She bundled Jana and put her in the carriage. On the way to the hospital, Poldie cried and prayed more fervently than she ever remembered praying. Her heart broke to see her baby so ill that she could not even hold her little head up. "You can even take my life if it means the baby will live," Poldie prayed.

After an examination at the hospital, the doctor delivered more bad news: Jana had an infection in her stomach and bowels and had to be readmitted. Poldie tried to keep her emotions together. It was like a dream to meet Alois and then to be married and have a life together. Surely, they were not destined for a tragedy now, she reasoned.

When the Hufs took their daughter home from the hospital the second time that summer, they were incredibly relieved. Poldie stroked Jana and said, "Don't you worry about anything, my little angel. Your mommy is going to take good care of you. She is going to nurse you back to strength in no time. You'll see." Little Jana looked up into the eyes of her mother and seemed to understand every word.

By the end of the summer of 1953, things were going well. Jana's health was better, and she was even learning to stand. Every Sunday, Alois and Poldie would put Jana in her carriage, and they would go, along with Poldie's youngest brothers, Willy and Karl, to Monrepos. Located about a mile from Altach, it was a beautiful outdoor gathering with a castle that sat at the edge of a lake. Many people enjoyed going there on the weekends. Alois would treat everyone to ice cream. When they got back home, Alois would join Poldie's brother Tony outside. They had a picnic table that they used for table tennis, and they played for hours while Alois puffed on a cigarette. As the sun set and the breeze blew, Alois reflected on his life. While this was not what he had planned when he left Czechoslovakia, it was a happy life. He had a beautiful family, he had reconnected with his own family back home, and all was well.

The US Army motor pool moved from Bad Cannstatt to Kornwes-theim. It was a welcome change for Alois because his commute was shortened by one hour. He liked packaging-related errands because the scrap wood the army discarded Alois would reclaim. The Hufs and Kellners needed enough fuel to keep them warm in the winter.

Christmas 1953 was fast approaching. Now that the Kellners were finally residing in housing that felt like it belonged to them, Johann delighted in taking the task of decorating for the season into his own hands. He ventured into the nearby woods and found just the right tree. After chopping it down, Johann brought it home and set it up in the room where Jana was born. He kept the specially decorated tree hidden from the other family members until just the right moment. When he unveiled the tree, the family was in awe. They all enjoyed the Wiener schnitzel and potato salad Anna prepared and then retreated to the living area to sing Christmas carols.

Alois gathered the dozen younger children living in Altach. He owned a trumpet again and wanted to share the joy and memories of music with them just as his uncle Jenda had done. Alois taught the children Christmas carols and even some Czech love songs. Together, they regaled the community with their choruses. On Christmas Eve, Alois took his trumpet to a hill and at midnight played "Silent Night." It made Alois thankful that he and his family were part of the community after so much hardship in Germany.

◆

In 1954, Jana began walking and saying a few words. One day in March, Poldie greeted Alois when he came home from work and told him quietly, "I think I am pregnant again." They were happy but felt the gravity of a new addition to their family. Poldie worried about what her parents would say, since there were already thirteen people living in their unit.

Alois was reassuring. "God gave us this child, and He will provide for us what we need," he said. "And I hope we have another girl, since we already have clothing for a baby girl," he added. They kept the news to themselves for a while, but Anna was quick to pick up on the pregnancy. The whole family was excited about it.

Alois began thinking about providing for two children. He thought, "I better start saving up for the baby." He had become a heavy smoker. Even though he was able to get cigarettes for a low price through the GIs, he got the idea to buy tobacco and smoke a pipe or to roll his own cigarettes. His GI friends bought him a one-pound can of Half and Half tobacco, which was inexpensive. Poldie tried to persuade him to give up smoking altogether, but Alois was not willing.

Every day in the evening, Johann and Anna went out to the parcel of land they rented, which was only 150 yards away. They had accumulated a few goats, chickens, and rabbits. Jana liked going with her Oma and Opa on those excursions. They needed to bring food home for the animals, so Johann cut the tall grass with a sickle, and Anna filled her tall basket to the brim. The carrier had handles on both sides, so Opa and Oma put little Jana on top of the grass in the basket and carried her back home to feed the livestock. Jana loved the rides they gave her. Anna showed baby Jana how to feed the animals, and the little girl squealed with delight as they took the grass in their teeth.

Residing in the country was favorable for the family. They could eat better and had abundant provisions. Johann worked for the Autobahn, and during cherry season, he would stop along the road on his way home from work and find full branches with cherries dangling from the limb. He would break a whole branch off with fresh, juicy fruit on it and bring it back for the children.

------------------------◆------------------------

In September, Frau Batz, the midwife, began checking on Poldie every few weeks. She lived in Eglosheim, about two miles away. While she was not known for being exceptionally friendly, Poldie trusted her and took comfort knowing that the caretaker was looking out for her. During her mid-November checkup, the midwife told Leopoldine and Alois that everything looked stable and that the baby would not be born for at least six weeks.

At about 4:00 a.m. the following day, November 14, 1954, Poldie woke Alois. "Call for my mother," she said.

Anna came in and conversed with Poldie briefly. She turned to Alois. "Go and get Frau Batz. Hurry!"

Because the midwife said that Poldie wasn't due for another six weeks and because he was still half asleep, Alois asked, "Are you sure you couldn't wait until later in the day? I'll be waking somebody out of hibernation."

Poldie was not amused. "Just go—and fast!" she said in an uncharacteristic command.

About fifteen minutes later, Alois arrived in Eglosheim. He knocked on the midwife's door and waited. Finally, the midwife appeared. She was in her nightgown and looked displeased. "What is it?" she asked.

Alois began to apologize but hurriedly got to his point: "Leopoldine and her mother told me to come and get you and to hurry. They said the baby is coming."

Frau Batz raised her voice: "The women are crazy, and so are you! I checked her yesterday, and I'm sure that it will take six more weeks for the baby to come."

Alois thought of his wife and mother-in-law waiting for him. "Frau Batz, that is what I told them, but they just told me to get you and to hurry," he replied.

The woman fumed but told Alois to wait and that she would be right out. Alois heard her mumble some choice words as she went back inside. Sure enough, she reappeared, this time pushing a moped out into the yard. To Alois's surprise, she invited him to hop on the bike behind her. Alois held on and tried not to agitate the stern woman with any more words. A few moments later, they were back in Altach. As they pulled up to the house, they saw Mrs. Kellner waving them in. "Hurry!" she said.

Only five minutes later, a beautiful little girl was born. The tiny baby weighed only five pounds. Because the infant was so small, the birth went very smoothly.

"There's nothing to it," Alois remarked. "I think we are going to have a lot more babies if it's so easy."

About a week later, they took their youngest daughter to a Catholic church to be baptized and named her Marie Anna for two reasons. First, Marie was Alois's mother's name, and second, the Brunner family, close friends of the Kellners, had an older daughter named Marie.

Marie Brunner held the newborn baby girl at her christening and was asked to be her godmother too. Alois and Leopoldine gave little Marie the middle name Anna, after Poldie's mother. Alois began calling his daughter "Maruska," as was his mother's nickname in Czech. Jana was speaking a few words and called her "Makiku." Everyone in Altach loved the new little addition. Opa was proud of his two granddaughters, "Janule" and "Makiku."

Following the entry of his second daughter into the world, Alois began thinking more about his family's long-term situation. Staying with the Kellners was a blessing, but Alois worried about wearing out his welcome as the family grew in number. Staying in Germany would make things difficult for housing and other opportunities.

In January of 1955, Alois contacted the American Fund for Czecho-slovak Refugees (AFCR) to see if his family could immigrate to the United States. The fear of rejection was always in the back of his mind, but he tried to ignore it. After all, he had already had a few dreams come true—he had an excellent job, a beautiful wife, and amazing children, and he had finally reconnected with his family back home.

The organization confirmed that it would be possible for his family to go to the United States of America. President Dwight D. Eisenhower had just signed permission for a new quota of Czechoslovak refugees to immigrate. Alois immediately completed the necessary documents and was told by an AFCR representative that the organization would contact him as soon as they knew something. As hopeful as he was, Alois remained guarded against disappointment.

Within two months, Alois received a letter asking him to submit chest X-rays of himself and Poldie so they could review them to clear the couple for possible acceptance to the US. Alois and Leopoldine had the X-ray images taken and submitted. Alois again checked with Poldie. They already had the conversation before—if Alois arranged for the family to go, would she go? Poldie always assured Alois that wherever he wanted to go, she would go with him. It helped persuade her too when she could see how hard it would be for the family to attain their very own place in Germany. Neither of them wanted to be a burden to Poldie's parents, although the Kellners were always welcoming.

While the couple spoke openly with one another about making a transition for their future, Alois never disclosed to Poldie what had happened with his past immigration rejections. He rehearsed the conversation in his mind with the CIA officer when he learned he was on their watch list. He held the hope that the agency would lose interest in him, especially now that he was a husband and a father of two. In his agonized thoughts, Alois did not know that his prayers could be more than expressions of worry. He and Poldie did not know the verses "Trust in the LORD with all your heart and lean not on your own understanding; in all your ways submit to him, and he will make your paths straight" (Proverbs 3:5-6, NIV).

◆

As the two families—the Hufs in Czechoslovakia and Alois and Poldie in Germany—continued their correspondences, they gave basic details of their lives and updated each other on how everyone was doing. Alois's mother, Marie, was pleased that her son's family was attending church. When she learned the young couple only had a civil ceremony, however, she urged them to be appropriately married in the Roman Catholic Church. Honoring her request, in the spring of 1955, Alois and Leopoldine dressed up and went to the church in Asperg to officially marry in the chapel. When they arrived, the priest asked them who their two witnesses would be. No one in Poldie's family was interested in attending, since they concluded the young couple was already married two and a half years earlier.

The priest called upon a few people from his congregation to stand as witnesses. Poldie and Alois stood and looked into each other's eyes with a more profound love than when their relationship began. Poldie held a bundle of flowers and looked as beautiful as ever. The ceremony was even more meaningful for them than the first one, after the thrill of infatuation had faded and the permanence of commitment had settled.

After the ceremony, the two of them walked back home hand in hand. Alois and Poldie reminisced about their joyful times during the past three years. When they arrived home, they hugged little Jana and

Marie. One of Poldie's brothers snapped photos of the couple with Jana standing at their side.

Alois's mother was quick to express her delight at their wedding ceremony. At least now their consciences would not bother them anymore, since their religion commanded this, she wrote. Alois and Poldie wanted to do right in the community and with the church. They did not think about what was right before God, Himself, such as what is taught in the verse "And whatever you do, whether in word or deed, do it all in the name of the Lord Jesus, giving thanks to God the Father through him" (Colossians 3:17, NIV).

---◆---

Poldie stayed busy with her two children. In many regards, she had been a mother all her life. She took care of her younger siblings for as long as she could remember. Only having two children did not seem to be as much work as it would have to some mothers. Each day when baby Marie fell asleep in her crib, Oma Kellner would keep an eye on the baby while Poldie took Jana on the bike seat and pedaled to Asperg to buy fresh milk and food. Since there was no refrigeration, each family would go to the market daily, and the Kellners had a place in the basement where they kept their milk and produce.

One day, when Poldie was working in the kitchen, she let Jana play in the other room for a few minutes. When she did not see the toddler in the house, she asked her mother if she had seen her. Poldie went outside and saw Jana's figure off in the distance about a quarter mile down the road. Poldie ran to Jana quickly and saw that the little girl had a shopping bag dragging behind her tiny, blowing dress.

Poldie asked breathlessly, "Wo gehst du, Jana?" (Where are you going, Jana?)

The little girl looked up. "Ich gehe einkafen zum Karger," she said. (I am going shopping to Karger.)

Poldie picked up the little runaway toddler and gently scolded the girl. She told her she should never leave by herself. As Poldie carried Jana home, she laughed about her little shopper. When Alois got home, he chuckled about their runaway shopper too.

In August of 1955, Alois received word from the AFCR that they had a sponsor for him in the United States in a city called Chicago. They would be sending his application to the American consulate. Both Alois and Poldie were excited, although the thought of change was a bit scary.

About a month later, a young American couple came to Altach to meet Alois, Poldie, and the girls. The jovial couple told them that the American consulate had sent them to investigate what kind of people the Hufs were. The couple liked little Jana and Marie, and they had a pleasant visit. The guests even invited the Hufs to go to the American bowling alley in the Robinson Barracks in Stuttgart for the evening. The two couples had cake and coffee after while talking about the US. After hearing about the country and having a good time with the Americans, more than ever, Alois and Poldie agreed they should go.

A month had passed when another American couple came to visit Alois and Leopoldine in Altach one weekend. The Autobahn housing complex where they lived was fenced in and gated. The couple drove up to the gate and announced themselves. They were looking to locate the Hufs. When the weekend attendant allowed them entrance, someone from the front office went to Alois and Poldie's room upstairs and alerted Alois that the couple was outside waiting. They parked their car in the front yard. A man in his sixties exited the vehicle while his wife remained in the car. He asked again for Alois Huf. Alois hurried downstairs, thinking that the American consulate had sent another couple to continue the vetting process. Alois was sure they came to find out more about them and what kind of lifestyle and morals they observed. Alois identified himself to the man, and they walked outside near the table where the guys often played table tennis. Alois was at once taken aback when the man spoke to him in the Czech language. The man proceeded to introduce himself and his wife as Charles and Edna Lukesh. Mr. Lukesh began a unique conversation about Jesus Christ. Alois decided to be extra cordial, even though he was a little annoyed with all the religious talk. It seemed very curious to Alois to talk about Jesus outside of the context of the church. This seemed very strange—who were these people, anyway? Alois was puzzled why the American consulate would have sent someone to interrogate them about spiritual matters.

As Mr. Lukesh talked more about Jesus, Alois recalled the only memories he had of this person called Jesus. Images of a priest and an altar boy carrying the holy book to the altar came to his mind. He remembered how the priest would read a few lines out of the Gospels about something that Jesus taught His disciples. The priest would sing Latin lyrics out of the book, and the congregation would give a response, although most did not understand what they were saying in the ancient language. There was always the depiction of Jesus on the cross at the front of the chapel. Alois had always felt sorry for Jesus, seeing Him in agony. He wondered how the Roman soldiers could be so cruel and crucify Jesus. Alois knew few details about the Bible and even less about this Jesus of whom Mr. Lukesh spoke.

As Mr. Lukesh continued to gradually question Alois about God and Jesus, Alois became quite defensive. What was all this talk about Jesus without discussing the importance of the Catholic Church and religion? Alois quietly thought, "No one will take me from my religion!"

Alois intervened: "Mr. Lukesh, you need to go see our neighbors. They don't attend church at all. My wife and I are okay. We go to church every week."

The man gently responded, "Alois, if you would die tonight, where would you go?"

"This is easy to answer if you are a Catholic. No one can know until you die," Alois said.

Mr. Lukesh asked, "If I could show you that you could be sure of your destination when you pass on from this life, would you listen?"

Alois thought for a moment. Poldie was inside, and no one else was around. "Yes," he said. Mr. Lukesh opened his Bible and encouraged Alois to read a verse he pointed to with his finger. How interesting to have one's own copy and to read the Holy Scripture in one's own language, Alois thought. "Jesus answered, 'I am the way and the truth and the life. No one comes to the Father except through me'" (John 14:6, NIV). Alois read and then stepped back slightly and again thought quietly to himself, "No man comes to the Father *except* through me." It occurred to him that if Jesus was the way, then no prayer or church routines would be adequate to get him into heaven. "If this is right, then—I don't have this."

Still, Alois felt guarded. The Catholic faith was good enough for his family, and it was good enough for him. He resolved that nothing would pull him from the traditions that had been his companions throughout his life.

The more the man talked, the more Alois began to doubt the consulate sent him and his wife. The young American couple that came to see Alois and Poldie before had talked about little else than fun and parties. Never in his life had anyone talked about Jesus like this, and it was so strange to Alois that he wondered what other religion or church they had in mind.

The two men conversed a bit more, and Alois was both intrigued and offended. He felt a sort of war begin to wage in his heart. He was not sure if he should listen to someone who did not wear a priest's collar. Besides, if it meant turning his back on the Catholic Church, Alois was not at all interested. Still, Alois's curiosity spurred him to ask a few questions. When the two men concluded their conversation, Alois said, "Come again." He hoped they would not take his invitation seriously; it was just a polite turn of phrase, and he had determined that no one would detach him from the Catholic Church. Most people in Germany knew the invitation was a sign of gentility only and was never intended to be taken seriously. And with those final words, the Lukeshes left.

CHAPTER NINE

TWO HEARTS FOREVER CHANGED

For some reason, after that visit, Alois continued pondering the question Mr. Lukesh had posed: "Where would you go if you died today?" Also, what the missionary read from the holy book about Jesus being the only way to heaven was a strong statement. Did no one gain entrance into heaven without Jesus? Alois tried his best to recount the conversations with Mr. Lukesh. He realized he never said anything derogatory about the Catholic faith during the entire talk.

When the Lukeshes reappeared at the door the following Wednesday, Alois felt more confident that they were not attempting to threaten his faith. They arrived after suppertime, and Poldie invited them inside. Mrs. Lukesh's interactions with Jana and Marie were grandmotherly. As Marie sat on her lap and nibbled on a piece of cake, a crumb fell in Mrs. Lukesh's lap. Unfazed, the stranger popped the morsel into her mouth and continued conversing. The multilingual couple made a point to speak Czech to Alois and German to Poldie. Again, Mr. Lukesh was direct. "We are American missionaries, and everywhere we go, we tell people about Jesus," he explained. Alois found it hard to resist the couple's kind and loving demeanor. They were different from anyone he and Poldie had ever met. They expressed everything with such joy and talked of God with hope and love; it felt like a beautiful, living faith that they possessed. Mrs. Lukesh told the Hufs about their missionary adventures. Right after World War I in 1918, Mr. Lukesh immigrated to Chicago from his homeland of Czechoslovakia at eighteen years old. Soon after arriving, he was out hunting when his gun fired, and he accidentally shot himself in his foot. Unable to work and with little to occupy himself with, one evening, he came upon a tent meeting in Chicago.

He heard the Good News of the Gospel being presented and decided to commit his life to Christ.

After that, he enrolled in the Moody Bible Institute. At Moody, he met Edna, who was several years his junior. They married, and the two of them became missionaries to South America. At the close of World War II, they moved to Czechoslovakia to serve as missionaries. They hosted Bible studies at their house in Znojmo and even adopted twins: a little girl and boy. Sadly, when the little boy grew up, he joined the army and was killed during the war. Their little girl met a man from Znojmo, and they immigrated to Canada. When the communists took over, the Lukeshes' home was confiscated, and they were forced to leave. They decided to continue their work in Germany.

At the heart of the Lukeshes' messages was Jesus's love for everyone. They shared how Jesus extends salvation to all through being born again. The Lukeshes talked of Jesus with such grateful hearts and fervor—as if He were a real person they knew intimately. Mrs. Lukesh even told the little girls about the angels in heaven. Still, Alois and Poldie proceeded cautiously during that second visit. Before the Lukeshes left, they gave Alois and Poldie two small booklets. One was in Czech for Alois, and the other was in German for Leopoldine. Alois looked down and read the author's name on his booklet: Kristina Royova. Alois was unfamiliar with this author. He and Poldie would soon learn more about her passionate work. A Slovak protestant and revivalist, Kristina dedicated her life to pen literary works that, after her death in 1936, were translated into thirty-six languages. While still alive, the Communist Party in Czechoslovakia made several attempts to shut her work down. The Socialist Party blacklisted her so that her writings could not be included in the school curricula, and the Christian literature she authored and published was among those continually confiscated by the state security service.

The missionaries promised to come back the next week. After they left, Alois and Poldie discussed all that was shared, and Poldie admitted to Alois that she was still unsure of what a "missionary" was.

The conversations with the Lukeshes were unlike any that Alois and Poldie had ever conducted with other people. Alois remained guarded, but he also felt a sense of trust and connection with the older couple. Much of what they shared was interesting, and neither Alois nor Poldie had ever heard anyone recall so much scripture. The next morning, when Alois left for work, he took the booklet with him.

When he had some spare time between assignments, Alois began reading. The book described two groups of people living in Slovakia in the early 1900s—the Catholics and the evangelicals. Most of the people in the two groups lived according to the rules required of them and went to their respective churches on Sunday. While they followed the prescribed rules, there was no love lost between the people. In fact, there was a hornet's nest of dislike, gossip, and jealousy. Even the priests and ministers were among this wayward bunch.

Still, every Sunday, the words emanating from the altar and the pulpit were about God and His pristine ways. The people's hearts were far from God. The author wove a story about a man in his thirties named Martin, who came to the Slovak village to visit his elderly mother. He had lived in America for several years. The people in the town long remembered the man and his reputation as a youth. He was a drunkard and a fighter. Not a week went by when Martin had not been in trouble. He was a thorn in his mother's side; he caused her to cry many tears.

When Martin moved away, he left behind a wake of trouble with the townspeople and the police. For years, nobody heard anything else about Martin. Even his mother did not know where he went or if he was still alive. Alois paused for a moment. Although he was not rebellious, he related to this story immediately. He empathized with the mother in the story, who felt as if she had lost her son. Several years after Martin's departure, his mother received a letter from America. It was from Martin. She cried as she pored over the pages. Martin asked her for forgiveness for the heartaches he caused her. He wrote how the Lord Jesus Christ had forgiven him when he received Him as Savior. Martin was a new man now, he penned.

Not long after, Martin reunited with his mother and invited his old companions over. He told his story of subsisting on alcohol and living on the streets, even in the US, until a man asked him to join him for a hot meal. The man, Josh, shared Jesus's love with Martin, and Martin realized that he had never heard such a message. Josh said, "Jesus loves you so much that He was willing to die for you on the cross, and He will forgive all of your past and make a brand-new man out of you."

Martin explained how he accepted Jesus as his Savior and gave his life to Him. Martin promised that he would one day return to his village and tell everyone what Jesus did for him. Standing before his countrymen, Martin asked for their forgiveness. He said to them that Jesus would change their lives too. No one congregated had ever heard such a riveting story before. Their minds were full of the doctrines of baptism and keeping regulations. Sunday mornings and Saturday nights were worlds apart.

One of the men at the gathering asked Martin if he could return the next evening to hear more. The man brought his fiancée the next day. She was hesitant to marry the man because he was intoxicated weekly. She did not want to repeat the life of her mother. They both heard the message that God so loved both of them that He gave His Son to die on the cross for them. If they believed, they would not perish but would have everlasting life. Both of the visitors gave their lives to God. The young people came back, bringing their friends with them. More and more people in the village wanted to hear about this saving love of God.

The owner of the village pub was not pleased that the young men were going to Martin's house instead of his establishment. By now, even the older people in the village noticed the changes in these young people. They were not rebelliously engaged in fighting and drunken nights, as before. Instead, they were interested in being kind to one another. Peace spread over the village; many people who, for years, had not spoken to their neighbors found it in their hearts to live in harmony with one another. Members of both religious factions wondered why their leaders had never told them the simple message that Jesus alone can make a difference in someone's life.

When Alois finished reading the booklet, he ruminated over it and then opened it again. It reminded him so much of the village life in Drozdov. He felt as though he were reading about his father, grandmother, neighbors, and church. He wished someone had shared with his family and neighbors about the difference that Jesus could make.

Alois read the booklet twice more. As he thought about its message, he concluded that he was religious but that he did not have the peace that the villagers had in their hearts at the end of the book. And then there was that nagging question Mr. Lukesh asked: "If you died today, where would you go?" While the message of salvation through Jesus moved him significantly, Alois still struggled internally. He liked what he read but felt it would mean tearing down the secure fortress of religion he had built in his mind and heart. He presumed he would continue in good graces with the church and God as long as he did what was taught to him since childhood. But this message was saying that he could be in good graces with God—even if it meant doing things differently than the Catholic Church did—by trusting in Jesus Christ alone for salvation.

It was a problem to reconcile the opposing sides. Alois's religion had been with him all these years. He had prayed to Mary, the mother of God, adoring her and believing she was the queen of heaven. He had extolled her sinless nature and implored her on behalf of her Son. The Hail Mary prayer was as ingrained in Alois's consciousness as his own name. He did not want to give up that concept. It felt like disowning or at least disrespecting a dear aunt.

Had Mary made a significant difference in his life? And what about the many people who followed the religion in Drozdov? The more Alois reasoned these things out, the more it appeared to him that religion and Mary did not change people. It appeared that people adhering to this religion would vie for the favor of the holy mother as if she had only so much goodness and answered prayers to go around. Alois searched his heart and could not remember hearing any teaching about forgiveness and love in the church. He did recall that when parishioners had pressing needs it looked like Mary was not solving, sometimes the priest directed them to seek a shrine of Mary elsewhere. "You need to go to the shrine to the Virgin Mary in Czestochowa, Poland," he recollected the priest saying once. On occasion, if people were struggling with physical ailments, the priest counseled them to make a pilgrimage to Our Lady of Lourdes in France.

As Alois drove throughout the day and interacted with others, he was the friendly, easygoing fellow everyone knew. But internally, Alois was analyzing, weighing, thinking, and rethinking. He had never crucially examined the holy sites and shrines in his mind. He just knew that his fellow villagers were so poor that such expeditions would drain whatever resources they had left. And why could the spirit of Mary do different things at different locations? Again, he thought back to the priest saying Mary hears all prayers, no matter where the petitioner was.

What about the verse that Mr. Lukesh read to Alois about Jesus saying that He was the only way, the only truth, and the only life and that no one could come to heaven and to the Father except through Him. If Jesus was the only intermediary between God and man, then why was he taught that Mary was the one whom everyone should address? Where was that directive in the Bible? Maybe Mary was the other way to heaven. The thoughts pressed him, and Alois decided he would engage with Mr. Lukesh more the next time he came and ask him about these concerns.

When Alois arrive home from work that evening, he was subdued and not as talkative as usual. After greeting the children and Poldie and eating dinner together, he convinced Poldie he needed to go for a walk by himself that evening. Poldie looked slightly disturbed, but Alois assured her he just had something on his mind that he must think through. Poldie acquiesced; she knew their immigration status was probably causing him some anxiety.

By the time Alois was halfway to Monrepos on foot, he was surprised to see the fleeting shadows of the sun. It was a thirty-minute walk, and he was so deep in thought, he could scarcely remember the journey thus far. Putting his hands in his pockets, he continued his slow pace, letting the chill of autumn breezes gently wash across his face. He began working through the points in his mind. Number one, he believed the Bible was the Word of God. He affirmed this to Mr. Lukesh. Second, the Bible's message was unlike what he believed—he had no comprehension that all people were invited to accept Jesus Christ as Savior, go to Him, and ask Him to change their lives. Again, he considered the crucifix, the suffering visage of Jesus, ever crucified on the cruel cross. Alois envisioned a new image—that of a resurrected Jesus, walking around and well! The thought was such a shock; the cross was only the beginning.

It felt as if time stood still. Alois looked up at the black sky lit with innumerable stars. He wondered if God was there behind the stars, ready to hear a simple human like him. He pictured the throne room of heaven. Something or someone was drawing Alois toward something he had never felt before. Overcome with emotion, he prayed, "God, if

You can hear me, I need Your help. There is a battle going on inside of me. I believe in You. Part of me desires to cry out to Jesus to save me, and the other part wants to hold on to the religion I've always known. I am afraid to abandon what I was taught. Please help me."

In quiet desperation, Alois recalled a verse Mr. Lukesh quoted: "Come to me, all you who are weary and burdened, and I will give you rest. Take my yoke upon you and learn from me, for I am gentle and humble in heart, and you will find rest for your souls. For my yoke is easy and my burden is light" (Matthew 11:28-30, NIV). Alois visualized Jesus with outstretched arms, inviting him to come. At that moment, it was as if Jesus was saying, "Give me your religion, and I will nail it to the cross. Instead of religion, I will give you salvation, peace, and joy, and I'll never leave you."

Alone and defenseless, Alois dropped to his knees. He prayed, "Jesus, I believe that You are the Son of God and that You died on the cross for the sins of the world. I believe that You died there for me also. Forgive my sins and come into my heart. I receive You as my Savior. Thank You that You hear my prayer." Alois waited a moment in the quiet. He felt an inexpressible peace rush over him; the battle raging inside had stilled. Once again, he saw Jesus as alive and no longer as a body forever hanging on a cross.

A deep sense of God's love for Alois became instantly ubiquitous. He saw Jesus's crucifixion as a moving expression of that love. God's acceptance of him permeated his being. The fear of leaving the religious pattern departed and was replaced by confidence to pray to the Lord based on the work of Jesus and not based on Alois's own good works or religious formulas.

Another line of thought presented itself while Alois rested on the ground. He looked out over the quiet, dark countryside and contrasted his current peaceful state with the despair he experienced a few years before, when his attempts at leaving the country were denied. The desolation and helplessness Alois had faced were still fresh as he evoked memories of himself crying on the train and lying on his bunk, feeling trapped. After saying good-bye to his second group of friends, he had assumed his life was over, thinking that there was nothing left to live for. Several years had transpired since he left his family in Czechoslovakia, and he was sure that they thought he was dead and that they were moving on with their lives.

All at once, small signs of spring emerged from the frozen terrain of his life. First, obtaining the driver's license from the kind lady who pushed it through right during Alois's inquiry and the steady job with the US Army had been sheer miracles. Meeting Poldie, the love of his life, and gaining a family of two little girls were priceless gifts. Finally, Alois was able to reconnect with his immediate family. He saw how each of the dead places in his heart and life experienced a kind of resurrection. Tears streamed down his face. Dead things could come back to being just as the illustration of the cross demonstrated! Alois confessed he had held a bit of a grudge toward God for a long time for not letting him leave Germany. Now he was beginning to see things differently. What would his life have been like as a lonely shepherd in Australia? Would work in the mines of Canada have been a hopeful one? What would have become of him fighting in the US Army?

It was as if a hundred puzzle pieces were coming down from the sky and finally fitting together. Alois now saw with clarity how his life in the darkest days of living in the refugee camps was preserved. It was God's sovereignty that kept him from leaving Germany, he acknowledged. Even when the denials felt like a death sentence to his weary heart, God kept Alois from being crushed by the weight of it. In fact, the very blessings that were waiting for him would not have been possible if he had received his wish to leave. He thought of his loving wife, his two children, and all the things he had learned working for the US Army. And then God brought the Lukeshes. The peculiar entry of the couple into his and Poldie's lives caused him to seek God for himself in a way he had never done before. Alois was overwhelmed by the goodness of his heavenly Father.

Reflecting on the previous years, Alois replayed scenes in his mind—crawling through the snow and hearing the border dogs bark, saying good-bye as his friends left for a new life, wincing in pain as the doctor examined his hand. Thinking about the heart-wrenching moments of the past, Alois felt thankful. Somehow, God overruled all the plans Alois attempted to create for his future, and instead, He set in order what was best for Alois—rehearsing all the ways God provided for him and made way for him through Jesus and gave him hope and confidence for the future. Alois was still determined to leave Germany, but he felt a peace and a sense of release with whatever happened regarding his immigration request.

Upon standing to his feet, Alois felt refreshed, like he was a brand-new person, and his outlook was different. He began the thirty-minute walk back to Altach and continued his conversation with God as though he had seen a distant friend's face for the first time. He wanted immediately to share God with others. Alois prayed for Leopoldine. He said, "Lord Jesus, Poldie needs to be saved, along with our families. Use me to bring them the Good News that Jesus saves."

When he finally arrived home, Alois greeted his wife with tenderness. As they prepared for bed, Alois said nothing of the decision he had made but said, "The booklets the Lukeshes left are excellent. They talk about how we need to receive Jesus. You ought to read yours tomorrow."

Poldie promised she would, and with that, the couple kissed and turned off the lights for the night. Poldie held back from disclosing to Alois that she already read the booklet during the day while he was away at work. After Alois left for work that morning and while the children were still asleep, she stayed tucked in bed but with the booklet in her hands. She read the powerful stories and felt a sense of spiritual conviction come over her. She had never thought of herself as a bad person, but she immediately realized she was a spiritually empty, lost person who needed a Savior. Throughout the day, the message written in the booklet continued to enthrall her. Later in the day, Poldie made a fire in the potbelly stove in the room. As she added more coal, she felt the heat and saw the iron of the stove turn red. The intense heat reminded her of what she read about the great white throne judgment of God. She learned that all of one's life was like a vapor, and in eternity, only the redeeming work of Jesus Christ would allow a person to stand as holy before God. The ones whose names were not written in the Book of Life would be cast into the lake of fire (Revelation 20:15). The heat coming from the hot stove in front of her gave Poldie an entirely different picture of what she just read. She then remembered how Mr. Lukesh drew attention to their fiery stove and told them things Jesus said about eternal separation from God and hell. "According to Jesus's words, hell will be like the fire in that stove for some," Mr. Lukesh lamented.

Poldie rotely said her prayers, and she did believe in God, but she recognized for the first time that she had never put her faith in Christ or truly given Him her life. She knelt beside the warm fire and thanked God for providing Jesus as the sacrifice for sins. She asked God to forgive her sins and for Jesus to be her Savior. She thought about the change in the people she had read about. She remembered her past. There were so many days and nights when Poldie suppressed childhood worries and fears about the future. She fretted often about whether or not her family would survive the hardships and hunger after the war. But they did. And then she met Alois, and God gave them two beautiful children. Poldie was thankful for her life and so appreciative that she had met Edna Lukesh and her husband, Charles. Poldie kept the events of the day hidden in her heart and would not reveal the decision she had made to Alois.

The following day at work, Alois's mind was on Poldie as he drove. He had a transformative peace of the assurance of his salvation for the first time in his life and of God's love for him. He wanted that for Poldie. He prayed, "God, please draw Poldie to Yourself. She needs to come to You too; she needs You, Lord Jesus." He then thought of his parents and how they needed Jesus. He started to look at the men he worked with differently. Everyone needed Jesus, he realized.

When Alois arrived home from work that night, it was Poldie who gave Alois a piece of fantastic news upon greeting him. She could no longer contain her excitement and told him that she read the booklet the day before and accepted Jesus as Savior. She admitted that she fretted over confessing her decision to Alois because of his devotion to the Catholic religion. Poldie conjectured that Alois might be angry with her for making peace with God. Instead, a broad smile spread across Alois's face, and he hugged her. "I did too!" he said. "Last night, at Monrepos, when I went for that evening walk. I had hoped that you would too!"

Poldie chuckled. She remembered how uncertain Alois was when the missionary couple first arrived. Now he was the one thankful that Poldie accepted the Gospel. They recalled the scripture Mr. Lukesh read to them once, quoting John 1:12: "Yet to all who received him, to those who believed in his name, he gave the right to become children of God" (NIV). Alois and Poldie were joyful and could not wait to share with the Lukeshes what they had done.

The following Wednesday, the Lukeshes came again to visit. Both Alois and Poldie welcomed them with a new warmness. When they sat down, the young couple shared that they both received Jesus in their hearts. The missionaries were thrilled and told them they fervently prayed that God would open their eyes and enable them to see their need for Him.

Alois wanted to have some of his questions addressed. He asked, "How is it that I was taught to honor—almost worship—Mary and pray to her?"

Charles smiled softly and surprised Alois with his answer: "I think I honor Mary even more than you." Alois waited, and then Mr. Lukesh continued, opening to a page in his Bible. "I don't want just to tell you my opinion. Look at what the Word of God says. In Luke 1:38, we read that Mary called herself 'the Lord's servant.' Then in Luke 1:46–48, it says, 'My soul glorifies the Lord and my spirit rejoices in God my Savior. From now on, all generations will call me blessed'" (NIV). Mr. Lukesh looked up from the open Bible at Alois. "Mary is honored among all Christians because she was willing to be used by God as His servant," he said. "This is the reason that Christians count her as blessed."

Alois nodded, absorbing the scripture passage. "What about the worship of Mary? Why were we always taught to adore her and pray to her, especially in May?"

"If God would want us to worship Mary and pray to her, I feel confident He would have asked us to do that in His Word," Mr. Lukesh said.

"I don't know much of anything about the Word of God. But I believe that God would have told us who we are supposed to worship and pray to," Alois said.

"Let's look at Acts 1:14 [NIV]," Mr. Lukesh said, turning pages in the Bible. "'They all joined together constantly in prayer, along with the women and Mary the mother of Jesus, and with his brothers.' We read about Mary here for the last time in the Bible." Mr. Lukesh held tight to the pages of the Bible. "That same verse mentions two of Jesus's half brothers, James and Jude. They did not believe in the divinity of Jesus until after His resurrection, when He appeared to James. That brother wrote the book of James. The other half brother, Jude, wrote the book of Jude. Even in these two books, there is no mention made about their mother, Mary. But every page in the New Testament is about Jesus."

Alois leaned back and thought about what he was hearing and reading. He looked at Mr. Lukesh as if to compel him to keep explaining why the Bible was different than he had assumed. It seemed more practical and less mystical. He did not hear messages about going to certain shrines or saying a chosen prayer over and over.

"Jesus did honor his mother and father, but he did not assign a personal, spiritual level to them. In Acts 4:12 [NIV], it says, 'Salvation is found in no one else, for there is *no* other name under heaven given to mankind by which we must be saved.' In Isaiah, a book that contains prophecies about the Messiah, it reads in chapter 45, verse 22, 'Turn to me and be saved, all you ends of the earth; for I am God, and there is no other.' In Psalm 138, verses 1 and 2, we are told that we should not worship others."

Alois's thoughts were still about the shrines and relics. He knew how special items and places were revered. "What about bowing down to items, like pieces of the cross or pieces of the burial shroud of Jesus?" Alois remembered that sacred items were passed among the Catholic churches and regarded with awe. Sometimes parishioners were even directed to worship such things.

Mr. Lukesh was never condemning of other people, but he knew his Bible thoroughly. He turned to the front of the Bible. "Well, God addresses that very thing," he said. "In Exodus chapter 20, it says, 'You shall have no other gods before me. You shall not make for yourself an image in the form of anything in heaven above or on the earth beneath or in the waters below. You shall not bow down to them or worship them; for I, the LORD your God, am a jealous God'" (Exodus 20:3-5, NIV).

It was making sense to Alois. He misunderstood and assumed some of the rituals were imposed by God, but he saw more clearly that the religious acts were just means for humans to try to reach God instead of receiving what He had given them. Jesus, the Messiah, had been prophesied, and when He came, He claimed divinity and proved it by performing miracles and rising from the dead. It seemed odd now to Alois to give such attention to Mary.

"The New Testament speaks over and over again to us about Jesus, who created all things and holds all things together as the books of John and Colossians tell us. He even intercedes for us to God as it says in Hebrews 7. He alone is someone who came as a human who deserves honor and praise," Mr. Lukesh said.

It was logical to Alois. He was concerned that pulling away from the sacred observations of Mary, the saints, and the reverence for holy objects would make his faith in God less real to him. But he found the opposite to be true. When Alois thought of God alone as the One from whom everything stems, it made him even more in awe of the Creator God. Alois was satisfied with Mr. Lukesh's explanations through the Bible passages and felt ready to pray to and worship Jesus alone.

Even though Poldie was quieter than Alois, she listened intently and took everything to heart. She always loved school and learning about God was a new quest entirely. She wanted to read this book, the Bible, for herself and learn all the things she did not know before.

When it was time for the missionary couple to leave, Alois sincerely requested, "Please come back." He meant it this time, and they knew he did. In just hours with Mr. Lukesh, Alois learned more about the Bible than he knew his whole life. Like Poldie, he wanted to read the Bible for himself. As Mr. Lukesh demonstrated, everybody can read the Bible, and a regular layperson can understand it. Still, Alois craved the guidance and wisdom that Mr. Lukesh brought as they examined the Bible verses together.

Mr. and Mrs. Lukesh continued to come at least once a week, and Alois and Poldie gathered the children of their little community in Altach. Mrs. Lukesh had flannelgraph, which she'd attach to a propped-up board. About fourteen children gathered for a Bible lesson. The Hufs enjoyed the stories as well. They had not heard the tales of Samson's strength, or David slaying Goliath with a stone, or Peter walking on water to Jesus.

On one occasion, Mrs. Lukesh told Alois about a special meeting at a church in a neighboring city where a female preacher from Switzerland was speaking. She said, "Alois, I will fetch you and drive us to the meeting." Alois wondered what "fetch you" meant, but he soon came to understand this language. Mrs. Lukesh came to "fetch" Alois while Poldie remained behind with their two children. Mrs. Lukesh drove Alois the hour drive to Böblingen, Germany. The preacher spoke in German and gave a powerful message to the crowd of inquisitive seekers. Alois was able to travel there with Mrs. Lukesh on two occasions, and during the long rides back and forth, she taught him more of the English language, for which he was grateful. The two spoke much about the ways of God and spiritual matters.

For both Alois and Poldie, a relationship with God rather than an adherence to strict rules and routines changed their prayer lives and their perspectives. Each of them found fulfillment in reading the Bible and discovering more about the faith they knew so little of throughout their lives.

Poldie's family tolerated the Lukeshes, but they were not very interested in their message. Concerned for their family members, Alois and Poldie yearned for them to experience the same faith and source of strength in Christ. Alois thought about all the times in which Poldie wrote letters on his behalf. Perhaps he should put aside the fear and intimidation brought on by the communist government and write, he decided. Alois sat down and penned a letter in his own handwriting, telling his family how much he loved and missed them. He wrote that Jesus had become his Savior. He added that Jesus is the only way to heaven and is available for all who put their trust in Him. Putting his newfound faith into words, Alois wanted to share relevant Bible verses. If only his family could read the Bible for themselves, he thought, they would know this faith was real.

Alois copied John 3:7 out of the Bible: "You must be born again." He believed his loved ones would be interested to know they did not have to worry about their eternal destinies. He copied a passage he felt was unusually clear, 1 John 5:11-13: "And this is the testimony: God has given us eternal life, and this life is in his Son. Whoever has the Son has life; whoever does not have the Son does not have life" (NIV).

When Alois sent the letter, his heart was full of joy in sharing the Good News he had found; he hoped his family would receive the message with the same eagerness he experienced when he realized that Jesus died for him so that he could have a relationship with God.

Alois and Poldie received a quick reply, this time from Maruska. When Alois opened the letter and read the Czech text, he felt the anguish of rejection. His sister wrote, "As I can read from your letter, I see that you have turned to Jesus Christ, proving to me that you took on the Protestant religion."

Inside, Alois felt disappointed and frustrated. His family thought he was going from one religious system to the next. They were not getting the point; he was telling them about a person and a relationship—living water. Alois penned a reply explaining that the Lord Jesus had taken religion from him, and instead of only the observation of religion, he had a personal relationship with God and the assurance of salvation. Those are things that religion could not give, he wrote. Alois paused for a moment, praying for the right words to convey his newfound love for Jesus: "I don't consider myself religious. I have Jesus, and He is all I need. I am praying for all of you to believe in Jesus. He's the only One who offers us eternal life." It was all up to God whether or not his family would take his words to heart, but Alois knew that he could not contain the truth he discovered. It was love for his family that compelled him to write out a Bible verse on the letter. He wrote John 3:16: "For God so loved the world that he gave his only begotten Son, that whosoever believes in him should not perish, but have everlasting life" (KJ2000).

Poldie hoped her family would also believe. The Kellners did not see the need for incorporating faith into their daily lives. When Alois and Poldie talked with them about Jesus, it seemed the conversations became uncomfortable quickly. Alois's confident and outspoken personality prompted him to take a risk and be a messenger of the truth about God and Jesus. Poldie was always discerning but purposefully delicate with her family about sharing her new belief. Alois, on the other hand, found it surprising that people were not always readily convinced they needed a Savior. The more Alois learned of the Bible, the more God's Spirit continued to teach him new things, and he was grateful in many ways for the way for his religious upbringing. Even though he did not adhere to the rituals and the trappings of a religion without a relationship, he knew he became a person of prayer and faith with the help of the foundation that was laid. He had always feared God and believed there was some divine hand guiding his life.

With each letter he wrote to his family back home, Alois hoped his words conveyed kindness and encouragement and that they would be received well. The last thing he ever intended was to express anything that might give the idea that the Hufs or the Kellners were terrible people. Alois believed precisely the opposite. Both his family and Poldie's were some of the finest folks he ever knew. But no matter where people are in life, they will starve spiritually if they do not eat from the bread of life in Jesus. The disappointment continued as Alois continued receiving written responses from his family. They did not understand or accept what he was trying to convey. How could they without having a knowledgeable messenger to bring them the truth as the Lukeshes did for Alois and Poldie? Letters filled with news of family members and happenings were interspersed with overt sadness, especially from Alois's mother, Marie. She could not comprehend why Alois left the Catholic religion he had followed all his life. Each letter she wrote ended with a prayer to Mary that she would protect Alois and his family in Germany. Alois and Poldie had only one option: turning into intense prayer warriors for their families and loved ones rather than trying to win ideological arguments.

CHAPTER TEN

PREPARING FOR A NEW SEASON

T he Christmas holiday of 1955 was fast approaching, and both Alois and Poldie took extra pleasure in hearing the Christmas carols and observing the sights of the season. It was very real to them that the holiday was a celebration of Jesus Christ. For the first time in their lives, the words of the messenger angel in Luke chapter 2 to the shepherds in the field resonated in their hearts and minds: "I bring you good news that will cause joy for all the people." The news was for the poor and the rich, the young and the old, the healthy and the sick, the educated and the simple, the remembered and the forgotten. Jesus was the Savior to all.

After Christmas, the Germans anticipated celebrating New Year's Eve, known as Silvester in Germany. The festive holiday honors the fourth-century Pope Sylvester I, who was sainted by the Catholic Church, and is observed every December 31. However, regardless of the holiday's Christian connection, the history goes back even further to the pagan practices of the heathen German tribes. These practices were called Rauhnächte.

In previous years, Alois and Poldie anticipated participating in Silvester's rather rowdy celebrations. The partying would continue throughout the day and into the night in wild and noisy social gatherings. The champagne and liquor were ubiquitous while people took in the festivities. Most Germans were unaware of the real reason behind why it was so crucial for tons of noise to accompany the celebration. It was meant to drive away a host evil winter spirits, but the people were too busy drinking, becoming intoxicated, and acting unruly to comprehend the purpose.

This Silvester was different from any Alois and Poldie had ever celebrated. From their tiny room, after both girls fell asleep, Alois and

Poldie cuddled in bed and heard the yelling, singing, and commotion from outside. While Christmas was a special family celebration for them, they decided to spend that evening praying for the year to come. They both read from the Bible the priest gave them when they married in the Catholic Church service. The Hufs appreciated the gift from him, but with no instruction, they went home and never opened the book. They had no idea what was in their possession the entire time—God's Word, which gave them the truth. Poldie stroked Alois's arm. He was a good companion, father, and husband, and she told him so.

Alois looked toward the window for a moment and thought of the countless times his father came home, stumbling about, speaking in mumbled phrases, and smelling of alcohol. He remembered feeling afraid at first and then worried as he heard his parents fight and listened to the cries of his mother. He recalled his grandmother and how she liked to cradle the bottle in her hand as if it were her last treasure on earth. The atmosphere in their home was often unhappy. Alois went back to that unforgettable childhood memory when walking home from Mass with his mother: "Mother, when I grow up, I will not drink," he had promised. He had the potential to become like his father, but he knew the Holy Spirit would help him keep his promise. He assumed by the look in Poldie's eyes that her heart was full.

Alois and Poldie stayed up until midnight and wished each other a happy New Year. When the lights were turned off and the echoes of celebration could still be heard in the distance, Alois thanked God for the salvation of Jesus and also for his beautiful family. Poldie fell asleep quickly, but Alois had too much on his mind to sleep. The plethora of disappointments continually replayed in his mind: the forest service rejection, those many days in the camp, and the times he was hindered from immigrating. He thought of the gnawing hunger he feared might never subside.

Again, Alois realized a solitary life in Australia or Canada and an uncertain fate in the US Army would not have allowed him to live his current life. He wanted to jump out of bed and shout for joy. It had indeed been Jesus—divine intervention—that had led him down his life's road. "Alois Huf, report to the office," he remembered hearing. That voice was not rejection at all but an intervention, he realized. He wanted to laugh. He prayed, "Thank You, Lord, a thousand times, for loving me so much and caring for me all this time. I trust You for the future—whatever the future will bring."

———————————————————◆———————————————————

In January of 1956, Alois received a letter from the AFCR. Alois opened the envelope with Poldie at his side, hoping for good news. The letter instructed him and Poldie and their two children to appear before the American consulate in Munich in three weeks. It also confirmed that there was an employer who was willing to sponsor Alois in Chicago. It was a Polish restaurant where Alois would secure employment as one of the dishwashers.

Poldie looked at the letter to confirm the day they were to appear in Munich: February 6, 1956. As she contemplated having to raise three-year-old Jana and one-year-old Marie in a strange city, she became hesitant. As much as she felt hopeful about a future in the United States, they had a nest and a comfortable lifestyle in Germany. Even though she did not want to stay with her parents too long, and she knew opportunities were limited in Germany, Poldie felt she belonged. It was comforting to have family around and be in a place she was familiar with and understood the language. She uttered her fears to Alois: "At least you speak a lot of English; I don't know any!"

Alois encouraged Poldie: "I'll start teaching you some words. You will learn!" His enthusiastic and positive outlook put Poldie at ease. They were young, and now was as good of a time as any to make a change, she realized. It would not be easy to move across the world with two small children, but this could be a great opportunity. Mentally, Poldie began to prepare.

That week, the Lukeshes visited. Alois eagerly shared the news about the letter. Charles reminded them that he and Edna attended the Moody Bible Institute in Chicago, and they knew the city very well. Poldie, who generally listened more than she spoke in conversations, deliberately joined in. It was vital for her to understand more about the city and what it would be like raising two small kids there. When Mrs. Lukesh heard about the job assignment, she said, "Your wages will be very minimal.

You will only be able to afford a very small apartment with a tiny kitchen, bathroom, and one or two small bedrooms. There will be no laundry facilities, and you will have to wash your clothes in the bathroom and then hang them to dry on a small balcony on clotheslines."

Poldie's mind began racing. In Germany, they had a yard and lived in the beautiful countryside. Alois's current job was better than being a dishwasher, but it was the land of opportunity that he was ultimately seeking. "Oh, Mrs. Lukesh, I'm so scared of the big city," she said openly. "How am I going to raise my little children there? I would be so happy if I could live somewhere in the country."

Mrs. Lukesh certainly understood. She suggested they pray to the same Jesus who saved from sins. He was also the One who would direct their futures, she encouraged. They all prayed together that God would specifically lead the Hufs and make a way to the place that was best. Edna had brought her portable organ. She played a Christian song, and they sang together before praying. Mrs. Lukesh's hopefulness made Poldie feel somewhat better, although there was still a knot in her stomach. She wished for the faith of the Lukeshes and the optimism of Alois. After the Lukeshes left, Poldie quit complaining to her husband. She knew that he had wanted to go to the United States for years, and she felt she should practice turning to God in the fervent prayer that Mrs. Lukesh modeled.

As the Lukeshes drove away that evening, Edna turned to her husband: "When we were praying, I felt the Lord impress on my mind to ask some of our supporting churches back in the US to help this young couple whom we have come to know and love." Charles nodded and agreed that they should pray more about it and seek the Lord's direction.

In the days that followed, Poldie and Alois prayed together about the upcoming visit to the consulate as well as the specific location they will settle in America. Alois wanted Poldie to be happy. He did not realize how much the images of the big city hovered like a storm cloud over her mind. She pictured being cooped up in a cramped high-rise with two children and venturing out into chaotic streets among hundreds of strangers whose language she could not understand. In her private prayers, she begged the Lord Jesus to prepare something different than Chicago. She reasoned in her frustrated mind that she was already giving so much up by agreeing to go to a whole new country. Why could she not go somewhere that made her feel more at ease?

Poldie and Alois processed their feelings without sharing the extent of them. Visions of the various refugee camps her family endured resurfaced in Poldie's memory. Eventually, they ended up in a place that felt like home. She tried to anticipate the best outcome. Alois prayed through his intimate feelings. He never disclosed to Leopoldine about how he was prohibited three times from leaving Germany. He did not want to worry her, but he was also concerned that even his wife might speculate untrue things about him. The reactions of the men in the barracks when he was sent back tormented him. They had gotten to know him, and yet even they assumed that Alois must have done something incredibly wrong to be turned away so decidedly.

Alois planned to share the full account of his previously failed immigration attempts with her, but he would do it after they left Germany. It would be too much for Poldie to process and would add to her concerns. For the time being, he took his angst to God. "My Lord Jesus," he prayed, "You know how much I would like to take my little family to the United States. Here in Germany, we do not have a place to live on our own, and it will be hard for us to acquire that. You gave me great in-laws who welcome us, but there is not enough room. Lord, Poldie and I have been married now for more than three years. Could You give us a place to call our own?"

Alois continued to pray: "Lord, if the CIA decides to send me back after we have traveled to northern Germany and boarded the ship, it will be confusing to Poldie. She won't understand after she has prepared herself to leave. If that is what is going to happen, please allow something to happen sooner, like the American consulate rejecting visa applications. Please keep my family from experiencing the trauma of deportation as I have in the past. And if we are rejected for immigration, Lord, please provide an apartment for us in Germany. Whatever You have for us, we will receive it gladly from Your hand." Alois remembered how Jesus prayed to His Father. "Not our will, Lord, but Your will be done," Alois added.

The Lukeshes returned weekly during January to call on Alois and Poldie. Each visit was an opportunity for Alois and Poldie to learn more about God, Jesus, and the Bible. Now the two couples shared a tender closeness and treated one another like family. Poldie, always the consummate hostess, baked sweets for their visits. The Lukeshes did not drink coffee, so Poldie grappled with finding other appropriate drinks to serve. One such time, Poldie added a shot of rum in Mr. Lukesh's tea. A gesture such as this one was customary to Poldie, and she had no intention of offending him. As he brought the cup to his mouth, he repeatedly sniffed it and made a bizarre expression. He had difficulty with his sense of smell and blurted out inquisitively, "Is there rum in my tea?" Poldie confirmed, to which Mr. Lukesh fired back, "Thank you, but that is alcohol, and this is not for us! I will not drink this; I want plain tea!" Poldie appreciated the Lukeshes' natural joy and happiness but found them to be quite strict. Alois encountered some curious interactions with the couple as well. Alois had taken an interest in ice hockey while he still lived at home with his parents in Czechoslovakia. The Czechoslovakian men's team proved to be gifted and become the first-ever team from his region to win two World Championships, one in 1947 and the other in 1949. Alois recalled how exhilarating it was when the heroic team shut out Belgium 24-0 on February 21, 1947. The entire country was ecstatic about their beloved team's success and showed their total allegiance to them, especially in the face of heartbreaking tragedy. In 1948, the team was invited to play an exhibition game in the UK at Wembley. One day before the event, eight members of the group traveled ahead of the others. The remaining six players chartered a flight the next day, November 9, 1948, to join their teammates. The Beechcraft airplane, flown by Mercure Airlines, took off from Paris and headed for London. It unexpectedly and tragically crashed in the English Channel off Dieppe, France. All six players perished, including one of their star members, Ladislav Troják, who scored thirty-seven times in the seventy-five games he played for the team. In leaving his homeland, Alois held only a few treasures close to his heart: his love for his family, his loyalty to his favorite hockey team, and his devotion to his religion. Certainly now, even though he committed his life to Christ, he could still appreciate the excitement of sports and the enjoyment of smoking. Mr. Lukesh was intolerable toward both, and his candid judgments were abundant.

When the Lukeshes arrived for another visit on Monday, January 30, the 1956 Winter Olympics, hosted in Italy, was at its height. The Czechoslovakian ice hockey team advanced to the final round, undefeated in their preliminary pool, along with Canada and the Soviet Union. Alois was determined to capture the thrill of what he hoped would be a win against Canada for his cherished home team. It was the most thrilling time in the world of ice hockey competition. The Canadian team had for thirty-two years dominated Olympic ice hockey until 1952, when the Soviet Union proved to be contenders. As the couples socialized, Alois intermittently vanished into the Kellner family's compact kitchen, where a small radio sat on the cabinet. It was the first game of the final round, and the Czechs would be battling the Canadians for the win. Alois adjusted the antenna and played with the dials on the transistor, attempting to gain a clear signal from Radio Prague. The transmission signal was so weak, Alois awkwardly hunched over and finally brought the radio to his ear to hear each play. Mr. Lukesh was irritated at being left alone while Alois struggled to listen to the game. He finally interrupted, saying, "Do you think you will listen to ice hockey in heaven?" Alois tolerated Mr. Lukesh's comments that night and was saddened when the Canadians defeated the Czechs 6–3.

Since the age of sixteen, Alois enjoyed smoking. And he did not see the urgency in giving this habit up when he became a Christian. To Alois, smoking was pleasurable. Poldie wanted him to quit, but it was an addiction that proved hard to kick. Mr. Lukesh strongly disagreed. Alois briefly drove vehicles in the evening for the Autobahn, where Poldie's father worked. One of the drivers from the Autobahn was waiting at the bus stop for a ride home after his shift. Mr. Lukesh and Alois were in Mr. Lukesh's vehicle on the way to the Ludwigsburg packing company to have the Hufs' items boxed for the trip to the US. Mr. Lukesh saw the worker waiting for the bus and offered to give him a lift. When he hopped into the car with Alois and Mr. Lukesh, he lit a cigarette. Mr. Lukesh was astonished and blurted out, "Yah was ist das? Was gibst?" (Yeah, what is that? What gives?) Mr. Lukesh continued, "Glaubst du, du darfst im Himmel rauchen?" (Do you think you will be allowed to smoke in heaven?) The worker fired back, "Ja, wenn ich kann, würde ich gerne." (Yes, if I can, I would like to.) Alois took pity on the man because he too struggled with the addition, but eventually, with a lot of effort, Alois finally put the cigarettes away for good.

The Lukeshes' visits were mostly delightful. Edna and Charles attempted to equip Alois and Poldie spiritually because they had such little time. They utilized every opportunity to provide them with proper theology, along with spiritual and practical guidance. The Hufs treasured their time with the Lukeshes, whether their visits were serious or even comical. One such laughable visit involved a strange odor. Alois worked long hours during the wet winter months, and upon arriving home from work, he pulled his boots off and uncovered his very damp and smelly socks. When the Lukeshes appeared, Mr. Lukesh put that old nose of his to the test again and started sniffing until he queried, "Was ist das fur ein Geruch?" (What is that smell?) "Das riecht nach sauren Gurken!" (That smells like sour pickles!) Alois was embarrassed, but he and Poldie got a good laugh out of it.

On the Lukeshes' latest visit, Mr. Lukesh brought a camera. Alois guessed that he wanted a photo of the family for memory's sake. The Hufs did not have a sofa in their tiny room, so Alois and Poldie sat on one of the two single iron beds and put the girls on their laps.

Mr. Lukesh snapped a few pictures. When the visit ended, the couples prayed together again, this time that the Lord would allow the people at the American consulate to be compassionate.

Poldie began preparing the necessary things the family needed for traveling. She washed the girls' dresses and prayed that Jana and Marie would remain healthy and that the family's trip to Munich would be safe. February 6 was a workday for Alois, so he arranged to take the day off. The family arose at 1:00 a.m., and Poldie prepared sandwiches to take with them. She put Jana and Marie in their cutest dresses and coats, and Alois double-checked his list of required documents to take along. Before they left, Opa Kellner urged Poldie to watch over the girls as they traveled, and then he saw them out the door. The family set out in the chilly air at 2:00 a.m., Poldie pushing Marie in the carriage and Alois carrying Jana. They walked to the Ludwigsburg train station, and at 3:30 a.m., they boarded the train to Stuttgart. From that stop, they transferred to an express train to Munich. Marie slept, but Jana was wide-eyed, taking in the sights and sounds of the train ride.

At 6:30 a.m., Alois, Poldie, Jana, and Marie arrived in Munich. Together, they waited at the train station until 8:00 a.m. The US consulate was located a distance away, and their appointment was not until 9:00 a.m. The train station would be an excellent place to kill the extra time they had before hopping a streetcar to the consulate. The family arrived thirty minutes before their appointment. Once checked in, they were shuffled from room to room and heavily vetted through a stringent interview process. After all the questions seemed to be satisfied, the officials asked them to complete specific paperwork, and then they were informed to wait. Alois reflected about the time he visited the CIA and tried to prepare mentally for rejection. He glanced over at Poldie and the children. Poldie seemed slightly nervous, but she smiled back at him. Their daughters were well behaved and looked so pretty in their beautiful clothes.

A doctor examined each family member and instructed them to go before the chief consul in the late afternoon. He would be the representative who would decide if they immigrate to the US. After reporting to his office, the man gave a quick review of the Hufs' documentation. He interacted primarily with Alois. After the interview session, the officer stamped Alois's and Poldie's passports, indicating they were accepted and good to go.

Finally, they had accomplished it! The family walked out of the consulate building and breathed a deep sigh of relief. Alois whispered a silent prayer: "Thank You, Lord Jesus, for being so good to us." Poldie thanked God too, but her fear of moving to Chicago tempered her excitement. She focused on attending to her children instead.

The family of four had already eaten the sandwiches Poldie packed. When they got back to the train station in Munich, the girls were hungry and crying. They scurried over to one of the station restaurants and ordered a quick meal. Since the establishment did not serve water, milk, or hot chocolate, they ordered German beer. When the waitress set the glasses on the table, little Marie reached for one of them. She was so thirsty, she swallowed half the drink. People at surrounding tables looked on as the little girl gulped the amber liquid. She set the glass down, tapped herself on the chest, and breathed out a loud "Agghhh." They all laughed. Jana had to drink the beer too, since there was no other beverage option. Alois and Poldie chuckled at their darling princesses. The girls were incredibly patient and well mannered during the arduous day of interviews and doctor's appointments. Enjoying a little levity and celebrating the victory, even if only for a moment, was a welcome diversion.

The family ate and then boarded the 8:30 p.m. train back to Stuttgart and later on to Ludwigsburg. From there, they set out on foot and made it back to Altach after 2:00 a.m.

Opa Kellner, the consummate father and grandfather, watched from his upstairs window as they walked into the yard. He yelled, "Da sind sie schon!" (Here they are!) He was so happy to see them—especially his two granddaughters.

The following day, Alois notified the immigration office at the AFCR that his family was accepted and given entry visas into the United States. The representative advised them to make preparations for departure to the new continent, which could happen shortly. They would be notified soon of the departure date.

Alois had accumulated four weeks of paid vacation. He asked his supervisor if he could continue working and be paid for the vacation time. The supervisor denied the request and told Alois he was not allowed to collect the money; he would have to use the vacation time instead. The road commission where Alois's father-in-law worked needed extra help, especially in the winter months. Alois went to the commission manager and inquired if there was an opening for four weeks of employment because he wanted to save as much money as possible for the upcoming journey. He was accepted and immediately went to work with Opa Kellner. When the snow arrived, they were called upon at any hour of the day or night to run the snowplows and salt trucks.

The job educated Alois even more about Germany's recent dark history and the devastating effects of World War II. About twenty-five miles from their house, there was an Autobahn tunnel by the city of Leonberg. Cars and trucks waited in lines to use the tunnel, taking turns in traffic direction, since it only had one open lane. The highway department stored sand and salt for winter months in the closed section of the tunnel. Some of Alois's coworkers who were alive during wartime informed him that the Germans transformed the tube into a factory for wartime supplies.

The Nazis used foreign laborers to work inside the tunnel around the clock in inhumane conditions. Many of the workers starved to death, and they buried them beside the highway in a crude cemetery.

Occasionally on his lunch hour, Alois walked through the cemetery and looked at the rudimentary wooden crosses. At least the gravesites were dignified, with the names of the perished. It looked like just about every European country was represented. When he loaded sand and salt into his truck, Alois thought about those who were there before. He could have been one of them or one of the young men slaughtered in the villages of Czechoslovakia. Even though he had always tried to guide his destiny, he realized how little control he had. It encouraged him to trust God with what the future held in the United States.

The Hufs received a letter from the immigration office letting them know they were scheduled for departure to America on Thursday, March 22, 1956. Alois was delighted to learn that; because of the temporary job he took with the road commission, they had four hundred extra German marks for the journey.

That very week, the Lukeshes came by. Poldie again conveyed her continual anxiety regarding living in Chicago. The missionaries urged the young couple to pray for God's will to be done in the matter. Edna was a good friend to a dear Christian lady who lived in Michigan. Her stepson and his wife, the Joneses, lived in a small town. They too were tremendous believers and held their membership at a church in Hudsonville, Michigan. Unbeknown to Alois and Poldie, the Lukeshes wrote a letter to this married couple. They explained how the Hufs became Christians a short time before and would soon be departing Germany for America. The letter outlined their arrival date in New York on April 2 and explained their sponsor was in Chicago. In the letter, they requested if the Joneses would consider finding employment for Alois and a place for his family to live. They explained their fear of the young Huf couple and their children heading to Chicago to begin a new life in an unfamiliar country. The Lukeshes enclosed the photo they took of the Hufs sitting on their bed.

Mrs. Jones received the letter and photo one day when she was home with her infant daughter. She read the letter and then studied the picture. Mrs. Jones felt compassion for the young European family. She looked outside over the fields of her family's onion farm and prayed that God would help provide a location for the Huf family. She wanted to help, but her own family had limited resources.

Later that evening, when Mr. Jones arrived home from working in the fields, she shared the letter and photo with him. "Do you think you could investigate around Hudsonville and see if any of the businesspeople have work for the young man and a place to live?" she asked her husband.

He pondered for a moment. "Let's pray about it," he said. "And as we pray, yes, I will go see if there is an opening and a place for the four of them."

As preparations for their journey across the Atlantic continued, the Lukeshes were an enormous source of comfort and assistance to the Hufs. One of the next items on the to-do list was preparing their two boxes of belongings for shipment. Alois purchased a small washing machine for Poldie specifically with the US 110 voltage. There were plenty of options for inexpensive washing machines in America; however, Alois was not aware of this and thought he was quite clever in obtaining one in Germany to take with them. The washer would be placed in one small crate and the other crate would hold Poldie's sewing machine. Mrs. Coutch, a neighbor who lived on the main floor of their housing complex, taught Poldie how to sew. It was rewarding for Poldie to make pajamas and a few other clothing items for the children. Mr. Lukesh helped Alois load them in his car so he and Alois could drive them to the plant to pack everything in wooden crates. The company imprinted the destination address on the boxes. As the two men were putting the boxes into the back of the car, it was as if their eyes fell on the imprinted letters at the same time.

They paused for a moment, and Mr. Lukesh pointed to the address on the box. "This address says that you will end up in Chicago, but let's pray that the Lord will send you where He wants you to go," he said.

Alois did not understand the implication of that statement. Unlike Leopoldine, he had no apprehensions about living in Chicago; he knew the employment at the restaurant was secure for at least the next two years. And while he always agreed in prayer for God's will, Alois felt the matter was settled. He thought Mr. Lukesh probably felt the same way. So why did Mr. Lukesh now have this perspective? Alois kept his thoughts to himself.

When the time for departure was imminent, Alois told Mr. Lukesh they had saved altogether about 1,200 German marks. He asked for advice on the best way to exchange the marks into US dollars. Frugality was one of the Lukeshes' strong points, so he advised Alois, "If you go to the bank, they will charge a fee for the exchange. I have an idea. You can give me the German money, and I will give you a personal check based on my account at a Manhattan bank in New York." At his suggestion, Alois gave him the 1,200 German marks, and Mr. Lukesh gave Alois a check for the exchange rate of 300 US dollars.

With each passing day, their imminent departure became more real. Poldie especially cherished the time with her family. She knew she might not see her loved ones for a long time, if ever. In the final days before setting sail for America, Poldie gathered what few possessions they owned. Anna helped occupy her granddaughters so Poldie could pack undistracted.

In the depths of her heart, Poldie struggled with multiple fears. She remembered a childhood adventure that was meant to be a day of fun but ended up being a terrifying experience. Back in her Wachterhaus home by the railroad in Hodonice, Poldie, eleven at the time, and a few of her adolescent girlfriends went to the river nearby to play. Poldie and her mother often came to this same spot to wash their clothes in the river and then spread each piece out in the grass to dry in the sunshine. On that day, two Czech boys had arrived out of nowhere, picked Poldie up, and threw her in the river. Poldie could not swim, and the river current was strong. Poldie's head was continually bobbing in and out of the water while she gasped for air. Miraculously, she reached out her hand and grabbed a portion of an uprooted tree. She hung on with every ounce of strength she could muster. One of her girlfriends jumped into the river and helped Poldie to safety. Poldie's fear of the water and not being able to swim was now at the forefront of her thoughts. Her precious family was also days away from boarding a large ship that she was unfamiliar with. She likened any large vessel to the British passenger liner *Titanic* that sank in the Atlantic years earlier.

On March 21, 1956, Alois and Poldie began the morning in prayer on bended knee. They asked God to guide them through the unknown adventure and committed their steps to him. While taking time to say proper and lengthy good-byes with each member of the Kellner family, Poldie intentionally expressed a cheerful attitude, smiling as much as possible. She wanted her family to remember her with a beautiful countenance and a happy heart. However, inside she was torn, tentative, and tender.

At 2:00 p.m., the Lukeshes arrived at the housing complex. All the family gathered around so Mr. Lukesh could capture a final family photo. One more time, the family hugged and expressed their farewells. Opa and Oma Kellner held tightly onto their granddaughters. People in the Altach housing community came to see the Hufs off to America. A large gathering of family and acquaintances all lined up one by one for a hug. When Poldie hugged her mom and dad, she wept desperately, attempting to hold it together. Her siblings took their turns hugging and wishing for Alois and Poldie to "bleib gesund" (stay healthy) and stay safe.

Poldie noticed someone was missing—her young brother Walter was nowhere to be found. He was present during the final family photoshoot just moments earlier and yet now disappeared. Walter was a gentle, tender young boy. He was a favorite child of all of Anna's children and never declined an opportunity to assist Poldie with things like running errands on his bicycle to the market if she needed milk or other items for the children. Poldie loved Walter dearly and was brokenhearted when she could not find him and would have to leave without saying good-bye. Poldie later learned the fourteen-year-old had hidden because he did not want to be seen crying in public. Opa Kellner embraced Alois, and they both felt the warmth of one another's love. The two men never argued or faced a turbulent relationship. Johann and Alois had, especially in the absence of Alois's own family, become like father and son. "If it's possible, let us come to the US to live with you, Poldie, and the children," Johann told Alois.

Alois promised he would endeavor to find a way to have the Kellners join them in America. Finally, Alois, Poldie, Jana, and Marie joined the Lukeshes in their car, and they drove away extra slowly. The Hufs held their children tightly and looked at one another with tentative and wet eyes. The road leading to the Autobahn was about a quarter of a mile. When the heartbroken couple turned around to look out of the rear window, they saw Opa Kellner running along a hill that was a shorter path than the car would take. It was the very same hill Alois gathered the group on to play his trumpet during the Christmas celebration just a few months back. Poldie's father kept running and waving until the car took its final turn onto the Autobahn and soon disappeared from his view. The image of Opa running toward the vehicle was forever engraved into Poldie's and Alois's memories. Unbeknown to them, it would be the last time they ever saw Opa alive.

Poldie squeezed Alois's hand, remembering that this was his dream. Then she shifted and tended to their children as tears streamed from her eyes in an unsuccessful attempt to distract herself from the agony of leaving her home.

Frightened but trusting her husband, Poldie looked to the future, as this was now her dream too.

When the Lukeshes dropped the family off at the Stuttgart rail station, they lingered a bit to reassure the Hufs. Poldie's brother Sepp arrived at the terminal with his new girlfriend, Milla, to bid them farewell. Poldie and Alois were mere acquaintances with Milla. She stood back along the wall, not wanting to impose during the tender good-bye between brother and sister. Poldie's oldest brother, Johann, who the family called Johnny, worked for the railroad and took a few days off work to accompany them on their journey to the northern German town of Bremerhaven. Since he worked for the railroad, he traveled at no charge. Having family around for a short period at the station helped ease the transition for Leopoldine and made the break from her home less emotionally raw.

The Lukeshes expressed a sad but hopeful good-bye. They promised to offer a prayer for their friends' safe journey and to commit them to the care of the Lord. The missionary couple was like spiritual parents to Alois and Poldie. God surely used Charles and Edna to lead them to Christ; they

PREPARING FOR A NEW SEASON

had changed the trajectory of Alois's and Poldie's lives. Alois wondered where they would be without the enduring influence of the Lukeshes. Without indicating the reason, Mr. Lukesh repeatedly emphasized that they should please not forget to look for a letter from them when they arrived at the port of New York.

With a final good-bye to the Lukeshes, the Hufs and Johnny entered the train, and it left the Stuttgart station. Its destination was Bremerhaven, a harbor seaport city of Bremen. It was Europe's most important harbor for passage out of the country. Anticipation filled Alois's mind, but Poldie tried not to think into the future that far. It was an enormous change, but having her husband by her side and Jesus in her heart gave her the peace that she would not be alone. Jana and Marie were thrilled to be on the train again. For the children, it was an adventure. The children eventually fell asleep, and Poldie lay coats on the train bench and put the girls next to each other. She turned off the lights to help everyone sleep.

Neither Poldie, Alois, nor Johann felt like chatting. Poldie was contemplating, "Will I ever see my family again? What will it be like crossing a huge ocean? What kind of life is awaiting me on the other side?"

Alois's immediate thoughts had not journeyed past the ship port. He mentally reviewed the next two days. He had so much more at stake now than he did as a single, young man. He had a wife and two small daughters who were dependent upon him. Alois willed himself to be strong and to act as if he were not disturbed. Internally, he had to turn his worries into prayers over and over again. The next two days would truly determine their future. Would the CIA let them depart Germany? Or would their names be announced over the ship loudspeaker in a nightmarish turn of events? As the train continued to roll on, Alois prayed quietly, "God, it will be devastating to me to be turned away again. But I have to believe that You care about my family and me, and You have everything under Your control. Whatever Your intentions are for us, please let it be for our good only."

His thoughts then quickly drew him back to Czechoslovakia, where his mother, father, and siblings had grown accustomed to hearing news of Alois and his family. Alois had purposely not informed them about the potential of traveling to America. Even when Alois, Poldie, and the children were accepted to move to the US, he guarded the information. Partly he knew the Czechoslovakian communist government might pry into his letters to them, but even more than that, he did not want to talk about immigrating and then potentially have to explain why he couldn't, as what happened the last time he attempted to immigrate.

Alois encouraged himself to think positively. Once he reached the shores of the United States, he would certainly send his family in Czechoslovakia a letter updating them of their whereabouts. Alois looked at Leopoldine. She was beginning to drift into a light sleep. While Poldie was positive about the US in general, Alois knew she would never have made this huge life change if it were not for him and his optimistic plans. Poldie wanted a happy home, and together they could raise their children to know Jesus and the love of God. Alois felt partly guilty for not confiding in Poldie about his past rejections, but seeing her upper eyelashes close and touching her cheeks and looking at the quietly sleeping children nearby, he felt he had made the right decision. Once his family reached the open sea and the ship was far from the port, he would finally be honest with Leopoldine about the burden he carried for the past seven years. For now, they would just take the process one day at a time.

◆

The train arrived in Bremerhaven the next morning at about 10:00. The group of five loaded a bus and went to a large barracks complex. Voluntarily going to barracks once again seemed ironic to the Hufs, but this was just for the day and night. They were assigned a small room with four bunk beds. Johann stayed with them throughout the day, and Poldie was grateful for an extended good-bye with her oldest brother. By evening, Johann bid his farewell to his sister, nieces, and brother-in-law and boarded the train to return home to Stuttgart. This time, Poldie held no emotion back. She hugged him and bitterly wept as she watched him depart.

Poldie took time getting the girls ready for bed and then tucked them in. Finally, she and Alois were able to communicate their feelings—they were both nervous about the next day. This was going to be their last night in Europe! Poldie quieted her fears. How would they adjust on the ship for the ten-day trip, and would they suffer from seasickness? Alois struggled with many what-ifs in his mind. He knew he did not want to be a dishwasher long term, but the job was just a start. It would open the door to what would be a more significant opportunity and a better life for their family—he had faith in that.

Alois suggested, as they thought about the unknown, that the best thing for them to do would be to bring their concerns to God in prayer. Poldie agreed, and they fervently brought their hopes again to the Lord Jesus in prayer. In the petition, they committed themselves, their children, and their future to their loving Lord. They asked for His guidance. Poldie, exhausted from the lack of sleep and her eyes swollen from the tears, fell asleep readily.

Alois grappled with too many thoughts and could not fall asleep as quickly. He kept thinking about the worst-case scenario: his whole family being treated like fugitives and being marched off the ship. He visualized the impending pain on Poldie's face and the confusion in his children's eyes. He imagined them returning to Altach, having to give an account of their rejection. He would have to try to get his job back. Alois's emotions overcame him when he thought about being sent back. He whispered into his pillow, "Please, Lord, don't let it happen again. Please, Lord."

At that moment, he wished Mr. Lukesh was present to give him specific promises from the Word of God. Something like Jeremiah 33:3: "Call to me and I will answer you and tell you great and unsearchable things you do not know" (NIV). God knew the future, even if humans did not. Alois did not know the scriptures well, but he did remember that Jesus had promised to give His presence and peace. He thanked God for that constant presence and allowed himself to drift into sleep finally.

In the morning, both Jana and Marie were distraught. "Where's Oma and Opa?" they asked. They did not know where they were, and they wanted to go to Oma's kitchen for breakfast and the comforting embrace of their grandparents. Poldie explained to three-year-old Jana that their family was going on a big ship. That ship would take them across the water and to their new home. Later, Oma and Opa would also come to live with them, and they would all be together again. Jana turned to Marie and attempted to explain this promise to her baby sister. Poldie hoped with all her heart that her parents could soon join them.

The family dressed and went to the camp dining room for breakfast. Afterward, they attended an orientation meeting to learn the protocol for the next day. They understood that it would take six hours before processing and that the departing families would be registered in alphabetical order. Next, they reported for one final medical exam. The doctor checked everyone to see if they were healthy enough for the ten-day voyage.

The Hufs appeared before the German immigration officials who checked their papers. They stamped Leopoldine's passport, which stated she was a German citizen. They instructed her that she was eligible to return to Germany within one year if, for some reason, the US did not meet her expectations. When Alois stepped forward, he presented his passport, which included their two daughters, classifying the three of them as homeless refugees. They did not extend the same offer for Alois and the two girls to return to Germany within one year. Alois thought it peculiar that he was still considered homeless after all these years. The permanence of the move settled upon him in a more significant way. He was ready to travel to a new land that would allow him to be a countryman, a citizen. Alois watched as they stamped Poldie's passport different from his and the girls; she had no comprehension of the future ramifications.

In the afternoon, the Hufs reported to the transportation hall. Ship authorities asked passengers to line up to obtain their identification tags. Each of them received their two-by-three-inch numbered tags and strings to tie through a buttonhole. Each passenger was assigned a number. Alois and Poldie attached tags to Jana's and Marie's coats as well as their own. The wide-eyed girls looked like dolls for sale with their tags hanging from their coats.

Like all the camps Alois temporarily lived in before, this site had loudspeakers that sounded announcements every few minutes. A voice yelled through the speaker to remind passengers about policies or to call for one of them to report to the primary office. Alois pursed his lips when the loudspeaker interrupted his thoughts. He remembered how, some six years ago, in the northern town of Emden, his dreams of leaving Germany were dashed. Would he receive devastating news again? Alois reminded himself, "Whatever the Lord has is good. He knows what is best for us."

At around 4:00 p.m., buses arrived at the camp. Drivers were responsible for transporting two thousand passengers to the ship. The Hufs boarded a bus and made it to the shipyard. Poldie looked through the bus window and read the name on the side of the vessel: *General W. C. Langfitt*. The ship was previously utilized for transport for the US Navy during World War II. Now, like a sword beaten into a plowshare, it was used for peaceful purposes: the transportation of immigrants. Memories of moving as a child were unpleasant for Poldie. She hoped this time would be different. Even if she didn't quite believe it yet, she would receive it by faith as she walked with Alois and her daughters to board the ship.

The ship had only bare-bones accommodations. Poldie and the children were assigned to a cabin in the heart of the boat. Another mother and her child were also given the same cabin to share. Husbands were not allowed to stay with their wives and children. The men slept in a large room near the bow of the ship, where there were endless lines of bunk beds.

Alois and Poldie found a black-and-white postcard with the vessel pictured on the front with room to pen a last-minute message on the reverse. The caption on the front of the card under the ship's photo read, "Letzer Gruss aus Bremen vor der Uberfahrt." (Last greeting from Bremen before the crossing.) Alois added his personal cutline, "With this ship, we will drive." On the backside of the card, Alois quickly wrote, "We are good. We all came here okay. We are all healthy. Jana cries because she wants to always go home." Poldie took advantage of the remaining two inches to write, "Dear Oma and Opa, please come to America. Lots of greetings from Bremen. Before we depart, many greetings for my siblings." Alois addressed the card to Poldie's family in Eglosheim, and it was stamped March 24, 1956, before being mailed.

At about 6:00 p.m., the ship was full of passengers. The ship's loudspeakers crackled, and Alois felt the hair on the back of his neck stand on end. Then a voice bellowed, "Passengers, please make your way to the dining room for the evening meal." The small vessel made the number of passengers seem enormous. There were people at Poldie's elbows all the time. She was thankful that Jana and Marie clung tightly to her. They had never seen so many people gathered.

The Hufs joined the crowds assembling in the dining room and made their way through the serving line. The food was good and plentiful, offering comfort for the travelers. They sat around metal tables on metallic benches bolted to the floor. Alois ate hesitantly, hoping that the ship would begin to move and set sail for America. As long as the boat remained in the harbor, he felt tense and enslaved.

After supper, the voice blaring from the loudspeakers directed everyone to report for a safety drill. The staff provided all the mothers and children with life vests, and Poldie slipped hers on as directed and then proceeded to put on Jana's and Marie's. The commotion on deck, the slight movement of the ship, and the crowds of people bothered Marie. The little one screamed in horror. Poldie attempted to quiet Marie, but it proved useless. She and the girls took their assigned position at their designated lifeboat. Alois received orders to report to another part of the ship and remain there. The group listened as two seamen instructed them on the procedures in case of an emergency. Poldie looked around to find Alois. Why would they not allow a woman's husband to be with her? Leopoldine tried to be strong, but by the time the drill was over, she, Jana, and Marie were all crying. Jana and Marie were calling out for their Oma and Opa, and Poldie wished she could be back in Altach.

CHAPTER ELEVEN

SAILING WEST TO AMERICA

When the evacuation drill was over, Alois joined Poldie and comforted his wife and daughters, even as he faced his own inner turmoil. Through tears, Poldie begged, "Please stay with us. Don't leave us!"

Alois explained that the vessel was operated as a military ship, and they would get in trouble if they did not follow the rules. "It's really for the safety of all the women and children that they have the rules," he said, trying to reassure Poldie. She reluctantly agreed, knowing that other women were in the same predicament as her.

The couple and their little girls walked around on the deck and then found shelter inside from the cold air. An announcement from the speaker indicated the ship would leave port sometime that evening. The girls were tired and fussy, so Poldie bid Alois good night at 7:00 p.m. "We will see each other in the morning," Alois said, trying to sound positive. He walked to his bunk area at the other end of the ship and felt his stomach tighten in a knot. If only the ship would set sail, then he would know the CIA had let him depart in peace.

Alois greeted the other men around him as he entered the bunk and repeated over and over in his heart, "Lord, have mercy on us."

Lying down, Alois stared at the ceiling of the room. He remembered a passage in the Bible he read, Psalm 42:5: "Why, my soul, are you downcast? Why so disturbed within me? Put your hope in God, for I will yet praise him, my Savior, and my God" (NIV). Maybe the time to put his hope in God was the time he least felt like doing so, he mused. Alois turned on his side and began silently praising the Lord and thanking Him for His goodness. He replayed the good things God had blessed him with. He remembered the words of Psalm 34:8: "Taste and see that the LORD is good; blessed is the one who takes refuge in him" (NIV).

Over the next several hours, Alois's consciousness kept vigil, facing every possibility with hope. He lay on his bunk, frequently tossing and turning, wondering if the ship had left the harbor yet. Finally, he felt more movement of the boat, much stronger than he had sensed when they were in the port. He could hear crackling noises from below. Several men came into Alois's cabin. The fellows talked about how they were on the deck and waved good-bye to their friends and relatives who saw them off. They continued to wave at family until the light of the harbor, illuminating the figures on the shore, faded away.

Alois sat up and listened, looking for an opportunity to join the conversation. He saw the swollen eyes of the men who had cried tears of good-bye. Alois decided not to stand on the deck of the ship for several reasons. There was no one waving good-bye onshore, but more importantly, Alois was still anxious about being seen. And he had not wanted to hear his name if called. He walked over casually to a group of his bunkmates.

Alois cleared his throat and asked one of them, "Are we really on our way?" One of them nodded affirmatively. Alois could hardly contain his excitement. "How far are we from the shore?"

A man near Alois said, "We're already at least five miles from the harbor."

Alois thanked the man and returned to his bunk, feeling his spirit quiet within him. "Thank you, Jesus!" he exclaimed in his heart. The second half of verse 11 of Psalm 42 came to him: "Put your hope in God, for I will yet praise him, my Savior and my God."

It was as if an enormous burden had been lifted from Alois's heart. He knew with certainty that he was in the clear now. The CIA would not turn the ship back for somebody like him. Alois wanted to laugh and cry at the same time. No longer would the threat of a faceless foe taunt him. He knew he had made his peace with the CIA. If people would not have thought it strange, Alois might have jumped up and run a lap around the ship. Instead, he thought of how he would tell his story to Leopoldine in the morning. She would understand him fully, and she would be so happy. With the ship swaying beneath him, Alois sank into a profound sleep.

The next morning, the passengers were up early and reunited with their family members in the dining room. Poldie noticed Alois looked fresh and happy. He must be genuinely thrilled about this change, she thought. Poldie kept praying through her fear of the transition and encouraging her children; although they were out of their routine, everything was okay, she told them.

Standing in the serving line for breakfast, the Hufs were amazed at all the delicious food laid out for them. They did not expect to eat like kings on the ship, and the eggs, bread, and fruit were like nothing they were accustomed to. They sat down at one of the metal tables, and the girls enjoyed the scrumptious fare.

"How did you sleep?" Alois started.

Leopoldine's countenance showed a bit of fatigue and unhappiness. "I didn't sleep well. The other woman and her child were fine, but I was worried, and I just kept wishing we could stay together on this journey," she said. "Don't you think the four of us should stay together? Isn't there any way?" For Poldie, ten days sailing on the giant ocean sleeping in a cramped room with strangers made her feel even farther from home.

Alois understood and tried to convince Poldie to endure the hardship. "Leopoldine, look around. You can see that you and I are not the only couples who were separated at night," he said. "Besides, I have something wonderful to share with you that will cheer you up. Let's wait until we can sit down outside on the deck, and I'll tell you."

Jana and Marie seemed to be adjusting to their new environment and were in good spirits when they all walked out on the lower-level deck. The air was chilly, but the sun's rays provided promising warmth. They walked over to the railing and marveled at the beauty before them. In the distance, they could see the White Cliffs of Dover, the magnificent coastal site. The lovely sight felt like a promise from God and His confirmation they were on the right track.

"Where are we?" Poldie asked.

"We are going through the Canal La Manche, the English Channel. On the east is France, and on the west, England," Alois explained. Poldie had never journeyed so far away from home in her life. It was hard to imagine that they were just getting started on their journey to becoming American citizens. She took in the beauty across the horizon for a few moments and watched the girls' faces as they too were enthralled. Poldie remembered what Alois said in the cafeteria and turned to Alois, ready to hear his story.

As safe as he felt, Alois subtly checked to ensure no one was listening. Alois began to recount how, six and a half years before, he had wanted to immigrate to Australia. He described his first attempt to leave the country and how he was turned back. "I was so devastated to have to leave my friends and be forced to return to Ludwigsburg alone," he said.

Poldie did not look sympathetic. Her mind was moving faster than the ship beneath her as she held on to the railing with one hand. Had this whole desire of his to leave the country been because he was in some kind of trouble? Why hadn't he told her this before? Maybe Alois had fled Czechoslovakia for some dark reason. "What? Why did they send you back?" she asked breathlessly. "You must have done something terrible. Well, who did I marry anyway? I thought I knew you, but now I don't know what to think!" Poldie was not at her best, and this story wasn't helpful.

"Well," Alois responded, "that is exactly what other people thought about me." He explained how he sought out every authority to find out why he was sent back, but he had no luck. Then he explained that late that same year, in 1949, he attempted to immigrate to Canada, but when he boarded the train, the US military police had entered the car and called his name and then drove him back to the refugee camp. Again no one would tell him why.

Poldie's cheeks were hot. Her voice was loud enough now for other passengers to hear. "You must have done something bad to be sent back twice! You must have done something bad like robbing a bank!" she exclaimed with exasperation. "Just tell me! What did you do?"

The ship was rocking above the waves below, and Alois could tell Poldie's world had spun out of its normal balance in the past few days. Maybe this had not been the best idea to say to her now. However, he had to finish. Alois tried to show extra kindness and patience. "My dear, that is exactly how I felt—like I was a criminal. It seemed like I was a bank robber or a murderer. In my heart, I knew that I did not hurt anyone at all or commit a crime. Nevertheless, my life was devastated as if I had."

Alois looked for indications from Poldie's face that she was receptive. He could at least tell she was listening. "A few days after the second rejection, I had to decide what to do. I realized that if I wanted to live like a human being, I would need to find a good job. You moved around a lot with your family in Germany. The refugee camps were a dead end, as you know. I worked in construction for a while. And you know how the German population despised us. Do you remember?"

Poldie's heart seemed to be softening as she remembered who was talking. Alois told Poldie how God had sent an angel in the form of the woman in the German Transportation Department and how it was only a miracle that he had received a German driver's license. The license allowed him to get a good job with the US Army, and his lifestyle changed from that point. He had felt like a normal person again. He described how, after about two years at his job, he had applied to join the US Army and was rejected while his friends were accepted.

Then he explained how not long after they met and started dating, he visited the CIA headquarters in Heidelberg to find some answers. He spoke to an officer who told him it was because of the time he had trained with the CIA for an information-gathering assignment. He described how before he could even serve, they received word that the assignment had been canceled, but by then, he had a change of heart and decided not to take the position. He continued, "When I put the CIA experience behind me, I did just that. I thought of it like declining a job—that was it in my mind. But to this officer, it was the reason my name was added to a watch list. From the CIA's administrative perspective, 'Alois Huf' was someone who signed up for espionage, went through a very brief training, and then disappeared. What could a kid like me have done with no power, no money, and no knowledge of what they were doing? I do not know, but they still categorized me with potential enemies."

Alois touched Poldie's hand and hoped Jana and Marie would cooperate a little longer so Poldie could focus her attention on what he was trying to say. "Here, let's sit down on this bench," he said. "When I knew I loved you and wanted to marry you, I told the officer that I wanted to know that we would be free to immigrate together. The officer could not assure me that there would not be any hindrances to keep us from leaving, but he did say that, as a husband and father, the CIA would probably lose interest in me."

Alois continued, "When we got married, I felt God had not wanted me to leave Germany. I know now that I stayed where I was for a purpose—God destined me to meet you. When Jana was born, and Marie, and when the Lukeshes told us about Jesus and we became born-again Christians, I knew it was the Lord who did not allow me to leave for Australia or Canada or to join the US Army. Just like He watched over you and your family and led you to reside where you did, He led me too. I believe the Lord brought us together."

Poldie smiled tenderly. She wanted to say that she agreed, but she was listening intently and processing everything. "Poldie, I wanted to tell you all this before," Alois said. "I did not because I was afraid that if you knew this backstory, you might be afraid to immigrate to the US. Now that our ship is under way, many miles from the German shores, I don't think anyone would send us back. I wanted you to see how God has led each of us, individually and together, to this point."

Poldie concurred. "I'm sorry for getting upset with you. You are right; I would have been extremely nervous if you had told me this story before we left Germany," she said. "And I can perceive that God watched over us—first when we left Czechoslovakia and the Sudetenland and then when we lived in Germany. I'm so glad I met you."

They hugged, and Alois promised he would help make sure Poldie and the girls were always safe and cared for. "If the Lord has done this much for us already, surely He has a life for us in this new land. We can serve Him with joy and let our lives bring glory to Him," Alois said. Together, they looked down at Marie, who gazed at them sweetly. Jana, who did not comprehend anything her parents were discussing but saw how happy they were, crawled into Alois's lap, hugged him, and then reached over to hug her mother. Even the children felt the beauty, peace, and love that enveloped them.

Poldie looked again as the White Cliffs of Dover disappeared from their view. She knew trusting God was going to be an active choice and a daily one. She realized how much her familiar surroundings and the presence of family had given her a sense of security. Now far from land and estranged from any semblance of home, Poldie was learning that the presence of God was the positive, constant force in her life. Lonely and separated from Alois during the night on the ship, her faith was tested. Poldie prayed again that God would give her strength and perspective for this adventure.

The rest of the day was peaceful, and they allowed themselves to dream of a hopeful future. What would it be like to have their very own place? Alois and Poldie hardly knew. They reminisced about the Lukeshes and laughed at Alois's early, insincere invitation for them to return to their home after the tentative first visit. Now they knew, as it said in Revelation 21:27, that their names were written in the Lamb's Book of Life. Through Jesus Christ, both of them had eternal life and the assurance of God's presence. Poldie was thankful Alois had told her about his past. Knowing how God guided each of them settled her heart and made her feel this journey was meant to be.

A peaceful breeze blew across the deck of the ship, and the sun shone throughout the day. A good portion of their time was spent waiting in line for lunch and supper in the cafeteria. Passengers around them were envisioning life in America, and the atmosphere was one of expectancy. The mealtime food was surprisingly good. Alois and Poldie were unaccustomed to eating such scrumptious and abundant cuisine. After suppertime, it was dark outside. Alois carried Marie, and Poldie led Jana by the hand back to Poldie's cabin to help put the girls to bed. Alois said good night, and added, "We will see each other in the morning."

There was not much to do in his cabin; Alois lay awake on his bunk, occupied with his thoughts. He thought how much his life had changed in just the past few years. And it was about to change again! He silently voiced his thanks and praises to God. The quiet was interrupted by the ship's loudspeaker. A voice alerted the passengers that the ship was expected to encounter a storm overnight. "Please tighten your bunk safety belts," the voice directed. Alois looked in the dim light at the seat-belt-like device hanging from the side of the bed. It was hard to believe there was any future problem; the boat rocked gently as it sailed. Nevertheless, Alois made sure the belt was tightened around him and prayed that Poldie and the girls were settled and unafraid. He turned toward the ship's wall and went to sleep.

During the night, the rocking of the ship jolted Alois awake. He looked around and saw that the other men were awake as well. The men discussed among themselves how they hoped the storm would quiet down in a while. But within hours, the wind hurled, and the rain intensified. The ship rocked back and forth dramatically. Alois tugged at his safety belt and thought of Poldie and his daughters. "God, please let them be okay," he prayed. In the flickering light that illuminated the room, Alois could see the feet at the end of his buckled legs swing up, only to go far below his head a few seconds later. He felt the sensation of fear, but mostly he was thinking of his wife and children. Some of the swings were so drastic, Alois felt as if he were standing up in one instance and standing on his head in another. Could the ship sustain this kind of rocking?

Alois wished he could communicate with some of the men around him to derive some human comfort, but no one was in a state for conversation. Some of the men were groaning, and the odor of vomit was strong. Alois did not feel well either, but he managed to keep his supper down. He was thankful that his family was positioned in the lower center of the ship. Hopefully, they would not feel the ocean's jolts as much as the men did who were positioned at the edge of the vessel.

Added to the wild rocking was a sound that startled everyone. Each time the front of the ship went down, they could hear a terrible roaring sound from the back of the boat. "Did we hit some rocks or an iceberg?" one man dared to voice. Alois had heard of the *Titanic*.

There was murmuring until an older man spoke up. "It's the propellers," he managed. "Every time the front of the ship dips down, the back is lifted so that the propellers are completely out of the water, and they are producing that sound." Because there was little resistance in the air, the propellers would spin violently in the air, sounding like roaring thunder.

Alois closed his eyes for a moment. That news made him feel a little better, but there was no getting used to the noise and the rocking—it felt like the gigantic ocean could swallow them in an instant. The movement of the ship and the anxiety it brought caused a wave of nausea over Alois. A memory came to him, and Alois trained his brain to settle upon it. He remembered how Mrs. Lukesh would bring her portable organ and sing. The song that Alois remembered was "What a Friend We Have in Jesus." The stanza sang on in Alois's mind: "O what peace we often forfeit, O what needless pain we bear, / All because we do not carry everything to God in prayer."

Alois fixated his energy on prayer. "Lord, I believe that You can quiet this storm. But if You do not, please give us the strength we need to endure the storm and the voyage," he pleaded. "Give extra strength to Leopoldine, because she will need it to care for the children."

No one, it seemed, in Alois's cabin slept for the remainder of the night. When a stream of light signaled that morning had dawned, Alois tried his shaky legs and held onto the bedposts while he slipped on his clothes. Eagerly, he took several stairways to get to Poldie's cabin. He used the rocking of the ship to his advantage. When the vessel tilted downward, he would lean forward, holding onto the stair rails and using the momentum to move. Finally, he arrived at Poldie's door and knocked. She opened it, and Alois found her and the girls dressed. They had been unable to sleep.

Alois spoke quietly so as not to disturb her roommate and child. "How are you doing?" he asked.

"We are okay," Poldie replied. "I heard there was a storm, and we could feel it. How about you?"

Alois's face was ashen. "It was a rough night at the front of the ship. Many of the men are sick. I feel nauseous, so I don't plan on going to breakfast in the dining room."

Poldie tilted her head and used her motherly voice. "Do you remember what Mr. and Mrs. Lukesh told us about being on the ship? Eat—even if you do not feel like it at all. Eat lots of dry bread without butter."

Alois remembered. "Please lead the way to the dining room; I will follow," he said. Alois, Poldie, Jana, and Marie set out for the dining room. On their way, many of the passengers were sitting or lying on the ship's floor, vomiting. Many women were crying. It had been a scary few hours, and the ordeal was not over yet. Only a day before, families looked happy, clean, and neatly dressed. Now they were sprawled in their vomit and did not have the energy to care how they appeared. Alois and

Poldie wanted to offer help if they could, but they were hardly better off themselves, and there was no assistance they could offer. Jana and Marie could feel the tension around them, and they were frightened. The girls began crying. Alois and Poldie comforted them as they cried out again for their Oma and Opa.

When the family reached the cafeteria, there was a small group gathered for breakfast. Alois wanted to be curled up in bed, but he battled through nausea and kept his eyes on his family. Somehow, the four of them made it through the cafeteria line holding on to each other. Poldie and Alois set their trays down on a table and were glad to be seated. It did not take long for a giant tilt of the ship to cause some of their cups and plates to tumble to the floor. The dishes shattered. Marie screamed, and Jana pleaded, "Why don't we go home? We don't like it here." Even Alois felt the same at the moment, but he responded with some encouraging words about enduring for a short while.

The ship's loudspeakers came on every few minutes, instructing the passengers to go to the dining room and eat something if they could. "You will feel better," a voice assured. But most people did not feel well enough to go. As Alois and Poldie forced themselves to chew and swallow, their daughters were not eating. A kind Chinese man who oversaw the cafeteria made his rounds throughout the room. When he walked up and could see that Jana and Marie were not eating, he picked up a spoon and began feeding them. Since it was a stranger and an imposing authority imploring them to eat, the girls obliged.

Alois looked over at his wife. The loudspeakers made another announcement about food, and he said, "I wish they would not even mention food for a while."

Poldie was the stalwart and would remind him, "Remember what the missionaries told us." Alois still had a hard time swallowing. "We have to force ourselves to eat so we can take care of the children," she said.

After breakfast, they decided to go outside for some fresh air. Due to the storm, the bottom deck was sealed off. Poldie and Alois went to the second-floor deck. The family sat on a metal bench that abutted a wall of the ship. The huge waves in their vantage point were equal parts mesmerizing and alarming. Suddenly, a stream of strange liquid came down from the top deck. A gust of wind picked it up and blew it in Alois's direction. He realized in a moment that his face and shirt were covered with someone's vomit. Poldie gasped, and Alois felt like jumping into the sea to cleanse. Thankfully, the men's showers were available, and Alois went down and scrubbed his face and clothes. He put on a change of clothes and rejoined his family.

By the fourth day of the voyage, the storm had become even worse. Poldie felt as if she were living in a nightmare. All semblance of control over her life was gone. The only thing that kept her heart still was a prayer to God and holding on to her husband and children. Each day, fewer passengers were in the dining room. But Poldie made sure her family was there. The cafeteria supervisor came around the children and told them, "Eat, eat." Jana and Marie were afraid of him, and it helped Poldie's admonition because the girls ate when they saw him.

Walking around on the ship felt depressing for the Hufs. People were in such misery. Seasick passengers would sit or lie throughout the boat, hoping things would get better for them soon. The men did not want to stay in their bunks since their location bore the brunt of the storm. Only the top deck of the ship was open, so the Hufs found a place in the center of the ship where the turbulence lessened. Watching the enormous waves, they could not help but think of the worst scenario. They prayed to God, who had created the oceans, for protection and peace.

When the Lukeshes gave them a Bible, they first read Genesis and then the Gospel of John. The Bible told of how, in the beginning, God created the heaven and the earth, and how He spoke all things into existence through the power of His Word. Alois and Poldie knew God was love, and the impact of the waves showed His mighty power. The young couple was comforted in knowing His presence was there.

As they sat outside, Poldie had her arms crossed over Marie in her lap while Alois was taking everything in. Suddenly, his eyes darted to Jana. She had slipped passed a barrier, and only a thin guardrail was between her and the stormy sea. She was hanging on the rail with one hand and was leaning over the deck. Horrified, Alois raced to her and grabbed her arm, pulling her up quickly.

Alois held Jana tightly. It seemed she disappeared in only a split second. Alois looked at Leopoldine, who was already shaking and sobbing. "Come to me my schaetzchen [treasure]," she said. "Just now, we could have lost you, Januli. What would we do without you?" Poldie and Alois both thanked God for His protection of their daughter and prayed for shelter against any sinister forces that would seek to harm their family. Alois realized even more the responsibility he had; his wife chose to believe in his dream of going to America. He realized how much Poldie had risked for him.

While the Hufs fared better than many passengers due to their faithfulness to eat, Alois began to feel seasickness come on. During the last few days, Poldie suggested Alois stay with her and the girls in their room. Jana slept with Poldie nightly, and Marie slept in the crib, so the left upper bunk was available. Poldie encouraged Alois to hop into the bed, lie facing the wall, and pull the covers up under his chin with only the back of his head exposed. She reasoned that if security came by to check in the room, Alois would appear to be a woman with those lovely locks of blond hair. Alois agreed and slept soundly in Poldie's room.

The next day, the waves were higher than the previous days. Alois and Poldie worked to calm themselves. A person could go insane in conditions like this, especially when the mind irrationally attempted to convince a person to leave the ship altogether. Together, they breathed deeply and asked the Lord to shorten the remaining days on the ocean somehow.

Alois continued to sleep in Poldie's room the remaining nights aboard the ship. One evening as the storm was raging, Marie stood up in her crib just as the force of a massive wave tilted the boat. Marie was thrown against the metal crib and sustained a gash on the back of her head. Alois and Poldie quickly took her and Jana to the infirmary. Poldie tried her best to keep her emotions in check. This journey was just as rough as her experiences with her family as a child during the war. Back then, they were surviving. The medical professionals cleaned the wound and stitched the cut. When they arrived back at the cabin, little Marie pointed to the crib and said, "Nein." (No.) So Poldie, Alois, and Marie all lay on their tiny bed until Marie was asleep and could be laid back in the crib.

Getting through the incessant leaning of the ship was a challenge, but Alois and Poldie drew strength from stories they had read in the Bible. Most of the time, Poldie remained calm, but she despised the emergency drills the ship officials conducted. It made her feel as though they might be in genuine danger. Leopoldine and the children reported to a lifeboat in the center of the ship, while Alois's boat was at the front of the ship. With shaking arms, Poldie put the girls' life vests on, and then fastened on her own. Jana and Marie seemed to pick up on her fragile emotions, and soon, all three of them began crying again. Thankfully, Poldie was less worried about Jana running off. While Poldie held Marie and waited through the drill, Jana held on to one of Poldie's legs as if her life depended on it. Poldie had to pry little Jana's hands off so they could walk and follow the crew's instructions.

It was hard for Alois to see Poldie and the girls struggle. He knew they were on this journey because of him. He did his best to convince them that beautiful days were ahead. Alois continued to stay in Poldie's cabin, and the children appreciated their father's company. At the end of each day, they thanked God for seeing them through another twenty-four hours and keeping the ship safe. There were still many people who were ill, and collectively, they wished the voyage to a close.

The last day of the ocean trip, like the first, was clear skies. Passengers awakened to a calm sea. After so many days of shaking, it was a strange sensation to walk around without having to grip the railings. But people still did not feel well enough. The Hufs went down for breakfast. They heard the loudspeakers announce that the ship would be arriving in about two hours in the New York Harbor. A speaker urged all the passengers to line up on the decks to see the breathtaking view of the Statue of Liberty.

The Hufs went out early on one of the decks to survey the clear skies. Alois could feel the excitement building in his chest. As the ship neared the harbor, the passengers at the railings could see the Statue of Liberty in the distance, holding her flame high. Almost paralyzed with awe and wonder, Alois and Poldie felt goose bumps running up and down their arms at the sight of this beautiful lady. Alois took a few brief minutes to educate Leopoldine on the history of Lady Liberty as the USS *General W. C. Langfitt* gradually cruised by Liberty Island. The massive statue was gifted to the US in 1886 from France and represented the Roman goddess of freedom. At no point in Alois's twenty-five years of life had the immanency of true freedom seemed more a reality than at that very moment.

It was as though Lady Liberty said to everyone, "I will leave the light on for you all so you can find your way to me through the storms of the sea and the storms of life and darkness. The light will guide you to me, the Statue of Liberty. I assure you this light will guide and welcome all of you who were oppressed for your religious or political beliefs. It welcomes all of you who are hungry—either physically hungry or hungry for freedom. It is here for the poor, the discouraged, the sick, and the lame. All of you who are willing to work hard and are willing to become part of us are welcome. Here, we do not care where you came from, what language you speak, or how poorly your dress. All that I, the Statue of Liberty, require from all the passengers who have ever sailed by me in the past or will pass by me in the future is only one thing—honesty! I welcome you all to be part of us, because I, the Statue of Liberty, am part of America."

Alois remarked to Leopoldine, "Finally we are going to be in a country that we can call our home. People will no longer look at us as homeless refugees. In five years, Lord willing, we'll be American citizens!"

Poldie looked at Alois; tears welled up in their eyes. It felt like the journey of their entire lives had been leading them to this point. In spite of her fears, Poldie felt eager to start their new lives. She could not stop staring at the Statue of Liberty. She represented a promise that the light would not go out for them, the storms of life would subside, and her family would have a home. They continued to sail past other small islands within the harbor, including Ellis Island.

When the ship docked, the city skyline was like nothing they had ever seen. Poldie found herself clinging to Alois as Jana and Marie clung to her. All two thousand passengers disembarked and entered a vast hall. Each of them was met by officials who examined their passports, fingerprinted them, and completed medical examinations for the final

Figure 1. Six-year-old Alois (top row, third from right) with first-grade teacher Ms. Kinychova and his other grade school classmates in 1937. Air raid survival drills occurred daily.

Figure 2. Harvest festival in Czechoslovakia, 1946; fifteen-year-old Alois played the trumpet with Mirek (left).

Figure 3. Czechoslovakia Forestry Appreciation Day, 1947—Alois (right) in the uniform he left prior to his escape in 1949. Friend and neighbor Pepa Josef Kovarik is on the left.

Figure 4. A miraculous turning point—Alois was granted a German driver's license on July 10, 1950, which allowed him to drive for the US Army.

Figure 5. The Czechoslovakian general civil identity mandatory ID card issued at sixteen years of age; a penalty occurred if it was not carried at all times. Alois escaped in March 1949.

Figure 6. The displaced persons refugee camp Krabbenloch-Kaserne, in Ludwigsburg, Germany, where Alois was interned from March 1949 to 1951.

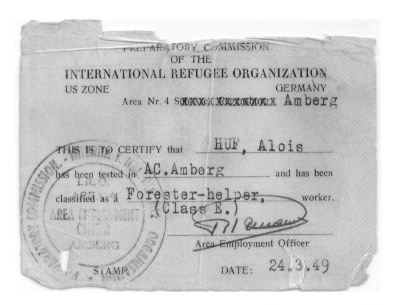

Figure 7. The International Refugee Organization, Amberg, Germany, enrolled Alois on March 24, 1949, three days after his escape.

Figure 8. In 1949, Alois penned a sad song in his pocket calendar during days of loneliness and depression.

Figure 9. Alois (left), wearing secondhand clothing, in the displaced persons refugee camp with friend Frank (right) six months after his escape. Frank immigrated to Australia with Alois's second set of friends.

Figure 10. Leopoldine Kellner, sixteen years of age, in Ludwigsburg, Germany, in 1951.

Figure 11. Alois driving for the US Army in 1953. The US soldiers gave him the military jacket pictured.

Figure 12. Alois and Leopoldine's wedding picture, October 4, 1952.

Figure 13. Charles and Edna Lukesh—the missionary couple who shared the Good News of the Gospel of Christ with Alois and Poldie Huf.

Figure 14. Mrs. Edna Lukesh was known and loved for her children's Bible school ministry, Czechoslovakia, 1937.

Figure 15. Leopoldine Kellner Huf in 1953.

Figure 16. Alois, Poldie, Jana (left), and Marie (right) in Germany, 1955. Mr. Lukesh took this picture in the Hufs' one-room apartment and mailed it to Hudsonville, Michigan, to request sponsorship in the United States.

Figure 17. Alois and Leopoldine with the Kellner family and Mrs. Lukesh on the day of departure for the United States, 1956.

Letzter Gruß aus Bremen vor der Überfahrt Mit ... Letzten ... W.... ... "General W. C. Langfitt"

Figure 18. The USS General W. C. Langfitt, the vessel Alois, Leopoldine, Jana, and Marie sailed to the United States.

Figure 19. Leopoldine, Marie (lap), and Jana (right) on the deck of the ship where Jana slipped and almost fell overboard.

Figure 20. In Hudsonville, Michigan, 1961: (left to right) Jana, Joey, Alois, Debra, Leopoldine, Cristie Jo, and Marie.

Figure 21. Alois Huf, Certificate of Naturalization, May 18, 1962, Grand Haven, Michigan.

Figure 22. Leopoldine Huf, Certificate of Naturalization, May 18, 1962, Grand Haven, Michigan.

Figure 23. The Huf family, 1963: (from left to right, back row) Marie, Leopoldine, Susan, Alois, and Jana; (front row) Debra, Joey, and Cristie Jo.

Figure 24. The Huf family with Josef and Marie on their visit to the United States, March 1966. This was the first time the Huf grandparents met Leopoldine and the six children in person.

Figure 25. Cristie Jo holding two Czechoslovakian dolls given to the Huf girls by their Czech grandmother.

Figure 26. Jerry and Cristie Jo Johnston with Poldie and Alois Huf on August 2, 1996.

Figure 27. Leopoldine and Alois on their fiftieth wedding anniversary in October 2003.

Figure 28. Alois with Chaplain Matt Hanson (right); Alois here is being honored for his many years of service to the inmates of the Ottawa County Jail by the Forgotten Man Ministries in Allendale, Michigan.

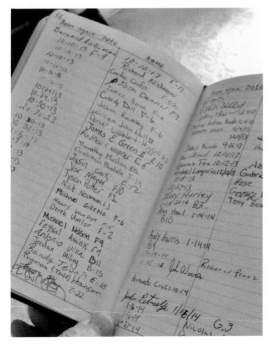

Figure 29. Alois Huf's unique Lamb's Book of Life in which he asked inmates who received Christ into their lives to sign their names as a written record.

Figure 30. Leopoldine and Alois at Poldie's eightieth birthday party, May 16, 2014.

time. The Huf family had stayed healthy overall on the trip, but when they were on solid ground, Jana began vomiting. The medical examiner was kind and told them that the symptoms were typical—many passengers became sick on the sea, and some found their bodies out of equilibrium when they were back on solid ground, he said.

Poldie constantly attended to Jana. It made her forget her own anxiety momentarily. She looked around the processing station and noticed many of their fellow passengers being welcomed by relatives and friends and being given flowers, hugs, and kisses. The Hufs had no welcoming party. The raw emotion of the experience began to show. Poldie held the children tightly while she wept. "Is this a mistake?" she thought. "We do not know a soul in the United States." The loneliness started to set in all over again. "What will our lives look like moving forward? Everything feels strange and foreign." Poldie wiped the tears from her rounded cheeks, pressed her lips together, and studied her family. Alois wanted to be strong for Poldie but could not keep the tears from welling up in his eyes. Although they had one another, being in a foreign environment with no friends or family members was a shock to their system. Pitifully, they stood huddled in a corner by themselves for about half an hour, holding tightly to one another while waiting for the next step in the process.

CHAPTER TWELVE

CONTEMPLATING CHICAGO AND REDIRECTED TO MICHIGAN

After waiting and watching people around them, two men came out from the crowd and approached the Hufs. They introduced themselves as officials from the AFCR and confirmed they would be assisting the family to their final destination. Alois was happy to see what appeared to be friendly faces. The men presented the Hufs with two airmail letters addressed to them that the AFCR recently received. The AFCR opened them, as was procedure. One of the letters, they relayed, was from a Mr. Jones in Hudsonville, Michigan. The other message was from the Lukeshes in Germany. It felt comforting to realize they had some connections and a welcome in America after all, even though it did not arrive in a bouquet or involved hugs from family.

Alois intently listened as they translated the letters to him in Czech. "The man says there is a job on a farm in Michigan for Alois and a house for the family to live in there. He invites you to come," one of the gentlemen said. Alois was speechless. The man continued, "Your sponsor is in Chicago, and you have the dishwasher job at a Polish restaurant, which you will need to stay at for two years. If you choose to go to Michigan, the procedure is a little different. You will have some flexibility and will not necessarily have to stay in the same job for two years. And another thing, if you go to Michigan, we could take the work assignment in Chicago and help other refugees."

Alois understood and thanked the men for this news. He turned to Poldie and translated their message into German. Poldie's eyes lit up. She was all for the idea of settling in Michigan right away; she had never wanted to end up in intimidating Chicago. Alois and Poldie communicated back and forth for a little while, but Jana interrupted them when she became sick again. The men kindly suggested that the Hufs stay the night in New York City and allow little Jana time to recover. They encouraged Alois and Poldie to utilize the extra time to further discuss and think through these two opportunities. Alois and Poldie readily agreed, and the family went with the men to a Broadway hotel. When they dropped them off, the men highly recommended that Alois and his family get plenty of rest. The men handed Alois the two letters and promised to return the following afternoon.

When they unloaded their two wooden crates and bags, Poldie looked at her family. She was relieved to be safe and have her daughters and husband back on solid ground. Poldie wanted to kiss the pavement beneath her feet, as it was the first stable ground she felt in the past ten days, but this new place felt more foreign to her than anywhere she had ever been. In the hotel room, Poldie immediately drew a bath for Jana and Marie and was thankful to see Jana settling down and feeling better.

She and Alois opened the letter from the Lukeshes, which they penned to Alois in Czech. He read it aloud and translated it for Poldie:

We have been praying and asking God to provide another place for you to live and work instead of Chicago. We wrote to our friends, the Jones family, in Hudsonville, Michigan, near Grand Rapids, and asked if they would be willing to find employment and a place for you to live. They wrote back to us and promised they would go to work on this right away. The Joneses are members of a Baptist church of about three hundred members in the same city where they live. Mr. and Mrs. Jones promised they would involve the entire church in the project and see if they would be successful in finding employment for Alois. They agreed that if they did, there would be a letter waiting for you in the New York Harbor upon your arrival.

Poldie began to feel upbeat and smiled as she listened.

We have been praying for the Lord to open a door in Hudsonville among the believers. This will be so much better for you, we believe,

than the city of Chicago. Believe us, we know, since we lived in
Chicago for several years. We pray God's blessing on you all.

Sincerely, Edna and Charles Lukesh

Before they had a chance to discuss the letter, Alois moved on to
the letter from the Joneses, which was written in English. Alois was
not fluent, but he could speak and read well enough to understand
it. He read,

With the Lord's help, we were able to find a job for Alois with a
farmer. Alois can be employed as a farmhand. There is a large, empty
house on the farm. Several church members will have some extra
clothing and used furniture for you. We do hope you will consider
coming to Hudsonville. If you decide to do so, please send us a telegram
from New York. You are quite welcome here. May the Lord bless you.

Sincerely, Mr. and Mrs. Jones

Leopoldine's smile broadened widely by the end of the letter. She
mentally rehearsed the message Alois interpreted. She imagined the
farmhouse—an entire house just for them! In Germany, there were fifteen
family members in three rooms. Interestingly, she noticed Alois did not
seem as happy with the offer in Michigan as she was. "Alois, please, let's
go to Hudsonville!" she said. She pictured the welcoming countryside
in contrast with a bustling city like the one she and Alois were currently
spending the night in. "I am terrified of Chicago."

Alois listened, but he was not ready to commit to going to Michigan;
he was not much enthralled about the idea of farm work. He remembered the toil of his childhood and how difficult it was to carve out a
living. He did not see Chicago as threatening as Poldie did. His dreams
took him beyond the dishwashing job to further horizons. It seemed
like a more substantial city could mean more vocational prospects. He
was not excited about working in the restaurant, but he was afraid a
small town would present limited opportunities.

Poldie watched Alois's face, trying to see any evidence that he was
on her side. She began to tear up as she begged him to agree to move
to Hudsonville. It was still the afternoon, but Alois was tired from the

journey and from the weightiness this new option presented. He knew Poldie was exhausted, and her emotions were high. "Let us get some rest. Let's think and pray about it some more," he said. "By tomorrow morning, we will decide."

Poldie and Alois bathed, marveling at having a bathroom all to themselves. In Altach, they only took a bath once per week in a room shared by dozens of others. After the family napped, they went to the hotel lobby, and Alois asked if there was a restaurant nearby, and the attendant confirmed there was one around the corner.

The girls were hungry. Alois took Marie in his arms, and Poldie led Jana by the hand as they walked down the street. At the restaurant, Alois helped Poldie order a meal. It was so strange to be in a place where she could not speak or understand the language. Inwardly, Poldie determined that she would not be left out linguistically. Alois and Poldie were surprised when the waitress brought four cups with ice and water and set them on the table. In Germany, restaurants did not serve ice water but usually served patrons beer. He asked the waitress for a glass of beer for both himself and Poldie.

The waitress laughed. "Sir, for beer, you are in the wrong place. You will need to go to a bar for that," she said. "We don't serve it here."

Alois was curious and asked her why, since it was commonplace for people to drink beer at restaurants in Europe. She explained that in the US, only establishments with a liquor license were allowed to serve beer. Alois and Poldie noted this first cultural difference they encountered. Also, in Europe, people usually did not receive water unless customers requested it. The bottled water there was almost as expensive as beer. During the meal, they also learned that Americans call the morning meal *breakfast*, the noon meal *lunch*, and the evening meal *supper*. In Germany, they called the noon meal *dinner* and the evening meal *supper*.

Poldie was excited; she was already learning new vocabulary words and customs. Back at their hotel, they prayed as a family, thanking God for His guidance and safekeeping thus far. The children offered short prayers that felt like music to Alois's and Poldie's ears. In their hearts, they prayed for the Lord's guidance in the decision they needed to make the next morning. Neither Alois nor Poldie knew many verses yet, but the message of Psalm 37:4–5 still rang in their hearts: "Take delight in the LORD, and he will give you the desires of your heart. Commit your way to the LORD; trust in him, and he will do this" (NIV).

When the children fell asleep, Poldie tried to rest but felt that she was still on a ship and the world was moving beneath her. She and Alois went over everything that happened for the past ten days and concluded that their family had fared amazingly well given the rough passage and long journey. Alois usually called Poldie by his pet names for her, like "Broucku" and "Kocicka," but today, she resisted those overtures when he confessed that he still wanted to live in Chicago.

"Chicago?" Poldie asked loudly. "Listen, I am the one who has to raise the kids and take care of many things at home. I will be terrified in a big city!"

Alois did not feel like arguing again about either opportunity or how Poldie would adjust. She just wanted to go to Hudsonville. At that point, as Alois turned over to face the wall, all he could think about was cigarettes. Ever since they received Christ in Germany, Mr. Lukesh strongly encouraged Alois to quit smoking, since he felt it was a weak testimony to others. One evening in Germany, Alois determined to stop. But all the next day at work, he thought he might jump out of his skin if he didn't have a smoke. When he got home, he begged Poldie for just one cigarette. For the next two weeks, he chewed lots of gum. Sometimes, when the urge became extremely strong, Poldie purchased three packs—each containing only three cigarettes—for him in Altach. Alois was proud of himself that at least he was smoking less.

When they were on board the ship, Alois felt too sick to smoke. Still, he reasoned that smoking might make him feel better and take the edge off. He purchased a whole carton of Marlboros. As he puffed away while leaning on the ship's rail, he hoped that American Christians smoked so that he would not feel bad about it.

Poldie confessed to Alois when she saw him fiddling with a carton, "I will be delighted if you quit smoking."

Alois rebutted, "I think the Christians in America also smoke, as I've seen in the movies. Anyway, I'm just going to finish what I have left of the carton, and then I think I'll quit."

Alois fell asleep and rested dreamlessly.

In the morning, they all rose early, and Poldie dressed the girls. They were contented with a full night's sleep. The family walked down to the restaurant they visited the night before and ordered breakfast. Later, they returned to the room, and Alois left Poldie and the girls in the hotel, promising to return shortly. He asked in the hotel lobby how to get to Downtown New York to the Manhattan Bank. The receptionist gave him directions, which he wrote down. He arrived a short time later at the bank.

Alois strolled inside the big-city bank and presented the personal check from Mr. Lukesh to the clerk. It had a German address on it, giving the clerk pause. After studying it further, the clerk asked Alois to wait a moment. She returned with the manager of the bank. He motioned for Alois to follow him to his private office. Alois sat down with him and wondered what was going on. The manager inquired how Alois received the sizable check from Germany. Alois answered all his questions, explaining how he left Czechoslovakia and became a Christian in Germany, accepting Jesus Christ as Lord. He said that the missionary couple, the Lukeshes, exchanged his German marks with a check so he could obtain the American dollars. The manager was intrigued and satisfied with the answer. He called the bank clerk in and asked her to bring three $100 bills.

As they prepared to part, Alois mentioned to the manager that sometime in the afternoon, his family would board a train to either Chicago or Michigan. The manager immediately warned Alois not to show anyone the large bills he was carrying, especially on the subway. He divulged there were gang members who would kill for as little as $20.

Alois's eyes widened, and he was instantly shocked. "Is it that bad in America?" he probed.

"You would not believe what people will do here for money," the manager replied. The man reiterated that $300 was a lot of money to carry around. He motioned to the inner pocket of Alois's jacket and said that pickpockets travel the subway.

Alois thanked the manager for his kindness and went on his way. Internally, Alois was reeling. What had he gotten himself and his family into? As much evil as he had witnessed in his life, Alois was still naïve and innocent in many respects. Outside of war conditions and in a prosperous country, wouldn't things be better and safe? Riding in the subway, Alois was especially conscious of the people around him. As he walked through crowds and as people zipped by, Alois paid close attention and kept his jacket and coat wrapped tightly around him. When he arrived back at the hotel room, he kissed his wife and daughters and expressed utter joy to be with them again.

Poldie was glad to see him and did not mention that she had been praying about their final destination incessantly while he was on his errand. Instead, she tried not to be overeager. "How did it go at the bank?" she asked.

Alois gave a smile and motioned to his pocket that the mission had been successful. He decided as he rode the subway that he should not alert Poldie to what the manager said about the pickpockets and gangs. It will frighten her, because it certainly scared him. That warning from the bank manager might have been precisely what Alois needed at that very moment. He began to backpedal on the idea of living in Chicago.

Poldie lost her composure and tried again. The morning had passed, and they were running out of time. "Can we please go to Michigan?" she pleaded. "It sounds so much better. I am afraid to go to Chicago." She hung on to his hand as if he were her last hope.

Alois cleared his throat. He was not ready to admit why he agreed with her. He simply smiled. "If you want to go to Michigan, my dear, then to Michigan we will go," he said.

His words felt like a proclamation of freedom and joy! Poldie hugged Alois tight. Surely, God had heard her prayers. As she looked over at Jana and Marie, she felt hope rising in her again. She could do this; they could do this together.

Since it was nearly noon, they decided to go back to the restaurant for lunch before the men from the refugee organization came to pick them up. For Poldie, the meal was a celebratory one. She wasn't sure how Alois felt about Michigan, so she subdued her enthusiasm. As Poldie studied Alois's expression at lunch, however, she began to think that maybe he was not disappointed at going to Michigan after all.

◆

At 2:00 p.m., while the Hufs waited in the hotel lobby, the men returned to the inn. They asked about Alois and Leopoldine's decision: "What will it be? Are you going to Chicago or Michigan?"

Poldie was so pleased when Alois confirmed that they chose Michigan. This choice gave her a sense, in spite of everything that was out of her control, that she still could determine her own destiny. While Poldie did not understand the Czech language, she could tell the two men were gratified with the answer. It meant room for another family to take advantage of the restaurant opportunity. More than that, she sensed that they also felt Michigan would be a better fit for the young family.

The men drove the Hufs, along with their two wooden crates, to Grand Central Terminal. As the vehicle approached the terminal at the Forty-Second Street entrance, Alois and Poldie were captivated with the massive building. The structure's exterior was designed with intricate detail and towered over them. The thirteen-foot clock featured statues that seemed to reach to the heavens. Once inside at the ticket window, the men ordered four tickets to Grand Rapids, Michigan. They handed Alois a business card and asked him to let them know how everything was going and to forward their new address. The men reminded him the refugee organization would stay in touch with them for several years. Finally, they suggested Alois send a telegram to the Jones family in Hudsonville to alert them about their arrival time.

After saying good-bye, Alois and Poldie were overwhelmed with the station. It seemed to engulf them amid the sea of faces. There were crowds of people with so many different ethnicities, and they were bustling every which direction. Alois and Poldie were no strangers to groups in trains, but they had never seen anything like this. There were masses of bodies coming and going. Alois observed how frightened Poldie looked; she clung to Jana and Marie, and the children clung to her. Alois realized for the first time just how important going to Michigan was for her. She left all she knew, and now she was going to have to create a new sense of home and family. Alois began to feel homesick too. But he quickly shook it off. While collecting their thoughts, Alois and Poldie barely had time to take in the magnitude of the structure before them. The edifice's interior was 125 feet high and seemed to grow taller as they stood mesmerized at its ornate beauty. The four-faced brass clock peering at them from above the information cubicle reminded them of the last leg of their journey.

Alois leaned in close to Poldie and said, "I know you are afraid and homesick, but trust me, everything is going to be just fine. But I need to ask you a favor: please be patient for a short time. I must find a telegraph office so I can send a telegram to the Joneses in Hudsonville. I don't know where the telegraph office is or how long it will take, but hopefully, it won't take long."

Alois proceeded to place the two wooden crates in a corner and then set the children on top. Leopoldine stood beside them, wishing that Alois did not have to leave. He instructed her to stay there no matter what. "Otherwise, we would have a hard time finding each other among so many people," he said.

Then Alois asked at the ticket counter where a telegraph office was. He found it quickly, but the line was incredibly long and moved painfully slowly. He wished his English were better so he could ask someone to hold his place. He wanted to check in on Poldie and the girls and alert them that it would take longer than anticipated. Poldie held on to the girls with her life. God forbid one of them disappeared into the crowds; she would be lost forever. Her mind seemed to be racing as quickly as the crowds around her. Her thoughts paused on every unanswered question. She tried calming herself by memorizing the terminal. Before her stood a massive marble staircase, and arched windows surrounding her seemed to push the ceiling into the sky. On the horizon were too many ticket counters to count. Poldie kept eyeing the brass clock and watched the minutes pass by. The minutes turned to a half hour, and the half hour turned to hours. "Where is Alois?" Poldie thought.

After more than two hours, Alois finally reached the window at the telegram counter. The process took a while, and Alois asked the clerk several times to confirm the details. He wanted to make sure the telegram went to the correct address.

When the telegram was sent, Alois hurried back to the train station corner where he had left his family. As he approached, he saw Poldie and the girls huddled over the wooden crates, weeping uncontrollably. "What's the matter?" he exclaimed. "Why are you all crying?" He thought something awful must have happened in his absence.

Poldie looked both irritated and relieved to see him. "I thought," she said through tears, "I thought you abandoned us and ran off."

Alois shook his head. "Leopoldine, what are you saying? How could you think of something like that?" he asked, feeling insulted. "You are not being helpful. I could not take you, the children, and two wooden crates with me to the telegraph office to stand in line. Why would you think that of me?"

Alois's response impacted Poldie, and she continued to cry. She explained that there was a young woman she knew in Germany who married a foreigner, and they immigrated to the United States. As soon as they reached New York, her husband disappeared and left her alone. She had to return to Germany. "I thought that you also left us here," Poldie said, her lips quivering.

Alois put his hands reassuringly on Poldie's shoulders. "I love you, and I love our children. I would never leave you. It does hurt a little that you would think something like that about me," he said. "Besides, we both love the Lord. We are going to stand strong together, and even more so now. In this new country, it is only you, our children, and I. We love each other, and we are going to stand together." Poldie was satisfied with his response but scolded Alois further because she and the girls had to use the bathroom and could not the entire time he was away. Alois conveyed his regret and offered an apology for not being able to get back to them faster.

After everyone had a chance to collect themselves, Alois reviewed the details of their departure time. He was ready to get his family to their new home.

That evening, they boarded the train to Grand Rapids. They stopped only briefly in their train car before making their way to the dining car. That night, they all rested quietly. It felt liberating to depart the crowded city, and the mild jolting of the train was nothing compared to the tumult of the ocean. Alois looked at Poldie, Jana, and Marie. His family and their two wooden crates were everything he had in the world. Alois prayed he had made the right decision and asked God to guide his family in Michigan. In America, he would have an extra responsibility to help make sure Poldie was happy as she learned a new language and environment. As long as he had known her, however, Poldie seemed to take responsibility for her own happiness. Her emotions were delicate and raw sometimes, but she was still a strong woman, capable of looking after herself and the children well.

After a refreshing night of sleep, the train slowly came to a halt in Grand Rapids at 10:00 the next morning. Poldie assured the girls they were about to be finished traveling; her assurances were partially directed to herself. She was ready to conclude their long journey. Yet not knowing the future had been a comfort in a way. Soon, she would have to face the new reality of her life—whatever it may be. She looked out the window, eager to discover her new home.

Upon disembarking, Alois and Poldie immediately noticed this station was much less congested than the one in New York City. They appreciated the quieter pace that was closer to what they were familiar with. A man dressed in overalls was there to greet them. Alois thought he must be the farmer, but he introduced himself as Mr. Jones. He came across as a straightforward, quiet person. After Alois paid the train clerk extra for the oversized crates, they loaded them onto Mr. Jones's pickup truck bed. Together, they all piled into the front seat of the cab. First Mr. Jones, then Alois with Jana in his lap in the middle, and finally Leopoldine in the passenger seat with Marie on her lap.

It was quiet in the truck except for the sound of the tires hitting a few bumps on the road. Finally, Mr. Jones asked, "Do you smoke?" Alois realized his jacket probably smelled like smoke since going through the pack on the ship. Alois said he did but followed it up by stating his intention to quit.

Mr. Jones said, "Smoking is not a good habit for Christians. It would be noble if you'd quit." Alois was surprised at his directness. So American Christians didn't smoke like he thought, after all. Alois decided again that he would plan to quit.

Mr. Jones turned his forthright attention to another matter as they drove to Hudsonville. "Four days ago, we had a tornado pass through Hudsonville," he said. "There were several people killed and many homes destroyed."

Alois felt his back straighten as Poldie jerked beside him. She knew a few English words, but *tornado* needed no translation. "What did he say about a tornado?" she asked. Alois was compelled to explain in German what he just heard.

Poldie looked as if she'd been betrayed. "Tell Mr. Jones to turn around and bring us back to the station," she said. "I want to go back to Germany now!"

Alois took a deep breath. "Kocicka, just wait and see. Maybe tomorrow everything will look better," he said calmly. "Besides, how can we go back to Germany? We don't have that kind of money. The $300 would not be sufficient for the trip home. Just trust me, everything will be all right."

Poldie calmed, and Alois repeated his reassurance in his own mind. He was not sure if everything was going to be all right, but he had to be stable for the three souls who depended upon him. The ride was quiet most of the way to Hudsonville, and Alois was sending up prayers in his heart that God would give his family strength for whatever they would face in the new town.

As they passed the city-limit sign that stated they had reached Hudsonville, Alois and Poldie were surprised to see soldiers standing guard along the streets. "Mr. Jones, what are the soldiers doing here?" Alois asked.

"Those are the Army National Guard watching for looters," he replied.

Alois did not know what a looter was, so he asked. "Soldiers are guarding areas destroyed by the tornado. All the belongings of the homes hit scattered throughout a large area. Some people were looking through it and stealing whatever they could find," Mr. Jones explained.

It was the second time hearing an American describe a crime, and Alois was shocked. It just didn't fit the idealistic image of the country he had in his mind. "Would people here really do this? Would they steal from those who just lost everything?" he asked incredulously.

"Yes, there are people who would do this," Mr. Jones said plainly. Mr. Jones slowed the truck as they made their way around a long procession. There was a funeral going on for all the people who were killed by the tornado. Just four days earlier, an F5 tornado hit; it had the strongest winds recorded anywhere that year. The twister touched down and carved a path forty-eight miles long and as wide as a football field in some areas. After the storm had passed, thirteen people in Hudsonville were recovered dead.

All the sobering news at once felt overwhelming, even for Alois. He knew that if he felt trepidation, Poldie felt it all the more. But they had both been through horrible circumstances in their lives. And they prayed every step of the way as they decided to make this transition to America. It was important for Alois and Poldie to remain positive and to show their children that everything was well and that there was nothing to worry about.

The pickup truck turned down a quiet road, and Mr. Jones said, "I am bringing you to our house; my wife is preparing a meal for you." The truck stopped before a large yard in front of his farmhouse. As they filed out of the cab, Mr. Jones pointed to a field a quarter of a mile away. "We had a house over there that we rented out. It was destroyed by the tornado this week," he said. "Four things happened to me that I was not prepared for. The first one was the tornado, and the second was losing the house. I had a new car ordered and delivered to me, but when the tornado came, I did not want the car anymore. And lastly, you all came."

Alois was not sure how to respond. Grouping his family's arrival with a tornado and destruction was not welcoming, but Alois realized Mr. Jones had just endured significant loss. Alois was glad he would soon be working and would not have to be a burden to anyone.

The Huf family followed Mr. Jones through the front door, and Mrs. Jones gave them a much warmer reception, embracing each family member while she grinned widely. Mrs. Jones introduced them to their five daughters and one son. The youngest child, a girl, was Marie's age at eighteen months. Alois took the lead in translating and was happy to discover the Joneses knew Dutch, as Poldie could at least understand more of what was said in Dutch than in English.

When they had all introduced themselves, the Joneses had a hard time pronouncing Jana ("Yah-nuh") and Marie ("Mugh-reeeh"). They began calling the girls "Janie" and "Mary." They called Leopoldine by her nickname or "Mrs. Huf." And as for Alois ("Aloy-es"), the Joneses began referring to him as "Al." Alois did not mind the Americanized versions of their names. He was pleased that the children had companions to play with. He also was glad to see that Mrs. Jones was taking an interest in Poldie. She told her, "Don't worry that you can't speak English. I will teach you that and other things you need to know."

Even though Poldie couldn't communicate very easily, she felt the warmth conveyed in Mrs. Jones's words and their interactions. The woman was kind to the children, and her welcome made Poldie and Alois feel better after driving through the tornado-torn town. Poldie tried to help with the final meal preparations. Both families sat down to lunch and prayed, and Poldie took note of the table. It was a hearty lunch, with bread and butter served with the meal. Poldie had never seen it served with a meal. The families talked with the help of Alois's basic translations. When the meal ended, Mrs. Jones went to the counter and grabbed a large bowl of pudding. She served it in small bowls. It was the most delectable dessert Alois and Poldie had ever tasted.

"What is the name of this?" Alois asked. "It is so good!"

"Jell-O," Mrs. Jones replied.

It was a unique word, but one that Poldie and Alois would remember. After lunch, Mr. Jones said he would take Alois over to introduce him to his new boss. His name was Les Schneider, and he owned several properties in the Hudsonville area. They took a short drive in the truck to another farmhouse. Mr. Schneider answered his door in a gruffer manner than Mr. Jones. He and Alois shook hands, and they walked over to an empty house nearby. It would be the Hufs' home.

Mr. Schneider showed Alois the herd of beef cows and a large barn. He demonstrated how to feed the cows, distributing hay with a pitch-fork. He gestured at one milk cow that was in the pasture. "If you know how to milk, then all the milk from the cow is yours," he said.

Alois remembered milking cows from his upbringing in Czechoslo-vakia. The farmer described the remaining duties with the property, depending on the need and the season of the year. Alois was confident he could do a good job and learn what needed doing.

Mr. Jones and Alois drove back to the Joneses' house and picked up Poldie and the girls to take them to their new home. When they reached the house, Poldie got out of the truck and looked at Alois to be sure this was going to be their dwelling. As they stepped inside, Mr. Jones explained that some members of the Baptist church had donated furniture for them. There were a few chairs and a sofa. The bedrooms had beds with mattresses and a baby crib.

Poldie heard her heels click on the wood floor and echo as she walked. She had grown used to living in a space that was not much larger than a bathroom and sharing a bathroom with dozens of neighbors. This house had four bedrooms, a dining room, a living room, a bathroom, and a kitchen! The many doorways made Poldie feel as if she were in a mansion.

When Mr. Jones left, Alois and Poldie put the two beds and a crib in one bedroom. It seemed strange to have so much room, and the children would be comforted in having their parents' presence close in this large home. Alois went outside to explore the land and to review his new job duties. While he was gone, there was a knock at the door. Poldie answered; from what she could understand, the two women before her were from the church. Poldie invited them in. They took a look around at the bare space and said they would bring "curtains" the next day. Poldie thanked them; she understood from her limited English lessons that they were coming back but got confused about what they meant by curtains.

When Alois returned to the house, Poldie exuberantly told him the ladies from the church were going to bring them a *kredenz* (credenza). She was already dreaming of a china cabinet and buffet table that would make her castle even more magnificent!

The following day, Alois worked on unpacking their crates before venturing outside. A knock came at the door, and Poldie welcomed the two women who had visited the day before. Poldie noticed they arrived in a car. She was bewildered because a china cabinet wouldn't have been able to fit in the car, and they didn't have a man with them to help move it in. The women carried paper bags inside and set them down on the floor. They took a trip to the car and returned with metal rods and a toolbox filled with screws, nails, and assorted tools. Poldie and the girls watched closely. Poldie concluded in amazement that they must be putting the cabinet together using only a few rods and the items in the paper bags.

Instead, the women were turning their attention to the windows. They fastened metal pieces on both sides of each window toward the top of the frames. Next, they pulled long cloths out of the paper bags, inserting rods through the ends. Together, they fastened brackets at the top of the windows along the wall. Poldie was grateful, but she was still wondering why they had talked about a "kredenz" the day before.

When they finished, one of the women pointed and said, "Nice curtains." Immediately, Poldie realized she had just learned the English word for *vorhang*–curtain. She was sure she would always remember it.

CHAPTER THIRTEEN

A WHOLE NEW WORLD

W hen Alois returned to the house, the Hufs decided to walk to the grocery store. Alois felt ready to start his job the next day, but on his last day off, it was nice to enjoy a stroll in the afternoon sunshine. He spent some of his time outside the house puffing on his last cigarettes and preparing to give them up this time. The air was clear and the sky blue as the family of four made the half-mile trek to the market. Poldie pushed Marie in the baby carriage they brought from Germany that Poldie was so proud of. Each time she used it, she remembered how she had saved money to purchase it for her first newborn. Alois carried Jana in his arms. He and Poldie noticed that the people who drove by were staring at this new addition to their community. The Hufs were unsure why residents were so fascinated by them and why no one else but them was walking.

When they entered the store, Poldie and Alois were surprised at the selection of items. Several women approached them as they shopped. The ladies wanted to know where the pretty baby carriage came from. An American couple pushing their carriage approached them to compare strollers. The American one had large wheels and stood much higher, whereas the German carriage was better quality and had prettier craftsmanship. Its slight height was perfect for Poldie. She learned a few additional words in English: "Nice carriage." As soon as Alois explained that they had purchased their carriage in Germany, several people surrounded them. The inquisitive shoppers wanted to know more about these strangers. People were friendly. This was so much better than the big city, Poldie assumed.

Alois and Poldie walked the isles of the store and selected several things, calculating costs and determining how much each would be in

German marks. When they paid for the groceries, the total was $8. They did not buy milk or butter; the total felt like a lot of money to spend. When they returned home, they checked each item and compared it to the receipt. Alois double-checked the pile three times and could not understand why there was one more item on the receipt than what they received. They counted one more time to be sure. Finally, they put the groceries back into the bags and set back out on the road to rectify the issue at the store.

The owner of the store, who introduced himself as Mr. Dunn, looked surprised to see the Hufs return so soon. Alois explained that when they got home, they counted one less item than the receipt showed.

The owner promised he would make it right. "Please show me the item on the receipt that you did not receive," he said.

Alois pulled out the receipt and pointed to the line at the end of the ticket. "I did not get this item," Alois said.

Mr. Dunn said, "That's a tax."

Alois was not sure the man understood. "We did not take any tax, and we did not want any," he clarified.

Mr. Dunn chuckled, and his laughter became even more hearty when he caught sight of Alois's bewildered expression. "It's sales tax," he explained.

"That is what you told me, but we did not take any tax," Alois said.

Mr. Dunn explained to Alois that the government imposed a "tax" on items for sale. "Everybody who purchases anything pays sales tax," he said.

"Oh," Alois said, relieved the store was not intentionally charging him for something incorrectly. He told Mr. Dunn that in Europe, the tax had to be calculated into the final price of the products sold.

That day, he and Poldie learned an important English word: *tax*. As they made their way home, Alois and Poldie talked about life in Michigan. There was so much that was new—from the barren landscape of the tornado-hit land to the language and the customs.

Approaching the farmhouse, Poldie noticed for the first time that there were two large sets of windows on the second floor of the house. "I don't remember seeing stairs anywhere," Poldie commented. Her imagination began to wander. "I remember seeing American Westerns with train robbers and looters," she said. "I wonder if people like that could hide in our house."

The two high windows fascinated Alois also. "I don't think anyone could hide in there, but let's see how we can get up there."

Inside, Jana and Marie were happy to join their parents on a journey throughout the house. Jana, especially, felt as though she were in a giant structure. After looking in every room, Alois and Poldie were stumped about how to access the high windows. They went outside to see if they could find a clue of how to get up there.

"Americans are full of surprises," Alois said. "First, tax at the grocery store, and now hidden rooms."

Alois had an idea. They needed to check every closet and corner. Alois walked into a bedroom closet and looked around for some crack on the floor or wall. "Look up there!" Poldie exclaimed, pointing up. There it was—lines that looked like a 1.5-by-1.5-foot hidden frame in the ceiling.

Alois hurriedly brought in one of the donated chairs and stood on it. He pushed on the space that looked like a large picture frame on the ceiling. As he did, it gave way. Poldie and the girls excitedly squealed. "Oh, wow," Alois said as he pulled the wooden board down and peered into the vacant space. It appeared to be a spacious, vacant upstairs room, with four windows casting streams of light across the floor. He described his vantage point to Poldie. It was a relief that no cowboys or Indians were hiding in a dark corner. It was only then that the Hufs realized that the upstairs space was an attic and not another apartment.

Alois closed the portal and climbed down. He and Poldie shared their amazement at the massive size of their home. They felt it was much too big for them. What would their loved ones back home think when they saw that one small family had several bedrooms, a living room, a kitchen, and a bathroom all to themselves? That night, they prayed and thanked God for the blessings of their beautiful home and Alois's new job.

The next morning, Alois rose at 6:30 a.m. and enjoyed breakfast with Poldie before walking over to the barn. The cattle looked as though they were expecting him—all fifty cows stared at the gate with hungry eyes as he walked through. He felt his heart rate quicken. Alois milked dairy cows before, but he had never interacted with a herd of animals. In his mind's eye, the cows numbered five hundred instead of only fifty and were angry longhorn bulls waiting to trample him. He climbed over the gate, intending to make his way between the cattle to the silo. He would then throw the silage down to the herd.

He began climbing, but the snorts and moos of the animals frightened him. He stepped back to the safety of the grassy ground. Alois looked around and found two pitchforks, then went back to the house.

Poldie looked up when she saw Alois come in. "You won't believe it, but those animals are mean," he began. "Could you please go with me and stand watch with this pitchfork?" Poldie chuckled, which offended Alois. "Don't laugh! You wait until you see those huge monsters with the big horns. You won't be laughing when you see them."

Poldie left the girls sleeping and followed Alois back to the herd. The cattle were even more agitated at the appearance of Alois and Poldie. Alois stood at the fence and turned to Poldie. "When I jump in, if they go after me, you poke them with a pitchfork and yell for help if you need to."

Alois scaled the gate, holding on to his pitchfork, and quietly dropped to the ground on the other side. The eyes of the animals were intent on him now. He moved stealthily through the pack, waiting at any moment to defend himself from the would-be predators. In a short time, he realized he had reached the silo and he was still in one piece. His heart calmed as he climbed up the silo.

"See, there was nothing to it!" he heard Poldie say. He was not a chicken, he thought.

Alois threw the silage down to the hungry cows. It took a while to distribute enough to all the animals assembled. Poldie waited patiently. Finally, Alois climbed back down and walked through the herd. All the cattle were chewing on their food, uninterested in him. By the time he made it to the fence, he knew he would not need Poldie to stand guard again.

———————————————◆———————————————

It took a little time for Alois to learn the routine of the farm work, but he got the hang of it. His workdays were from 7:00 a.m. to 7:00 p.m. After he fed the cows in the morning, he rode the tractor and tilled the ground in preparation for planting corn. One day, as he was raking the field with the machine, pulling a four-by-four-foot drag harrow, Alois came to the end of a row and turned the vehicle sharply. He looked back and saw that the tractor's right wheel had caught the chain that pulled the drags. As the wheel turned, the right side of the drag harrow was being hoisted powerfully. In a second, Alois slammed on the brakes and leaned forward.

He took several deep breaths and heard the tractor come to a stop. Alois looked back again. If he had not stopped when he did, the drag harrow would certainly have smashed his head with a fatal force. He felt sure his guardian angel had warned him just in time. "Thank you, Lord," Alois said aloud. He untangled the chain carefully and got back to work, this time making cautious turns.

That evening, when Mr. Schneider came to inspect the field, he seemed satisfied with the work. God's intervention so moved Alois during the day that he asked his boss, "Are you a Christian?"

The man eyed Alois and replied, "I'm trying to be one."

There were always things to do around the farm, and Alois learned that most of the time, he was the one to figure out how to do it. At least Mr. Schneider trusted him to do the work, he thought, even if the days were very long. At times, Alois wiped his brow and thought back to the driving job he had in Germany. There, the work was relatively easy, and the people were friendly and helpful. Things were different in Hudsonville, but Alois concluded that the job suited him far more than being a dishwasher in Chicago.

On the first Sunday in Hudsonville, Mr. Jones came to the house to pick up Alois for the church service. Poldie stayed home with the girls in the morning. With his Czech Bible in his lap, Alois took in the American church service. His English was not sufficient to carefully follow the message, but he discovered something interesting. When the pastor stated where he was going to read in scripture, Alois followed along in his Bible. He could put two and two together and readily learned new vocabulary words.

The church service was much different than the Catholic Church services Alois had attended. The people were devout, but the service was less formal, and there was a lot of singing. The choruses reminded

Alois of the folk songs he used to sing back home. After the congregation sang a closing song, Mr. Jones said they were going to Sunday school. Alois had never heard of Sunday school but discovered it was just a small Bible study group.

Alois returned home and conveyed to Poldie how much he enjoyed the service. That evening, Mrs. Jones picked Poldie up for the evening service, and Alois stayed home to watch the girls. As the choir sang in the loft, Poldie sat motionlessly in the pew and felt like they were angels sent by God to serenade the parishioners. There were few words that Poldie understood, but she still felt that her heart sensed a presence. There were songs of faith and joy, and they lifted her spirits.

Evening services at church in Germany were usually very brief and only had a few attendees. In Hudsonville, the congregants were serious about church. The choir sang several songs, and people stood to share impromptu testimonies; upon finishing, the congregation clapped. The pastor delivered his sermon, and Poldie followed along in her German Bible. When a church member stood to sing a song in closing, Poldie thought she must be in heaven to be with such lovers of God.

By the time Mrs. Jones dropped Poldie back off at the house, Alois was worried. Jana and Marie were restless, and Alois had never heard of a Sunday evening service lasting so long. "There you are!" he said as Poldie walked inside.

"Oh, Alois," Poldie said. "I did not really understand, but I received such a blessing from being there at church. I thought I was in heaven."

"I am so glad. With how long you were away, I thought you were back in Germany by now," Alois teased.

"It was just beautiful," Poldie continued. She described the testimonies, the sermon, and the spiritual songs. Although she did not understand much of the service, she was sure she was in the presence of the Lord.

◆

Alois felt safer in America to correspond with his parents and family in Czechoslovakia; he was far from the tentacles of the communist government. He had not told his family they were leaving Germany; the news of their settlement in the United States would surely be a surprise. Poldie wrote to her family first, letting them know that they were all safe and doing well. A letter took at least ten days to reach Europe.

Thoughts of Poldie's family consumed her at times. She daydreamed about how nice it would be to have her mother's reassuring presence, her father's watchful eye, and her siblings' fun rapport. She told herself they would all be reunited eventually, but she did not know when. Eighteen days after she mailed the letter, Poldie made it a habit to walk to the post office each day with Jana and Marie. In her best English, she inquired of the postmaster if a letter had arrived. It had not, and he tried to tell her something about a mailbox close to her house, but Poldie did not understand. Finally, after six weeks, a letter arrived.

The Kellners were doing well and expressed their happiness that they had received word from the young family they so cherished. Soon after, a letter came from Czechoslovakia. This letter had a dourer tone. The Hufs had hoped the situation between Germany and Czechoslovakia would improve and that they would finally be able to visit Alois in Germany and meet his beautiful family. Now with all of them an ocean apart, they felt sad at the prospect of being separated by such a distance.

Alois felt a strong pull in his heart when he read the letter. He did not doubt, however, that he made the right decision. Alois had examined his situation in Germany in every way he knew how and had determined that America was their future home. For Poldie, however, it was not so simple. More reserved, she had been content to remain in Germany with her parents—coming to the United States was not her dream; it was Alois's dream. She sometimes felt upset when she would compare what she had in her former life to the difficult adjustments of her current one. But Poldie believed that she would make her own dream with Alois, and they would build a life together.

There were a lot of things different about the United States, including what people owned. Even though the people around them were not rich, it didn't seem like they were impoverished. The dairy cow helped supplement their grocery allowance. Early on, Alois showed Poldie how to make butter. They would collect the milk for about five days and put the cream in a metal milk can. After sealing the container, Poldie would shake the cream until it morphed into butter and buttermilk.

The Huf family used the butter on delicious boiled potatoes and drank the buttermilk.

For about a week, the Joneses came by the house to pick up some of the milk. But frugality prevailed for the Joneses when the family concluded that they would save on gas money and time if they allowed the milkman to resume delivery. So Alois and Poldie repeatedly had to pour out a portion of the remaining milk. It felt wrong to do so. Both thought sadly of all the people in Germany who would have utilized it.

One day, when Mr. Jones was picking up Alois for church, he said, "Al, you need a set of wheels to get around."

"What do you mean by 'set of wheels'?" Alois asked curiously.

"You need a car," he clarified.

Alois did not immediately see the need. "We don't need a car. We are from Europe, and people there don't mind walking to the store. How can I use a car here on the farm?" he inquired. "Besides, I only get paid $200 per month. With that kind of income, I don't see how I could afford one."

Mr. Jones persisted: "Sometimes you can get a decent car and for rather cheap. I'm going to keep my eyes open for one."

Alois agreed that Mr. Jones could look but doubted the probability of obtaining a used but good car. Besides, he did not have time to drive anywhere. Alois usually worked twelve-hour days for six days a week. On Sundays, he fed the cattle in the morning and evening, which added up to four hours. After the fieldwork finished in the spring, Mr. Schneider would pick Alois up and take him to the warehouse to load trucks with other men.

There was always something to do—working in the fields, loading trucks, cleaning cattle stalls, and clearing the livestock trailers. At 5:00 p.m., the other men at the warehouse punched out and headed home. Alois would walk the half mile back to the farm, or Mr. Schneider would drive him. Once home, Alois would continue with chores until 7:00 p.m.

The week after Mr. Jones suggested the idea of a vehicle, he came to Alois's door with two other men. They exchanged greetings, and Mr. Jones said, "This is Mr. Varga, a car salesman. And this is Don Hall, an insurance salesman. Mr. Hall brought you a car."

The three of them walked outside and looked at the vehicle parked in front of the house. It was a 1949 black Oldsmobile. From his experience as a driver, Alois thought it looked like a good car. The group explained to Alois that he could buy the car for $100 and even pay it off through monthly payments and that Mr. Hall would insure him. That sounded like an excellent deal to Alois, so they shook hands on it.

Shortly after, Alois went to the Department of Motor Vehicles. Since he already had a US military driver's license, after the staff checked his eyesight and he passed an exam on US traffic signals, they gave him a driver's license. Back at the house, Alois cleaned the car inside and out, just as he had in the military.

The next Sunday morning, Poldie and the girls, in their church dresses, climbed into the vehicle, and Alois drove them to the service. Alois felt a sense of pride to be behind the wheel again and to own his own automobile. He also realized that Mr. Jones was probably eager for Alois to have his independence. It was a win for everyone.

On the following Monday, Alois was awoken early by the sound of a horn. Since he had just purchased the car, he felt disoriented at first. But the horn blast came again, and Alois rose and looked out the window. It was Mr. Schneider's truck. Alois ran outside to see what was wrong.

"Hurry!" Mr. Schneider ordered. "One of the homes on the property caught fire, and we need your help."

Alois ran back inside to put on his clothes and shoes. He joined Mr. Schneider and several other men in the vehicle. Mr. Schneider told the workers that a house had all but burned down. As they approached, they saw that there remained little left of the structure. The air was gray and challenging to inhale as the men got out of the truck. What once was the floor and foundation of the house were red-hot embers of debris. Mr. Schneider instructed Alois and the other men to pick up all the smoldering pieces of wood and throw them in the fire. None of them were wearing gloves.

Traversing the hot ground in his thin-soled shoes, Alois could feel the burning on the bottom of his feet. He and the other men picked up the pieces gingerly at first but moved faster when they heard Mr. Schneider's voice compelling them to hurry up. Alois and the others felt they had no choice but to comply. He remembered how things were in the US military: safety first. He could hardly believe that a man was asking his employees to perform work in such conditions.

For days after that, Alois felt the sting in his hands, and his shoes were all but ruined. He saw clearly that he could not rely on Mr. Schneider. He knew he would have to make his own way vocationally and would have to discover what that looked like.

One day at dinner, Alois had a suggestion and voiced it to Poldie: she should learn how to drive their car. Poldie looked up at him from her plate as if he had just insulted her. Very few women in Germany drove, and they were not expected to drive themselves.

"What?" she asked incredulously.

"Poldie, I just want you to be independent. Imagine, for example, if I was injured or if I was away," Alois reasoned. "Wouldn't you want to drive?"

The look on Poldie's face said she would not. She was already trying to learn English and adjust to a new country. Would she now have to learn to drive herself? "You cannot ask this of me!" she intervened.

Alois suggested that they try driving on the farmland. This way, Poldie could practice with no traffic around and have all the space in the world to learn. Poldie reluctantly agreed. Not long after, the entire family sat in the car, and Alois began his lessons. The vehicle was not automatic, so it might be difficult for Poldie to navigate the clutch and gearshifts. Poldie followed his instructions, but it was not easy. As they began making their way down the road, Poldie objected again to driving. Alois ignored her complaints and kept thundering out instructions, sometimes with a tinge of frustration. For Poldie's sake, Alois was determined to keep at it and make sure his wife developed the competency to drive and to have her own driver's license. Alois felt the responsibility of looking after his family and wanted Poldie to have some sense of independence and an ability to take care of herself if needed. At the end of her first lesson, Poldie cried and thought Alois was far too demanding of her.

Shortly after that, Alois took Jana for a ride to the Joneses' house on an errand. The passenger-side window was partially open, so he asked Jana to close it. "Sure," she replied and then reached for the door handle by mistake. The door swung open and the little girl with it, flying out of the vehicle. Alois caught a flash of her rolling in the rearview mirror as he came to a quick stop. Horrified, Alois jumped out of the car, afraid he had run over his daughter. Jana was screaming, but other than a hurt ankle from the fall, she was uninjured.

Upon arriving home, Alois alerted Poldie what had happened. She was alarmed, and then she and Alois paused to thank God for His protection over little Jana.

After about six weeks of warehouse work, Alois gained the friendship of one of the young men who worked there, Jim. Each day when Jim and the other employees left at 5:00 p.m., Alois continued to work. He wondered about the different treatment he received compared to the other employees. Alois decided to ask Jim how much his group earned by the hour. He learned that the starting pay for the warehouse workers was $1.67 per hour. Alois thanked him for sharing and continued working.

Later, when Alois had time to reflect, he did the math. With all the time he was putting in each week, Alois was working about seventy-six hours. At $200 per month, that meant he was making around sixty cents per hour. Alois thought about his abilities and how he had not performed this type of labor for long. Some of the other men were a lot stronger. Still, Alois knew he worked hard and did an excellent job. He began thinking of a way to reconcile the difference in pay rates. He decided to ask for a raise to $1 per hour.

The next workday, when Alois found a private moment with Mr. Schneider, he broached the subject of compensation. Alois mentioned that he was doing farm work as well as spending many of his hours at the warehouse. He asked if his boss would consider a raise.

Mr. Schneider made the same expression he had the morning of the fire when he callously led the men to burn their hands and feet. "You agreed to work for $200 a month," the foreman said. "That means from sunup to sundown."

Alois knew that was the end of their conversation. After that, Mr. Schneider was mainly stony to him for daring to challenge his pay. Alois thought about what Mr. Schneider said. He interpreted from his response that Mr. Schneider assumed he owned Alois day and night. In his heart, Alois let his mind drift back to Germany. At least there, he had had a job in which he was respected and treated humanely. Alois tried not to dwell on the past. He had to keep moving forward. He whispered a prayer to God: "Lord, I don't like being treated like a slave. Please, Lord, open up some other way. I would be so thankful."

About a month later, Mr. Schneider picked up Alois and told him they were going to the large house he was building. Two other men were working at the site when he and Mr. Schneider arrived. They were all raking the ground to prepare for grass seeding. Alois's job was to collect the roots, stones, weeds, and leftover construction wood and remove them from the property in a wheelbarrow.

In the middle of the afternoon, Alois was picking up the debris when Mr. Schneider approached the other men. They all turned to Alois, and he could see Mr. Schneider gesturing at him. They all started laughing hysterically, and something snapped in Alois; he dropped the wheelbarrow and approached the group.

"Mr. Schneider, if you have anything to say about me, tell me to my face," he said. "Don't talk and laugh about me behind my back."

Mr. Schneider was as mad as a hornet. His face turned red, and he spewed, "Nobody ever tells me off! You agreed to work for $200 a month, and you are going to do as I please. Do you understand?"

"Well," Alois said, "I don't like it when you laugh at me and gossip about me behind my back."

"If you don't like it, you are fired," he said.

Alois replied, "Okay, I quit."

Alois began walking back to the farmhouse when a vehicle stopped next to him. It was Mr. Schneider. The foreman said, "Come inside."

Alois opened the door and sat down. "You can't just quit like that," Mr. Schneider continued. "Come on back to work."

Alois shook his head. "I don't think so. First, you only pay me about sixty cents an hour, while the other guys get $1.67. I work right along with them," Alois said boldly. "At 5:00, they punch out and go home, and I go home and do more chores for you until 7:00. On top of that, you laugh at me behind my back. I don't think that I would like to work for you anymore."

Mr. Schneider was unmoved. "If your mind is made up, then you have to pay me $60 per month to stay in the house."

"Okay," Alois said. "I will look for a smaller place, but in the meantime, I will pay you."

Alois felt proud of himself and yet disturbed when he got out of the truck. Poldie could see his downcast countenance as soon as he entered the home. "You're home early!" she said. "Is everything okay?"

Alois got right to the point: "I don't have a job anymore." He explained to her what happened.

Poldie was sympathetic but very worried. "What are we going to do?" she asked, glancing over at their daughters. "What if you can't find another job? What will we do then?"

"Poldie, we will just trust the Lord for another job," Alois said. "The $200 that I have been getting is not a lot of money. I would think that I would be able to get more than one job. And if not, I'll just write the refugee organization and say the job did not work out."

That evening, Mr. Jones came by. Alois guessed he had learned of the disgraceful termination from Mr. Schneider. Mr. Jones seemed worried and hinted that Alois should consider trying to go back. Mr. Jones sat on the donated couch in the Hufs' living room. He leaned forward and let his elbows rest on his legs. "Al, what are you going to do?" he asked.

Alois ached for the old job he had with the US Army in which he was regarded as a colleague and was able to work regular hours. "Tomorrow, I am going to go look for work," Alois replied.

"I know a man in Zeeland who owns a hatchery," Mr. Jones said. "Maybe he can give you a job." Alois nodded in agreement. "I will pick you up early in the morning."

The next morning, Mr. Jones arrived early, and Alois rode with him to Zeeland, which was around six miles from Hudsonville. The two of them walked to the office of the hatchery. John Vanderslug was the man in the office. He and Mr. Jones exchanged greetings; Mr. Jones had previously worked for him. Mr. Jones told him about Alois and that he required a job.

Mr. Vanderslug explained that there was no need for hatchery workers at the time but that there were always workers needed at the poultry processing plant about half a mile away. After a friendly parting with the supervisor, Mr. Jones and Alois drove to the plant. The boss there greeted them. He told Alois that he would make $1 per hour and he could start immediately. Alois was not wearing work clothes, but the man said employees donned a white overcoat over their regular attire and wore a cap.

Mr. Jones turned to Alois. "If you would like to start today, I will go to my friend Joe, who works at the Zeeland feed mill. He usually works until 6:00 p.m. He could come to pick you up at the end of the day and bring you home," Mr. Jones offered. Alois agreed.

The boss took Alois to the punch clock and directed him to fill out a time card. He asked Alois if he knew how to cut chicken legs off. Alois said he had cut a few in the past.

"Here, you need to be very fast," he told Alois. "We kill fourteen hundred chickens per hour."

Alois observed the operation. Two men cut the legs, and another hung the chickens on a moving belt with hooks. There was a hook every foot, and none of the hooks were empty. It was fast work, but Alois was happy to have a job. He was pleased too that he could be making $1 per hour.

That evening, Mr. Jones's friend Joe drove Alois home. When he dropped him off, he told Alois, "I will pick you up again tomorrow, that way you will get acquainted with the route. Then you can drive your own car."

CHAPTER FOURTEEN

A Home to Call Our Own

Alois walked through the door tired but pleased that he was back to work so quickly. He told Poldie about the new job. She was skeptical that a business could slaughter fourteen hundred chickens per hour. Secretly, Poldie wished that maybe Alois could be home for a short while. She disliked that the farmhouse did not have locks on the doors. To ease her fears, Poldie took chairs and jammed them under the door handles. Still, she was thankful Alois had a job so soon.

The next day, Joe picked up Alois again. At the processing line, there was no room for mistakes. Every thirty minutes, an attendant brought the men freshly sharpened knives so they could sever the chicken legs in one swipe.

At lunchtime, the boss pulled Alois aside and asked if he would like to drive a truck in the evening to pick up chickens on the chicken farms. "Sure," Alois said. "I would like to work as many hours as I can get."

The boss explained that he would need a chauffeur's license to drive a big truck. That afternoon, he drove Alois to the Zeeland police station to take a short exam. Alois passed and earned his chauffeur's license. The boss wanted Alois to haul chickens the same day, but Alois explained that he was scheduled to ride home from work with Joe.

That evening at supper, Alois told Poldie about the opportunity to drive the truck after hours. Poldie frowned on that idea because evenings were the one time when they could be together. She felt isolated and lonely without anyone to communicate with, and she missed him. Alois assured her that if the chicken farms were closer, he would be able to come home for dinner. The trucks often did not arrive at the farms until after dark.

Alois adjusted to his new work schedule. At 7:00 a.m., he began work on the poultry processing line. The line ran steadily until all the chickens that were brought in the night before were butchered. Then Alois would prepare the truck bed by loading it with about 150 crates. When time permitted, he drove home for supper. At 7:00 p.m., the trucks would set out for the farms. Usually, it was after midnight by the time the chickens were all unloaded at the factory.

Alois's workweek was around eighty to ninety hours. He earned more money than if he was a farmhand. When it was time for his first week's pay, he estimated he would make at least $80. But instead of $80, the check said $60. Alois entered the office and asked for the boss. "There must be some mistake," Alois said.

The boss looked at the check and then called the primary office. The party on the other end of the receiver communicated specifics to him, and the boss began laughing. Alois was confused. The boss hung up the phone and explained that the payroll department thought Alois was a woman, and women were paid seventy-five cents per hour. Mistakenly, they thought it was a lady with a name like "Lois." The payroll department corrected the mistake and made up for it in the next paycheck.

Alois contemplated whether or not the farmhouse was the best for his family. To pay $60 per month for a farmhouse rental was not exorbitant, but the space was too ample for them. Alois and Poldie were like marbles rolling around in a vast area, never to meet. A one-bedroom apartment cost about $25 per month. Alois conferred with drivers where he worked to see if they knew of an apartment for a family of four. One day, one of the men who lived in Holland, a city close by, told Alois he saw a lovely little house on Twenty-Fourth Street.

The next time Alois drove through Holland, he went by the house. It had a huge "For Sale" sign on the front lawn and appeared well kept. Alois jotted the telephone number down. The next day, he used the phone at work to call the number. A real estate agent answered, and Alois asked how much the house cost. The man on the other line, Mr. Burg, suggested that Alois bring his wife on Saturday afternoon to look at it and discuss the home further.

On Saturday, Alois worked until noon and then went home to pick up Poldie and the children. The real estate agent met them at the house.

The tiny two-bedroom home was very appealing to Poldie, with its beautiful kitchen, plenty of cupboard space, and its bathroom neatly kept. After touring the home, the Hufs went back to the agent's office. At first, they just talked about their personal stories, and Mr. Burg was interested to learn more about their faith.

Finally, they began discussing the home—the house listed for about $8,000. Mr. Burg asked how much money they had to put down. Alois said he only had $300 in savings bonds. Mr. Burg said that would be fine since he was the owner of the house. "Would you be able to make a $50 payment each month?" he asked.

Alois and Poldie looked at each other. They believed they could, and this way, they would own a home. Mr. Burg suggested that Alois give him a $50 deposit. He said he would prepare the necessary papers to close the sale in three to four weeks.

The next day at church, Alois saw Mrs. Jones and told her about the plan. Another acquaintance, Mr. Panski, told the Hufs that he and his wife would take them to the Baptist church in Holland, located near their future house.

Mrs. Jones was not keen on the idea of the Hufs relocating. "You can't move away from us!" she said. "We love you and want you to stay in Hudsonville so we can keep an eye on you. I have been working with Poldie and helping her progress in her English."

The Hufs were thankful for the kind words but accompanied Mr. Panski the next Sunday to the Emmanuel Baptist Church in Holland. They met people there who were kind and welcoming like their churchgoing friends in Hudsonville.

A few days later, Mrs. Jones came for a visit. She told Alois and Poldie she would be sad if they moved to Holland. She mentioned a small house a friend had told her about. It was four miles outside of Hudsonville on Port Sheldon Road, and a preacher named Barnett owned the house. Mrs. Jones offered to take Poldie to see it the next day.

When Alois arrived home the next evening, Poldie told him about the house and how she liked it. If they bought it, they would live only four miles away from the Joneses. For Poldie, Mrs. Jones was her primary friend and took the time to teach her English. Every Saturday, the Joneses came over to the house so the children could play together, and the women curled Poldie's hair for Sunday church. Alois and Poldie knew if they moved, they would be starting over again socially in some respects.

That evening, Mrs. Jones came over to talk about the other house. Alois confirmed he had already signed the papers for the Holland house and had given the real estate agent a $50 deposit. She asked who it was. As soon as Alois gave her his name, she said, "I know him. He is a Christian. I'll call him tomorrow and will explain everything to him. He will understand when I clarify that you should live in Hudsonville rather than in Holland. I am going to ask him to tear up the papers and give you your deposit back."

Just as she said, Mrs. Jones requested he destroy the agreement, and the next evening, the real estate agent tore up the contract and returned the deposit. The following evening, the Hufs went with Mrs. Jones to look at the other home. Alois and Poldie liked that it sat on two acres of land. There was a sizable hole dug in the ground behind the house. The agent told them the previous owner had a problem flushing the toilet, and he was about to put in a new septic tank. The real estate agent said the seller needed $700 down with $50 monthly payments. The total cost of the house was around $8,000. Mrs. Jones noted Mr. Barnett was a friend of theirs. She offered to ask him if he would be content with only $300 down. But the next day, the salesman said the $700 down payment was still required.

Mrs. Jones was not satisfied, so she tried negotiating with Mr. Barnett through a friend of hers. Still, the $700 requirement remained. Mrs. Jones was persistent, and the next time she saw Alois, she said, "Come with me. My husband will be home. I'm sure if I ask him, he will gladly loan you the $400 that you need. He is a good Christian man."

Feeling uneasy about the idea, Alois objected. "Just come," Mrs. Jones insisted. "You will see that my husband will gladly do it. You don't have to say a word. I will do the talking."

Alois followed her in his car, and when they walked into the Joneses' home, Mr. Jones gave him a kind greeting. After they all sat down, Mrs. Jones began explaining the situation to her husband. Mr. Barnett needed a $700 down payment, and Alois only had $300. The house was the perfect place for the Huf family, she explained, if only Alois could make up the $400. "I told Alois that you would be more than happy to loan him the $400," she concluded.

Mr. Jones's friendly demeanor quickly vanished. He pointed his finger in his wife's face, and his voice rose several octaves. "Don't stick your nose into their business!" Then he turned to Alois and pointed with his other hand, saying, "I don't have any money to loan!"

Alois stood up and turned to Mrs. Jones, feeling mortified for her. "Ma'am, I'm so sorry to have caused you any trouble and this humiliation," he said. He turned to Mr. Jones. "Please forgive me that I came. And please, do not hold this against your wife. I do not want to cause any problems between you. Thank you for everything."

When he got in the car, Alois raised a prayer. He had no intention of asking for a handout, and now he felt awful that Mrs. Jones had done so on his behalf. Hopefully, this had not damaged the couple's relationship as a result. "Please help them so they do not argue," Alois prayed. "I will wait on you. I will go to Mr. Barnett this evening. If he won't consider my offer, please help us find a small apartment."

Alois drove to Mr. Barnett's residence and was glad to see that he was home. After they exchanged pleasantries, Alois explained his situation. "Mr. Barnett, all I have is the $300 in savings bonds. I promise that if you sell us this house, within three months, with the Lord's help, I will have the extra $400 that you need," he said. "I will ask my boss for extra hours to work."

Mr. Barnett just said, "There is no way you can save $400 in three months."

Alois paused. "Yes, we can," he said. "I am going to ask my wife, and we are going to eat just bread, milk, and potatoes. We did not have much more than that in Germany, and we can do it again. I believe that is how we will save up the money—if you give us a chance."

The older man looked as if he was weighing the offer. He studied Alois. Finally, to Alois's amazement, he accepted.

Alois was elated as he walked out the door. No longer would he and Poldie have to live in the shadow of Mr. Schneider. When he told Poldie the news, she nearly squealed. Once the property was theirs, Poldie eagerly entered their new place and started cleaning, and with a neighbor friend's help, they cleaned the house from top to bottom.

The rent on the Schneider house was paid through Wednesday, July 4, and since it was a holiday, Alois was off work that day until the evening. So on Independence Day, he and Poldie put chairs in the trunk of the car and tied the trunk door with a rope. When they got to the new house, Mr. Vanderbell, their new neighbor, offered to help. He drove to the Schneider rental house in his truck and helped move the rest of the furniture. The kind gesture did not go unnoticed. Alois determined to steer clear of asking Mr. Jones for help. Alois walked over to Mr. Schneider and asked him to check on the rental house to ensure it was in excellent condition. Alois then thanked him for allowing his family to stay an extra two months.

At work, Alois asked his boss if he would allow him to work as many hours as possible. The operation was a busy one, and the boss was glad to oblige. Alois worked as many as twenty hours per day at times. The hours took their toll physically, but Alois was too driven to focus on his fatigue. He wanted to keep his word to Mr. Barnett and pay off the down payment. Poldie was concerned for her husband but knew he had a strong work ethic, and she knew that once he made a promise, he intended to keep it.

A few days after they moved in, Poldie complained that the toilet would not flush. The water did not drain in either the toilet or the bathtub. Alois asked Poldie to be patient for a few days because the agent who sold them the house had promised the previous owner dug the hole to install a new septic tank and drain field. Alois was exhausted from working so many hours; he and Poldie decided to give it a little more time.

Alois and Poldie were concerned after three weeks went by with no change. Alois came home one Saturday evening, and Poldie said, "Something strange is going on. The former owner of the house who was supposed to bring the new septic tank came by this afternoon with a shovel. I saw him cover up the hole that he dug up for the new septic tank!"

After church, the Hufs drove to the real estate agent's house, and Alois rang the doorbell while Poldie and the girls sat in the car. The Hufs intended on finding out what was going on with the septic tank. He waited a few minutes for the salesman to come to the door. Alois said, "I hope you don't mind me disturbing you on a Sunday. Since I am working almost all day and night, I thought you would not mind me stopping here after church."

The man snapped back, "What do you want?" Alois was surprised to hear the sharp tone in the man's voice when he had been so friendly the day he sold him the home.

"Okay, I'll make it short," Alois said. "My wife has to wait hours for the bathtub water to drain, and the toilet isn't flushing either. You promised me that in a few days, the former owner of the house was going to come and install a new septic tank and drain field, but instead, he came yesterday and covered up the hole where they were supposed to go."

The salesman began yelling: "Don't you ever come to my house on Sunday again—which is our Sabbath! Besides, do you have it written in your land contract that the septic tank and drain field would be coming? If it is not written in the contract, then you can't expect anything."

"But, sir, you gave me your word," Alois pleaded. "You said it would be done. Besides, you typed up the land contract, and you should have put it in—if you think your word means anything! I trusted you."

"Don't ever bother me again on Sunday," the man said.

Alois tried again: "But what about the toilet problem? What are you going to do about it?"

"That's your business," the man said. "I don't care what you do. Just don't ever bother me again—especially on Sunday! I'm a Christian."

Alois was teary eyed when he entered the car. He struggled to explain to Poldie what had just happened. It was evident that many people who said they were Christians did not act like it. He wished they would come to know the true faith that he had fully embraced.

Poldie let the harsh reality sink in for a few moments and then asked, "What are we going to do with the bathtub and toilet water? How can we fix it?"

"Let me think about it until tomorrow. I will figure something out," Alois said reassuringly.

Alois was feeling weary, but his mind had taken over any protests of his body. Even though it was Sunday, he still had to pick up chickens.

The Monday-morning line had to be supplied. He left home at about 10:00 p.m., ensured that the chicken crates were tied down, and stopped to gas and weigh the truck.

Alois looked down at his information ticket, which showed the location of the chicken farm. It said to arrive at midnight—that was unusual. His truck rolled to the farm, south of Zeeland, and he arrived at about fifteen minutes till midnight. Alois looked at the farmhouse; its front windows lit up. He saw about six young men inside. They must have been waiting for him, Alois concluded. He walked up to the door and knocked. When the farmer answered, Alois said, "The truck is here; we can start loading the chickens."

The farmer looked annoyed. "You just sit in the truck and wait," he said. "It's only 11:45. We have to wait fifteen minutes because we are Christians and don't work on Sundays."

While Alois was ever polite with customers, he felt irked. "I am also a Christian," Alois countered. "My wife and I, while in Germany, were visited by American missionaries. They led us to a saving knowledge of the Lord Jesus. I also don't want to work on Sunday. Yet you, the farmer, did not have the driver in mind at all when you decided not to work even one minute before midnight." Alois was channeling his remaining energy into getting his point across. "You could have requested the truck to be here at 2:00 a.m. I had to come to work at 10:00 p.m. to get the truck ready and be here on time. Yet what would you have said if I drove into your yard at 12:30 a.m. instead of midnight?"

"If you came here half an hour later, I would have called your office demanding from them the wages I had to pay for the six young men I hired to be here at midnight," the farmer retorted.

Alois just could not help himself from exposing the man's hypocrisy. "You think, in the sight of God, it's not okay for you to work on Sunday, but it is okay for me to work?"

The man answered, "The difference between you and us is that we are covenant children and you are not. So just wait in your truck until midnight."

As Alois walked back to his truck, he was puzzled by the phrase "covenant children." Whatever it meant, the man's approach had a similar ring to it as the real estate agent who stiffed him on the septic tank.

About a week later, Alois knew he could not put off the septic tank problem anymore. On Monday afternoon, he had a few free hours before he would need to return to work, so he began digging outside of the house near where the previous ditch had been. It did not take him long to find something that looked like a big metal barrel. It was covered with a layer of black crust—corroded with time. He began cleaning some of the coating with a shovel, and immediately a hole appeared, and water burst out of the thin drum. Alois called to Poldie and asked her to try flushing the toilet.

She ran out and cried with joy, "It's working! It's working! How did you do that?"

"All I did was make an opening for the water to come out of the old barrel," he said. "We still need a new septic tank and drain field, but this temporary fix will have to do. We need to pay off the $400 to Mr. Barnett first."

At times, Alois pondered how he had to be the one to take the high road with Mr. Barnett, with the real estate agent, and with the Sabbath-occupied chicken farmer. He gained comfort in prayer and told himself and Poldie that they had to answer to God alone, as did the other men.

There were days when Alois worked as many as twenty-two hours in one day. Behind his exhaustion was the memory of life in the camp, when he would have done anything at times just to have a job. Living in America might not be easy, but at least he had opportunities here. Poldie had readily agreed to live on milk, bread, and potatoes for the time being; she also remembered a time in Germany when they could barely afford the basic essentials to survive.

The day finally arrived when the $400 was saved up for the down payment. It was about three weeks earlier than promised. Alois delivered the money to Mr. Barnett, who was shocked Alois could accomplish that feat in such a short time. Even if others did not keep their word, Alois took pride that his pledge still meant something.

After the down payment was taken care of, Alois turned his attention to the septic problem. He called a septic tank company and told them what the house needed. The representative promised to come out in the evening and look the situation over. The man arrived and told Alois that if he could dig out the hole himself, the company would be able to bring in a small septic system and some tiles and gravel for the drain field. It would cost about $125.

Alois agreed, and through the week, he spent several hours here and there digging the hole by hand. The day the company installed the septic tank was a good one. Alois was pleased to see Poldie so happy. They finally had their own functioning home.

Frugality was an ingrained part of the Hufs' lives. Now that they were in a new land and a new home, saving money and spending it wisely was critical. When Poldie peeled potatoes to prepare specific recipes, she threw the peelings in the trash. Alois was hesitant to throw anything away, even the skins. If they had a pig, he thought, they could feed it leftovers. There was already a coop on the property. Alois knew a coworker who raised pigs. He arranged to purchase one for $6.

One afternoon, Alois came home with a wiggling burlap bag. Jana and Marie gathered around him to find out what it was. They screamed in delight when Alois pulled out the pink little pig. He told Poldie and the girls that when the pig got bigger, they could butcher it and have their own meat. The girls did not seem as excited about that.

Alois built a fence around the coop in the backyard so the piglet could have room to run around. Jana and Marie immediately loved the little oinker. They called her Lisa. When the girls called her name, she came running out of her coop for a petting. That darling little pig was more blessing than bother.

Poldie had a real knack for making the house a home and grew to love the location and their piece of land. She sometimes thought about Chicago and felt so grateful that God allowed them to settle at a place where they could have considerate friends and a community church, be homeowners, and even have an animal. She worried about Alois working such long hours, but he continued assuring her that all was well and that he was doing it for their future.

Although there was plenty of work at the chicken processing plant, sometimes Alois was called upon to help in the hatchery he had first been introduced to through Mr. Jones. One of his duties at the hatchery was to examine the eggs under an incubator light. The eggs that were not viable would be discarded. Alois asked the manager if he could take a pail full of the broken eggs home for his pig.

Lisa loved the eggs and quickly grew to about 150 pounds, becoming a mature gilt. Alois asked Jana and Marie if they would like little piglets. Poldie thought Alois had lost his mind. He always had plenty of ideas about projects. Alois called a farmer with a boar, and he came to mate the two.

Sometimes in the hatchery, if there were leftover chicks, the company workers would put the ones they could not sell in a barrel and pour water over them to drown them. Alois felt sorry for the chicks, and he did not like the waste either. He was used to making something from nothing all his life, but so many where he lived seemed to make nothing from something. Alois asked the manager if he could have the unwanted chicks.

When Alois came home with yet another surprise, Poldie asked, "What are you bringing home now? Where are you going to put those poor little things?"

Alois prepared a space for the chicks in the attic above the garage. During the day and at night, the family could hear their new neighbors rustling around. Alois eventually built roosts in the coop with Lisa and put the chickens outside. He found out the Michigan Bakery in Grand Rapids sold barrels full of day-old bread for $1. Bread soaked in water was the perfect treat for the chickens.

A couple of months after moving into their home, Poldie began feeling that common illness in the mornings. She announced to Alois that she was pregnant. The new baby would arrive in mid-April 1957. They were excited to be adding to their family, and Alois was glad they had a proper home now for their growing brood. Poldie's growing responsibilities reminded Alois that she did not have a driver's license. Alois brought up the idea again for discussion.

"Not as long as you have that old car with a clutch," she replied. "I am not even going to try it!"

Alois tried to ease Poldie into using a stick shift, but she never took to it. Poldie had been such a trooper through the entire move, leaving her family and all that she knew behind, that Alois wanted to surprise her with a car of her own. So he drove to Zeeland to a used car dealership and carefully selected a 1953 two-tone green Chevrolet Bel Air four-door sedan complete with an automatic transmission. The car cost $700, and Alois was grateful the payments were totally manageable for their budget. When the car showed up at the house, Poldie's excitement over the beautiful car thwarted any fear she had about learning to drive it. Alois suggested that Poldie learn and obtain her driver's license before the baby arrived. Poldie agreed, and once behind the wheel again, her previous lessons kicked in, and she picked up the automatic vehicle quite well.

When he thought she was ready, Alois took Poldie to the Zeeland police station to take the driver's exam. The chief of police was strict. Alois asked him if he could sit by his wife during the exam to help translate the written test. The chief agreed that Alois could translate but said he could not help her with the answers. He added that he spoke Dutch and would be listening in to make sure the couple did not cheat.

Poldie aced her written exam, and then came the time for the practical test. "She has to take me for a ride, but you cannot be in the car," the chief told Alois.

Alois uttered a silent prayer as the two of them took off in the car. Poldie was sure she understood enough to follow the chief's instructions. About fifteen minutes later, the car returned. Alois waited for the report. The man was satisfied and in a lighter mood, although he ribbed Alois about her stopping past the stop signs. With a new driver's license, Poldie drove Alois home.

When they got home, Alois said, "Since you have your driver's license, do you want to drive by yourself to Grand Rapids to pick up the bread?"

Poldie was surprised. "Do you trust me?" she asked. "Do you think I could go by myself? Aren't you scared that I could crash the car?"

"No, you will be fine," he said, and Poldie took off with the girls.

Alois worked around the coop for about three hours. He was glad when he heard the sound of the car engine approaching. He greeted Poldie and the girls as they emerged from the car.

"Look," Poldie said, "not one scratch on the car, and I got three barrels of bread—and doughnuts!" The bakery staff gave the girls doughnuts. Poldie loved her Chevy and was proud of herself for taking the trip without Alois's help.

The poultry processing plant had its own crew who raised turkeys. Turkeys were raised in coops until they were twelve weeks old and then released to roam on acreage. There were many acres of forest outside the village of nearby Hamilton, and the turkeys occupied lush areas under the boughs of trees. They moved the rafters (turkey groups) around like herds of cattle, letting them graze on fresh, grassy areas until the ground was depleted.

In early fall, the manager at work told Alois the company was going to be installing large metal feeders for the turkeys. The feeders would replace the simple wooden ones, which were about twelve feet long, one foot wide, and one foot high. Management asked Alois if he would like to clean up the leftover feed in the wooden feeders and use it for his pig. By now, Alois had a reputation for not wanting anything to go to waste.

One Saturday afternoon, Alois and Poldie took the girls in each of their cars and drove to the Hamilton woods to pick up the unused feed. By the time they had cleared out all 150 of the wooden feeders, they had filled up eight burlap sacks, which Alois had loaded in the two cars.

The next week, the men at work asked Alois if he had cleaned out the feeders. When he told them he did, they said, "Good, now we can burn the feeders."

Alois stopped for a moment. "If you are planning to burn those feeders, could I take the feeders apart and keep the lumber?"

The management agreed to it as long as Alois cleared the lumber within the next few weeks. The following two Saturdays, Alois spent his time taking the feeders apart. He loaded the boards in the trunk of his car. It took three trips to get all the lumber to their home.

From the scrap lumber, Alois expanded the chicken and pig coup, which also had become home to several turkeys. Later in the fall, their pig Lisa delivered twelve piglets. Everyone thought they were so cute. Alois bought a few more gilts. He was planning to earn more money so the family could have enough for a down payment on a small farm nearby. Alois had decided that having his own farming operation was the way to go.

In March of 1957, the processing plant moved toward securing an on-site poultry inspector. The company leadership wanted to improve the label on their products, since they sold thousands of chickens and turkeys. Alois was ambitious, and the company owner asked Alois if he had any interest in completing a three-week course at Michigan State University for poultry meat inspecting. Alois was honored and asked what would be required. The foreman said he needed to live on the university campus and be away from his family for three weeks. If he completed the course successfully, Alois would be issued a license for poultry meat inspecting. He would be paid by the State of Michigan in addition to being compensated by the company. The result would be that Alois would make $2.50 instead of $1 per hour.

Alois thanked the owner and said, "Let me talk with my wife, and I will let you know tomorrow."

When Alois mentioned the offer to Poldie that evening, she was supportive. "I am all for it, except I am a little worried because of the pregnancy," she said. Poldie was due to deliver sometime in mid- to late April.

Alois assured her his boss knew about the baby coming and that he promised Alois could call home daily and leave an emergency phone number where he could be reached. "If you need me, I can be home in about an hour and a half by car," he said.

The next day, Alois confirmed that he would go to the training provided that he could come home if his wife were to go into labor.

The following Monday, March 25, 1957, at 8:30 a.m., Alois reported to Michigan State University. He registered and was then told where to go. Classes were from 9:00 a.m. to 5:00 p.m. each day. That sounded like time off to Alois compared to his usual schedule. When he walked into the classroom, there were about thirty students from throughout the state.

Two days into the three-week course, Alois realized it was going to take more than the classroom instruction time for him to learn the material, especially since his English was still rough. He began studying for hours in the evening. Alois learned one of his professors spoke German. Since the students had to take a written test once per week, Alois asked the professor if it was permissible to write some of the answers he did not know in English in German instead. The instructor readily agreed, saying it would help him brush up on his own German.

Each evening, Alois called Poldie to see how she was doing and to check on the welfare of the children. Poldie said all was well. "Hopefully the baby will delay until you get home," she added.

Occasionally the helpful professor would say a German phrase to Alois during class to help clarify a concept. After the three weeks, when it was time for the exam, Alois again asked the professor if it would be possible to write some of his answers in German. The kind man agreed, and Alois said a prayer, "Lord, I don't want to disappoint my wife and the people who put their confidence in me. Please help me do well on the exam."

Alois passed the exam on Friday, April 12, 1957, and as he drove home the next day, he expressed his thankfulness to God. He was excited to be with Poldie and the girls again and also looking forward to the birth of their third child.

CHAPTER FIFTEEN

DISCOVERING AN UNEXPECTED
VOCAL HARMONY

I n spite of certain hurtful experiences with some Christians, Alois
and Poldie were blessed by the genuine friendships they made. A
month before her due date, a lady from their church invited Poldie
over for what she assumed was a social gathering. She took Jana and
Marie along for the adventure. When they arrived, several women from
church were present. The ladies sat around conversing with Poldie. At
one point, Poldie noticed numerous gifts in the corner of the room.
They then announced it was a "baby shower," but Poldie did not know
what that meant. The women presented Poldie with various presents,
including baby clothes and cloth diapers. Poldie cried at their generosity;
she had never experienced friendship so tangibly and sincerely.

Two days after Alois returned from his university classes on April 15,
1957, he began his new job as a state meat inspector. He was responsible
for the fourteen hundred chickens per hour that were transported on
a moving chain line at the processing plant. His duties involved examining each chicken and also inspecting the livers. Alois calculated the
amount of time he was allowed for each chicken; it was about three
seconds—2.57 seconds, to be exact. In those few seconds, Alois had to
decide if each chicken was healthy enough for human consumption. If
he saw any that did not qualify as food grade, he pressed a stop button
on the wall so he could remove the unfit ones from the conveyor. At
the end of the line, each chicken was packaged and stamped with the
words "Inspected for wholesomeness by the Michigan State inspector."

Alois took great pleasure in his promotion to meat inspector and
particularly the pay increase that came with it. In the evenings, he

continued to go to the chicken farms and deliver poultry to the plant. He was still paid only $1 per hour for his evening employment.

A few days later, very early in the morning, Poldie went into labor. A family from church allowed Jana, four, and Marie, two, to stay with them while Alois took Poldie to the Zeeland hospital on Good Friday, April 19, 1957. Dr. Eiff was on call and ready to bring this new little one into the world. This was the first time Poldie delivered a baby in a hospital. Men were not allowed to be present during the baby's birth, so Alois took a seat in the waiting room, anticipating good news. He was excited to hold his newborn baby, but not until he or she was already bathed and swaddled up. Alois loved to touch the baby's delicate, soft skin and study every inch of its tiny features.

In no time at all, Poldie gave birth to a healthy baby girl at 6:35 a.m. Alois was overjoyed when they delivered the news. Poldie and Alois agreed to name their daughter Debra Elizabeth. The Hufs did not have any health insurance, so Poldie only stayed in the hospital for two days, which was unheard of at the time. Usually, new mothers spent five to seven days in bed at the hospital. On Easter Sunday morning, Alois checked Poldie out of the hospital with a promise to pay the $150 charge on a payment plan. He and Poldie departed immediately to retrieve Janie and Mary. Poldie was homesick for her girls. They hugged and kissed when greeting. Alois and Poldie were amazed at how quickly their daughters picked up English when they talked with their new friends.

After the baby's birth, Alois worked as many hours as possible to pay the hospital bill. On the evening of Easter Sunday, after making sure all his girls were home and secure, he was back out to get a load of poultry. Poldie, only two days into her recovery from birthing her third child, did not have much time to rest either. She had a full schedule of childcare and housework.

By mid-May, the family had settled into a new routine with baby Debra. When the sun would come out, Poldie would bathe the baby, dress her, and put her in the pretty German carriage. She set the carriage outside by the window, as was the custom in Europe. Occasionally, Poldie went out to check on the baby while the infant was sleeping and breathing fresh air. Once, when Poldie went outside, she saw something slithering in the bush next to the carriage. It was a snake!

Poldie quickly pushed the carriage inside and ran next door to their elderly neighbors. She told the man, "There is a big snake out there in the bushes."

"It can't be poisonous," he said. "We don't have poisonous snakes here in Michigan." But he obliged Poldie and grabbed a shovel. The snake went to another bush, and the man took care of it for good. Poldie was confident the snake would bite her baby. She never left a child alone in a carriage again.

When Debra was four months old, Poldie began experiencing that familiar morning sickness again. At first, she doubted it would be another pregnancy. Soon, Poldie realized she was indeed pregnant again! At twenty-four, she would be the mother of four children.

Alois was upbeat about the news. He always envisioned having a large family, but Poldie asked, "What are we going to do? There are only two small bedrooms in this house." Poldie had grown accustomed to the American way of multiple rooms for a family, and she saw their two-bedroom house, for the first time, as small.

Alois said, "By the Lord's help, we might be able to move to a small farm by the time the baby arrives in May."

At this time, the Hufs had six sows with piglets. Each week, Poldie and the three girls picked up three or four barrels of old bread from the bakery. The processing plant also ran a feed mill. The manager called Alois any time there was a feed spill. Between the damaged hatchery eggs and the leftover feed, Alois took home a haul for his animals. Every animal he was raising would help him accumulate a down payment on a larger home, he reasoned.

Mrs. Beld, a neighbor who lived two miles away, befriended Poldie and came to visit often. The Beld family had children who were close in age to the Huf children. Mrs. Beld was a gracious person and at just the right time would bring over hand-me-down clothes for the Huf girls. Grateful for every blessing, Poldie still struggled through periods of loneliness and depression and suffered from pounding headaches. Her mother, Anna, also experienced horrible migraines, and Poldie remembered how they imperiled her at times. When the migraines were at their worst, Poldie wept and longed for her mother the most. She had little time to feel homesick for Germany, and the friendships made her feel more at home.

True to her word to be a good neighbor, Mrs. Jones often visited when she had free time from the onion farm. Mr. Jones came along as well but to teach Poldie and Alois how to study the Bible. He even showed them places where the Old Testament foretold of things that happened during the New Testament period. Alois and Poldie began to memorize verses of the Bible.

The Hufs maintained contact with the Lukeshes in Germany. It brought Mr. and Mrs. Lukesh great pleasure to know the Hufs were doing so well. To help develop Alois's English, Mr. Lukesh suggested Alois write letters in English. Three weeks later, Alois received a reply, along with a corrected version of his English letter.

Mr. Lukesh proposed Alois, Poldie, and the children make a tape recording for the Kellners. The Huf family recorded an update of their lives in America and shared how they were growing with the Lord and sent it to the Lukeshes. Mr. Lukesh took the tape to Poldie's family in Altach. When Opa Kellner heard everyone's voices, he began crying. The Hufs started a tradition of sending voice tapes. It was more fulfilling and more natural than writing in their broken English.

Alois continued to correspond with his family in Czechoslovakia as well. It took a long time for mail to travel to Czechoslovakia and then back to the United States.

Since Alois was busy at work, Poldie took more of the responsibility with the chickens and pigs. When a sow delivered, Alois created his own technique. He placed a heat bulb in the middle of a fifty-five-gallon barrel and positioned it in the coop, separate from the sow. When the sow delivered, Poldie took each piglet away and placed it under the heat bulbs. Once they were dry, the piglets could run and move freely, and the sow would not be able to lie on her offspring and accidentally kill them.

One of the sows delivered twelve piglets, and one of the twelve was very tiny. Each time the piglet tried to get a drink, the other piglets pushed it away. Alois put the piglet in a box in the garage, and the family gave the piglet a baby bottle. They named her Luchala. The piglet became very attached to all of them; she followed Poldie to the mailbox each day and played with the girls like a puppy.

After ten weeks, Alois decided the piglet was ready to go back into the coop. Later, he looked all over and could not find the little animal. Finally, he caught sight of a trampled young pig in the mud. Most likely, the other pigs did not accept it back. Alois reached down and pulled the lifeless little one from the muck. He held the piglet in his arms and walked to an area of their property where he could dig a small grave to bury it. Poldie, Janie, and Mary ran outside to learn of the loss of their pet piglet. The girls cried and participated in the brief funeral for little Luchala.

In the fall of 1957, it was nearing turkey slaughter season for the upcoming Thanksgiving holiday. In the mornings, the plant typically slaughtered chickens and moved on to turkeys later in the day. The turkey line did not move quite as fast as the chicken line, but still, the plant slaughtered about four hundred turkeys per hour. Alois performed two inspections on each specimen. The first was the antemortem inspection, which was to visually look over the live poultry that came from the plants. The second was the line inspection of the carcasses.

In late October, the plant brought in a load of turkeys. The procedure was for management to notify Alois of the new load, but this time, for some reason, Alois was never alerted. The first time Alois saw the turkeys from the load was as carcasses on the line hooks. In all the time Alois had been doing his job, nothing had shocked him as much as what he saw that day. The dressed bodies did not look like turkeys at all but lean birds with bones and skin. Even the color of the skin was bluish and sickly.

It was not just a few of them either; every bird that came down the line was like that. The carcasses looked sick and unfit for human consumption. Alois was a stickler about the rules and did what he was taught to do in the state inspection school. He pushed the button to stop the line.

The manager of the processing plant came running to Alois. It was very unusual to stop the production line for any reason. "What seems to be the problem?" the manager asked.

"Where did these turkeys come from?" Alois asked. "And why was I not notified before they started the slaughter?"

The plant manager said that a turkey farmer brought the load of turkeys and that a partial shipment was still outside. Alois went out to the loading dock to examine the remaining amount. Every single turkey looked ill and skinny.

Alois went back inside and found the manager. "If you run these turkeys, I will have to reject every single one of them on the other end," he said matter-of-factly.

The manager called the main office and factory owner. Within ten minutes, the owner was on-site. He viewed Alois's behavior as a challenge and started a heated exchange. It was evident that the owner cared little about the unhealthy turkeys and was more concerned with the hundred or so workers who were now standing idle while earning an hourly wage. "Start the line up again and run these turkeys through," he ordered.

Alois resisted. "I can't do that, sir," he said. "I am responsible to the State of Michigan, and that is who we will call to make the decision." Alois proceeded to call the oversight office of the state inspectors. Alois explained that there was a whole load of sick-looking turkeys and that almost one hundred workers were idle. The official on the other end said someone would be there in two hours. The owner was fuming and especially irritated that all his workers would be getting paid for those two hours. He was cross and cold to Alois, but Alois knew he was doing the right thing.

Two hours later, a gentleman from the state office came. It was Dr. Weisner himself, one of the professors Alois met at the school. He introduced himself to the owner, greeted Alois, and immediately began inspecting the turkeys on the line. He turned to Alois. "They don't look even passable, do they?" he observed.

Alois then showed him the livers hanging out from the carcasses. They were discolored white instead of dark red and were full of tumors. The owner was silent as he observed the turkeys and the conversation.

The three of them walked back to the plant office. After they sat down, Dr. Weisner said to the owner, "You are correct to slaughter these turkeys, and Alois is also correct when he refuses to pass them as inspected for wholesomeness."

Alois could hardly believe what he heard after the painstaking training he had received at the school. "How could we both be right?" Alois asked him. "At school, you showed pictures of what kind of poultry carcasses have to be rejected. I think those turkeys today looked worse than the bad examples in the pictures!"

Dr. Weisner replied evenly, "Alois, the first thing you have to do when you have completed the inspection course is to forget half of the things we taught you and use your common sense."

Alois was stunned. "Professor, I don't believe I'm hearing you say this. Would you buy one of these turkeys in the store for you and your family to eat?" he asked.

"No, I would not," the man replied.

Then Alois turned to the owner. "How about you? Would you eat those turkeys?" he asked.

"No, I would not," the owner said. "And I don't have to."

Alois addressed both of them with a furrowed brow: "If I have to use common sense, then my common sense tells me that I should quit this inspection job as of now. I was pleased to be the meat inspector as long as I will not be restricted from doing my job honestly. But you are asking me to close my eyes as some of the sick poultry passes by me on the line. The unfit meat would carry the stamp 'Inspected for wholesomeness by the Michigan State inspector.' I could not do that with a clear conscience knowing that someone would see these unhealthy turkeys in the store and say, 'What inspector would let something like this pass through?' No, gentlemen, I will not go on like that. I would sooner quit."

The owner of the processing plant said, "You can't quit, and we don't want you to quit. It took lots of planning and expense to put you through school, and we are proud to have a state inspector in our plant. This, by itself, has improved sales considerably. No, you do not want to quit."

Dr. Weisner also encouraged Alois to stay, and he promised to find a solution that would satisfy everyone. The owner and Dr. Weisner talked between themselves and concluded that they would process the load of turkeys, but they would not put the inspection stamp on those. They would pack this load separately and mark the meat as "Grade C." They also assured Alois that he would not be hindered from doing his job correctly as he had been instructed in school.

Although Alois preferred they did not process the turkeys at all, he was satisfied with the compromise and felt thankful he did not have to claim the meat had passed inspection. He did not understand why, in a land of plenty, people were willing to cut corners, but he was glad, for now, that he could continue doing his job.

◆

By the spring of 1958, Poldie was preparing for the birth of their fourth child. Sunday, May 11 was Mother's Day. Poldie was in awe mothering three—soon to be four—children. She was only five days away from turning twenty-four years old and about to deliver another baby. On May 20, Poldie ushered in the day with labor pains, so the Hufs prepared to find caretakers for their three girls. They took Jana and Mary to stay with friends Ike and Lavon and arranged for Debra to stay with a woman they knew from church named Marvina. Poldie and Alois were grateful for these precious friends who cared for them like family. Although they missed their own family—especially Poldie—these new friends had become like family to them.

Dr. Hager was on call at the Zeeland hospital, and later that day, a son was born. Alois, as was customary, waited in the waiting area until he summoned back to the hospital room. Poldie, elated, was so thankful to finally have her little boy. Both Poldie and Alois were so happy to have a son after three girls. Poldie hoped he would look just like Alois.

"I like the name 'David' for him," Poldie said.

"Oh, I was thinking of 'Josef,' after my father," Alois said. "But if you want to name him 'David,' I am okay with that." He squeezed Poldie's hands and kissed her forehead.

After holding the baby for a while, Alois said good-bye and went home. The neighbors were outside and asked him about the baby.

"We had a boy!" Alois told them.

"Oh, really? What is his name?" they asked.

"David," Alois said. The neighbors were pleased because they also had a son named David.

The next day after work, Alois visited Poldie and his son at the hospital. When he arrived, Poldie showed him the birth certificate. Alois read it and then reread it. It said, "Josef Alois." "What happened?" Alois asked. "I thought we agreed on 'David'?"

"Well, you seemed disappointed when you left, so I told the hospital his name is Joseph," Poldie said.

Alois smiled. "I already told our neighbors that our son's name is David, but I am glad you decided on Josef," he said. "How are you and the baby doing?"

Poldie said, "I'm most homesick for the other children."

"Well, get strong in a hurry so you can bring our son home," Alois said. "Here, I brought you something that will make you healthy." Alois proceeded to open a plastic bread bag and pull out two apples.

Poldie chuckled at the gift. "You should have brought me some flowers," she suggested.

Alois did not know much about bringing flowers. "Back home, the family always brought apples or some fruit," he explained, realizing he was not very romantic. He did not have much time or money for picking flowers, he thought.

Poldie left the hospital in about four days. When they went to Marvina's house to pick up thirteen-month-old Debra, she held on to her father and mother and wept bitterly. This made Poldie cry too. She stroked Debra and said how much she missed her little girl. Marvina told them Debra had continuously cried. Marvina offered to keep the child longer while Poldie recovered, but Poldie took Debra home. The little girl pointed to her little brother and said, "Baby, baby." The Hufs affectionately called their new son Joey. Jana and Marie stayed with friends for several more days before the family was together again.

In the summer of 1958, the processing plant began to slow down. The company had a hard time selling dressed chickens. Most of the workers were laid off, which no one anticipated. Alois was called to work two to three days per week. The struggling company needed a meat inspector and did not want to lose his services.

Alois still intended to buy a farm. He knew of a teacher who owned an eighty-acre farm a half mile down from their house at 6061 Port Sheldon Drive, Hudsonville. The farmhouse was empty, and the teacher and his family lived nearby. Alois visited one day and asked him if he would be interested in selling. The man replied that he was not interested in selling all the land; he had planted fifty-five acres with Christmas trees. The government paid him a set amount per acre if he planted those trees—referred to as "soil bank." He did indicate he was willing to sell the farm, which included a large, old barn with a silo; a couple of small sheds; a house; and twenty-five acres of land.

Alois thanked him and inquired if he could bring Poldie back to view the property and farmhouse. Alois and Poldie returned and looked it over. The house was larger than where they currently lived, but it was old and would need substantial work. The kitchen had only a hand pump in the middle of the sink and no running water. Poldie thought the house had great potential. For Alois, the barn held the most promise. He envisioned converting the space into a three-story barn to house his own chickens.

They returned to the owner, and Alois began to negotiate about the price. The owner said he would sell the twenty-five acres with all the farm buildings for $12,500 with $2,000 down. Alois thanked him and asked if he could have two weeks to think about it. The man agreed.

Alois had always made decisions quickly—leaving Czechoslovakia, marrying Poldie, coming to Hudsonville, and quitting his farmhand job. While those turned out for the best, he also nearly got into a mortgage on a house that wasn't a fit for the family. After offering so quickly on the first house in Holland and becoming more discerning since, Alois decided to wait and pray for a little while before making a big decision.

One day while Alois was feeding his pigs and chickens, he started calculating what he would get if he sold all the piglets and kept the sows. He and Poldie had been praying earnestly. The young couple did not think it would be easy to sell their house in a challenging market. They learned their neighbor's brother was about to be married and was looking for a place to rent. He offered to pay the Hufs $50 per month to rent their house, which is the amount they would need to keep making the bank payments on it.

Things seemed to be falling into place, so Alois revisited the teacher and told him they would like to proceed. So they put together a land contract and decided to close the deal in two weeks. Alois went to the livestock sale and sold the piglets; with the transaction, he was able to come up with the $2,000 down payment.

Before the family moved, Alois was glad his work schedule allowed him to do some repairs on the dwelling they just purchased. He took the hand pump out of the kitchen sink and installed a used water pump and motor. He also obtained a water heater and found a used kitchen sink with cold and hot water faucets. Then he turned his attention to the bathroom, which had a door with steps that led outside. The wooden steps had massive rot. Alois did not want that entrance, so he tore down the steps and sealed the door.

He looked over the first floor, which consisted of the kitchen, bathroom, living room, dining room, and one bedroom. From the dining room, stairs led to two more bedrooms and another room with shelves on the second floor. From that room, there was a door that opened to exterior stairs leading to the ground floor. In the past, the upper floor was a separate apartment, thus necessitating the private exterior entrance and exit. Those rickety stairs were also old and rotten. Alois tore that set of stairs down and also sealed the door.

Outside, Alois observed that much of the wooden siding was worn and rotten. Birds made cozy nests in the crevices. It was a big job, and Alois tried to figure out how he would fix it by himself. However, he knew the house needed repairs before the cold winter arrived.

The family moved into their new home. There were so many rooms, Poldie felt like she was in a mansion. The children loved the stairs, but Poldie had to watch their play. Outside, there was plenty of room for their animals, and Alois imagined again how much potential that old barn possessed.

Alois called a few companies specializing in exterior siding. One of the company representatives, John, came out. He agreed new siding was necessary and said insulated siding would keep the house warm. He told Alois that if he was given the job, the Hufs could pay him over time. Alois and Poldie agreed at once.

John started the job and did exceptional work. When he came to a window area, he noticed that his nails went through the casing much too easily. He tested the casing with a hammer swing, and the material crumbled. John approached Alois with the problem diplomatically but told him, "I really can't continue the job unless we do something about the windows."

Alois said, "I don't know what to do. I didn't expect this. How much more would this cost?"

"Well, if this were my house," John began, "here is what I would do: there are four windows in the living room. There are two on the east wall and two on the south wall. I would close the two east windows, fill the hole with some plywood, and fasten the siding over the windows. This would keep the house warmer. On the south wall, I would take both of the windows out and place a large picture window in the middle of the wall."

As Alois deliberated, John continued: "I have one more suggestion for you. The little house you lived in before—do you still own it?"

"Yes," Alois said. "We could not sell it, so we rented it out."

John said, "I believe there is enough property next to the house—large enough for a lot that I could build a house on. If you give me the lot, I would complete the job on your house, including the large picture window, for no charge. This would be an even swap. You would owe me nothing."

Alois liked the idea and excused himself to explain the offer to Poldie. She loved the sound of a large picture window opening up the view and agreed to it. Alois returned to John and said, "We will take you up on the deal."

That evening, Poldie and Alois thanked God for being so kind to them. He had provided much more for them than they had expected. They would never have thought of selling part of the lot next to their former home. It made sense now why it had not been a good time to sell the house. There had only been one bad offer—they had been offered a price a lot lower than what they were asking—but now it all felt right. The Hufs wondered at the wisdom of God in creatively providing.

The next day, John came with a sizable picture window. It was lovely, and the family liked it right away. That evening, Alois reviewed John's work. The structure nearly looked like a new home with the new siding and sparkling windows. As Alois was picking up a few scraps of wood that had fallen, a neighbor came over. He strolled up and scrutinized the house and Alois.

"I don't know how foreigners like you can afford to do this," he said. "Come from the old country, and right on out, install a picture window!" he said, gesturing at the two-story home.

Alois could hear the jealousy in his voice. He wanted to tell the neighbor that there was enough for everyone to achieve; they just had to work hard as he had. "The Lord provides" is all Alois said.

From that time on, Alois was aware that not all his neighbors were happy for him. Some even viewed his success as a threat to their own. Alois struggled with their rejections. His feelings were certainly hurt, since he only wanted their friendship.

Hudsonville Baptist Church started a sister church in the nearby city of Jenison at an old vacant schoolhouse. They called it Baldwin Heights Baptist Church. The new gathering numbered only a few people. One of the members asked Alois and Poldie to come to a church meeting and share about their experiences in Europe. They also understood that Alois enjoyed playing his trumpet, so they encouraged him to bring it along. After Alois played a tune for them, he and Poldie sang a few songs in

German, which delighted the listeners. One of their favorites was "Rock of Ages," which they learned from the Lukeshes and sang in German.

"You two harmonize so well," the friends commented. "You should be singing duets in churches! People would enjoy it." It did not take long for word to spread that the European couple sang and harmonized beautifully together. So not long after, Hudsonville Baptist Church asked if the couple would agree to sing for the young people that Sunday at church. The teenagers would meet in the church's basement during the Sunday school hour. That particular Sunday, Alois and Poldie stood before the group while someone held their little toddler, Joey, at the back of the room. Alois and Poldie selected the song "A Child of the King," written by Harriet E. Buell in 1877. The companion scripture text from the Bible is Roman 8:16–17. As the Hufs began to sing "My Father is rich in houses and lands, He holdeth the wealth of the world in His hands . . ." Alois put his trembling arm around Poldie's waist to calm himself. Poldie was always such a tower of strength in Alois's view, and she did not disappoint whenever they sang together. She encouraged Alois in all his dreams and plans, and although frightened herself most times, she agreed to be a team player when asked to participate in activities or ministry. As the first verse came forth from their lips in their tender, broken English, which seemed to astonish and engage the people, Alois felt a tight tugging at his leg. While continuing to sing, he looked down and found little Joey forcefully holding on to his leg. Without missing a line in the lyric, Alois leaned down to pick little Joey up and held him while he and Poldie finished the song. Alois and Poldie never realized how well they harmonized together before, but they received such fulfillment while doing it. The couple taught young Jana and Marie to harmonize along with them, and the two children often joined them when they sang in various churches around Michigan. The couple was grateful to God for allowing them to find their voice. With several small children, Alois and Poldie had little spare time, but they took any available opportunity to sing on Sunday nights. They generally included short words of testimony before they sang, and it felt surreal to Poldie that she was the one sharing about her life experiences. Alois helped her tell her story. People were fascinated by them and loved to hear how they became Christians in Germany. Singing for an audience reminded Alois a little of playing his trumpet as a youth. Hudsonville felt more like home than ever. Soon, Al and Poldie received invitations to sing in other churches in the area; people loved to hear them speak and harmonize.

◆

As 1958 drew to a close and 1959 began, Alois was being called in to work less and less. With the recent move to the farm property and all the renovations needing to be done, plus the fact that Poldie confessed to Alois that she was pregnant with their fifth child, Alois felt the pressure of providing for his family. The poultry processing plant was not as successful as it had been in times past. Alois learned that the plant would be required to change from a state meat inspector to a federal government inspector. Because he was not yet a US citizen, Alois was not allowed to be a federal government employee. The plant owner told him that losing his job was only a matter of time. He assured Alois that the plant would still need him in other places, but Alois knew it would not be enough hours or pay to support his family, especially with another baby on the way.

During the day when he had the time, Alois began looking for work all over the Holland and Grand Rapids area. Jobs were scarce, and Alois was unsuccessful at finding anything. The savings he and Poldie had accumulated began to disappear. One night as Alois lay in bed, he remembered walking outside of the camp in Germany as a young man, scavenging produce from the yard next door. He shuddered at the thought of being destitute again. He prayed every day for God to show him what to do.

Poldie trusted Alois, but she trusted God more. In her prayers, she interceded and asked for God's guidance. One day, Poldie expressed her concern. "What are we going to do?" she asked. "We have enough food for a couple of days, but that's it."

Alois did not know what to say. He learned of an employment office in Holland, so he drove there one day looking as sharp and fit for work as possible. When it came time for him to talk with an attendant, he said that he desperately needed a job and would be willing to take any reasonable responsibility he could get. Alois explained he had a wife and four children, with another on the way. "We only have food at home for a couple of days," he confessed.

The employment clerk asked him, "Didn't you work before?"

"Yes," he said. "I worked at the poultry processing plant in Zeeland."

"Are you drawing unemployment compensation?" the clerk asked. "What about food from the welfare office? Did you get any?"

"No," Alois said. "No one told me about this. Besides, I don't want to be a burden on anyone."

The clerk nodded. He helped Alois fill out the necessary papers for unemployment. He then told Alois that he was eligible to receive $14 per week for twenty-six weeks.

Alois thanked him. He came home and rejoiced with Poldie that they would be receiving temporary income from the government. This small amount would keep them afloat until an opportunity arose.

Each day, Alois looked for work. When companies were not hiring, he turned to ask people in the area if they needed help with anything. He landed a few odd jobs, including picking strawberries for a farmer. Sometimes he thought of the disingenuous words the neighbor had spoken to him. If only the man knew how difficult times were for them, he would not be duplicitous anymore.

◆

CHAPTER SIXTEEN

MAKING A WAY THROUGH HARDSHIPS

In the summer of 1959, with a meager but steady income of only $14 per week, Alois kept envisioning ideas of what the barn on the property could mean for their future. He hoped to have the resources to patch up the outside of the barn, extend the second floor, and perhaps put in a third floor to raise chickens. That might be the way out of his financial predicament. With what little he had, Alois began working on the project. He shared the idea with his friend Ike from church, which was significant because Ike's brother owned a sawmill. He encouraged Alois to go to the mill and explained that his brother, Joe, would be happy to supply the lumber that Alois needed.

Alois met with Joe at the mill and explained what he had in mind. "If you are willing to sell me the lumber on credit, I promise to pay it off in six months," he said.

Joe agreed and delivered the first load of beams the following week. He took measurements for the length of the massive support beams that Alois needed and promised to bring them in a few days. Alois agreed to bolt the smaller beams in place first.

When Joe and one of his helpers brought the second load of lumber, two of the beams were extremely heavy. Alois asked, "Since there are only two of us—my wife and I—who are reconstructing the barn, it will be impossible for us to carry and install these heavy beams. Joe, would you and your associate help me carry the beams to the barn and place them on the supports that I have already nailed in place? I have $5 left and would give you that money for helping me."

Without hesitation, Joe and his helper agreed. In about ten minutes, with the work of three men, the beams were in place. Alois surveyed the job and felt so pleased. "You can't imagine how much I appreciate it," Alois said. "I don't know what I would have done." Alois pulled out the $5, but Joe declined to accept it.

With teary eyes, Joe confessed, "Alois, I feel like I need to tell you what some of the people in your neighborhood think of you. Instead of wanting to help you, one neighbor learned of the barn renovation, and he came and strongly discouraged me not to give you any credit."

Alois was saddened but not shocked. He was confused at his neighbors' cruelty. "Joe, I'll never forget your help and kindness," Alois said. "May the Lord bless you for all your help."

That evening, Alois and Poldie discussed the sad matter with the neighbors' insolence and took it to God in prayer. The neighbor was not a Christian and needed Jesus, no doubt. It was difficult for them to believe there were people that resentful in Hudsonville. They determined to make their own way and provide for their family, no matter what their neighbors said.

In July of 1959, Alois was surprised to receive a call from the processing plant. The company management needed Alois to come back to work but indicated it would only be a temporary job. Alois accepted eagerly. They guaranteed he would receive at least forty hours per week plus health insurance. It was great news for his growing family, and Alois was overjoyed at his fortune. The insurance came just in time. Poldie was eight months pregnant and still spending long hours outside beneath a large maple tree wiring chicken nests together for hatching.

On Wednesday, August 26, 1959, Alois and Poldie woke to record-breaking heat in the Great Lakes area. The weather reports called for highs in the nineties with a humidity factor raising the heat even more. Alois headed to work, and Poldie, pregnant and with four children huddling around her, managed the household and farm in his absence.

The day had barely begun when Poldie felt the beginnings of familiar pains in her tightening belly. The scorching heat and un-air-conditioned house made it almost unbearable. Alois would not be home from his job that day until late, so Poldie began making plans. She called her neighbor and informed her that her contractions had begun and that she was not certain what time Alois would be home. Poldie confirmed that Alois's employer sent him to Detroit, a two-and-a-half-hour drive, to deliver frozen dressed chickens to various stores. With her pains intensifying, Poldie reached out to Jackie, her good friend from church, and asked if she would pick her up and take her to the hospital. Jackie dropped everything and made it to the farm in a flash. Poldie called another family, the Vrugginks, who lived just down the street and with whom they shared a sweet friendship, and asked if their daughter Helen could come to stay with the children. Jackie hurried to the hospital and dropped Poldie off. The attendants checked her in, and the nurses made arrangements to get her settled in a room and then called Dr. Ralph Hager and alerted him that the birth would be imminent.

Alone and afraid for her children, Poldie lay in bed and noticed her contractions stopped. She waited for them to begin again, but nothing happened. Poldie called the nurse to her room and pleaded to be discharged for the sake of her children at home. The doctor strongly discouraged her from leaving, but her mother's heart won out. She signed discharge forms releasing the hospital from any responsibility and called Jackie to come and pick her up. Jackie agreed and arrived in short order. As the car pulled over the railroad tracks at Seventy-Second Street and M-21 just a few miles away, Poldie's contractions started again, but it didn't matter to Poldie; she wanted to be home with her children.

Upon arriving back at the farm, Poldie thanked Jackie for her help and sent Helen on her way. Poldie prayed Alois would make it home soon and then gathered the children into the car and drove to the market down the street to shop for some groceries for Alois and the kids. While at the store, Poldie's pains rapidly intensified. As each new contraction ripped through her midsection, she begged God to have mercy. She grabbed hold of the metal rack that held the grocery items neatly in place in the isles. Panting through the contractions while holding her legs tightly together, Poldie tried not to draw attention to herself. She continued gathering as many items as she could while rounding up her four little ones and then proceeded to the cashier. The storeowner, Don, was checking customers out and could immediately sense Poldie was in labor. "Don, may I come back later and pay you? I have to go. I'm in labor, and I feel like the baby is coming," Poldie pleaded.

Don said, "Oh my goodness, Poldie. Are you certain you will make it home safely?" He graciously consented to add the amount to the Hufs' account and helped rush Poldie out the door.

Upon arriving home, Poldie sequestered the children in the house and put away the few grocery items while pausing to struggle and breathe through the escalating pains. It was nearing evening when Alois finally arrived home. Poldie announced, "Alois, I'm having this baby now. Take me to the hospital!" Excited but composed, Alois told Poldie he had to take a shower first. She frantically ordered Alois to get in the car and take her or she would call their neighbor, Mr. Vruggink, to take her instead. Alois hurried to drop Poldie at the hospital just in time. He returned home to watch the children while Poldie walked the long hall to readmit herself. All at once, Poldie's water broke, and a mixture of fluid and blood drained to the floor. The nursing staff panicked and raced with a wheelchair to greet Poldie, rushing her into the delivery room. In a matter of minutes, the clock struck 8:21 p.m., and Dr. Hagar announced that Poldie delivered a healthy baby girl who weighed seven pounds and one ounce and was nineteen inches long. By the time Alois arrived back home, the telephone rang, and the nurse revealed that he was a father to another baby girl. Alois and Poldie were both grateful for another healthy and beautiful baby girl. The day proved to be a harrowing one, but it had a happy ending. Poldie hugged her little newborn to her breast and thanked God for the mercy he showed her this day.

The next day, Alois loaded the four children in the station wagon and set out to the hospital to see their new addition. Since children were not allowed in the hospital, Alois found Poldie's first-floor room and gathered the children around her window. He lifted the children to have a clear view of their mother and new baby sister. As the little ones peered into the window, they cupped their hands around their eyes to prevent the glare of the sunny day from obstructing their vision. Poldie asked Alois if it would be agreeable to name the baby Cristie Jo, after Jackie's toddler daughter. Alois was okay with the name and eager for Poldie to recover so she could come home.

With Alois working fixed hours during the five days Poldie spent in the hospital, he asked their good friend Pearl Errinson to watch the children during the daytime. Joey was a lazy toddler and not walking yet, so Pearl set out to teach him. When Poldie arrived home with the new baby days later, Joey headed straight for his mother, and to Poldie's delight, he was walking on his own. Once Joey saw the baby, he tried to pronounce her name, but all that he could say was "Teetee." From that point on, the newborn was nicknamed "Teetee."

For the next few months, Alois stayed busy in the processing plant. Additionally, his employer paid him six cents per mile for driving a truck to neighboring states around the Michigan area. They gave him a daily per diem of $1.50 for meals. Alois was gone from the family for large amounts of time and missed them dearly. While on several deliveries, he decided to save his daily allowance for food and instead take bread from home to eat; he wanted to purchase a special dress for Poldie. When he had saved enough, he marched into a Robert Hall department store while delivering in Ohio and asked the clerk for a dress for his wife. The clerk asked what size he was looking to purchase. Alois was naïve and did not have a clue what size Poldie was. The clerk encouraged him to look around the store and find a woman who looked about Poldie's size. Soon, a woman about Poldie's petite size walked by, and Alois said, "That's it!" He picked out the perfect dress and took it home to Poldie. She was genuinely surprised and thanked Alois for his love and thoughtfulness.

As the business wound down, Alois was once again in the employment office. This time, he could only draw about eight weeks of unemployment compensation. Alois took the opportunity to work odd jobs, such as cleaning up barns, as he was needed.

As 1960 launched, Alois became discouraged. In his prayers, he reminded God of the promises in the Bible for Him to provide. The family had never run out of food, but things looked bleak. Alois was afraid. Adding to his stress, Cristie Jo became incredibly ill at six months old. She struggled to breathe, hacking and coughing uncontrollably. When Poldie took her to the doctor, the physician told Poldie the baby needed hospitalization. Poldie arrived home to update Alois with the upsetting news. Alois had workers helping him at the rear of the property and could not shake loose to help Poldie. Frustrated at his current struggle and having to manage the men, Alois asked Poldie to make sandwiches for the crew before bringing the baby to the hospital. Poldie was appalled at his unreasonable request but acquiesced and hurried to focus on her little one. Poldie laid her baby across the front seat and wept while driving her darling to the hospital. Cristie Jo was admitted and immediately put under an oxygen tent in the Zeeland hospital, where she stayed for ten days healing. On the drive back home, Poldie had flashbacks of when their eldest daughter, Jana, had also been admitted to the hospital for a similar illness. Poldie wept bitterly and wondered how she could make it through another heartbreaking ordeal—leaving her baby behind in a hospital. She cried out to God and asked for him to heal her precious little Cristie Jo.

At the end of Cristie Jo's stay, a hospital administrator called Alois and Poldie into his office. He wanted to know who would pay for the hospital bill before the baby was released. Alois told him they could not pay since he was unemployed. The administrator sent them to the welfare office in Holland with the bill. The Hufs went, and by some miracle, the welfare office called the hospital and said they would pay the bill. The hospital then released Cristie Jo into the care of her grateful parents. The ride home was a somber one. Alois and Poldie were thankful to have their little one back in their arms, but the reality of their dire financial situation was stealing away some of their joy.

Alois looked for work with a new desperation. He especially hated asking people whom he had already asked. But he didn't have a choice. If there was some chance they would say yes this time, it would be worth it.

One day, a representative of the telephone company stopped by. Without a word, he clipped the telephone line. Alois was embarrassed; he could not pay the monthly fee of $2.50.

Alois stood in his yard and prayed to heaven: "Have You forgotten me, God? And have You forgotten my poor wife and our precious five children?" Alois remembered Psalm 43:5: "Why, my soul, are you downcast? Why are you disquieted within me? Put your hope in God, for I will yet praise him, my Savior and my God" (NIV).

Somehow, Alois and Poldie managed to scrape together enough money to get the phone lines reconnected. It was a must in case employers phoned for Alois to come in for work.

Strawberry season came, and the farmer whom Alois had previously helped, Mr. Novak, asked Alois to pick strawberries again. Alois was thrilled to have the work. He had applied for a job at Reynolds Metal Company and was hoping he would be hired. At Reynolds, they guaranteed at least $2.50 per hour. Harvesting the strawberries outside in the dismal and damp conditions, Alois caught a significant cold. He continued picking for long hours as his cough worsened in the plummeting weather. Alois petitioned God to continue helping him persevere.

To Alois's delight, Reynolds asked him to come in for an interview and medical exam. Alois reported on a Tuesday. He explained he had a cough but was well otherwise. Alois was relieved when he was hired and told to report for work for the night shift starting the following Sunday at 11:00 p.m.

The timing of the new job was perfect, Alois concluded. He would have a few days to recover from the cough. On Thursday, however, the owner of a repair shop, whom Alois knew from church, called and asked if he wanted to work for half a day. Alois was not feeling well, but his family needed the money badly.

When he arrived, the shop owner told Alois he needed him to take a bulldozer apart. To do so, Alois had to lie on the rain-soaked ground. The job took much longer than anticipated. Alois worked all that day and part of the next day. By Friday evening, the cough and cold intensified, and Alois felt hot with a fever.

By Sunday morning, Alois huddled in the warm bed and hoped the fever would subside and he would feel better by his 11:00 p.m. shift. But by 5:00 p.m., he was burning and had a sharp pain under his ribs. Poldie called the family doctor, Dr. Hagar, at his home and explained Alois's symptoms. He asked Poldie to bring Alois directly to the hospital in Zeeland and that he would meet them there. Poldie assisted Alois into the car. He was weak and felt depleted of any energy. Every breath brought piercing pain beneath his ribs.

Once at the hospital, the doctor ordered an X-ray. After some time, he told Poldie and Alois that it was pneumonia and pleurisy. Poldie was even more devastated than Alois. Her husband finally found a job, and now he was in the hospital with no insurance and no money.

As Alois was admitted and placed in a hospital room, he spoke clear directions to Poldie: "I need you to drive first thing on Monday morning to Reynolds in Grand Rapids. Tell them what happened and ask them to please give me the job as soon as I get better."

Poldie agreed. There was very little food at home. She was concerned about Alois and also worried about the children.

Poldie prepared to leave early Monday morning to make it to Reynolds. She hoped to give a good impression. A friend watched the children, and in her quiet voice, Poldie rehearsed what she would say in English as she drove there.

The staff welcomed Poldie into the building, and she asked for the manager. She smiled a strained smile at him and explained that Alois was looking forward to working there. She informed him that Alois was very ill and asked for another chance when he got better. The manager made no promises but said he would keep Alois at the top of the list when he was able to work again.

As she drove home, Poldie burst into tears. She longed for the warm presence of her mother or father or the familiar words of a brother. At that moment, she felt very alone. Once again, she had to put her emotions aside and think of her husband and five small children.

Alois recovered slowly in the hospital, surprised at how poorly he felt. One day, John, a church board member, came to the hospital. After he sat with Alois and small-talked for a few minutes, he said, "Al, the church is going to take care of the hospital bill."

Alois turned and reflected on the words. "They are?"

Alois and Poldie had never asked for any gifts or remuneration when singing and sharing their stories. John explained that a few Christian friends from the churches where Alois and Poldie sang came by the house and gave Poldie several $20 bills when they learned Alois was sick. Both Poldie and Alois were astonished at their friends' kindness and how God was still providing.

After eight days, the hospital discharged Alois. He went home but felt very weak and frail. Just walking around the house made him nauseous at first. It took about six weeks before he felt well enough to get out again. On that day, he drove to Reynolds and told the manager he was ready to start work anytime they could use him. The manager was receptive but said there were no openings at the factory. He assured Alois he would call if anything opened up.

Back at home, a friend of Alois called and said there was a position available at the local furniture factory and that Alois could start the following day. Alois thanked him and began work there the next morning. The starting wage was only $1.50 per hour. While Alois was more than thankful for the job, he still hoped that Reynolds would hire him. There, he could make a dollar more per hour.

Having an income again seemed to settle the whole family. Poldie made a way to live on very little, but she was much more comfortable knowing her children would not have to go hungry. She gave thanks to God for all the help they had received along the way.

Two months into the furniture company position, Alois received a call from Reynolds. The manager told him he could start working there the following Sunday at 11:00 p.m. for the night shift. He added that since it was the night shift, the pay was bumped to $2.76 per hour. Alois accepted readily. When he got off the phone, he did the math. For forty hours of work, Alois could net $103. That was a good income. He would have medical insurance too. When he told Poldie, she touched his shoulder and said, "Wow, thank the Lord."

Alois began working there in October 1960, and the shift was from 11:00 p.m. to 7:00 a.m. The line workers handled extruded, hot metal with heavy gloves. They oversaw the cutting of fifteen- to twenty-foot sections of the aluminum and then lay it on cooling racks. Once cooled, the sheets were lifted by crane to the stacks to be inspected by engineers, who would approve them to be shipped out. It was a hot and dangerous environment with no room for error. Alois learned the job quickly and took to it.

During the day, he put the finishing touches on the barn. Joe, a friend of Alois who worked for a hatchery in Indiana, asked Alois if he would be interested in housing hens in his barn so they could produce for the hatchery. Alois said he would, and Joe said the hatchery would arrange for hens to be brought. They would even bring the feed and all the supplies that Alois would need to feed the chickens. Alois thought this was an excellent way to make some extra money and agreed. The hatchery began to work with Alois in early 1961.

Things were going well at Reynolds, but five weeks in, Alois's faith was tested. While Alois liked the job, workers there had complaints. The employees wanted higher wages and decided to go on strike with their union. Alois was in his six-week trial period and was not part of the union. The plant shut down temporarily, and during the strike, the union paid all workers $14 per week. Alois was worried that he would be let go since he was still on trial.

He and Poldie had also hoped this Christmas would be better for the children. There had not been much in the way of gifts for a long time. It saddened Alois and Poldie that they were not in a position to give their children the basic toys and other modest playthings for their fun and development. The Barbie doll was marketed by Mattel beginning in March 1959, and it would have been wonderful to gift their daughters with the famous toy. Any hope of unique presents would have to wait for the appointed time when extra money would no longer be an issue. Finally, after ten weeks, Reynolds called to tell Alois to report back to work.

Poldie continued to manage the farm and children. She was grateful to a dear church friend, Betty, who was an incredible seamstress. She sewed beautiful matching dresses with puffy short sleeves for the four girls. The light-blue fabric accented with a dark-blue velvet waistband and two matching vertical buttons at the collar was stunning. Each dress had a fringe of white lace sown inside that hung below the hemline to accent the garment. She crafted a matching pair of high-waisted pants for Joey accented with suspenders and a white shirt with a long tie. The children wore identical red-and-white saddle shoes. Poldie was so pleased to present her family at church with these special outfits.

◆

In March of 1961, a representative from the hatchery in Indiana called and informed Alois to prepare for the delivery of the hens for egg production. He said the company would send someone to inspect the barn. An inspector determined Alois needed to cover the outside of the barn with tarpaper because the cracks between the boards would not insulate adequately when the chilly wind blew. The man also confirmed that the barn needed windows for ventilation.

Alois secured an estimate for how much it would cost to insulate the barn. For such a large structure, the price was more than $2,000. The contractor required assurance that he would be paid as soon as the job was completed. Since Alois had been out of work so long and had only been paid strike wages for two months after he was hired, he had no choice but to apply for a loan.

In a Zeeland bank, Alois discussed his needs with a loan officer. The man was courteous and directed him to fill out the necessary paperwork. He told Alois that he would call him within a week.

After he worked the night shift, Alois busied himself preparing the barn. He needed about thirty windows in total, so he went to a scrap wrecking company and bought used windows for about $1 each. Alois ran on adrenaline and little sleep as he hurried to cut holes for the windows and to frame and install them.

A week after he applied for the loan, a bank clerk called and asked Alois to come in. At the bank, the loan officer asked Alois to sit in his office. He said, "Al, your loan has been approved, and whenever the contractor is finished with your barn, the $2,000 will be ready for him to pick up."

Alois was grateful. "I appreciate you so much for helping me secure the loan," he told the man.

"There is one more thing I would like to tell you, and believe me, I am telling you with a heavy heart," the banker said. "Some of the people in your neighborhood are expressing disdain for you. One of them even came to the bank and asked me not to loan you any money. I guess he heard about what you were doing." The man paused. "You seem like a very nice man. I probably should not have told you this because I knew it would upset you. But I think you deserve to know how a few of your neighbors feel about you. I would be careful about them."

Alois's joy about the loan approval sank. It felt like someone was stabbing him in the back. How did such talk circulate so quickly around town, and why did someone try to sabotage his efforts? Alois wanted to collect himself, but tears began to roll down his cheeks. He stood up, realizing his exhausted state made him more sensitive. "I can't find any words to respond," he said. "It does hurt deeply. I will treasure your friendship." Alois shook the man's hand and left.

In his car, Alois sat for a while before turning on the ignition. He let the tears roll freely. "Lord," he prayed, "this is the same man who went to the sawmill and asked them not to give me credit. Now he has gone to the bank to tell them not to loan me any money. What else is he saying about me? Lord, You know how much it hurts to be so opposed like this. The only thing I have done is tried to make my own way. Lord, You told us to forgive the ones who hurt us. Lord, help me to forgive him and to pray for him and the others who don't like me."

Alois remembered he had made plenty of friends in the area, but at the moment, it did not seem to ease his hurt. He wanted to defend himself, but he knew there was nothing he could do to change the man's mind about him. On his way home, he thought of how he felt when the ship had entered the harbor in New York. He felt relieved from any persecution as he had in Germany. The Statue of Liberty had welcomed him with her torch.

Why did some of these American people dislike foreigners so much, he wondered? He came to the United States of America lawfully, he reasoned. "It's the same hatred I endured for seven years in Germany," he confessed to God. "Don't these people see I am just trying to make a living and raise my family? My success—whatever I have—does not take away from their successes. But they seem to be afraid that I will do well or even better than them."

Alois waited in silence for a moment for an answer or an impression. A verse came to his mind: "And forgive us our debts, as we also have forgiven our debtors" (Matthew 6:12, NIV). What a perfect, fitting answer, he thought. "Lord, You have forgiven me of my sins," he said. "Yes, I can forgive those who dislike me too. Thank You, Lord, for loving me and forgiving me. I know that You will take care of us, and I thank You for it."

◆

The contractor was able to complete the insulation job in late March of 1961. Soon after, the hatchery approved the barn and filled its three floors with about three thousand hens and some roosters. Alois worked at Reynolds at night, and in the morning, he fed and cleaned up around the chickens. By late afternoon, he bathed and slept some before leaving for the night shift at 10:30 p.m.

About three weeks into the operation, the hens began laying eggs. The eggs could not be washed with water. It was necessary to keep the nests filled with dry wood shavings. Poldie helped with this; she and eight-year-old Jana carried the shavings in baskets and refilled the nests once per week.

The family members collected eggs with care. Each harvester rubbed the eggs with a dry towel and placed them in cases. The hatchery sent a truck twice per week to pick up the eggs. Alois and Poldie kept incredibly busy with the entire operation. It was not a substantial income they were making, but it was what Alois had envisioned doing for a long time. He could not turn the extra money down. Between the chicken operation and the Reynolds job, Alois felt confident he could finally provide well for his family for the first time in a long time. That made him conclude that the extra work was worth it.

Poldie became wholly independent since they moved to the United States, driving around and speaking English with the neighbors and at church. Alois chuckled to himself the first day he came home and saw her wearing pants. He did not like it at first; he had not seen women wearing pants for almost all his life. Soon, he got used to it and decided it was okay and practical for their lives.

◆

The hatchery business slowed down in February of 1962. The company notified Alois that the laying hens would stay in the barn for only the remainder of the year. Alois was disappointed. He had insulated the barn thinking it would house a long-term operation. He began thinking of ways to utilize the space.

With his friend Joe, he went to visit a farmer who kept chickens for egg production in wire cages. Alois liked what he saw there. It seemed to be a neat, well-run system. The farmer, Don, also told Alois that a farmer in nearby Middleville was quitting the chicken business and that he had used cages to sell. Alois felt like he was following the bread crumbs that led to what he should do next. He drove to see the man who was leaving the business. The man had cages in twenty-foot sections that were in excellent condition. He offered them for a reasonable price. Alois agreed to buy them by putting some money down and saying he would return to pick them up when the barn was cleaned out.

When it was finally time for the chickens to be cleared out and taken back by the hatchery, Alois worked double time cleaning up the barn. He borrowed a flatbed truck and went to pick up the used cages. Back home, Alois benefited from Poldie's help. She climbed to the second floor of the barn, and he handed her the end of a twenty-foot cage section. She pulled them up. Once in position, Alois fastened hooks to the ceiling to hold up the cages. Alois continued thinking of ways to make the production as neat and efficient as possible.

One Saturday evening, Poldie alerted Alois that she felt a lump in her breast. "It has been there for some time," she said. Alois encouraged her to observe it to see if it changed in size or form.

Not long after, Poldie's friend Edna came over. Poldie showed her the lump. "How long have you had this?" Edna asked with concern in her voice.

"For about six months," Poldie said.

"Poldie, if you don't go to the doctor tomorrow, I'm going to take you," Edna commanded. "Did you know that you could have cancer and it could be too late?"

Poldie took a deep breath. She felt afraid. The next day, she went to see Dr. Hagar. He checked the tumor and confirmed it had to be removed. He called the hospital and scheduled surgery the following week.

Poldie told Mrs. Jones, who said she would call the church and put the surgery in the bulletin announcement so that everyone at church could pray. Mrs. Jones prayed herself fervently, and as she played the church organ on Sunday, she glanced at the row of pews and spotted the Hufs with their five small children. She pleaded with God while playing for the tumor not to be cancerous.

Alois was moved to the day shift at Reynolds by this time, and he was worried about taking off work—especially since the family needed every penny they could earn. Several ladies from Poldie's Sunday school class offered to take Poldie to the hospital and stay there during the surgery. Two other ladies from church volunteered to stay with the children until Alois arrived home.

On the day of the operation, Mr. and Mrs. Jones came to the house. Mrs. Jones stayed with the children while Mr. Jones took Alois to Saint Mary's Hospital in Grand Rapids. Mr. Jones parked the car, and they began walking in together. Suddenly, a car came from behind them and struck Alois in the hip. Alois was pushed to the ground and felt severe pain in his hip. Mr. Jones ran into the emergency room, and the staff came out with a stretcher. The driver was careless and inattentive but thankfully stopped just in time.

As Alois lay on the stretcher, he regretted he had not seen the car in time. Now Poldie and he might both be in bad shape. He just wanted to be by his wife's side and hold her hand. After the doctor took Alois's X-rays, he determined there were no broken bones and that the bruising would heal soon. When Alois finally limped to see Poldie two hours after he arrived at the hospital, she was happy to see him and expressed thanks that he was okay. Poldie shared that as far as the doctors could see, the tumor was benign. They all rejoiced the surgery went well.

Poldie was to stay the night at the hospital, but there were no empty rooms. She, along with several patients, was placed in the hallway on rolling beds. Poldie wished she could get some rest in a private or semi-private room but was thankful that the procedure was behind her.

The next day, a chaplain from a local church made his visitation rounds in the hospital. He came by in the hallway where Poldie's bed rested near the wall. He asked her how she was doing and asked if she was a Christian. Poldie shared her testimony of coming to the saving knowledge of the Lord Jesus. The chaplain and Poldie formed a friendship, and when she was well, she and Alois were invited to his church to sing and give their testimonies.

Poldie's homecoming was a joyous day, especially for the children. Alois was relieved and thankful. He realized even more just how much she did for their family and in how many ways he needed her.

While life was more than busy at home, Poldie especially loved having children and wanted more. When she could not get pregnant, she visited a doctor. She underwent a procedure to clear any blockage in her uterus. Immediately after, Poldie became pregnant with their sixth child.

May 18, 1962, was a hallmark day for Poldie and Alois. Poldie was two months pregnant, it was two days after she turned twenty-eight years old, and it was the day they were appointed to appear before a judge to become US citizens. A group of friends from church and close neighbors joined them in a courtroom in Grand Haven, Michigan. Alois, thirty-one, was good at conversing in English and answering questions, but Poldie still struggled. She was able to answer the questions on her citizenship test, but she still needed help when it came to conversing. Writing and spelling were an entirely different matter. The judge asked her to write something. "Write, 'I am a good cook,'" he suggested.

Poldie wished someone would help her as she jotted down the words. An intermediary passed the slip to the judge. Poldie had written, "I am good cock."

Without further ado, the judge passed both Alois and Poldie, sure that they were going to be good citizens. The Circuit Court of Ottawa County handed the Hufs their Certificates of Naturalization. They shed tears of joy, as did their friends. This was the day they dreamed of for many years. It was finally a reality.

That summer, Poldie was more tired than ever. With five young children, animals to tend to, and a pregnancy, she got little rest. She wished many times for the help of her mother as she had back in Germany. Now she prayed for her family's salvation even more than seeing them again.

That fall, ten-year-old Jana and eight-year-old Marie got into a routine with school. The girls would walk together to their elementary school, South Blendon School, about a half mile away. At lunch, they would walk home to eat before returning to class. One day, both girls arrived home crying.

"What's wrong?" Poldie asked.

"Some of the kids are always calling us 'Krauts.' They told us they would beat us up and chase us out of their school," Jana said.

When Alois learned of it, he thought the children must have watched or been influenced by the television show *Combat!* It depicted US soldiers and their fight during World War II. The children at school assumed the Hufs were German and therefore Nazis. Alois was upset about it. It was one thing if people were cruel to him, but the children did not deserve such ridicule. He told Poldie, "They won't do to my children what they've done to me!"

He told Poldie to keep the children home from school while he went and talked to the teacher, Mrs. Pyle. Alois arranged a meeting and told her what was happening. "We are US citizens," he said. "Now my children are terrified to even go to school. It isn't right. Unless the guilty children come to my farm and apologize to my children and to my wife and me, I won't let the children go to school, and I'll report this incident to authorities."

Alois's reaction was strong, but he was fed up. He had endured years of feeling like an outsider. He wanted so much more for his children. Mortified that the girls were threatened, Mrs. Pyle assured Alois she would talk to the offending children and their parents. She asked Alois not to report the incident further because it would be a poor reflection on a good school.

That same afternoon, before school was out, Mrs. Pyle and a group of children knocked on the farmhouse door. Several children apologized and promised they would not repeat such behavior in the future.

Poldie was exceptionally hungry with this pregnancy. She often woke up at 2:00 a.m. to get a cookie and a glass of milk. She felt sure she was carrying a big boy who would play with baby Joey.

December 1962 was very snowy. Almost daily, a fresh layer of snow christened the ground outside. Alois did not mind the precipitation except that he was worried about making it to the hospital in such conditions when it was time for Poldie to deliver. The road commission employed one of their friendly neighbors, Herm. Alois asked him, "If the roads are blocked, what could we do?"

Herm told Alois that he operated a snowplow. "If Poldie goes into labor and the roads are covered with snow, call me," he said. "You could follow behind the plow."

Alois felt more at ease. He and Poldie were also reliant on friends like Mrs. Jones, who called almost daily to check in. One of Poldie's friends, Jane, called every other day. By the time Poldie was about three weeks overdue and quite enlarged, she could not comfortably walk or even sit and felt frustrated.

One day Jane called and asked, "Are you still home?"

"Yes, I'm still home," Poldie said.

"Well, whatever it is, the baby has got to come out sometime!" Jane said.

"Thanks a lot!" Poldie said, and they both laughed.

In mid-December, Poldie went to her doctor, Dr. Keme. He advised, "We will wait one more week. If you don't have the baby by then, I will induce labor because the baby will be a month overdue."

CHAPTER SEVENTEEN

LOSING LOVED ONES

During the early morning of Sunday, December 23, as Poldie scrambled eggs for everyone's breakfast before church, her contractions finally began. They came consistently every five minutes, and Poldie felt like the baby might come quickly. She asked Alois to feed the children so she could take a bath and prepare to head to the hospital, but the pain was too intense, and she realized she did not have time. She called a neighbor, hoping to catch her at home before she left for church. She answered and agreed to come over.

The roads were clear on the way to the hospital. Since it was a Sunday morning and they had the children cared for, this was the first time Alois could totally focus on his wife's labor. Once again, he was not allowed to stay in the room with Poldie as she delivered. Alois was nervous for her, and in viewing the enormity of her belly, he confessed, "I would never let it come out. I think I would be scared."

"You sure are a comfort to me," Poldie quipped. "And at the right time too."

Dr. Keme examined Poldie and said, "The baby's position is wrong—it's in the breech position. It probably won't stay that way, but if it does, I will need to take it out by Cesarean."

Alois and Poldie both began praying. The nursing staff dismissed Alois from the room, and he waited expectantly by the door. A little while later, he heard Poldie scream once. He knocked on the door. "Is everything okay in there?" he asked.

A nurse opened the door. "Yes, everything is okay, Mr. Huf. The baby straightened out and delivered just fine. You have another baby girl," she announced.

The little girl was born at 9:24 a.m. She was beautiful and had lots of black hair. The doctor thought she was precious, and he and his wife wanted a child of their own. "I will give you $2,000 for her," he said. "You won't miss her; you already have so many children."

Alois and Poldie loved their newborn daughter and weren't at all interested in giving her up. They chuckled at his offer. The nurses combed the little girl's hair into a perfect dollop, and everyone thought she was a sweet, gorgeous baby. The Hufs named her Susan Ruth.

While Poldie and the baby were in the hospital, Alois did his best to take care of their five children at home. He was not much of a cook, but the kids needed to eat, so he prepared the only thing he felt comfortable making. With the chicken soup recipe stored in his memory, Alois took out a large pot, filled it with water, and diced a few carrots to throw in the mix. He grabbed a chicken from the freezer and prepped it for the broth. "Not bad for a second-rate cook," Alois conjectured. He placed the massive pot on the small dining table and then called the children to dinner. Alois served his special soup at every meal. After a few days, the children complained of the liquid fare, overflowing with thick noodles that continued to increase in size as the days passed. So Alois got creative and borrowed the girls' play dish set. When he put the soup in the small dishes and said it was a special meal, the children agreed to eat it again.

Alois knew Poldie was homesick for her other children but remembered the hospital did not allow anyone underage to visit patients. Poldie's room was ground level and had a window close to the street, so Alois brought the children to the hospital, and once again they looked through the window at their mother and new sister.

Each took their turn waving at their mommy and the baby and throwing them kisses, but when Alois raised little four-and-a-half-year-old Joey to the window, Poldie had just begun nursing the newborn. Joey struggled with this new little one cuddling so close to his mommy and blurted out, "What is the baby sucking on mommy for?" Alois and Poldie laughed at the innocence of Joey's query and filed that sweet memory away to hopefully rehearse it with him in later years. Alois and Poldie decided their family of six beautiful children was now complete.

In the last quarter of 1962, egg prices dropped because of overproduction. Many farmers in the area quit the chicken business altogether, determining that the cost of running the operation did not make sense. Area hatcheries had thousands of pullets. They offered them to Alois for a low price. He bought them on credit, thinking it was an opportunity to grow his business.

Alois drove to Grand Rapids to the main grocery store. He arranged a meeting with the owner and asked if he would be willing to buy eggs for the store from the Huf farm. They made arrangements for the store manager to visit Alois's operation. He liked what he saw because it was clean, with the chickens in neat, long cages. He told Alois that if the eggs could be washed, candled for cracks and blood spots, graded, and packed in one-dozen-size cartons, the store would take all the eggs Alois's chickens could produce.

The offer was an answered prayer. Alois purchased an automatic machine that conducted egg washing, candling, and grading. With the device in place and carton packages ready to go, Alois was all set.

Many mornings before school, Jana and Marie spent an hour candling eggs. Marie was the fastest at handling the eggs. She was able to take three in each little hand and place them on the moving belt. The belt stayed full, and it needed to so the person candling would not be exposed to the bright light shining from underneath the belt. As the eggs passed over the light beaming from below, the person examining them was able to determine their condition to see potential cracks and blood spots.

In early 1963, Alois had arranged the barn just how he wanted it, with the cages hanging from all three floors of the barn. Around that time, he was laid off from the Reynolds. The cyclical nature of business and competition had struck again. Alois was glad he had a backup plan. Now was the time to get enough chickens for egg production; perhaps from now on, he would no longer need the night shift work.

His friend Joe also suggested that Alois build a forty-by-one-hundred-foot chicken coop about five hundred feet away from the barn on his land. Alois went to the lumber company to inquire. The lumber manager told Alois they could prefabricate a building and deliver it in ten-foot sections for a reasonable price. The lumber company agreed that Alois could pay it off in reasonable, monthly installments. Alois hired a cement contractor to lay a foundation, and within a week and a half, Alois had his building up. In the mornings, Poldie and the older children helped Alois with placing shingles, and in a month, the coop was completed.

Alois ordered chicks from a hatchery and placed them under lamps to keep them warm for about six weeks until they grew their own feathers. He raised them to be roasting chickens. By the time they matured to thirteen to fourteen weeks old, he had sold them at the market. With the chicken business, Alois was able to pay off the building and pay his family's bills.

◆

In January of 1964, the manager of Reynolds Metal Company called Alois. The business had picked up, and they had an opening for him to work the night shift again. By this time, the chicken farm was taking a substantial amount of time, but Alois did not feel he should turn down the additional work. He had bills to pay and was eager to take the extra job.

In the mornings, Alois, Poldie, and the older children would run the eggs through the machine, and Alois would box them all up and deliver them in town. About the time the kids were getting home from school, Alois would lie down to get some sleep. It was not an easy task with six happy children running around.

Alois worked in this manner until May of 1964, when they again laid him off. The fellow who had previously sold him the chickens came to visit Alois and asked him if he could use some more eggs. He had quite a few chickens that were about twenty-four weeks old that he needed to sell. The chickens had started to lay eggs. The eggs were quite dirty, but he sold them to Alois for a discounted price.

Alois went out to the farmer and brought the first load of eggs home. Poldie, Jana, and Marie did not like it at all. The eggs were so dirty and covered with chicken poop from being on the floor. Alois put the eggs in the basement of the house, and Poldie and the girls had to run them several times through the washer. For the next two months, Alois continued picking up the eggs. When they were through that batch,

Alois also agreed to purchase the laying hens, provided he would have six months to pay for them.

Poldie did the best she could with clothing the children, especially for Sunday church. She wanted them each to have at least one beautiful set of clothes for occasions like Christmas and Easter. She needed to be creative with their tight budget. At times, people stopped by the house to purchase eggs from the Hufs directly. When Poldie collected the cash and Alois was away, she saved it in a hidden place. This allowed her to shop at the Arlan's store in town and buy cute outfits for the children. For the girls, she even purchased little white gloves, coats, and purses.

◆

When Poldie corresponded with the Kellners, it seemed to them that the Hufs had become wildly successful. They had a full family, land, a house, a chicken farm, and plenty to eat. In the back of his mind, Alois remembered the promise he made to his father-in-law that if at all possible, he would help bring them to the United States. Alois knew that his neighbor Herm had an eighty-acre farm only two miles from them. It was all set up for chickens and had a good-sized coop and a barn with two floors in it. Herm wanted to retire, Alois knew.

When he found the time, Alois went to Herm and asked him if he could rent the barn and the chicken coop. Herm replied that he would like to sell the farm. Alois then asked him if he could rent the place for six months with an option to buy the farm. Herm agreed.

Alois took the new chickens he had purchased and placed them in the other barn. Between both properties, the Hufs had a total of twenty thousand laying hens. Alois and Poldie were busy going back and forth between the two properties, but they did not mind, knowing they would soon be able to bring Poldie's parents over. At the end of six months, Alois would be able to purchase the property.

Alois estimated that in about a year, Poldie's parents would be in the US. They would raise chickens for Alois, and he would take the birds as laying hens. Alois was sure of his plan, so he told Herm that he would purchase the farm and make the first payment in six months.

In September, Alois sent a letter to them advising them to prepare for the move to the US the next year. Poldie and Alois were excited as they made preparations for the Kellners to come. Although they were Poldie's parents, Alois had long felt a kinship with his father-in-law and was looking forward to having family around. He and Poldie often prayed their family members would come to a saving relationship with Jesus Christ.

That fall, Alois realized he had become financially independent. If the factory called him, he did not have the time to go back. It was nice when he had medical insurance, but everyone in the family was doing well. It was a good feeling to know he had made it.

In February of 1965, Alois paid off the chickens he had bought and made his first payment on Herm's farm. Life had settled into a happy routine in Michigan. Many Sunday evenings, Alois and Poldie spoke at churches around Hudsonville, Holland, and Zeeland, and then they would sing with Jana and Marie.

Back in Altach, Germany, Opa and Oma Kellner, along with their youngest boys, were making preparations to come to the new land. Mr. Kellner had dealt with stomach ulcers for a long time, and he wanted to take care of the problem in Germany while he could. On August 10, Opa had a successful surgery, but recovery was slow. After twelve days in the hospital, Johann told the staff he wanted to go home. The doctor told him he needed to stay for at least three more days, but Opa insisted that he wanted to go back home.

"Okay," the doctor said. "Then you will have to sign a document that says you went home against the doctor's wishes." Opa signed it on August 24 and went home.

Wednesday, August 25, started as a typical day for the Huf family. The children were all enjoying the last of their summer vacation and playing around the farm. Poldie was going about her daily routine and planning little Cristie Jo's sixth birthday the following day. Alois made a quick trip into town to purchase some supplies. He hurried with his errand and returned to the farm quickly. When he pulled into the driveway and made his way up to the house, the older children ran outside in a frenzy, greeting him with screams. This was unusual, so he stopped abruptly and opened the door. "What's going on?" he asked.

"Daddy, Opa Kellner died, and Mommy is crying and feels very sick," the children shouted. At that very moment, Alois felt like someone physically punched him in his stomach. It was if all the oxygen had been sucked out of his lungs. He could barely catch his breath but knew he needed to go inside to console his wife. He tried to move but sat paralyzed in the truck for several minutes, gripping the steering wheel. In that first moment, many thoughts pelted his mind. He immediately wondered about Opa's spiritual condition and if he had given his heart to Jesus before he died. He thought of the family in Germany and how devastated they must be. And he thought of how heartbroken Poldie was. He knew that their plans to bring family over were now permanently annulled, and he thought of the farm he and Poldie had so lovingly prepared for the Kellners. Alois raised a prayer: "Lord, I need Your strength and guidance on how to handle this."

He entered the house and found Poldie crumpled and distraught. He held her and repeated, "I am so sorry." Poldie fell on Alois's chest, and her unrelenting tears soaked his work shirt.

"Why?" Poldie asked utterly weeping. "Why did this happen to my father?"

Poldie alternated between being hysterical with grief and lethargic, so Alois took her to the doctor. The silence was more present in the car; neither of them found any words to express the unbelievable loss. The doctor gave Poldie a sedative to help her calm down and sent her home with medication to last the next several days. Alois instructed the children to be quiet and let their mommy rest. He needed to be alone to think, so he set about completing work outside.

When Poldie awoke the next day, she was in an improved state of mind. Alois suggested they make a call to Altach. Alois called the road commission office that was in the same complex as the Kellners' dwelling. He asked to speak to Mrs. Kellner. All the children were with their mother, and Poldie was able to talk to her. "What happened?" Poldie asked.

"Opa was in the hospital for two weeks," her mother said. "He got homesick and left early. After about twenty-four hours, he seemed to be fine but said, 'Mutter mir ist es so kalt.' (Mother, I am so cold.) I covered him with some feather blankets, but he said again, 'It's coming from the bottom of my feet and feels like something is crawling up.' So I went downstairs and called the doctor. He came and gave him a shot. What it was, I don't know. When the doctor left, Opa said he felt better, except he was still cold. I put warm socks on his feet and made a fire in the kitchen stove. He lay there quietly for about half an hour, then said, 'It's coming again—all over my feet!' He turned his head and was gone."

The doctor had determined that Opa died of blood clots, Oma said. After speaking with her mother, Poldie talked with her siblings, and lastly, with her favorite brother, Walter. She still remembered when he hid himself the day Poldie left, nine years earlier, to keep from crying in public. Walter was now married and had a little boy of his own named Manfred. Poldie wished she could go to the funeral, but it would have been impossible to afford the trip. Poldie was in no condition to travel internationally. She told her mother that she and Alois would hold their own service for Opa. She consoled her mother as best she could and wept bitterly as she hung up the phone.

On the day of Opa Kellner's funeral in Germany, Poldie and Alois went to the farm that they prepared for the Kellners. They sat down on the steps of the house. The warm sun illuminated the farmland and peeked through the tall maple trees surrounding the house.

"We made this place so nice for them," Poldie said.

"Yes. It's a nice place now," Alois agreed.

"They are probably in church for the funeral now," Poldie commented. "Or maybe they are lowering the casket into the grave."

Poldie looked out in the cornfields and saw herself as a little girl, hiding as Johann's retriever, Tref, searched for her. The dog was there, wagging his tail and barking, and she could hear her father's voice praising him. She felt the thick hair on Tref's back as she petted him, and then she and the dog ran back to her father. Poldie and Alois shed tears.

Alois brought a Bible to the farm for their private service. He pulled it out and read a few verses he hoped would bring Poldie comfort. He invited her to pray, and together, they committed everything to God. It was hard for them to understand what had happened in the past three days. All their plans and all their investment seemed to be for naught. They both clung to the belief that God doesn't make any mistakes and is in control, even when they did not understand.

As they made their way back to their house, Alois said, "Poldie, now that you are doing a bit better, will you tell me details of how you found out your father died?"

"It was a telegraph," she said. "The telegraph office called and said they had a telegram from Germany. The person said that he could not read the words but that he would spell it for me. I reached for a pen and paper and wrote down each letter. It was 'Vater Gestorben, Beerdigung.' (Father Died, Funeral.) There was more information about the funeral, but I did not hear anything else."

Alois put his arm around Poldie. Her father was only fifty-nine years old. They had hoped their children would all learn to love him and know him for the wonderful grandfather he was.

"If only I knew my daddy was with Jesus, I would not be so sad," Poldie cried.

"As difficult as this is for us, we just have to trust the Lord," Alois said. "We should take comfort that we sent them the tapes. The ones where the children sang songs in German and we told them what it means to be saved and how to receive Jesus as Savior. We know from the Lukeshes that they played the tape at Altach and that when Opa heard the tape, he cried. We don't know what happened in his heart, but we know the Word of God does not return to Him void. The Word always accomplishes what God pleases. This is our comfort—that God is in control, in spite of anything we see to the contrary."

Poldie was thankful for Alois's kind words. She slowly let herself absorb a new reality—her parents and siblings would not be in Michigan nearby as planned. When she called her siblings a few days later, they told Poldie their mother was taking things very hard. They suggested that it would be good for Oma Kellner to come and stay in the US for a few months. Poldie told Alois, and he agreed. They sent her a ticket to come by plane.

Oma Kellner flew to Chicago alone. It was much farther than any other place she had ever traveled in her life. When they picked her up,

Poldie and Alois could not believe what they saw. Oma appeared to be a shell of who she was. She was not the lively person they remembered. Poldie was thrilled to see her mother, but Oma was unable to give much in their interactions. They tried to keep her busy with the grandchildren, but her mind and heart kept going back to Germany. Her emotions were tender and still so raw. Any little thing triggered a response.

After only a week, Oma asked to return to Germany. She was grieving the loss of her husband and talked about visiting Opa's grave. Poldie pleaded with her to stay at least a few more weeks, but her mother had her mind set. Poldie could not help but be upset. She missed her mother's company and longed to be together.

"Mother, don't you love your daughter anymore?" Poldie asked. "I don't have any relative here. It would make me so happy if you stayed for a few weeks."

Oma was unmoved and said she was returning to Germany. The original airline ticket Alois purchased was one way because he had planned on his mother-in-law staying for several months. Now he had to buy a return, one-way ticket for immediate departure. The impromptu international plane ticket put a strain on him financially, but he had no choice.

After they dropped Mrs. Kellner off at the airport in Grand Rapids, Poldie cried for some time and agonized over the separation. The break from her family finally felt complete. She knew that she would not know her parents as she had before.

The chicken farm on both properties kept the entire family busy. Alois and Poldie initially planned for Mr. and Mrs. Kellner to be operating the other farm, but God intervened. Alois believed that to get the most out of the chickens, he must keep the second operation going for another year and then put the property on the market.

◆

In October of 1965, a car drove into Alois and Poldie's yard. It was not one they recognized, and through the window, Poldie noticed that the license plate read "Ontario." She backed away from the window as she saw a group approaching the door. The visitors knocked, and Poldie and

Alois answered. A man and woman introduced themselves as Mr. and Mrs. Springel, and a second man introduced himself as Mr. Kratochvil, and he spoke Czech.

The group accepted the invitation to come inside. Alois was especially attentive to Mr. Kratochvil. He had not had a conversation in his native language with someone in a long while. Mr. Kratochvil said he was from Alois's village of Vikyrovice. Alois was even more intrigued to learn that the man knew his parents. Mr. Kratochvil said he had been visiting Canada for three months and soon would be returning to Czechoslovakia. Both the Springels and Mr. Kratochvil were Christians. The family and their new acquaintances had an immediate bond and enjoyed sharing stories of their lives during the extended visit.

Alois asked Mr. Kratochvil how he was able to get out of the communist country to visit Canada. Mr. Kratochvil explained that the Czech government permitted people to visit relatives who lived abroad.

"Do you think they would allow my parents to visit me here?" Alois inquired. "Or would they not be able to because I escaped from Czechoslovakia?"

"Well, are you a US citizen?" the man asked.

"Yes," Alois said.

"The government there would not have interest in you anymore," Mr. Kratochvil confirmed. "Especially since you've been out of the country since 1949. I do think the government would permit your parents to visit you—and if not both of them, at least one."

Alois was elated at the thought of his parents coming to see him and to meet Poldie and their children. Having Mrs. Kellner come had made him wish even more that his own family could visit. The death of his father-in-law made the desire even stronger.

Mr. Kratochvil brought a movie camera with him. He suggested that he film everyone and show the film to the Hufs back in Czechoslovakia upon his return. He shot the family members inside, and then Alois took him outside to capture the chicken operation while Alois demonstrated how the farm operation functioned.

As the visitors prepared to leave, they gathered around Alois and Poldie, and they prayed together for the Hufs, for Czechoslovakia, and for God to lead all their plans.

The next day, Alois wrote a letter home, telling his family of Mr. Krato-chvil and inviting his parents to visit. Alois wrote that he wanted both of his parents to come but knew his mother might be frightened to fly. He remembered her saying once that she would rather die than get on a plane.

He then went to the Dutch Immigrant Society in Holland, Michigan, and asked for help with securing the proper documentation for Czech visitors. The office offered to take care of the needed paperwork with the Czechoslovakian government.

Later that month, on October 20, 1965, Alois and Poldie's spiritual father in the Lord, Mr. Lukesh, passed away. He was eighty-three years old and being cared for in the one-room apartment he shared with his precious wife, Edna. Mrs. Lukesh wrote of the experience to the European Harvest Field agency, "Charles Lukesh, my dear husband, fell asleep in Jesus." She was with her husband to the very end of his life and said, "It is especially hard to part with him." She stayed with him and held his head on her arm and gently stroked his forehead, continually repeating the name of Jesus until he took his last breath.

Christmas 1965 was fast approaching, and though it was just four months after the death of her father, Poldie was looking forward to the holiday. As was their custom, Alois went to a specific part of their property where several pine trees grew, selected the best tree, cut it down, and took it into the house. The children prepared red apples as ornaments and hung them on the evergreen. Poldie creatively shaped dough into ornaments and put them in the oven to harden. The children delighted in threading them and placing the decorations on the tree. A traditional Christmas tree in Germany was strung with real wax candles and only lit for a few moments on Christmas Eve. The children would watch the flames flicker while Janie read the Christmas story out of Luke. The family would sing "Silent Night" before gathering around the tree and blowing out the candles.

Alois taught the children German and Czech songs. He showed them how to loop arms and sing the tunes with a partner, as he used to do. Poldie liked to join in with the songs she knew.

This Christmas Eve was unique because the neighbors across the street invited them over. They were from the Netherlands and did not have family nearby. The Hufs could undoubtedly relate to that and accepted the invitation readily. The family was getting ready to leave the house at around 4:00 p.m. when the phone rang. Alois answered.

"Are you Alois Huf?" a voice asked.

"Speaking," Alois said.

"This is Western Union. We have a telegram for you," the person said. "It is written in German. We cannot read it, but we will spell it for you. Please get a pencil and paper."

Alois could feel his stomach sink as he prepared to write. The message about Poldie's father had been delivered to them this same way, he thought. "Okay, I am ready," he said.

"Here is the spelling: 'Walter Toedlich Verungluckt Begraebnis.' A written copy is coming to you by US mail," Alois heard.

The person on the other line hung up, but Alois continued pressing the phone to his ear as if he could decipher something more. Walter, Poldie's favorite brother, died. Alois wondered how he would tell Poldie that her beloved little brother had passed away.

Poldie saw Alois with a scrap of paper, placing the phone down slowly. "What's wrong?" Poldie asked, but Alois was quiet. "What's wrong?" she asked again. "Did something happen?"

Alois wished he could protect her from this horrible news, that he could undo it altogether. All he could do was lift the piece of paper and hand it to her. Poldie read the words and screamed out, "No! Not again! No, no! It can't be." She felt as though she were in a nightmare. Her father had gone too soon, and now her brother, in his early twenties, was gone even sooner! She was distraught.

Alois called the neighbors and told them what happened. He called the doctor and took Poldie in to get her something to calm down. When they arrived home, the children were concerned about their mother. Alois felt sorry for them. The children were so excited about Christmas and opening the few presents under the tree. Christmas and the days following passed on with mourning instead of celebration. As soon as Poldie was able to call her family back in Germany, she found out about the details surrounding Walter's death. It was Christmas Eve, and he and his wife argued. Walter wanted to spend some time with his mother because of her heartache from Opa Kellner's recent passing. He drove off on his motorcycle to see her but stopped at the pub first to have a beer.

When he entered the tavern, three acquaintances of his were present and extremely intoxicated. They became aggressive and began to pick a fight with Walter. Things rapidly escalated out of control. They ganged up on Walter and severely beat him. When they finished throwing their last punches, they picked him up and threw him outside on the street in front of the pub. A lady who lived nearby heard the agonizing screams coming from the imperiled man in the street. It was dark, and there was a small hill just ahead of a bend in the road, making it difficult for oncoming traffic to see ahead. While Walter lay struggling, an oncoming car rounded the hill and ran him over, fatally wounding him. When news got back to Oma Kellner, she was once again devastated. That had been the most painful year for her. She lost her husband and beloved son. Walter's remains were unrecognizable, so the mortician decided to keep the casket closed. Poldie's eldest brother, Johnny, had to make peace with himself that Walter was indeed departed. He demanded to have the coffin opened to him privately so he could confirm without a doubt that it was indeed Walter who was lying in the casket and gone from their lives forever.

After a while, Poldie was grateful she had her children's bright spirits to help slowly pull her out of the dark sadness she felt over the deaths of her father and brother.

◆

When Mr. Kratochvil returned to Vikyrovice, Czechoslovakia, he visited the home of the Hufs and reported that he had visited Alois and his family in America. He told the family he would bring a projector the following week and show them the film he had made with the Hufs in Michigan.

Alois's parents were happy at this news; they arranged to have all their adult children who had left home, along with their families, return and watch the movie on a set day. The Hufs welcomed Mr. Kratochvil into the happy gathering the next week, and he set up the projector. There were smiles and tears as he played the film. They had photos, but to see Alois and his family in such a vivid way and to hear his voice was so special. At the end of the film, they immediately asked Mr. Kratochvil to play it again. They watched the movie several times.

Marie Huf, who had previously vowed never to fly on a plane, had an infusion of courage upon seeing her son. She turned to her husband and said, "If you go, I also would like to go." The next day, they sent a letter to their son saying they both would like to come. Alois was surprised and very pleased. He went to the Dutch Immigrant Society and added his mother to the invitation.

It was soon arranged for Alois's parents to visit in the coming months. He told Poldie, "Surely when my parents come and we show them in the Word of God that Jesus is the only way to Him, they will also gladly receive Him as Savior." Al and Poldie began to pray even more fervently for their family members' salvation.

--------------------------------◆--------------------------------

The day finally arrived: on Monday, March 7, 1966, Alois and his family piled in their blue Ford station wagon and set out on the nearly three-hour drive across Michigan to the Detroit airport to meet Alois's parents. It had been seventeen long years since seeing his father and mother—half of his life had gone by from the time when he escaped Czechoslovakia. So much had changed since then.

The anticipation of meeting his parents again left Alois excited and nervous. His stomach growled and felt like it was turning somersaults. On the way to the airport, Alois recounted memories of his parents to the children, and they became eager to meet them. The family arrived at the airport two hours early, but no one minded. The kids loved watching the planes take off and touch down from the outside fence.

At 11:30 a.m., they saw an airplane land. Alois began to choke up the moment it did. He could barely hold back the tears. The family observed as the ground crew pulled a set of mobile stairs up to the plane so the passengers could disembark on the tarmac. Alois and the family watched expectantly from the exterior fence line as the passengers began to deplane. One by one, the people were exiting the aircraft and grabbing hold of the railing on the mobile stairs. Finally, Alois recognized his father and mother as they appeared from the aircraft door and began walking down the stairs. Alois felt a thousand emotions as he studied his father first. He was thin as always, and his mother was hunched over and walked with a limp. Josef was sixty-three, and Marie was sixty-one. They too lived a hard life and struggled to provide for their family and make a modest living. It appeared to Alois as if the wear and tear of life had almost done them in. He voiced a quick prayer of thanks to God. How many years had it been that they all had prayed they would see one another again?

When Josef and Marie entered the customs processing area, Alois and the family darted inside the terminal and hurried to the receiving gate. Once his parents finished at customs, they appeared at the exit gate. When their eyes locked, Alois took in a large breath and raised his chest, immediately exhaling with a sigh of relief to finally embrace them. He pulled his mother aside and squeezed her for what seemed like an eternity. They wept, partly for the joy of finally being together and also for the years they missed out on. Marie stroked Alois and said, "Lojsku jsi to ty?" (Alois, is that you, my love?)

Then Alois took his father in his arms and wept with him. "Konecne, konecne, konecne tebe vidin!" (Finally, finally, I see you again!), Josef said.

The Hufs hugged their daughter-in-law, Poldie, and each of the children warmly. After he loaded their luggage in the car, Alois took them all to a nice restaurant in Detroit. This was quite a treat for everyone. The children tried out some Czech phrases they had learned. One would ask, "Dedecku, babicko, mas me rad?" (Grandpa, grandma, do you love me?) Then both grandparents would reply, "Ma'm te rad moc, moc, moc." (We love you very, very much.)

It was dark when they arrived back at the farm in Hudsonville. Grandpa and Grandma Huf thought the house was beautiful. Even though the older couple was tired from the trip, they were filled with excitement and stayed up for a long time. Josef knew some German, so he was able to converse a little with Poldie. Marie kept telling the story over and over to her grandchildren, using hand gestures and tears, of how she had not seen her son in seventeen years. She tried to convey through Alois's translations how empty she felt when they knew nothing of his whereabouts for four years and how thankful the family was to learn he was alive. Finally, Poldie suggested they all get some rest, and they retired for bed.

The next day, a small local newspaper from Zeeland heard about the old-world visitors and sent a reporter out to cover the special visit by the Huf grandparents. The reporter asked many questions about their visit and the special reunion after seventeen long years. He took photos of the entire family huddled closely on the living room sofa. Joseph and Marie brought traditional Czech dolls in folk dress and national costumes for the girls. The dolls mesmerized Cristie Jo. They were not like any dolls she had ever seen. The photographer watched as she studied them with her big blue eyes. She was in her own little imaginary world when he interrupted her for a quick minute, asking if she would turn her head toward him and hold the dolls under her chin. He captured a memorable photo of Cristie Jo with her new companions.

The reporter continued interviewing Alois regarding his escape and what life was like for him in Czechoslovakia. When the paper arrived at the home the next week, Alois opened it up to see two pictures and a short article of the reunion with his parents. Alois was pleased the newspaper honored his family.

CHAPTER EIGHTEEN

RISKING IT ALL TO CROSS
THE CZECH BORDER

Alois's mother brought a flask of holy water from home. She informed Alois that she had been on a Catholic pilgrimage to Poland, and she acquired the flask in a place where Mary had appeared to someone. The Catholic Church built a huge shrine there, and people from all parts of Europe visited it. Alois took pity on her. He knew his parents did not have the money for such trips, and he wondered how much she had spent on the little flask.

People like Marie kept the bottles at home, and if anyone became sick, they rubbed some of the water on the afflicted person in the hopes the sufferer would heal. Alois recalled traditions like this from his childhood. People revered things like bits of wood that were said to have come from the cross and fragments of linen that had purportedly touched Jesus or the disciples. The sincere people worshipped the objects in and of themselves. Alois knew that since coming to a true Christian faith, his days of such superstition had ceased. He had the Bible and relied upon its promises alone.

Marie took the bottle and dipped her finger in it, then went around and made the sign of the cross on all the children's foreheads. She urged each child to take a swig of the bottled water. Alois knew she was well intentioned, but he did not like these practices. He stepped in and told his mother gently that they did not need these pseudoreligious things. Jesus had saved them from human-made religion and had given them His holy Word to trust in, he explained. His mother was offended.

Alois tried again to explain how eleven years before, when he was in Germany, God the Father drew him to Himself, and the Lord Jesus saved him by forgiving all his sins. He explained how Jesus took all the burden of religion, nailed it to the cross, and set Alois spiritually free. Able to trust in Jesus completely, he told his mother about the Ten Commandments and how people were to have no other gods or revere any image before God. Josef was listening with a half-raised eyebrow. "Since Poldie and I committed our lives to Jesus Christ, we have been praying for you to receive Christ too," Alois told them.

"And leave the Catholic Church as you did?" Marie asked. "We would never do that!"

Alois decided it was prudent to keep his thoughts to himself for a while, since he did not seem to be making any impact.

Usually after the family ate supper, Alois reached for the Bible and read a passage to Poldie and the children. With his parents present, he translated what he read. Marie could not resist interjecting something about Mary and how she had appeared to people somewhere. Alois referenced the first chapter of Hebrews and addressed how God in the Old Testament spoke through prophets, signs, and dreams and how God then spoke very clearly through His Son, Jesus. In response to this, Marie confessed that she believed a forester in Europe who claimed Mary had appeared to others.

Alois grew agitated. He said, "Ma, you believe others, but you do not believe me when I say that Jesus changed my life. If you don't believe your own son, then believe the Bible."

Alois realized that convincing his parents to become Christians might not be as simple as he had hoped. When the weekend rolled around, Alois offered to take them to a Catholic church if they would like. But they said they wanted to go with the family to the Baptist church instead. They attended but understood very little of what was going on in English.

An older farmer named Mr. Novak, who spoke Czech, lived near Alois. He learned that Alois's father had come from Czechoslovakia. On several occasions while his parents were visiting, Alois brought them to visit Mr. Novak, who was a retired Methodist preacher. The Hufs were happy to converse in Czech and sometimes stayed with him for hours. Alois hoped, of course, that Mr. Novak, being older, might have some sway on his parents. They always enjoyed their visits, but that seemed to be as far as it went. Alois and Poldie continued praying for their salvation and hoping that, during their three-month stay, Alois's parents would see their need for Jesus.

Jana and Marie's school planned a field trip to the city of Chicago. When Alois learned of it, he briefly remembered a younger version of himself choosing Chicago over Hudsonville. He was glad Poldie had prayed otherwise. Alois thought his mom and dad would like to see the city while they were visiting America. He scarcely had time to take them places because of his long hours operating the farm. Alois approached their teacher and asked if there were any extra seats on the bus and if his parents could join the kids. The teacher said there was room and that he would be more than happy to have Alois's parents on the trip.

Alois gave Jana extra money so they could all have a McDonald's lunch in Chicago. Alois and Poldie said good-bye to the four of them the morning of the field trip, and off they went. Jana and Marie took hold of their grandparents' hands and carefully led them from the bus into adventures like riding up the elevator at Sears Tower to look at the city skyline from the observatory. The Hufs had never seen anything like the city horizon and the views of Lake Michigan.

When the travelers arrived home that night, Alois asked them how the trip was. Marie said it was lovely, but Josef covered his ears and said, "Na tom autobus, tam bylo kriku." (On that bus, there was terrible noise.) Alois had not even imagined what the bus ride with children would be like for his parents, although they undoubtedly had an adventure.

Josef was especially interested in Alois's farm operation and equipment. Since utilizing horses in the days he worked as a farmer, he wanted to try his hand at plowing with the tractor. Alois wanted to plant about sixty acres of corn again on both farms. Alois owned one International Harvester (IH) tractor and one Ford, and he told his dad he would be glad to have his help. Alois showed him how to operate the IH and then watched his father climb up onto the big red machine and take a seat. Before he engaged the clutch and gears, Grandma Huf climbed on board the rear of the tractor. Quickly, two of the girls came running to join in for a photo opportunity with their grandparents. Marie leaped up and sat on the massive tractor wheel with legs dangling while Cristie Jo stood on the tractor's floorboard just to the side of where Grandpa sat. They all smiled big for the camera and then hopped off the tractor, allowing Grandpa to finally take off into the field. Josef liked operating the tractor so much, he scarcely stopped for lunch before climbing in it again.

Shortly after they planted the corn, Alois and Josef walked around to see where the cornstalks had sprouted. Josef was delighted to see how straight his rows of corn were. He even went to the house and brought Marie out to show her how impossibly neat the rows stood. Throughout the remainder of their stay, he continued helping Alois with the farming.

Throughout his parents' visit, Alois creatively and compassionately talked of God when he could. He told his mother and father, "It's not religion that saves but Christ." He wanted Josef and Marie to know the biblical promises that had grown close to his and Poldie's hearts.

On the final morning of his parents' visit, Alois wrote down several verses on a sheet of paper:

Hebrews 13:5: "Never will I leave you; never will I forsake you" (NIV).

Matthew 28:20: "And surely I am with you always, to the very end of the age" (NIV).

Titus 2:13: "While we wait for the blessed hope—the appearing of the glory of our great God and Savior, Jesus Christ" (NIV).

Romans 8:31: "If God is for us, who can be against us?"

John 10:28: "I give them eternal life, and they shall never perish; no one will snatch them out of my hand" (NIV).

Revelation 21:4: "'He will wipe every tear from their eyes. There will be no more death or mourning or crying or pain, for the old order of things has passed away'" (NIV).

Isaiah 55:1: "Come, all you who are thirsty, come to the waters; and you who have no money, come, buy and eat! Come, buy wine and milk without money and without cost" (NIV).

Ephesians 2:8–9: "For it is by grace you have been saved, through faith—and this is not from yourselves, it is the gift of God—not by works, so that no one can boast" (NIV).

John 1:12: "Yet to all who did receive him, to those who believed in his name, he gave the right to become children of God" (NIV).

Beneath the verses, Alois penned an explanation of the Gospel and put the paper in a sealed envelope with money. Alois felt like a missing piece of his life fell into place by reconnecting with his parents in person, and now they would be leaving.

The children took the day off school to see their grandparents depart from the airport. Alois and Poldie spoke little in the car. They were sad to see their dear parents go. The children repeated phrases they learned in Czech; they were grieving their grandparents' departure also. Alois wondered if he would ever see Josef and Marie again, especially with the political uncertainty in his native country.

He was not sorry he shared his faith so passionately, but Alois regretted engaging in arguments with his parents over religion. His intentions were pure, but instead, he wished he would have enjoyed their company and accepted them more as they were. The verse that Jesus said in John 6:44 came to his mind: "No one can come to me unless the Father who sent me draws them, and I will raise them up at the last day" (NIV). Alois and Poldie understood that they could not save anyone. Only the Holy Spirit could do the work in their loved ones' hearts.

At the airport, the children cried even more than their parents. Although there was a language barrier, they grew very fond of one another, and it was hard to say good-bye. Alois held on to each of his parents for several moments, wondering if he would have the opportunity to embrace them again.

As their plane began to taxi, Alois and his family stayed to watch until it took off and ascended and grew smaller and smaller and eventually disappeared into the sky. The family prayed and committed Josef's and Marie's lives and souls into the Lord's safety.

That summer, the two farms were abundant with eggs and corn, and Alois and Poldie were glad the children were home from school and could help more. Alois took daily trips into town in a white van he had acquired to deliver eggs to the grocery store. With vehicles, tractors, a sizeable house, and two properties, Alois recalled thoughts of downsizing from the first farmhouse owned by Mr. Schneider in Hudsonville and also telling Mr. Jones that he did not need a car. In the past ten years of making a new home in Michigan, how things had changed.

Saturday evenings became a tradition for the Huf family. Alois and Poldie gathered the children and took them for a special treat to the McDonald's in town. The kids thought riding in the white delivery van was an adventure. They climbed into the transport area of the vehicle and took the empty egg boxes and pretended they were tables and chairs. On the twenty-minute drive to the fast-food restaurant, the siblings spent their time arranging the cardboard furniture just right. Upon arriving, with great excitement, Jana, Marie, Debra, Joey, Cristie Jo, and Susan walked to the window of the McDonald's and ordered burgers and fries. Back in the van, the children ate on their makeshift furniture. Poldie looked back at all of them and smiled. She was so glad the children never had to go hungry as she and Alois had as children.

The family was making a modest living, and with the Lord's blessing, they were able to continue planning for the future. Poldie was used to wearing the same few dresses to church events and to sing in various churches around their area. One day, she and Alois went to Robert Hall near where they lived and did a bit of shopping for their growing children. There in the corner, Poldie eyed a beautiful two-piece sparkly silver dress with a matching jacket. The sleeve dress had accent chains hanging in a semicircle from one button to another. The jacket collar, pockets, and sleeves were outlined in beautiful trim. Alois purchased it for Poldie, and she treasured the dress for a long time to come.

Michigan always had the highest number of acres of corn. From the time when Grandpa Huf assisted Alois in planting about sixty-five acres of corn on both farms in the early spring, the crop had grown tall and lush. Alois knew it would be a symbiotic relationship. He could fertilize the fields with chicken manure and use much of the corn to feed the chickens. Alois and Poldie waited until the corn stalks were fully grown and towering high over Alois's five-foot-eight frame.

In August 1966, they dressed the children in their Sunday best and headed to their second farm down the street to take a picture. The family was excited to show Grandpa Huf how well the cornfield was doing that he plowed and planted.

The chickens on the second farm were done laying eggs. Alois sold them and began cleaning out the barn so he could put the farm on the market.

About a month later, a man named Bill stopped by; he heard of Alois's plans and asked if he would be willing to sell him Herm's old farm. Since Alois was still using much of the land to cultivate corn, he expressed that he would like to sell only forty of the total eighty acres, including all the buildings. Alois presented him a price, and Bill said he would think about it and be back in a couple of days. Two days later, Bill came back and agreed to purchase the farm. Alois was able to sell it and all the chicken equipment. With the income from the sale of the land and the equipment, along with the healthy corn harvest, Alois and Poldie felt incredibly blessed.

With one less chicken operation to run, Alois and Poldie realized how exhausted they had been. There was enough work even without the other chicken farm. Egg prices were reasonable, and Alois was able to continue providing for his family with his own farm. Poldie worked long hours alongside Alois on the farm. She struggled with helping out in the barn, wishing instead to be caring for the children. However, she was determined through it all to raise a healthy and spiritually conscious family. The only day she really had time in the house was Saturday—cleaning day.

◆

When Alois's parents returned to Czechoslovakia, the communist leader of their area visited them. He asked them many questions about Alois and the United States. Marie was not afraid; she was proud. She bragged shamelessly about how well her son was doing, along with his wife and six children. The man asked if Alois would be interested in returning to Czechoslovakia. Marie responded that since Alois had such a good life in the US, she could not imagine him wanting to return.

However, she added, if the government could issue him a visa to visit his homeland for a few weeks, he would be interested in that. She said he would need assurance that he would not be detained in any way by the government if he visited. The communist agent replied that the Czechoslovakian government would issue him a visa and would guarantee that he could return to the US. Mrs. Huf then said she would notify her son of the opportunity.

When Alois learned of this through his mother's letter, enthusiasm filled his being. He would love to visit his homeland and see his siblings and their families. Still, he was nervous about the communist regime. He called his congressman's office in Grand Rapids and asked him about the chance of visiting the country. Within a week, the congressman called back and gave Alois information: "If the communist government of Czechoslovakia issues a visa to you, they must guarantee that you can leave the country." The man also advised that, for good measure, when Alois went, he should let the US consulate in Prague know where he would be going and how long he planned to stay.

With such busy lives and a thriving farm, Alois could scarcely leave town for a day. Taking a long trip overseas would have been impossible. Alois thought this through for some time. He had been praying that all his family members would come to know Jesus Christ as their personal Savior. Perhaps this was his chance to tell them the Gospel in person. He also had seen how God had directed his steps and provided for him as he undertook new ventures and business opportunities.

After much prayer and discussions with Poldie, Alois called a real estate agent in Grand Rapids and said that he was thinking of selling his and Poldie's farm along with all the chickens and the egg business. The agent came the next day to look everything over. He asked Alois why he wanted to sell the farm. "I want to start something different," Alois said. He and Poldie were excited about starting a new venture on the remaining forty acres of woods they still owned down the street.

About a month later, the real estate agent brought a young couple to Alois's farm and showed them around. The couple liked what they saw and wanted to purchase the farm and move in as soon as possible. Alois purchased a mobile home and placed it on the forty acres. The mobile home was small for a family of eight, but it was only a transitionary place until their new home on the forty acres was finished being built and ready to move into.

After selling the farm, Alois started a new venture and became a part of an industrial cleaning company that specialized in cleansing greasy automobile engines and other household items. He was grateful for the transition from farm life and eager to be investing his time and efforts in a new undertaking.

In the summer of 1967, the new house was complete. It sat in the middle of their land, was surrounded by towering trees, and had a beautiful view of seasonal wildflowers. Alois and Poldie had friends from church that built a house nearby, and Poldie fell in love with it. It was a split level with yellow siding, taupe-colored brick, and brown window shutters. She and Alois decided to use the same floor plan and a similar exterior. The dwelling had plenty of room for their family of eight. Poldie was eager to move out of the mobile home and into their new home. On move-in day, they loaded up the furniture, which they had stored in an old schoolhouse building down the street, and set up a lovely home. Alois could not help but wonder what some of his meddlesome neighbors were thinking of him now with a new house—but he didn't dwell on it for long.

In the meantime, the government approved Alois's visa, and he and Poldie began to plan the upcoming trip to Europe. Because of the children's schooling and expensive ticket prices, they decided to take only three children, their youngest daughters. The Hufs planned an itinerary that outlined visits to Poldie's family in Germany for four weeks and then Alois's family in Czechoslovakia for two weeks. Before the journey to their homelands, friends invited Alois and Poldie on a business trip to the Bahamas in November. It would be their first airplane flight ever. They were both excited and nervous about traveling to a sunny paradise. When Poldie arrived home from their trip, she gathered the children and told them stories of what it was like to fly on a plane. The flight attendant served them coffee on board, and the liquid barely jiggled during the fight. The children sat spellbound and loved hearing details of their trip.

During the remainder of November, Alois and Poldie finalized their travel itinerary for Europe and confirmed childcare arrangements for the three children staying behind. The week after Thanksgiving, Alois, Poldie, and three of their youngest daughters departed for overseas.

Alois and Poldie had never done extravagant things nor taken a vacation since moving to the United States. Poldie dreamt of seeing her siblings, whom she said good-bye to ten years before, but Alois's excitement was tempered with some concern. He did not trust the communist regime; he had heard how the government continued to oppress the people of Czechoslovakia for the past eighteen years. Alois wondered if they would find a reason to detain him and keep him there.

He wasn't alone in his concerns. More than once, Poldie said, "Are you sure you want to go to Czechoslovakia? We could stay in Germany."

"I'm indeed a little fearful," he told her, "but I trust the United States congressman. He assured me that if my papers are in order and I have the visa in hand with specifics, I would have nothing to fear. I am a US citizen now, after all. I would have reason to fear if I partook in some anti-communist discussions or if I committed a crime, but that won't happen. When we arrive in Prague, I'll be sure and register there with the American consulate and take any final instructions."

The family departed from Grand Rapids and flew to Detroit. From there, they flew to Amsterdam and then on to Stuttgart, Germany. As the plane landed, Poldie realized she was a visitor in her own home country; she had been gone long enough that it no longer felt like home.

As the Hufs walked into the Stuttgart terminal, most of Poldie's siblings were awaiting them, eagerly greeting her and Alois and the three girls. The children spoke some of the German sentences they had prepared. Poldie's mother stayed home to prepare a meal for everyone. Alois decided that, instead of renting a car for six weeks, it would be more cost-effective to purchase a Volkswagen Bug for the stay for about $5,000. Then he could have it shipped back to the US and could sell it for a profit.

Poldie was happy to see her family, but things were not the same. She felt an emptiness with her father and Walter gone. After a heartwarming two-week visit, the Hufs drove toward the border of Czechoslovakia. Driving through Nuremberg, Germany, they could see barbed-wire fences with machine gun towers standing every few hundred feet. Before and during World War II, the city had been the site of Nazi rallies. After the war, it was the site of military tribunals that shocked the world in their exposure of Nazi atrocities—the Nuremberg trials.

The closer they came to the border of the two countries, the more Alois and Poldie could feel the tension within them. Going eastward toward Czechoslovakia felt like reentering the past. Poldie looked at the bleak scene of the Czechoslovakian border before them and turned to Alois. "This looks like a huge concentration camp. Are you sure you want to go there?" she asked.

Alois did not want to admit his trepidation. He remembered how cold he was eighteen years ago when he had crossed the border. A chill passed down his spine. It was bitterly cold again. For a moment, he could hardly believe he was willfully reentering the communist country he had escaped. Not only had he left, but he had also lost everything to do so. For a moment, Alois hesitated and had to make sure he wanted to do this. At that moment, Alois was reminded of the precious promises he had learned in scripture. He remembered Hebrews 13:5: "Never will I leave you; never will I forsake you" (NIV). He thought of Matthew 28:20: "And surely I am with you always, to the very end of the age" (NIV). Then he thought of the confidence Jesus imparted when he spoke in Acts 1:8: "But you will receive power when the Holy Spirit comes on you; and you will be my witnesses in Jerusalem, and in all Judea and Samaria, and to the ends of the earth" (NIV).

Alois felt strengthened by the Holy Spirit. "We'll be okay," he told Poldie. He wanted more than anything to see his family and to tell his siblings about Jesus. He brought everyone a Bible. He said a prayer silently: "Lord, help us cross the border safely so that we can see my family."

Alois pulled up to a guard post, and a German officer asked for their passports. The man checked each passport, and then said, "Ich wuenshe Euch Eine gute Reise." (Have a nice trip.) His light tone made Alois feel like everything was going to be okay.

Alois pulled up to the subsequent checkpoint, where a Czechoslovakian guard stood next to an iron barrier. The man approached the car window, and his voice was emotionless. "Pasy prosim" (Passport, please), he said. He looked at their passports and peered closer at Poldie in the passenger seat and the three girls in the backseat. The Czech guard ordered Alois to drive ahead to the next barrier, then lifted a heavy iron bar.

At the next checkpoint, another guard came to the window and said, "Pasy prosim a papiry od auta." (Passports and car registration, please.) This man also studied Alois's paperwork very carefully. "I see your passport says you were born in Czechoslovakia. Is this correct?" he asked.

"That's correct," Alois said.

"Please wait here," the man said and disappeared into a guard structure with Alois's passports and car registration.

Poldie wanted to know what was said, and Alois assured her it was nothing out of the ordinary. About ten minutes later, the man returned with what looked like a high-ranking officer. The Czech officer ordered Alois to park the car and have the other occupants stay inside. He then ordered Alois out of the car and told him to follow him into the building. Alois was grateful he had filled the car with fuel. It was a chilly December and too cold for the family to sit inside the automobile without heat. Poldie kept the car running while Alois was detained.

Alois uttered a few silent prayers as he followed the officer inside to his office. They sat down, and the man said in a warmer tone, "I hope you understand that I need to ask you a few questions."

Alois agreed to it, and the man began the conversation. He wanted to know where in Czechoslovakia Alois was born and where he was educated. He asked what year Alois left the country. When Alois told him it was in 1949, the officer asked, "Did you leave legally or illegally?"

"Illegally," Alois said.

The officer looked surprised that Alois dared to return to his home country after leaving without permission. But the man only casually asked where at the border Alois had escaped. Slowly, Alois began to get the feeling the guard was genuinely curious about how Alois had made a life for himself outside of Czechoslovakia.

"What kind of job do you do in the US?" he asked.

"I have done farm and factory work, and for the last four years, I had a chicken farm," Alois told him.

"You own a chicken farm?" the man asked.

"Yes. My wife and I had about twenty thousand chickens laying eggs," Alois said.

The man guffawed. "That sounds impossible!" he said. "One farmer owning twenty thousand chickens. Here, the state will only allow individuals to own maybe ten or fifteen chickens."

Alois listened as the man drew his own conclusions and waited for the next question. The officer pointed to the car registration on his desk. "This brand-new car was purchased just a few days ago," he said. "How is it that your name is on the registration? You, being an American citizen, come to Germany on vacation, and you can buy a car in a couple of days? This is not possible. We must wait for several years here to purchase a car."

"Well, sir, my goal is actually to save money," Alois said. "I knew that if I rented a car for six weeks, it would just be money spent. But if I bought a car, I could drive it on my visit and then ship it back to the US and sell it for a profit." Alois was honest and answered humbly.

The man was getting more intrigued. "And how many vehicles do you have in the United States?" he asked.

"I have a passenger car and two farm delivery vehicles," Alois replied.

Again, the officer shook his head in utter disbelief. He kept Alois in the office for two hours asking all about his life in America, how things worked, and how Alois had managed to be independently wealthy and successful. Finally, the guard concluded, "You people in capitalistic states have everything, don't you?"

Alois had not meant to brag. He also did not feel that he could criticize the communist lifestyle. He could only let the facts speak for themselves. Alois had his jacket casually open, and the man could see that Alois had five ballpoint pens tucked in his jacket pocket. He had a habit of putting one there, and then another, and ended up collecting them. Alois noticed the man kept eyeing the open jacket.

"Would you have an extra pen?" the officer asked. "My son is collecting those."

"Of course," Alois said. "You can have all of them if you can use them."

The man was quietly overjoyed to receive something so nice. Alois was hoping the interview was nearly over. The officer indicated that it was.

"I only need to look in your car, and you can be on your way shortly," he said.

Outside, Poldie and the girls were shivering from the cold temperatures penetrating the vehicle. The fact that Alois had been detained for such a long period caused them to worry and tremble even more. "What could be taking so long?" Poldie silently queried. She attempted to soften her concern for the sake of the children, and with the angst about to overcome her, she led the girls in prayers over and over again for God to keep Alois safe. As they finished their prayers, they were relieved when they looked up and saw him emerge from the building with the officer. The Czech officer and Alois approached the car, and the officer opened all the doors. The man's eyes fell directly on the stack of Bibles Alois had lined the dashboard with.

"What kind of books are those?" he asked.

"These are Bibles printed in Czech," Alois said. "I wanted to bring a Bible to my parents and five siblings."

The officer agreed for him to take the Bibles into the country, but he would need to look through each one. "About three months ago, a bus full of English tourists came to the border," the officer said. "They had a few boxes of Bibles, and when we opened one of them, they had anticommunist literature."

The officer asked what else Alois was carrying in the luggage. Alois told him he was bringing the family chocolate, coffee, and some of his used clothing. Alois had to explain the route they were planning to take. It would be to Prague, then Sumperk, and then to visit family.

"Okay," the officer said. "You will need to go to the bank window of this building over here. You must pay the equivalent of $15 for each person in your party—for each day you are here visiting."

Alois wondered as he walked to the bank if this was a legitimate fee the man was quoting him. It was a lot of money to pay for five people. At the window, the clerk did not give him a fair currency exchange rate either. But the government called the shots. No one would dare dispute such policies. Finally, Alois made his way back to the car and then drove out beyond the final iron barrier and into Czechoslovakia. As they pulled away, the family prayed aloud, thanking God for giving them His favor at the border.

On the way from the border to the city of Cheb, Alois pointed out to Poldie and the children where he and his three companions had crawled through the snow to reach freedom eighteen years before. The children were curious and fascinated, but Poldie remained uneasy. Alois's memories of his escape were still vivid.

An hour later, when the Hufs reached the city of Plzen, the family let Alois know they were all hungry. Alois found a roadside restaurant, and they went inside. The establishment had a bleakness to it that restaurants did not typically have, Poldie and Alois purported. The blandness of the eatery muted the delight of culinary nourishment. When the waitress came, Alois ordered for everyone in Czech. When he turned to translate a few phrases to his family, she wanted to know where they lived. "We are Americans," Alois said and smiled.

She disappeared into the kitchen, placing their order. When she reemerged, all eyes in the restaurant were studying the Hufs. It was as if the family was in color and contrasted against the rest of their black-and-white world. The eyes of the locals seemed to say, "You don't know how lucky you are. You can come and go. We are stuck here in a state-run country."

Alois and Poldie felt genuine sorrow for the people who looked at them longingly. They wished those souls would be able to travel only a short distance away and know what it was like to live in a place where a person could think and speak freely. The Czech people appeared to them like they were caged birds. Poldie and Alois said a prayer that God would free the beautiful nation from communist oppression.

From Plzen, they drove to Prague so they could appear before the US consulate. Alois could hardly wait to arrive because his sister Maruska had planned to meet them there. He remembered fondly how she had buttoned his sweater that last day at home and how hard it was to say good-bye to everyone. As they drove down the street near the consulate, Alois could see a woman strolling down the road. She was looking at every car that went by. When she saw the Volkswagen, she was almost sure it was her brother's vehicle. Alois waved out the window, which confirmed it.

Alois could hardly park his car fast enough. He had scarcely let himself hope to see his siblings again—and today was the day! Alois jumped out of the car and ran to hug Maruska, and they both cried tears of joy. Maruska squeezed Poldie and said, "Liebe, liebe Poldinko!" (Lovely, lovely Poldie!) She hugged all three girls in one swoop and said, "Vitam vas do Czechoslovakia!" (Welcome to Czechoslovakia!)

Inside the consulate, Alois registered his passport and told the US government agents where he was going and how long he would stay. An officer advised Alois not to participate in any political discussions and to avoid any confrontation with authorities. An official gave Alois a phone number and told him to call right away if he ran into any problems.

Maruska rode in the backseat as they drove to Vikyrovice. The children admired the stunning structures throughout Prague and thought it was incredible to sit beside their dad's sister. It was about a four-hour drive to the village in average weather conditions, but they encountered snow-covered roads along their route, making the trip longer. Alois drove cautiously; he did not want to speed or get in an accident in Czechoslovakia. Maruska spoke German reasonably well, and she conversed nonstop with Poldie on the ride.

It was dark when they arrived in Vikyrovice, and Maruska led them to the family home where Alois spent his childhood years. All of Alois's siblings had gathered for this special homecoming. When Alois stopped the car, it was a flurry of activity. Everyone came running out to meet the family they had only read about in letters and seen on treasured photographs. Alois cried and laughed with everyone. It was so good to see them. He studied each family member's face to see how time had changed him or her, but it didn't seem that anyone had changed all that much. He was so proud of Pepa and all his grown siblings.

Alois taught some words and phrases to Susan, Cristie Jo, and Debra, so they conversed a little in Czech with everyone. The children loved meeting relatives and helping their grandmother fill the kitchen stove with wood. The girls were so intrigued by the wood stove that they often volunteered to go to the woodshed outside and collect more wood. It was so fascinating to their little eyes to see their grandma cooking a meal on a stove with crackling fire beneath.

CHAPTER NINETEEN

NEW BUSINESS, NEW COUNTRY

Alois was required by law to check in to the local police station within forty-eight hours of arriving. Josef accompanied Alois to the station. It was surreal for Josef, who had been questioned by authorities after Alois left. A police officer took Alois's passport and disappeared behind closed doors for almost half an hour. Josef whispered to Alois that he did not like this at all. But to their amazement, the officer simply reappeared, handed the passport back to Alois, and told him he was all set.

The arrival of Alois and his family sent a small shock wave throughout the village of Vikyrovice. Old friends, friends of friends, distant relatives, and even curious neighbors all came by to see this mysterious man who escaped so long ago and reappeared to his family like an angel from heaven. Filled with curiosity about life outside their country and the impact of being an American, they asked many questions. Many knew German, so Poldie and Alois talked with guests all day and all evening for days. The three girls loved the new friendship with their cousins and spent hours frolicking around the property and in the nearby creek.

There was a small Baptist church with about sixty members, including Mr. Kratochvil, in the community meeting nearby. They were allowed to hold services unrestricted as long as no one spoke critically against the regime. Mr. Kratochvil remembered that Alois and Poldie sang in churches back in the US. On Sunday morning, when the Hufs visited the church, the pastor asked Alois to share his faith story and if he and Poldie could sing some songs for everyone in English. Alois joyfully accepted. The pastor invited them to return for the evening service to sing again. The congregants were blessed and asked them to sing the next Sunday as well.

Alois and Poldie understood it was not only the singing they enjoyed but also the spiritual hope the Hufs brought. Their stories reminded the local believers that even when things seem their darkest, no situation is impossible for God. While Alois recognized that most of them might never leave their country, they were still able to have a hope that lifted them above the darkness. Alois was especially proud that his siblings came to see him and Poldie at church. His parents did not attend, but he continued to pray that God would soften their hearts.

After a church service, Maruska reminded Alois and Poldie that she had breast cancer surgery a few years back, as Poldie had. Maruska had been cancer-free for five years and remained healthy.

"Do you think that Jesus healed me?" she asked them.

Alois and Poldie told her they prayed for her healing and continued good health and also prayed for her soul—that Jesus would save her.

"What do you mean by 'saving' me?" she asked. "I go to church quite faithfully."

"Church is not enough," Alois said. "If you want to go to heaven, you must be born again."

Maruska's husband, Slavek, was by her side. "Who started this conversation about religion?" he asked. "Let's just talk about something else."

Maruska whispered to Alois and Poldie that she would like to talk more at a convenient time.

The two weeks in Czechoslovakia quickly came to a close, and it was time to say their good-byes. All the family came to see Alois and his family off, and they wept at their departure. As Alois drove away, he contemplated how much he had changed from the time he was a young man. One thing that had not changed was how much he cherished his family. He prayed for their physical and spiritual well-being with great love as he tucked memories of the two weeks into his heart.

At the German border, a Czechoslovakian customs officer stopped them. Alois could tell the man was eager to see what he could get off them.

"Tell me what you bought and are taking out of the country," he ordered. "And do you have any Czech currency?"

Alois showed him the souvenirs given to them by family members and friends. "Okay, you'll owe three hundred crowns in customs tax for these items," the officer said.

"All the paper currency I had I gave to my parents," Alois said.

"That's fine. You can pay the tax in US dollars," the officer retorted.

Alois was frustrated; he had already been taken advantage of with massive fees entering Czechoslovakia. "Sir, all of these souvenirs were given to us as gifts. I did not want them or ask for them, and they don't have value in US dollars," Alois said. "I will gladly give you all of these." Alois began unloading items from the car onto the ground.

"Wait there," the man said. He disappeared and then returned with his superior officer.

"What seems to be the problem?" the second man asked.

Alois explained the situation and how he was offering to give them the souvenirs.

The man agreed with Alois and said he did not have to pay tax on the gifts. "The only thing we will need is any Czech money you have. That is not allowed out of the country," he said.

Alois reached into his pocket and offered coins to the officer.

"No—paper money," the man said.

"I don't have any paper money, sir," Alois said.

The man looked Alois and the car over. "Load up the souvenirs. You can go," he said.

Poldie breathed an audible sigh of relief when Alois was back behind the wheel and they were moving again. The entire stay was concerning, and she was elated to be heading into a free country. Once the family was in Germany, the only requirement was for Alois to show the family's passports and then they were free to proceed. Poldie had never been so happy to be back in Germany! She took her first relaxed breath in two weeks. Even the children felt the tension lift like a fading fog.

While they were all happy to leave the communist country, for Alois especially, their good-byes were tinged with deep sadness. He had hoped he would be able to show his family the living water he had found in the pages of the Bible and through a relationship with God. Alois wished his family members would receive Jesus as their Lord. It troubled him to learn of things they were told, like how their priest said that if they bought candles in church and burned them, their loved ones would spend less time in purgatory. They were encouraged to give offerings to the priest to expiate sin or heal hurt. Some of the most devout believers among the congregations were the most exploited.

Alois replayed the conversations he had with family members and the verses he showed them. It made so much sense to him, but they did not seem to absorb any of it. More than anything, Alois desired for them to know God the Father's love—a kind that had become so real to him. But Alois rested in his knowledge that God was always working and that for the first time, his loved ones owned a Bible they could read for themselves if they chose.

The Hufs arrived back in Ludwigsburg and visited friends and family. They spent a few days also with Mrs. Lukesh. She was seventy-one years old now and a widow after Mr. Lukesh passed two years earlier, but she was as joyful as ever and still serving in the children's ministry at the local church.

The last day of their six-week stay arrived, and the Hufs left early in the morning. Alois dropped Poldie and the girls off at the airport and then drove his car to a shipping agency not far from the harbor before rejoining them. The family had a pleasant trip and arrived back in Detroit on January 4, 1968. They were all happy when their plane touched down on the Michigan runway. Their friends along with Jana, Marie, and Joey were waiting for them at the airport.

Jana, Marie, and Joey were relieved to see their parents after such a long absence. "Mommy and Daddy, please don't leave us again," they said. Alois and Poldie had difficulty with the separation as well and assured them that next time, they would all stay together.

The trip brought closure of sorts. Alois left Czechoslovakia very haphazardly the first time, and for Poldie, it was helpful to see her family members and hug them after the loss of her father and brother. The visit awakened something in Alois; he saw a business opportunity in Germany. After being a successful entrepreneur in the US, he believed he could find a niche in the German market to produce the all-purpose cleaner he was selling, something that the Europeans were not accustomed to having. He began researching business opportunities that would require minimal investment.

A friend informed Alois about a company in Holland that produced a different cleaning product than the one he was currently selling named By-Pas. By-Pas was produced in concentrated form and marketed and sold to households as well as businesses. Alois's attention peaked, and he was fascinated when visiting the company headquarters to learn more. The product was quite remarkable—it removed stains and made soiled items look new.

Alois approached the owner and informed him there was an untapped market for such a product in Germany. He offered to purchase the formula to sell it in Germany. The company leadership agreed on a price and would arrange the paperwork and create a procedure and directions for him to formulate the product. Two days later, Alois returned to the company office. The two parties signed contracts closing the deal, and Alois was ready for business.

Alois conversed with Poldie about their plans, and they determined it would be best for Alois to travel to Germany first by himself to secure a place to live and to start the mixing and bottling process before the family joined him. Poldie had varied feelings about the new business venture, but she remained supportive. The United States was all that her children had known, and the family had many friends and a full life in Michigan. They had just settled in a lovely new house. She and Alois were not sure how long they would be in Germany. Alois saw it is a chance to both make money and allow his children to know many of their family members. He hoped too that the Gospel might have a more significant effect on their families if they lived nearby.

On March 9, 1968, Poldie and the children took Alois to the Grand Rapids airport. The neighbors were all speculating and talking among themselves now. First, Alois sold his chicken farm, and now he was packing up and heading off to Germany with his family. They were perpetually curious about all things Hufs, it seemed. When the family arrived at the airport, Alois hugged and kissed his family and then entered the terminal and waited to board the plane. Poldie and the kids rushed off to the upper outside observation area. They wanted to wave to Alois as he boarded the plane and watch it take off and ascend into the sky for as long as they were able. Poldie brought the eight-millimeter movie camera Alois had purchased and filmed Alois entering the plane and taking off. When the family could no longer see the plane, they gathered in the car and headed back home.

Alois settled in for the long flights to Amsterdam and, from there, to Stuttgart, Germany. Upon arrival, Poldie's brother Sepp picked Alois up from the airport. Her family was curious about what this Americanized entrepreneur had in mind. Sepp took Alois to Zuffenhausen, a Volkswagen dealer, and Alois purchased a Microbus. The prices were reasonable, and the dollar-to-marks exchange rate was favorable.

Alois found a real estate agent who showed him properties for lease. The agent took him to several different places, but none of them suited his family's needs. Alois explained in greater detail how they needed a garage to store chemicals and bottles and a room to mix his By-Pas cleaning solution, pack it in containers, and prepare the product for shipment.

"Okay," the real estate agent told him one day. "I think I have just the place for you. The only thing is that it's quite expensive."

"Let's go see it," Alois said.

As Alois rode in the agent's vehicle and took in the German cityscapes, he noted how different the city looked a few years after World War II. Back then, roads and buildings were damaged, and businesses limped along. Now the towns in that area of Germany were much healthier, and buildings and roads were rebuilt. They pulled into the Besigheim area, not far from where Sepp lived. The countryside village was nestled between two rivers, the Neckar and Enz, which converged in the city center. Rolling hills with vibrant vineyards flanked the landscape. As they drove through the city, Alois eyed the old buildings dating back to 1459. There were medieval towers ascending toward the sky and a large Gothic church. The center of town offered a charming cobblestone marketplace. They proceeded to a beautiful apartment complex built into a hillside on the opposite end of the city. There were six large apartments on each side of the dwelling. On the outside, steep stone stairs connected all the flats. The lower-level dwelling was the only one unoccupied. Alois liked the idea of only a few stairs for the children to have to climb.

The garages for all apartments were located on the main level of the apartment complex. The first-level apartment was equipped with a basement. The apartment had three bedrooms, two bathrooms, a small kitchen, and a living room. The living space was adequate, and the garage and basement were large enough to start the By-Pas business. Alois asked the agent if the owners would be willing to let him begin working out of the garage and basement right away. The agent said he would contact the owners and get back to Alois with an answer.

A few hours later, the agent reported to Alois that the owners were willing to sign a one-year lease, and after that, Alois would have the option to rent on a month-to-month basis. If Alois agreed to the terms, they had no problems with him operating the business there.

"Okay, that sounds good," Alois said. "Well, what will the monthly rental fee be?"

"It is quite expensive," the agent said. "It's why this apartment has sat empty. The monthly rent is five hundred marks."

It took Alois a few seconds to do the conversion in his head. That was about $120. It was very economical from an American's perspective. "I'll take it," Alois said. That evening, he wrote a letter to Poldie and told her about the beautiful apartment he had secured there.

It was time to get busy on the business, and Alois needed to find a manufacturer who could produce the plastic bottles needed and find the best quality yet inexpensive ingredients for the mixture. Next, he would need sprayers and boxes. As Alois planned it, each box would contain twelve quarts of By-Pas, six on each side of the box, and in the middle, twelve plastic empty pint bottles with a finger-trigger sprayer attached. Finally, he would need to secure a printing company to assist with labels and produce a pamphlet explaining the product.

Alois traveled all over West Germany by car, securing each part of the assembly and packaging needed. Some of the chemicals needed for the formula would have to be purchased from Holland and Belgium, and the ideal sprayers were shipped in from England. After weeks of planning and with much of the start-up obtained, Alois met with a travel agent in Stuttgart to purchase airline passage for his family's upcoming move to Germany. Alois had always been fascinated with Iceland and how it utilized mostly geothermal energy steam as a heat source for the land. The agent worked out a travel itinerary that included a stopover in Iceland so the Huf children could engage with the history and culture of that unique country. With the family's travel plans finalized, Alois drove his newly purchased VW Microbus from Stuttgart, Germany, to the Luxembourg airport. He parked the vehicle in one of the parking stalls so the family would have transportation when landing back at the airport in a couple of weeks. Then on that very day, March 26, Alois boarded a plane and flew back to the United States, happy to have accomplished all he did. He felt confident that he could make a go of the business.

It was great to be back in Hudsonville with his family. Alois and Poldie engaged in many discussions over their plans to live in Germany. They didn't know how long they would stay there, and Alois was not keen on leaving all their things in storage. Besides, if they sold all their assets, he could utilize the money toward the business start-up. He and Poldie drove to Zeeland and talked with an auctioneer about having a sale at their house. The auctioneer agreed that he would advertise heavily for ten days and then hold a public auction on the property for the household items.

The six young children had difficulty comprehending all that was about to happen. Nothing made any sense, especially the idea of leaving their home and friends. Even when Alois tried to sway their opinions by rehearsing the experiences and adventures they would have in Europe, they stood their ground in protest. Poldie objected too but took her concerns to God and trusted that all would be well.

The family spent the ten days leading up to the auction cleaning and preparing all their possessions for sale. Poldie and the girls went through the house and separated only the items they needed and could take with them. Alois and Joe polished and cleaned up the tractor, snow blower, and other garage items to look like new. They lined the garage with tools and pieces of equipment. Ten-year-old Debra had to have a growth surgically removed from the bottom of her heel, so Poldie tended to her as much as she was able while still preparing the house for auction.

On the day of the sale, people came from all around neighboring communities. It was a plus that their new home looked impeccable. It made everything inside seem even more appealing. The items were auctioned off one by one, including their year-old station wagon. It was surreal to see everything carried off by buyers. It might have bothered

Poldie more, but she had learned to never cling to things. As a child, she had little, and anything she had now was much more than she ever dreamed of having. She and Alois placed their home on the market, and that was more difficult to part with. Poldie reminded herself that the long-term plan was to start the business in Germany and then sell it eventually and return to the States.

By the evening of the auction, every room was empty. The exhausted family slept with only pillows and blankets on the carpeted floor. Alois was thankful that their furniture, car, and other items brought in $25,000. That's just what he needed to start the business in Germany. The airline allowed each passenger to have two checked bags. Alois utilized boxes instead, and with eight people, they were able to fit quite a bit into sixteen boxes.

The next day, the family headed to the Grand Rapids airport for their international trip. Poldie and Alois packed a ten-volume set of *The Bible Story* by Arthur S. Maxwell and divvied it up, placing a few in each of the children's carry-on luggage given to them by the airline. Since it contained 409 children's illustrated Bible stories, they assumed it would be an enjoyable diversion on the planes as well as the only English reading they might do during their stay in Europe. Once at the airport, little Debra had to be placed in a wheelchair because she was unable to walk from the surgery just days earlier. The younger children all took turns pushing Debra around the airport while they waited to depart for Detroit. They laughed and engaged in boisterous play in the terminal. Alois and Poldie smiled, realizing this was going to be an unforgettable adventure. Then it was on to New York. For the three younger girls who had just returned from the earlier trip to Europe, this was familiar, but for the other three children who had not yet flown, it was a grand adventure.

The family flew on Icelandic Airlines from New York to Reykjavik, Iceland. They stayed there for a day and took a four-hour tour of the city. They liked taking in the gorgeous scenery and were fascinated by the steam heating system under buildings. This was the vacation Alois wanted to take for years. It seemed like whole sections of his life, when he worked nonstop at the factories and the chicken farm, were blurs of exhaustion and sleeplessness. The children were not accustomed to the

Icelandic cuisine. The culinary delights, mostly consisting of fish, fish eggs, and fish stew, seemed bizarre, since they were American through and through and were missing their Saturday-night adventures to the local McDonald's for hamburgers and fries. The kids made unhappy faces and pulled up their noses at the menu selections. Some of them went to bed hungry because they just would not try the fish. The family stayed in a hotel for one night, and the children enjoyed pushing the buttons on the bedside wall to engage the automatic skylight shades since it was daylight until after 10 p.m.

From Iceland, they flew to Luxembourg, and Alois loaded all their boxes into the Microbus that he had parked there a couple of weeks earlier. With eight people and sixteen boxes, the vehicle was loaded to capacity. The trip to Stuttgart took three hours, and they arrived at their new apartment in Besigheim, called Terassenhaus. Poldie and the children liked the apartment and the surroundings, which helped ease the homesickness they felt.

The Hufs soon stopped to visit Poldie's family, who were eager to meet the three oldest children they had not yet met. Alois drove to the city of Bietigheim and purchased furniture and a washer and dryer. Each time he went to buy something, Alois noted that the exchange rate was reasonable, so he got great deals. In just a few days, the apartment looked like home.

Alois and Poldie needed to find a school for the children. As soon as the kids heard that they would be going to a German school, they wanted nothing of it. They only spoke limited German and wished to be around other children with whom they could relate. There was an American school for military families, but it would be costly for civilians. Alois could not afford tuition for six children, but since Jana was a high school freshman, he enrolled her in the school to attend from April until the end of the school year in June. Alois decided to let the other kids stay home, since the academic year was nearly over and summer vacation was around the corner.

With his family settled, Alois began working on the By-Pas project. He needed a mixer for the chemicals and a filling machine for the bottles. It took most of the auction earnings to get the business off the ground. The manufacturing companies there were not as eager to accommodate

Alois as American companies usually were. They wanted him to pay for a unique mold to form the equipment. Alois had another idea. He took a fifty-five-gallon metal drum and drilled six holes around the bottom, about an inch from the base. Then he took six water faucets and fastened them from the outside of the drum in each of the holes. He took a half-horsepower electric motor and attached a three-foot-long shaft with a three-inch propeller. With the motor fastened at the top of the drum, Alois was able to install a mixer and bottle filler for a fraction of the cost. One drum would fill up a 220-quart container or 440 pint-sized bottles. Once the mixture was ready to go, six people could sit around the drum and fill bottles. The children liked helping with that.

Earlier that year, on January 5, just a few months prior to the Hufs arriving in Germany, Czechoslovakia engaged in what came to be known as the Prague Spring. The communist country realized a brief stint of political liberalization and mass protest within its borders. Alois was cautiously excited to hear in the media that freedom might be coming to neighboring Czechoslovakia, which was under the leadership of President Ludvik Svoboda. Alexander Dubček was elected as the first secretary of the Communist Party in Czechoslovakia in January 1968 and immediately went to work bringing reform to the government.

Alois thought this window of openness in the country was the ideal time to visit again. He and Poldie and the children piled into the Microbus. Alois was amazed at how easy it was this time at the border. There were no questions and no delays. They only had to present their passports, and they were free to go. Alois still did not trust the government, but he at least wished for a reprieve from their past heavy-handed approach.

The Hufs drove to Prague, and Alois showed the children the beauty of the Prague Castle and St. Vitus Cathedral. There was a lightness among the people they met, as if everyone had been touched by hope. The Czechs had learned to hold onto hope loosely. Communists had ruled them for a long time, and many wondered if Russia would invade again.

When the Hufs arrived at the family home in Vikyrovice, there was a celebration. Alois's parents were thrilled that his son and family were now nearby. They stayed for a week, and Alois voiced his plans to visit every three months while the borders were friendly. Initially, they planned to stay for two weeks, but for some reason, Alois had a feeling that they should leave sooner.

Marie Huf asked Alois if he would take her to her birthplace in Crhov, close to the border of Poland. She, Josef, Alois, and his family drove there. Marie visited her sisters, and they stopped at the cemetery where Marie's family members were buried. The group walked around the cemetery for about an hour, reviewing the names and years of the loved ones laid to rest. Their reverent, peaceful walk was interrupted by heavy gunfire in the distance. The sound continued for several minutes. Poldie remarked that it might be the Russians, to which Alois's father said, "Hopefully not."

The following day, Alois and the family said good-bye, promising to return in three months. They visited Hodonice, Poldie's birthplace, on the way to Austria. The Hufs went through Vienna and Salzburg on the route back home to Germany. Usually, Alois turned on the radio to hear the news, but with six children in the car talking and asking questions, he did not.

When they arrived at their apartment in Besigheim, the neighbor who lived just above them came out and talked with Alois. "Isn't it terrible that the Russian tanks invaded Czechoslovakia?" he asked, knowing that it was Alois's home country.

Alois was shocked. "This can't be!" he said. "We just came from there."

"You better listen to the radio," the man said. "It's awful there."

Alois went inside and turned on Radio Prague. He quickly learned that the last ten hours had been tumultuous. The radio announcer was calling for anyone who was willing to fight to come and help stop the Russian forces. The political liberalization movement that began in January was escalating under the reformist Alexander Dubček, and by August 20, 1968, the five countries representing the Warsaw Pact invaded Czechoslovakia, calling later for Dubček's resignation. The pact consisted of the Soviet Union, Poland, Bulgaria, East Germany, and Hungary. Five hundred tanks, along with 250,000 Warsaw Pact troops, invaded the helpless country as the largest military force deployment since the end of the Second World War. The troops immediately seized control of the radio and television stations. When Radio Prague journalists rebelled and refused to surrender control of the station, twenty people were killed prior to its take-over. One hundred protesters were shot to death by Warsaw Pact troops, and more than five hundred people, including civilians, were seriously wounded. A total of 137 civilians were put to death during the invasion. The pact was on a mission to crush any freedom movement under way.

Unarmed people had tried to stop the Russian tanks, and some of them even threw themselves in front of the tanks in one last act of freedom. Alois could not peel himself away from the radio coverage. He was so disappointed for his family and all the people there.

Alois and Poldie were incredulous at the timing of it all. Vikyrovice, located close to the Polish border, was flooded with Russian troops within hours of the invasion. The US consulate in Prague was calling on all Americans in the country to come to the embassy. From there, they could be escorted to the border of Austria. Alois thought of his American family and of the US sticker he had proudly placed on his vehicle. He knew he would have had a difficult time making it to Prague from Vikyrovice in a nice car. They would almost surely have been detained. He thanked God for giving him the urge to leave the country just in time.

For the next three weeks, Alois tried calling his sister Maruska. He was worried about her and his other family members. When she finally answered, her voice had an artificial calm. She did not want to say anything negative against the communists, especially on an international call, which was especially prone to wiretapping. The Hufs prayed daily for their family across the border.

◆

The By-Pas business was growing slowly. It took Alois longer than he anticipated getting the product literature prepared and printed. A few stores were selling the cleaning product, but it was not enough to meet the family's needs. Alois could also see that his children had not adjusted to their new environment. They often talked of people and things they missed back in the United States. Once a week, Alois went to Robinson Barracks in Stuttgart. There they could purchase American-style food, and Alois could keep an eye on schooling opportunities for the children.

The post kept a bulletin board with news and area activity announcements in English. Alois saw that employees were needed in the commissary. Pay would be $1 per hour plus benefits like discounted rates, base privileges, gas coupons, and car plates issued by the US Army. If Alois took this job, the children would have all the privileges of a US Army employee's family, except schooling. Alois was used to multitasking; he and his family could develop By-Pas on the evenings and weekends.

Alois applied and was hired. The US Army grocery store was in Aldingen, close to Ludwigsburg. Most of the time, Alois ran the cash register. He was proud to get the US Army car tag, which meant he no longer needed to pay the German vehicle road tax. With gasoline stamps, traveling was much cheaper. The children liked being able to get items from the store as well. Alois worked at the store forty hours a week and developed By-Pas in the off-hours.

One day, some of the American customers complained that they had to bag their own groceries. That was not what they were familiar with. One of them suggested the store hire some young people, especially when it was busy on the weekends, to pack up the groceries. Alois immediately thought that would be an excellent job for nine-year-old Joey, who, along with the other children, was not in school. Alois and Poldie usually would not have allowed them to miss school, but they were lenient because they knew how much their children missed their friends and old lives back in Michigan.

The next day, Joey came to work with his father, and Alois showed him how to bag the groceries. Joey thought it was fun, and he began receiving tips for doing it. He certainly liked the work better than being in school. This went on for about three weeks, and Joey was averaging $8 per day in tips.

One day, when a man was getting groceries, the customer asked, "Son, are you an American?"

"Yes, I am," Joey answered.

"Then why aren't you in school?" he asked.

"I don't know, sir. You better ask my dad," Joey said, pointing at Alois.

The man took a serious tone with Alois. "I'm the superintendent of the American school," he said. "Why isn't your son going to school?"

"Well, sir, I came back to Germany to start a business. I have invested my money in the business and can't afford to pay for the American school," Alois said. "And my children don't care to go to a German school."

"How many children do you have and where do you live?" the man asked.

"I have six children," Alois said.

The man took a sheet of paper and wrote down their ages and family address. "You'll be hearing from us shortly," he said. Alois didn't mind giving the information. He thought the superintendent might be arranging a special deal for them to attend the school.

Two days later, two men from the school administration visited the apartment. Alois and Poldie were both home and explained they didn't have the money to send their children to the American school. The two men were not there to extend any special offers; instead, they gave the Hufs an ultimatum: if the children were not enrolled in a German school within three days, they would go to the US consulate and force Poldie and the children to return to the United States so the children could go back to school. Marie, Debra, Joey, Cristie Jo, and Susan, along with Jana, were all carefully listening. When the two men left, they said they would go to school.

Poldie enrolled the children in school the next day. Susan was too young to attend. To the children's surprise, they liked school from the start. It took them only a few days to find friends; they wished they had enrolled sooner. Joey remarked that he would miss his tips, however.

Each Sunday, the family attended the Temple Baptist Church, a military church in Ludwigsburg. After service, they went to Sunday school. There, the Huf children made more friends. After Sunday school, several families made it a tradition to go to a schnitzel factory for lunch.

Alois continued to grow his business by selling to companies and homes, and he was an excellent salesman. His strategy involved asking a home or business owner if there were any spots—on a carpet, for instance—in which he or she could not get a stain out. When that person confirmed that there was, Alois would clean the stain with his product, and if the potential customer liked the results, he or she would buy a bottle or case. Whether it was wine, ink, or any other kind of stain, Alois sprayed some of the cleaning solution directly in its center. Then he rubbed gently and wiped it up, lifting the soil and leaving a ring around the cleansed area. The customer would usually be impressed, and then Alois would explain how the solution could be used to keep all areas in the home looking clean. People purchased bottles and cases regularly. Alois was pleased to find that he did not get the cold shoulder nearly as often as he did before in Germany for having a foreign accent.

A little before Thanksgiving, Alois purchased a second car. It was an inexpensive convertible manufactured in Czechoslovakia; it cost about $100. Alois wanted Poldie to have her independence as she had in Hudsonville. One day, Poldie took Marie, Debra, Cristie Jo, and Marie's German friend Karen to see her mother, Anna, who lived minutes away in Ludwigsburg. As they drove through an intersection a ways from the apartment, an oncoming car failed to see the stop sign and struck the side of Poldie's car. The small convertible overturned and landed in a ditch. As the vehicle rolled over, eight-year-old Cristie Jo briefly caught a glimpse of the tumbling view and wished it would be over soon. She closed her eyes, pinching them together as tightly as possible, and at that moment, she saw an image of the words *The End* flash before her mind. She truly felt like this was the end of her young life.

When the car stopped rolling and hearing the girls' terrified screams, Poldie managed to pull herself out and then tug on the girls to get them out quickly to safety. Some of the neighbors rushed outside upon hearing the impact. One of them called the police instantly. Poldie was so grateful that none of the children appeared to be seriously injured. Once Marie, fifteen at the time, was free from the tangled vehicle, she shouted out to the other driver while he was checking to make sure everyone was okay, "You stupid idiot. You could have killed us!"

To her surprise, the man responded in perfect English, "I am so sorry; I didn't mean to." He was an American teacher in one of the military schools.

The German police came, and when they learned that both drivers were American, they notified the US military police. They, in turn, sent an ambulance for Poldie and the four children and took them to the military hospital for examination.

A man known as Master Sergeant Turgean, who lived in the barracks not far from the commissary and who talked with Alois regularly, came to the grocery store where Alois was working and told him that his family had been involved in a car accident. "They were taken to the military hospital in Bad Cannstatt," he said. "That's about all I know."

Alois left immediately. He prayed nonstop as he rushed to the hospital. When he asked for his family at the hospital entry, he was led to the administration office, where Poldie was. She greeted him and assured him she was okay. "I'm bruised in a few places, that's all," she said.

"Oh, thank God. And what about the children?" Alois asked.

"As far as we can tell, there are no serious injuries," Poldie said. "The doctor just wanted us to wait a little longer and make sure everyone checks out."

That night, they were all back home, and Alois and Poldie thanked God that everyone was okay, including Marie's friend.

CHAPTER TWENTY

HEADING BACK TO THE US

For Christmas 1968, Poldie's family gathered at the apartment to observe this special holiday. Finally, her dream to spend the holiday with family after so many without them came true when they came together to celebrate. But honestly, most days Poldie was unhappy about living back in Germany. It seemed ironic since it had never been her first choice to leave Germany to begin with. She remembered those early days in Michigan, when her younger self would travel daily to the post office looking for some sign from home. All her attempts to communicate with people left her frustrated. Her homesickness then was palpable. Living in Michigan might as well have been living on Mars.

But as the years flew by, things quickly changed. She loved her church, the friends she made, and the piece of land on which they had built a life. In some ways, she was more culturally a Michigander than a German now—especially when it came to her Christian world view. And many of the things she longed for no longer existed, she realized. When their real estate agent in Hudsonville called to say their beautiful house had sold, Poldie was disappointed. She stayed positive for Alois, and especially for the children, but in her heart, she often prayed that they would be able to move back soon to the United States and their home in Hudsonville. She kept in touch with good friends back in the United States.

Alois and Poldie wished Alois's family could visit them in Germany. Though it would be difficult for the Hufs to enter Czechoslovakia, they learned that it was often possible for relatives there to visit Germany. In January, Alois sent an invitation to Maruska and her family. It took about four weeks for the Czech government to finally grant permission for all five members of her family to come to Germany. The two weeks of their visit were so much fun for all of them, and especially for the cousins. Maruska could not get enough of browsing stores and malls and seeing how differently their neighboring country did things.

While living in Germany, Alois wanted to expose his family to as many cultures and historical sites as possible. It was important to both he and Poldie that their children learn by visually experiencing history. After his sister's family returned back to their home in Czechoslovakia, Alois made plans to take his family to West Berlin. He intended to educate the children on life behind the iron curtain in East Berlin. Realizing the children were young and most likely unable to grasp the entirety of what they were about to see, Alois did his best to share some critical insight about the effects of the war.

An American friend, a soldier named Rus who attended their church, came along too. Since Alois worked for the military, the family traveled in the military train. Each car on the train had sleeping compartments. Through West Germany, the cities and villages lit up beautifully at night. With snow-covered mountains, the vista looked like a painting, they thought.

A military bus took the Hufs from Stuttgart to Frankfurt, where they boarded a military train. The route then took them along Russian-occupied territory. The train was only permitted to travel in that area at night. The reason was probably that the Russians and East Germans wanted to hide the poverty and disrepair in the section. When the train stopped in East Germany, no one was allowed to disembark. Iron fences and Russian guards flanked the railroad tracks.

When the family arrived at Berlin, the region was under a severe snowstorm. Nearly three feet of snow fell in a short time. Alois planned to rent a car for their stay, but it was impossible to get around in such conditions. The military buses took tourists to see the Berlin Wall and Checkpoint Charlie at Friedrichstraße.

In August 1961, eight years before the Huf family visited Berlin, the citizens of East Germany woke to find barbed-wire barriers—which later became a massive concrete wall—separating the city. It was built to prevent citizens in the east from defecting into the democratic west. The Soviet-occupied territory leaders bound the people physically and ideologically to prevent an uprising. This came about because of the masses defecting from the socialist east to capitalist west for a better life.

These refugees included 61 percent of the working population, skilled in fields like education, medicine, engineering, and technology. The Soviet officials devised a solution for the people who took advantage of what appeared to be an open and uncontrolled border: the twenty-seven-mile Berlin Wall. Checkpoint Charlie was the Berlin Wall crossing point for those who were cleared for entrance, such as Allied diplomats, foreign tourists, and military personnel.

The outer Berlin Wall, which separated the city into east and west, was marked with crosses and wreaths. These were the places where East German citizens tried to escape and were shot and killed. On the interior was another concrete wall. The two walls were separated by a 160-yard space called the "death strip." Along this area, Russian soldiers guarded miles of trenches, guard dog runs, tripwire machine artillery, and watchtowers.

Irrespective of the heavy falling snow, the Huf family walked to the viewing tower and climbed the long wooden staircase to get high enough to see over the wall into East Berlin. An eerie silence followed as they looked over in the snow-covered landscape. Off in the distance into communist East Berlin, the children saw an older lady peering out from her window in a high-rise apartment. Naturally, the children waved. Alois and Poldie grabbed their children's arms and lowered them to their side. They didn't scold the children but cautioned them to be reverent and unanimated until they left the wall. Alois and Poldie did not want to frighten the children but wanted the experience to educate them about the communist and anti-God perspective. It made everyone so thankful for the lives they were free to live. They stayed in Berlin for several days. Alois carried Cristie Jo, and Rus carried Susie on his shoulders. They visited several essential sights, including where President John F. Kennedy gave his famous speech in which he said, "I am also a free man; Ich bin ein Berliner."

◆

By the end of February 1969, the By-Pas business began to grow. Soon, Alois did not have enough time in the evenings and the weekends to keep up with orders. He alerted Poldie that he would have to quit working in the US commissary store. Poldie understood. She had an idea: she could take his position as a cashier. This way, the family could still receive the benefits. Alois agreed, so he took it to management. They were willing to have Poldie work in Alois's place, so that became the new arrangement.

That spring, Alois's parents were able to leave Czechoslovakia and come to Germany for a three-month visit. Alois arranged for them to ride the train and stay with the family, and he was grateful the political situation allowed them to come. The stay was delightful for all of them. Alois and Poldie continued sharing about Jesus, but they did not try to push their faith or engage in too much debate about it this time.

The By-Pas business became more productive once Alois recruited salespeople under him. He delivered the product throughout Germany, and often his father came along for the ride while he was in town. Alois knew that nothing could make up for the lost time he was away, but he was glad to be able to build new memories and strengthen their bond.

As Alois built the business, his goal was to get it to the point that it would be desirable for someone to buy. He and Poldie were Americans now, and he wanted to get back to the United States eventually. He was pleasantly surprised when there was interest in his company so soon. In May of 1969, one of the salesmen revealed that he knew of a man who was interested in purchasing the By-Pas name, formula, production, and distribution for all of Germany, the entire operation.

Alois arranged a meeting with the gentleman and invited him to come to his house in Besigheim to view the simple production. He took caution to hold the formula secret. During the meeting, the man appeared genuine. Alois explained that while his mixer and operation were basic, there was little overhead cost, which allowed it to be more profitable. The man liked what he saw.

"What are your plans if you were to sell this?" he inquired to Alois.

"If someone purchased the distribution rights, I would take my family back to the US," Alois confirmed.

The buyer was interested. He requested a document from the By-Pas headquarters in the United States stating that Alois was the sole owner of the By-Pas business in Germany and that Alois had the legal option to sell it. Alois agreed to his request. The next day, Alois drove to the

Frankfurt Airport. He was able to get a civilian ticket on the military service plane for a reasonable price to fly to America to obtain the legal document.

Four days later, Alois landed back in Germany with a signed document in hand. He presented it to the prospective buyer. The man studied it and said he would give it to his attorney to review. Within three days, the man called Alois and confirmed his desire to purchase the distribution rights. When Alois talked about selling the business to Poldie, she was thrilled. In her mind, it was a quick answer to her prayer to go back to America. She told him she would be supportive of him no matter what happened.

The next week, Alois and the buyer sat together in the attorney's office and agreed to the deal. A part of the agreement included Alois remaining in Germany until July 30 to help transition the business. When all was signed and the deal consummated, Alois broke the news to his family that they would be going back to America in August. The children had made the transition to Germany and German schools quite well and were less eager to move back to Hudsonville.

In their remaining time in Germany, Alois wanted to make the most of being around family. He invited two of his brothers to visit. Pepa and his family came first, and he enjoyed accompanying Alois on many By-Pas delivery routes. He stayed for two weeks, and then Hynek and his family arrived for two weeks. Alois built memories with them and took their families sightseeing.

After the company sale, the By-Pas business continued to expand rapidly. The new owner called his business partners together for a meeting and invited Alois. The owner was concerned that the profit margin was much too high for the salesmen. The company operated like a multilevel marketing business, allowing its salespeople an opportunity to distribute products to consumers through a downline. Alois thought this was a good problem to have, especially since it allowed everyone in the business to make a good income. He was thankful God had blessed his endeavor and hard work.

He and Poldie began preparing for the move. Poldie asked her siblings if they wanted some of their household items, like clocks and knick-knacks. The relatives came by and picked up the things they wanted.

Alois wished to go back to Czechoslovakia once more before they left the continent. He went to the American consulate in Stuttgart and asked if it would be safe to visit Czechoslovakia for a few days. He was especially concerned since their Volkswagen had a US Army plate. They confirmed that the trip should go well as long as he had a visa.

When Alois's visa was approved and the July weather was beautiful, the Hufs set out in their VW Microbus to visit Czechoslovakia. Again, Alois questioned himself for going, considering the country was under Russian occupation. He remembered the time, many years ago, when Russian soldiers took his and Pepa's bicycle. Poldie had traumatic memories of the time as well. But this time, they were adults and American citizens. They prayed, and their love for Alois's family compelled them to visit.

The trip was going well until they left Prague and headed toward Sumperk. On their drive from the city of Hradec Kralove, they unintentionally found themselves in the middle of a long convoy of Russian military vehicles. They crawled along for two hours. No one stopped them, but everyone in the van was tense. There were no civilian vehicles around, and their van had US Army tags and a big US sticker on the back. Alois mentally prepared a script in the event they were stopped. He prayed they would not encounter any problems with the soldiers or on the road.

Finally, when they were near Sumperk, the convoy began turning off in another direction. The children, who had been quietly watching the military vehicles, breathed a collective sigh of relief. "Daddy, you have to promise that you will not take this road on the way back to Prague," someone said.

Alois assured them, "We will never take this road. We'll take a different road back, even if it's a lot farther. I promise you that."

For the next three days, Alois and the family visited loved ones. Everyone they met was so discouraged about the occupation. Josef confessed to his son, "The Russians will never release their grip on Czechoslovakia."

July 20, 1969, the day they left, everyone wept. The children grew to love the Huf side of the family, and they were concerned for their European relatives. Maruska and her husband rode with them in the van, and as they drove away, Alois and Poldie led the children in prayer for their family and all of Czechoslovakia, and they promised the children that they would see them again one day.

On the drive back, Alois took an alternate route with a much busier road. It took them out of the way, but they did not see any military convoys, which put the entire family at ease. They stopped briefly in the city of Plzen to drop Maruska and her husband at the train station so that they could travel back to their home in Uničov. Plzen is the Czech city made famous in 1842 by a Bavarian brewer who crafted the famous Pilsner pale lager beer.

Alois parked the van, and the family walked along the busy sidewalk toward the station. Masses of people surrounded a large television just outside the station. People were standing tippy-toed, and there was so much commotion, it was challenging to hear. Alois and Poldie wondered what was happening. They knew it had to be a significant event, so they joined in to see for themselves. That's when they realized they had spent so much of the last month entertaining family, selling the By-Pas distribution rights, packing for America, and taking this last-minute trip to Czechoslovakia that they had forgotten that something historic was happening: as their eyes glanced toward the TV, American astronaut Neil Armstrong had stepped foot on the moon. It was the live broadcast of the Apollo 11 landing, a global event watched by six hundred million people. That was an incredible day for America and the world and made the anticipation of going home to the US even more thrilling.

They said their tender good-byes to Alois's sister and her husband and then left in the van to the border crossing. After a brief wait, they were permitted back into Germany. The family breathed a sigh of relief to be back in a noncommunist country. However, their Czechoslovakian family members were continually on their minds.

Back in Besigheim, the family made final preparations for their move back to Michigan. While packing, Poldie said, "It's high time that we go home." Jana and Marie did not agree. They made numerous friends in school and had begun to like their home in Germany. Many of their German friends were listening to the Beatles, the English rock band from Liverpool. They had released a single in August 1968 called "Hey Jude," which was a number-one hit in several countries around the globe, including the United States. Their *Yellow Submarine* album had released in early 1969 and proved popular among the young. In January, John Lennon came under fire for his album *Two Virgins*, and it was declared as pornographic in the state of New Jersey.

Poldie and Alois took time to reflect on all the global events that took place in the fifteen months they had been in Germany. The television age began in 1968; personal television sets allowed for historic events to play out in the homes of people across America and the world. In April, Dr. Martin Luther King Jr. was assassinated on his Memphis hotel balcony. Later that same month, riots broke out at Columbia University protesting the Vietnam War. In June, Robert F. Kennedy was assassinated in Los Angeles shortly after winning the California primary. In October, the world witnessed the Olympic Black Power protest, and in November, Nixon won the US presidency and was headed for the White House. Days before the year's end, Apollo 8 orbited the moon.

The couple reflected on the events of the first seven months of 1969. The Boeing 747 jumbo jet took its first flight from Washington to New York, and the Concord took its first flight out of London. In February, Golda Meir had been sworn in as Israel's first-ever female prime minister. American actress Judy Garland, who won her way into the hearts of all as Dorothy Gale in *The Wizard of Oz*, died in London at the age of forty-seven. Back in the States, Senator Edward Kennedy drove his vehicle off a Chappaquiddick bridge, killing passenger Mary Jo Kopechne, who was only twenty-eight. As previously discussed, on July 20, Neil Armstrong set foot on the moon, and on November 10, educational television program *Sesame Street* debuted. As the Huf family was heading home, Woodstock was making plans for the rock 'n' roll event of a lifetime, attracting more than 350,000 young people. Only the future would reveal what the closing months of 1969 would bring.

As they made plans for their return back home, Alois was grateful that he and Poldie decided to retain thirty-eight acres of land and that they had only included two acres with the sale of their old house. Poldie wondered about where they would live when they moved back. They had managed in a mobile home before and could do it again until they made further plans. Alois wanted to purchase another new VW Microbus, so they went to the dealership and had it shipped to the New York

Harbor. The dealership agreed to take their old bus as a trade-in with the understanding that Alois would drive it until it was time to leave.

Three days before departure, Poldie and Alois resigned their positions at work. They made the rounds one last time to say good-bye to family and friends. It was especially challenging to leave Mrs. Lukesh, who had come over on many occasions to set up her flannelgraph to teach the neighborhood kids Bible stories. The time with her was always tender. They knew they would spend eternity with her, but she was aging, and the Hufs wondered if they would be together again at any point in the future. They also stopped by the city of Pforzheim to bid farewell to the new owner of By-Pas Germany. Then they said good-bye to Jana's and Marie's school friends.

On their last morning in Germany, the Hufs drove to Ludwigsburg, where they met up with Poldie's brother Toni and his wife, Gisela, who both accompanied them to the Frankfurt Airport. Toni drove his BMW alongside their Microbus, and in no time, he sped off into the distance on the Autobahn. Alois stepped on the gas to keep up and drove the Microbus at its max speed—about one hundred miles per hour.

There was no speed limit on this highway, but Poldie still gave Alois a concerned look and said, "You better not try this in the US."

They chuckled, and Alois gave up on trying to keep up with his brother-in-law. As the trip went on, Poldie turned to Alois again. "I'm so glad that the Lord heard my prayers and that we are now on our way home to America!" she said. "I know Germany is where my mother and siblings live, but I for one didn't like it here, and I would not want to live here again." She paused. "We just don't belong in Germany anymore."

Alois gave Poldie a knowing grin. "You're right," he said. "We both can be very thankful to our Lord that He was one who helped us to accomplish the task we came to Germany to do so quickly. It was always a goal to launch the By-Pas business here in Germany, work hard to make it profitable, offer the distribution rights up for sale, and head back to America. I never thought it would happen so soon."

When they reached the airport, Toni and Gisela had been waiting there for them for half an hour. After the Hufs got their plane tickets and checked their bags, they all went to an airport restaurant. Toni noted how well the six children had developed in their German. All of them, including six-year-old Susie, could hold a steady conversation. They had a pleasant visit and lots of laughs until it was time to say a final good-bye. In no time at all, they were off for the long flight back to the States. After crossing the Atlantic, the plane began to descend into the New York area.

As the plane touched down in New York on July 30, Poldie felt her heart leap. How different was it this time than when she had sailed into the harbor? She glanced at Alois. They owed their success in America to God and to her husband's hard work and her diligent work alongside him. God had blessed them, and they had friends who were there for them. It all added up to a perfect life.

That night, they stayed in a hotel in New York. The next morning, Alois and Poldie went to pick up their new VW Microbus at the harbor. Once all the children and belongings were loaded, they drove to Harrisburg, Pennsylvania, to visit Norm, one of Alois's friends. Norm was an American who had been stationed in Germany six months earlier, serving in Kornwestheim. He and his wife had gone back to the US shortly after Alois and Poldie moved to Germany. It was good to catch up, and Alois, like Poldie, felt happy to be back in the United States.

The six-hundred-mile trip to Hudsonville was peaceful. Alois's thoughts were on their future. Apart from the land they owned, they didn't have a home to go back to. Perhaps the more pressing matter was that there wasn't a job either. Alois began to strategize what he would do; always the entrepreneur, he had learned not to worry. With prayer and determination, things had a way of working out.

When the family rolled into Hudsonville, fond memories came back to them. They stopped first at Mr. and Mrs. Jones's house. They felt close to them and always credited them for coming to Michigan in the first place. They found a motel between Hudsonville and Zeeland that was only five miles away from their thirty-eight-acre property. The rooms were tiny, so Alois rented three bedrooms for the eight of them. It was a good thing Jana and Marie had their own room because it was soon full of their old school friends. They had gotten word the Hufs were back in town, and everyone was so happy to see them. The warm welcome made leaving their German friends a little easier.

The next day, Alois and Poldie went to Grand Rapids to purchase a mobile home. They chose a three-bedroom model, and Alois got busy preparing the land. Only the fourth day after arriving in the US, the mobile home was set up, and Alois quickly connected the water, sewer, and electricity. Their first night in the trailer house, Alois gathered everyone around for a special prayer of thanks for God's help along the way.

The following day, after the family got settled, Alois put a plan in motion for future employment. He drove to Holland and met with a senior member of the By-Pas company. He and Alois talked about the business in Germany and how quickly it had grown. The gentleman asked Alois if he would join the By-Pas operation locally. Alois inquired how business had been for the past six months. The man revealed their modest sales.

Alois tried not to insult the man, but he felt in his heart that he could do better. They were in prosperous America, and through diligent work, he'd made a steady go of the product in Germany.

"I don't think I'm interested in joining you," Alois responded. "But if you are willing to sell me what remains of the By-Pas company and inventory, I might be interested."

The man agreed to talk it over with leadership. When the phone rang the next day, Alois was surprised the manager asked him to visit their warehouse and look over the inventory. This could only mean good news. The two men walked down aisles of items. There were thousands of carton boxes, bottles, sprayers, and caps and a few chemicals. Afterward, Alois sat down with the leadership team. They were prepared to offer him the entire inventory and the name By-Pas Worldwide for a reasonable price. Alois thanked them and asked for a week to think it over.

Ever since the early days, after arriving in the US, Alois wanted to be his own boss. He and Poldie spent time discussing and praying through the decision. The next week, Alois phoned the manager at the By-Pas office and asked him to prepare the purchase contract. The transaction was simple, and in a matter of days, Alois was the owner of By-Pas Worldwide.

Poldie enrolled the children in school in September, and they readjusted to America quickly. In October, Poldie and Alois met with a builder, and they began construction of a four-bedroom house. This made Poldie feel so thankful after they had sold the house they'd built not long before.

With the successful launch of By-Pas in Germany, Alois had a new fire under him to make the American company just as prosperous. He understood things needed to be done differently. In Germany, they earned most of their income from domestic contacts. The bulk of the product sold in pint- or quart-sized bottles of concentrate. The consumer would simply dilute the concentrate with water and could use the solution for a long time before placing another order.

Alois talked with a salesman about reaching out to small and large businesses with the product. Satisfied business owners could be repeat customers in a quicker time frame. The salesman suggested appealing to enterprises with larger quantities, such as gallon-size containers with six to a box. He also advised that the product be available in five-gallon and fifty-five-gallon drums with only the quart-sized bottles available for retail stores.

Alois appreciated his ideas but concurred immediately with producing quarts for retailers. He went to work on creating the logo, brochures, and labels for the industrial product. By late December 1969, Alois and Poldie registered their business as By-Pas International Corporation.

They rented a warehouse in Overisel Township to set up production, and in the first week of January 1970, Alois had the business running and mixed the first batch of the By-Pas cleaner in gallons. The first full-time salesman loaded up his car with as many six-pack cartons as he could carry. He traveled around the city of Holland to small businesses, inquiring about their needs and showcasing the product. Three hours later, he was back with an empty car.

"How'd it go?" Alois asked.

"I didn't have too much of a problem selling it," he told Alois. "Most businesses are willing to try new things. The real test will come when we call on the same businesses for reorders."

From that time on, Alois and the entire Huf family helped fill gallon jugs one day per week. It became a family business. On Tuesdays, Alois and the other salesman loaded a van full of gallons. With about one hundred cartons in their vehicles, they drove throughout the state of

Michigan. This was a lot of effort, but Alois knew it was the way for people to learn about By-Pas and for the business to become profitable.

In March of 1970, the new home was ready, and the Hufs moved into the lovely dwelling. This was a wonderful time for Poldie and the children to get settled back into a real home with plenty of space for everyone. However, Alois wished he could be home to enjoy his family more; he was typically absent from Monday through Friday each week, conjuring up new business for the company.

Alois determined to plan vacations from time to time and make memories with the family. Once, they traveled up north to Mackinac Island, Michigan, and rented eight bikes to tour the island. Another year, they set out to Florida in the family van, pulling a camper behind it. There was always fun to be had when they were together as a family.

No matter how busy life in Michigan was, Alois and Poldie visited their family in Europe every other year for three weeks at a time. For a week and a half, they stayed with Poldie's family in Germany, then rented a car and drove to Czechoslovakia to see Alois's family. They boxed up used clothing from home to give away. It was startling how little the people had in the communist country.

In the right moments, Alois shared verses that told of salvation by grace through Jesus Christ and not through good works or remittance to a priest. He told his loved ones about Ephesians 2:8-9, which says, "For it is by grace you have been saved, through faith—and this is not from yourselves, it is the gift of God—not by works, so that no one can boast" (NIV). Amid all the bad news in their country, he wanted them to have this good news, if only they would accept it. Alois and Poldie would depart from those trips with grateful and yet grievous hearts, thankful for how God worked in their lives and yet sorrowful when family members showed little concern about eternity.

During Jana's senior year of high school in 1971, her classmates named her the Hudsonville High School homecoming queen. Sometimes Alois and Poldie had to do a double take at each of their children. How did they go from babies to young people so fast? It seemed like they blinked once and a year passed, and then they blinked twice and two more years went by. Alois and Poldie realized they were not perfect parents by any means, and they had their faults, but the most important thing for them was to raise their children to be people of character who knew the God of the Bible. With that foundation, they were sure to do well. Jana went on to enter more beauty pageants that same year and accepted a proposal to marry a young man with whom she attended school.

By 1972, both Jana and Marie were engaged to be married and planned summer and fall weddings. The girls were excited about this next step in their young lives. Jana married on one of the hottest days in July. The groom and groomsmen wore burgundy velvet tuxedos and struggled to keep from fainting in the non-air-conditioned sanctuary. Jana looked beautiful in her dress and veil. Marie married in mid-September and was just as beautiful as her sister on that day.

In October, Alois began to build a metal pole barn on a piece of their property for the By-Pas production. Joey assisted Alois more and more with the business and the new construction. One rainy day driving back from the Overisel property, Alois and Joey encountered a slick patch on the road, and the van began to slide around. It careened toward a ditch, where it rolled over several times and landed upside down. When it came to a stop, Alois felt Joey directly at his side. Joey appeared to be fine, but Alois suffered a dislocated arm. When the call came in that they had been in an accident, Poldie screamed and begged God to keep her husband and precious boy in His care. Alois required surgery to restore his shoulder and arm, and it took a year of rehabilitation before he could resume his regular workload. The family was grateful God had watched over their lives and that Joey continued to help build the business.

By-Pas products did well, and the business was productive. Regularly, Poldie and the children traveled to the production plant in Overisel, and while Joey mixed the formula, the girls bottled and labeled it. Poldie and the children were thankful when the construction of the pole barn on their property was complete. It meant they no longer needed to spend unnecessary time driving to and from work. Alois made arrangements with his children to go on an honor system with their work hours. He pinned up a list of their names, and each child was instructed to jot down their legitimate hours worked. Sometimes the kids got feisty and cheated the system, and they got some good laughs out of it, but all in all, the kids were trustworthy and hardworking employees.

On July 20, 1974, Alois and Poldie became grandparents for the very first time when Marie delivered a healthy baby boy, Michael Jason. Early that morning, Alois took fifteen-year-old Cristie Jo on the road with him to sell By-Pas and other items at fairgrounds throughout Michigan. They called home on several occasions to receive updates. Finally, she convinced her daddy to pack up and head home so they could welcome the little baby into their family. Alois and Poldie took to grandparenting right away, spoiling the baby with hugs and kisses and gifts. Poldie was the consummate grandmother, wanting to cuddle and rock the baby whenever possible. Marie appreciated Poldie's motherly wisdom and received it with joy on multiple occasions. Almost a year to the day, Jana gave birth to Alois and Poldie's second grandchild. Three years later, Debra gave birth to their third grandchild, Aaron, and the grandchildren kept coming. While Poldie spoiled her grandchildren, bringing them gifts as often as possible and playing games with them, Alois took them in his arms, faced them away from his body, and swung them back and forth and sang them Czech lullabies. The grandkids leaped into his arms whenever possible, asking to be next.

The years sped by, and by fall of 1978, three of the oldest children were married, and Alois and Poldie had a fourth grandchild on the way. A friend of Alois from Holland asked him to come to hear a young evangelist named Jerry Johnston, who was preaching in the area at a local church. When Alois found out the preacher was eighteen years old, he smirked but decided to go for the sake of his friend. On Sunday evening, October 15, Alois and Poldie and some of their children went to hear him. They filled the entire second pew of the sanctuary. There was nothing extraordinary about Calvary Baptist Church that night except for the way the Holy Spirit moved when the young man preached. Many members were cut to the heart. They began confessing sins after the sharing of scripture, the message, and prayer. Numerous members and visitors received Jesus Christ as Savior.

Alois and Poldie were moved as well to seek and serve God whole-heartedly, and they, along with some of the married children, attended the evening services during the Holland revival. During weekdays, people invited their unbelieving friends to church. On Saturdays, groups of young people, including Cristie Jo and Susie, went out sharing the faith with neighboring communities. Alois had never seen Cristie Jo so passionate about God and the Gospel.

An infectious love and a desire to serve God came upon the Christians in the area. Alois felt grateful for the light and fresh joy that Jerry's messages brought to the region. The last night of the crusade, Alois invited Jerry to come over to their home for snacks and fellowship. He was blessed by the young preacher and wanted to make him feel welcome in the community.

Jerry agreed and came over that evening and hit it off with the family—particularly Cristie Jo. Before he left that evening, he asked if he could call Cristie Jo sometime. That "sometime" soon became more than once per day. When Jerry came to preach in their region, Alois, Poldie, and Cristie Jo joined him for services. The two seemed to have a special connection and seemed to be falling in love.

In December, Jerry came for a special visit. He asked Alois and Poldie if he could marry Cristie Jo. Alois didn't expect Jerry to ask for Cristie Jo's hand in marriage so quickly. He suggested to Jerry, "You hardly know each other. Why don't you wait until next year at least?"

Just days later, in early January 1979, Jerry came for another visit and again asked if he could marry Cristie Jo. Alois was surprised. "I thought you were going to wait a year before getting married," he said to the young man.

Jerry replied, "I heard you tell me to wait until next year. That was in December, and now it is January."

Alois said, "Yes, it is 'next year' now. If you love Cristie Jo and both of you would like to get married, you have our blessing, as long as this marriage will not be a hindrance to your preaching ministry. You have a message that people need to hear."

To this, Jerry replied, "This marriage will strengthen my ministry because Cristie Jo will be right alongside me, supporting me. She'll travel with me wherever I go."

Poldie and Alois asked, "What is going to happen when Cristie Jo gets pregnant?"

Jerry assured them, "This won't happen. We'll at least wait five years before we start a family."

Jerry and Cristie Jo began planning a March wedding. It would take place in Overland Park, Kansas, a suburb of greater Kansas City. Guests from Michigan and Kansas attended the church wedding.

After that, Jerry and Cristie Jo traveled together for evangelistic crusades all over America. When the young couple came to a nearby town, Alois and Poldie met them to be part of the spiritual blessing. On one occasion, Jerry was to preach in Canton, Ohio, and asked Alois if he would drive to Steubenville, Ohio, to pick up one of Jerry's friends named Harvey and bring him to the service. Harvey was an older man who prayed intercessory prayers for Jerry and his ministry. He was aware of Jerry's marriage to Cristie Jo but had not yet met this new girl in Jerry's life.

After being stuck in traffic, Alois arrived at Harvey's home. Following a quick introduction, they got on the road again, and Alois focused on navigating through the congested roadways to get them to their destination on time. Harvey began to make conversation, but Alois was brief in his replies, giving yes and no answers to maintain his attention on driving.

The highly opinionated Harvey started in with "Jerry called me and told me that he was getting married to some girl from Michigan. He did, and I wonder what kind of person she is. Is she going to be good for him, or is she going to keep him from serving the Lord?" Alois remained quiet. "I do not know her, but I do not think much of her. If Jerry had called me before about this girl, I would have talked him out of this marriage. Women today are not as good as they used to be."

Harvey didn't seem to notice that Alois had very little to say in reply. When the two men arrived at the church, the service had already begun. They found a place in the front row and joined in the singing.

When Jerry approached the pulpit, he said, "With great joy, I would like to introduce you to my wife, Cristie Jo. Honey, would you please stand? I also would like to introduce my in-laws, Cristie Jo's parents, Alois and Poldie Huf. Would you please stand up?"

When Alois and Poldie stood up, Harvey wanted to crawl under the pew out of embarrassment. After Alois took his seat, Harvey leaned over and whispered, "Al, you rascal, you." After the service, Harvey ribbed Alois about their earlier conversation.

Alois and Poldie traveled to be with Cristie Jo and Jerry in the crusades as often as they could. They were grateful for their son-in-law's entrance into their family. Due to his influence, some of their children and sons-in-law either were saved or renewed their relationships with God. As the years passed, Alois traveled with Jerry to cities in the US and Canada for evangelistic crusades. There, hundreds of people came to Christ, and their lives were changed forever.

During the weekdays, Jerry spoke in the public schools of each city. He addressed controversial issues like substance abuse, suicide, and the lies of the sexual revolution. Jerry closed by inviting students to Friday-night meetings, where thousands would be in attendance. Hundreds of students gave their lives to Christ each week. After the Friday-night meetings, students stayed to eat free pizzas and socialize. Alois so enjoyed seeing lives changed for the better. He helped at the resource table after the sessions.

◆

Joey married in 1979 also, just four months after Cristie Jo's wedding, and in the same year, he joined as a partner in the By-Pas International Corporation. Even though times were changing, some traditions never changed. Alois and Poldie still sang duets and shared their testimonies in area churches, telling people how God graciously saved them.

◆

With each trip to Europe, Alois and Poldie saw their parents aging more and more. When they returned home, they anticipated, at any moment, that one of them would get a sad phone call. For Alois, this moment came in November 1981 in the form of a telegram from Czechoslovakia. It said, "Maminka zemrela." (Mother passed away.) Even though he knew her death would probably come soon, it didn't spare the heartache he felt. Alois learned his mother had been in a coma for eight days before she breathed her last. Because the visa visitation requirements necessitated time, Alois told his father they would not be able to attend her funeral but would send flowers and a wreath. On the day of the funeral, Alois and Poldie held their own memorial service for his greatly loved mother.

When Alois and Poldie visited Czechoslovakia the next year, Josef was still grieving over his wife, but his heart was much softer. He told Alois that he wanted to receive Jesus as his Savior! He prayed with Alois and asked God to forgive his sins and for Jesus to become his Lord. Alois cried tears of joy when he saw his father's eyes light up. He loved his dad so much. He marveled that his years of faithful prayer on his father's behalf were answered.

On the same trip, Poldie had a heart-to-heart talk with her mother. She said, "Mother, you are getting older, and we are so far away from you. If you passed, I would never see you again unless you know the Lord Jesus as your Savior. Have you received Him in your heart?"

"I go to church whenever I can, which is not too often anymore," her mother said. "But receiving Christ—I don't think I ever did."

"It's so simple," Poldie instructed. "All you have to say is, 'God, I believe that Jesus died on the cross for me. I ask Jesus to forgive me of all my sins and make me His child. Lord, come into my heart.' The Bible says, 'Whoever calls upon the name of the LORD shall be saved,' as we read in Romans 10:13 and Acts 2:21 and Acts 4:12. The Bible says that Jesus is the only name by which we can be saved and the only way to heaven for all people. All people means everyone: the Jews and Gentiles, religious people, nonreligious, Catholics, and Protestants. Whoever calls on the name of the Lord shall be saved."

Mrs. Kellner agreed to pray and to receive Jesus Christ as her Savior. After she did, Oma Kellner told Poldie, "Jetzt habe ich." (Now I have it.) She pointed to her heart and smiled at Poldie. Not long after that, she became senile and lost her memory. It was such a comfort to Poldie to remember that conversation.

In May of 1983, Alois and Poldie's youngest, Susie, was married. Poldie and Alois transitioned to life as empty nesters and full-time grandparents.

Poldie was forty-nine, and Alois was fifty-three; all six of their children were married, and they already had eleven grandchildren.

A year later, in May of 1984, Alois received another telegram from Czechoslovakia, this time letting him know that his eighty-one-year-old father passed away. Alois and Poldie processed the loss together. How grateful they were that they had visited so often during their parents' final years and, even more important, were used by God to share the message of Christ's salvation.

In October 1986, Alois and Poldie attended one of the regular Sunday-morning worship services at their church in Hudsonville. Usually before the service began, members would read over the program notes or announcements provided in the church bulletin. To the couples' great sorrow, their eyes fell upon the message that was reprinted from a letter from Germany indicating that their precious friend and spiritual mother in Christ, Mrs. Edna Lukesh, had passed away on September 21, 1986, at ninety years old. Alois and Poldie were deeply moved and grief-stricken about the news. They had visited her in the nursing home in Leutenbach, Germany, on one of their earlier trips to see family. It was there in the Haus Elim Christian retirement home that she spent the remaining four years of her life. Their time with her that day was filled with tears and tenderhearted moments. Mrs. Lukesh asked about the children and their lives and wished that they could have corresponded more. Poldie thanked the wheelchair-bound Mrs. Lukesh for caring enough to bring her and Alois the Good News of the Gospel when they were just in their early twenties and needed spiritual direction in their lives. Mr. and Mrs. Lukesh served their missionary years with such commitment and dedication, even to the point of refusing to come home to the United States for regular furloughs. They felt that if they left Europe to come home and give reports about their work, the ministry would be hindered, and they were not willing for the people in Germany to go spiritually unattended.

The Lukeshes spent the war years in Minnesota, laboring for the Lord. In 1946, they returned to their headquarters in Znojmo, Czechoslovakia, where they encountered many difficulties: the authorities made only a part of their old home available to them. But still the work of the Lord went on. The people welcomed the Lukeshes with tears of joy.

Terrible stories were told of the rule of the Gestapo. Despite the efforts at restoration, the effects of the war were still plainly visible everywhere. There were many accounts of seemingly miraculous escapes from bombings. It was almost impossible to have ruined homes rebuilt. There was much work to be done, and the resources were inadequate. Mr. Lukesh could have used a car, if he had had one, to visit more towns and hold meetings there. People said to him, "We are waiting for you to resume the tract publication." They had no radio. The common things we in America take for granted were still lacking in that war-torn land. Mr. Lukesh wrote of their needs and their work at that time in 1947: "It is interesting that we keep getting messages asking if we have resumed our tract work and from people who have read some of our messages ten years ago. As to the articles of clothing that have so kindly been given, so much time is taken in fixing them for individual needs that we cannot write especially about them all. Then we have to gather lots of our Sunday school children from the street, and it is a task for Mrs. Lukesh to handle forty or more at a time. They want to come during the week also, and we are short of rationed fuel, not to speak of other supplies. But praise the Lord for evident signs of His grace working among us, and that encourages us to keep on before the night cometh, when no man shall work." When the Czech officials banned the preaching of the Gospel, Charles and Edna moved to West Germany, where they settled at Ludwigsburg, near Stuttgart, to continue their missionary work.

Both Mr. and Mrs. Lukesh died in the autumn, twenty-one years apart from one another. French poet and dramatist Edmond Rostand, who was best known for his play *Cyrano de Bergerac*, once said, "Look at the leaves there, perfect Venetian red! They know how to die. A little way from branch to earth, a little dear of mingling with the common dust—they go down gracefully, a fall that seems like flying." The Lukeshes lived well and died well.

In 1989, news of the breakup of the Soviet Union ricocheted around the world. The Cold War was coming to an end. Alois's siblings were overjoyed. For forty-one years, the people had longed to be free. Young people in Czechoslovakia and other communist bloc countries had never known life without oppression, but that had not stopped them from dreaming of freedom.

Not long after that, Jerry was invited by the US Army to speak to soldiers at the US military base in Mannheim, Germany. He asked Alois to join him on the weeklong visit, and Alois gladly accepted. Alois flew three days earlier to visit Czechoslovakia. Passing the border between Germany and his homeland had never been so easy. Instead of an hour or more, it took less than one minute. Driving toward Prague, Alois saw new businesses as evidence of the free-market system.

When Alois reached his siblings, they were all happy at their country's freedom. Alois wished he could bring so many Americans he knew to see his homeland; if they only knew what they had, surely they would never take it for granted. Alois spent the following week with Jerry in Germany and thought how amazing it was that he was given a chance to work with the US Army in Germany for the third time in his life.

CHAPTER TWENTY-ONE

THE CROWNING YEARS

Alois and Poldie discovered that being grandparents is still very much like being parents, especially when someone in the family is hurting. They weathered several health storms among their children, some of their children's spouses, and their grandchildren. At each turn, the family came together, and everyone pulled through.

In the early 1990s, Jerry orchestrated plans for Alois and Poldie to travel to Kansas City so they could record their voices professionally at a local studio. Jerry envisioned them singing hymns and sharing their personal stories of how they journeyed through the post–World War II events and then committed their lives to Christ. Jerry, Alois, and Poldie started recording early in the morning and managed to record their two life stories and ten hymns, which included the song "A Child of the King." In between the verses of that song, Jerry narrated a tender story called the Ditch Digger, which added an emotional appeal to the hymn. They completed everything by day's end, and when Poldie arrived home with the guys in the evening, she was suffering from a severe migraine. The three didn't have time to eat with such a tight recording schedule, so they went nonstop until the evening. When they burst through the door, sleep was all anyone could think about. When the recording went to production, it released in cassette form and was called *Glorious Old Hymns*.

In the summer of 1994, Alois and Poldie traveled to Europe. Poldie's mother, Anna, passed away on March 1 the year before, so it made this trip tender and tearful, filled with fond memories of their time with her.

Their first stop, as usual, was Germany. Poldie's brother Sepp picked them up from the Stuttgart Airport. Due to road repair on the Autobahn, Sepp decided to drive them through the city. Their route took them through a tunnel. The traffic congestion was terrible and eventually backed up for some time. They spent a full two hours inside the tunnel before it cleared enough for them to drive.

That summer, Germany experienced particularly hot temperatures, and Sepp's car did not have air conditioning. An annoying ring started to sound in Alois's left ear. He thought it might be the heat, or the tunnel, or the noise of the city. But during their two-week stay in Germany, he continually experienced ringing in that ear. Alois tried several basic home remedies, but nothing eased the sound.

When they traveled to the recently renamed Czech Republic to visit Alois's family, his sister, Maruska, was concerned about it and made an appointment with a local doctor. The doctor could not help but suggested Alois see an ear specialist when he returned to the US.

In spite of that maddening ring, which distracted him throughout the visit, they had a pleasant time with family. Once back in Michigan, Alois scheduled an appointment with a specialist. The physician proved helpless to provide a remedy. The doctor suggested the ringing was something that some people had to learn to live with, similar to tinnitus or Ménière's disease. Alois determined that he did not want to live with this irritating sound. It often made him feel off balance and frustrated. With nowhere else to turn, he found more and more comfort in the pages of scripture.

---◆---

In March of 1996, Alois decided that it was time to retire from By-Pas International. The corporation had experienced incredible growth, and its future appeared promising. Joey was prepared to take over the business after working under his father's guidance for several years. He planned a retirement party for Alois, and he and the other siblings knew in their hearts that the company would never have succeeded without Poldie's dedication and partnership. They honored their mother in their hearts that day for her incredible contribution. Their children, grandchildren, and friends came to celebrate with them. When Alois and Poldie looked around at the party, their hearts lifted as the family and guests honored them. God had truly blessed them.

On many occasions, while Alois drove from city to city for sales and deliveries within the state of Michigan, Poldie rode along and worked with him. After retirement, the couple envisioned that they would have plenty of time to do everything they wanted to do and then some. But somehow, they didn't have as much spare time as they had anticipated. They were adjusting to their new schedules. For the first time in their lives, Alois and Poldie slept in a little later in the mornings, but still time was different. What used to take Alois fifteen minutes to do in the mornings before retirement now took him two hours. Instead of performing a quick shave, he was thorough and took extra time to feel all over his face to determine if he had gotten all the stubble. One morning, he washed his face deliberately and then paused for a moment to look at his reflection in the mirror. He wondered where all the age spots and wrinkles on his face came from. Had they appeared that quickly, or was he not paying attention during those busy years? Alois neatly combed through his still full head of hair. It was graying, and so were his eyebrows. For the first time, he paused in front of the mirror long enough to view himself as an aging man.

Poldie looked at herself in a new way too. Time was gracious to both her and Alois, but their years of stressful hard work were also catching up with them. They were no longer the spring chickens they once were. Poldie giggled to herself when she thought of Alois calling her "my kitten" when they first met. Hopefully during their retirement years, she would hear that pet name often from her best friend and the love of her life.

Before retirement, she and Alois had morning devotionals together. They read the Bible and prayed together. When they were in the car on trips, Poldie sometimes read the Bible while Alois was at the wheel. If things were hectic, they would have their devotional time later in the day.

Now with an entire day before them, Alois and Poldie shared their devotions in the late morning. They never hurried the scripture readings. After a time studying the Bible, they would always hold hands and bring each of their children and grandchildren and their families in Europe to God in prayer. Prayer time was still time well spent and unrushed.

With a large family, there was always something to keep them occupied. One of the grandchildren would have a game or a school performance for them to attend. They had little time when their children were young, so it was special to be able to enjoy such events.

In August 1996, their first grandchild, Michael, married. Jerry and Cristie Jo and their entire family came from Kansas to attend. Jerry officiated at the wedding, and Jeremiah, their son, played his saxophone. Watching him reminded Alois of the years he enjoyed playing the trumpet, and now his grandson could strum a tune.

As 1997 ushered in and then came to a close, the ringing in Alois's ear persisted. He didn't always feel well and often woke up with a headache. Concerned, he began to think the symptoms were more than just a sign of his age. Without telling Poldie, he made a reservation for them to travel to Hawaii for a four-week vacation. If things turned out to be serious with his health, at least they could have a special time in a tropical paradise.

When Alois informed Poldie about the trip, to his surprise, she was not as excited as he thought she would be. "Four weeks?" she had asked incredulously.

"It's okay," Alois comforted. "Just wait until we arrive there. If you want to stay a couple of weeks only, all we have to do is call the airline, and we can depart earlier than planned."

"Well, what about the cost to change our departure date?" she asked.

"Yes, it will cost more," Alois said, "but then we will save money from not having to pay for the hotel stay, so it would balance out."

Poldie was satisfied with this answer and even began to look forward to the trip. In January of 1998, when Michigan was encased in frigid air and snow, she and Alois left Grand Rapids for Hawaii. Once arriving on the island, the weather was beautiful, and they both relaxed. Poldie quickly forgot about wanting to leave early. Instead of reading one Bible chapter in the morning, they had time to read four or five. When they went about, Alois distributed Gospel tracks to those who were resting in the lovely parks.

Together, they took in gorgeous sights and enjoyed walking along the beach, where the soft sand cradled their feet and the breeze blew gently. They often talked about some of their favorite memories and shared many fond thoughts about life and some laughs. Alois was proud of himself and decided he had improved at being romantic since the day he brought a couple of apples to Poldie's bedside after childbirth.

One day toward the end of the trip, during a walk, Alois brushed Poldie's hand. "My kocicka, this ringing in my ear has gotten worse," he said.

Poldie turned to look at her husband. She studied his face in the warm sunlight. He was still striking and full of life. She hated that the love of her life was suffering. "Let's call the ear specialist and go for a checkup when we get back home," she decided.

When they returned home to Hudsonville a short time after that, Alois called a specialist again. The office's first opening was in March. That would not work because he and Poldie had their Europe trip planned. So he scheduled an appointment for the first part of April.

On this trip, the Hufs flew to the Czech Republic first and then drove to Germany. As they were driving back to the Czech Republic, Alois confessed to Poldie that the headaches were coming more often and were on the left side, correlating with the ringing in his ear. Alois turned to Poldie and finally voiced the concern he hadn't said before: "I think I have a brain tumor."

Poldie would not hear it. She scolded him: "You do not have a brain tumor. Don't even think that!"

Alois's appointment was set up for two days after they arrived home from Europe. He and Poldie left early for a hearing test at Saint Mary's Hospital in Grand Rapids. While Alois underwent the examination, Poldie sat outside the door. During the hearing tests, a doctor spoke through a microphone and asked Alois several questions, including if there was any history of brain tumors in his family. That was the first time a specialist broached the topic of a brain tumor.

When Alois came out of the exam room, he confessed once more to Poldie, "I think I have a brain tumor."

Poldie argued, "Why are you saying that and thinking the worst?"

Alois revealed what the doctor had just asked, but Poldie was unmoved. "Don't even think something like that!" she said. "You do not have a brain tumor."

They had two hours before they would see the ear specialist for the hearing test results. Poldie suggested they go to lunch. Alois didn't feel like eating. He just sipped slowly on coffee and spoke a few sentences to keep the conversation going. In his heart, he knew the test result would confirm his suspicions.

He and Poldie arrived for the ear specialist appointment at 1:00 p.m. A nurse at the desk gave Alois an order for a blood test and told him to go upstairs for that first. That was the first time Poldie got a little worried and asked what the reason behind the blood test was. It was for cancer, the nurse told her. A rush of panic immediately flowed over her body. "Was Alois right all along?" she wondered.

After the blood test, Alois was finally able to see the physician. The appointment was brief. He told them the nurse was making an appointment for an MRI test. Alois was to undergo the MRI, and the doctor would call him with the results. Alois didn't mind getting the news through a phone call. He would rather be in the comfort of his own home when he found out what was going on than make another trip to the hospital.

All the tests were unnerving, and Poldie thought that Alois had been right all along about having a severe health problem. When it was time for Alois to go inside the MRI tube, a nurse asked him if he needed a sedative to quiet his nerves. Many people became panicked in the narrow tunnel, she told him. Alois said he didn't need it. He reminded himself that God was his strength and security. Inside the MRI tube, it was loud, with computerized blips that came in erratic intervals. It sounded much like a jackhammer gashing concrete. Alois could view beyond the tube by looking at a mirror above his eyes, and that helped alleviate the tightness of the enclosed space. After forty-five minutes, the technician pulled him out, but only to inject dye into his bloodstream, and then he was gently pushed back in the tunnel. Afterward, he and Poldie were told that the doctor would call in about a week with the results of the tests.

Back at home, Alois and Poldie turned to the comfort they had always found in reading God's promises in the Bible and praying together. By the eighth day, no word had come; Poldie decided to call herself. The wait was consuming their every thought. The office staff told her the doctor would call back within the hour. Alois felt afraid. He asked Poldie to please stay by the phone. He needed to take a walk, he said. Alois slipped on his jacket and headed out the front door. He began wandering down the street. He walked slowly; he did not want to be home when the doctor called.

Not long afterward, Alois saw their white van in the distance coming toward him. It was Poldie. "The doctor called, but he did not want to talk to me," she said. "He said he needs to talk to you."

Alois entered the van and sat in the passenger side while Poldie drove back to the house. The news must be severe, he thought. Finally, Alois broke the silence: "Poldie, you know what the doctor is going to tell me—that I have a brain tumor." Poldie was speechless and could think of no comforting words to say as they pulled up to the house.

A few minutes after they walked into the door, the phone rang. Alois answered, "Hello?"

"Are you Mr. Huf?" the doctor asked.

"Yes, I am."

"The MRI test revealed that you have an acoustic neuroma," he said.

Alois was silent for a few moments. He had never heard that term before. "Doctor, I don't know what you mean by 'acoustic neuroma.' Are you telling me that I have a brain tumor?" he asked.

"Yes," the doctor replied. "You have a brain tumor. I have already spoken to your family doctor, and both of us think that this type of tumor has only a four percent possibility of being malignant." The doctor went on to say that they were coordinating with a surgeon in Detroit who specialized in this intricate surgery.

In the past, Alois was always quick to understand anything, but now it was as if he could hardly process the information he was being given. He asked the physician on the other line, "Would you please relay all of this to my wife, who is here? I am not sure if what I am hearing is happening to me."

Alois handed the receiver to Poldie, and she took it all in while Alois sat motionlessly. The doctor explained to Poldie that the neurologist who read the MRI determined the tumor was relatively small—only two and a half centimeters in diameter. He told her there was not a rush for surgery and that they did not think it was cancerous. The appointment was scheduled with the surgeon in Detroit in about two months.

While the doctor had been as positive as possible, only God could bring comfort to their hearts. Poldie was speechless when she set the receiver down after the call ended. She walked over to Alois and rubbed his arm. She remembered finding the tumor in her breast and wondering what her fate would be all those years ago. Finally, she said, "Let's pray." Poldie and Alois came to God with a simple prayer and trust that He would work in this situation for good, as the Bible promised them in Romans 8:28.

Shortly after that, they shared the diagnosis with the children. The entire family was very supportive and offered to do whatever they could to help. Alois generally loved seeing his children and grandchildren, but he did not feel he had the energy to remain positive for everyone. He had been through a lot in his life, but this diagnosis was different than anything he had ever faced. Every health problem carried the risk of complications, but a tumor was in a whole other category. It would be a very delicate surgery, and if anything went wrong, the impact on Alois and the family could be devastating.

Day by day, Poldie saw the gravity of the situation weighing on Alois. After a few days, she said, "One thing I have not been happy about is that the doctor had scheduled the appointment with the surgeon in two months. Should we have to wait that long? We are going to be thinking about it day and night. Why can't we go there sooner? The surgeon would be able to answer all our questions and tell us what we need to know."

Alois thought she had a valid point. Poldie called the surgeon's number. When she was put through to the scheduling coordinator, the lady told her there had been a cancelation on May 15, which was a month earlier than the original date, so Poldie gladly accepted.

Jerry had invited Alois on a crusade in Myrtle Beach, South Carolina, but for the first time in all their years of traveling together in ministry work, Alois declined because of the health problem. With the appointment made, Poldie urged him to go ahead and join Jerry. "That way, you will get your mind on the Lord and off the brain tumor. It might be good for you," she said.

Poldie was right, and Alois decided it would be a good idea to go after all. When he boarded the plane in Grand Rapids, he buried his face in the Bible for the next several hours during the flight. How good it was to be refreshed with all the truth of the Bible. He wrote many verses in a notebook to study them and take the promises to heart. He started in Jeremiah and wrote the verse "I am the LORD, the God of all mankind. Is anything too hard for me?" (Jeremiah 32:27, NIV). Then Alois wrote, "Call to me and I will answer you and tell you great and unsearchable things you do not know" (Jeremiah 33:3, NIV).

As the plane flew from Michigan to Atlanta, and then on to Myrtle Beach, Alois searched for particular healing scriptures and wrote those down as well. They included verses about not being afraid, promises about God's power and love, and assurances of peace. While he copied the verses, he prayed the Word of God over himself. He also reflected on the many times God spoke to him and made way for him to survive and thrive. He felt the Holy Spirit's presence enveloping him in the love of God.

By the time Alois reached Myrtle Beach, he felt the joy that came from believing God's promises. God was omnipresent. He had created every cell in his body. Revelation 3:20 stood out in Alois's mind: "Here I am! I stand at the door and knock. If anyone hears my voice and opens the door, I will come in and eat with that person, and they with me" (NIV). Alois distinctly felt that Jesus yearned for fellowship with him, as the Father and Son had with one another. Alois and Poldie were always busy doing things for God, but Alois could sense that God wanted Alois to be still so he could be filled with peace and assurance. Even if surgery was not the route to healing Alois had hoped for, God was still in control, and He would be with him.

When he arrived at the hotel, Alois realized that Jerry would come several hours later. That would give him plenty of time to reread the book of Psalms. From there, he turned to the New Testament. He read Philippians 4:4: "Rejoice in the Lord always. I will say it again: Rejoice!" (NIV). Then he read 1 Thessalonians 5:18: "Give thanks in all circumstances; for this is God's will for you in Christ Jesus" (NIV). He took Philippians 4:7 to heart: "And the peace of God, which transcends all understanding, will guard your hearts and your minds in Christ Jesus" (NIV).

When Jerry arrived, they prayed together and committed Alois's health and the next three days of the church meetings to God in prayer. During the following days, hundreds of people responded to the message of repentance and salvation. Alois sat in the back of the auditorium at the resource table; he felt blessed to see people begin their faith journey or renew their commitment.

On the day of Alois's departure, Jerry drove him to the airport. They said a tender good-bye, and Alois made his way to the airline counter and presented his ticket. A clerk told him there had been a mistake. There were no seats available on the flight. Alois told the man he needed to get home to Michigan that day.

"If you want to take a seat and wait, it's up to you," the clerk said. "But I do not see how I can get you on."

Alois decided not to argue because he felt it would not be helpful. Instead, he sat in the departure area and silently prayed for God to open up a seat for him. Ten minutes before takeoff, the clerk called him up. "I can only get you to Atlanta, but from here, I can't find any open seats to Cincinnati and on to Grand Rapids," he said.

Alois accepted the offer of a flight to Atlanta. When he took his seat on the plane, Alois again bowed his head. "Thank you, Lord, for providing this seat for me," he prayed. "I trust that You will open up a seat for me from Atlanta to Grand Rapids."

At the ticket counter in Atlanta, Alois was once again informed there was no seat available on the outbound flight. The clerk told Alois to wait in the event a seat opened up. Alois sat and prayed again. A few minutes before the plane's departure, Alois heard his name being called from the speaker. At the ticket counter, the clerk handed Alois a boarding pass from Atlanta to Cincinnati and a boarding pass from Cincinnati to Grand Rapids. God answered his prayers to make it home to his wife.

As the plane flew above the clouds and Alois looked out at the billowy puffs below him, he felt the assurance that he was in God's hands. When the city of Cincinnati came into view, Alois could see buildings that looked like toys and cars on the highways that appeared like ants marching in a straight line. God's view and God's care of every creature were evident to him.

In his heart, Alois prayed, "Lord Jesus, You are the same One who walked the dusty roads of the Holy Land two thousand years ago. You healed, You restored, You provided. Lord, I believe You could just speak the word, and my brain tumor would disappear."

Alois sensed God's reply. God's presence had been so evident during the past several days. That day, God provided Alois with something as simple as multiple boarding passes to get home. The Holy Spirit inside of him assured him, "Trust Me with all your needs, including the one you worry most about. You wanted to bring glory to Me, and you will."

Alois remembered Matthew 6:33: "But seek first his kingdom and his righteousness, and all these things will be given to you as well" (NIV).

When Poldie picked Alois up from the airport, he revealed to her how full his spirit was. He apologized for being cranky and frustrated recently. He called his children and apologized for being short with them and asked for their forgiveness. Alois genuinely wanted his family to know how much he loved and appreciated them.

The day came for Alois's consultation with the brain surgeon in Detroit. Jana and Susan accompanied their parents to the appointment. At the doctor's office, Alois handed the folder containing his recent MRI scans to the receptionist. The group was directed to a small patient room and told the doctor would arrive in fifteen minutes. Alois felt calm in his spirit, assured that no matter what he learned, he was safe in God's hands.

The doctor entered the room and introduced himself. "I looked at your MRI images, and I'm afraid I have some bad news for you," he said. Alois felt his mind begin to race before the doctor went on. "The initial doctor who read the MRI wrote in the report that the brain tumor is small—only two and a half centimeters—and is growing slowly. He did not feel there was a rush for the surgery. I studied the MRI and measured the size of the tumor. I must tell you that the tumor is twice the size that was reported. It is five centimeters; that is about the size of a golf ball. It is already pressing against your brain stem, and we need to operate as soon as possible."

After the initial diagnosis, not much could shock Alois anymore. Still, he felt himself reeling. He was glad his wife and daughters had the presence of mind to ask essential questions.

He heard the doctor say, "This surgery, like any brain surgery, is not easy. It is taxing on the patient. With the size of this tumor, I think it will take a minimum of eight hours in surgery. Mr. Huf, you will need to prepare physically and emotionally for this surgery."

Alois thought that was good advice, but he did not believe anything could truly prepare him for the operation. All he could do was exercise, rest, and pray. Not even the doctor knew how quickly Alois would recover, and he could not guarantee that the surgery would heal Alois. Still, Alois felt a peace about having the surgery and giving himself the best chance at a full life in his later years. The office scheduled Alois's surgery for June 11, 1998—about four weeks away.

On the way back to Hudsonville, Jana and Susan commended their mother for getting Alois in to see a physician quickly. In the next weeks, Alois and Poldie spent many hours praying and reading the Bible together. They reminded themselves of the promise in Romans 8:28: "And we know that in all things God works for the good of those who love him, who have been called according to his purpose" (NIV).

Each day, Alois walked at least an hour. In his private prayer time, he pleaded with God to make the procedure successful. Cristie Jo invited Alois and Poldie to come to Kansas for their granddaughter's high school graduation. The couple had never missed any grandchild's graduation, and they were not about to let this upcoming surgery steal away any further joy. Alois and Poldie were grateful to spend time with their daughter's family. Over the years, they spent many weeks together praying and attending crusades, where they would witness God's blessing. It was a good time, and they departed from Kansas City looking for God to see them through the next part of their journey.

Two weeks before the surgery, Alois had blood drawn and stored so it would be at the hospital in case he needed a transfusion. The day before the operation, he and Poldie set out for Detroit early in the morning. Four of their daughters accompanied them, and Jana offered to drive their van. Sitting in the back of the vehicle, Alois looked out the window and struggled with thoughts like if he would be making the trip back home. He willed himself to give his worries to his Lord and Savior. Even if his life came to an end, Alois knew he would be in heaven with Jesus. No matter what happened, he would come out a victor. That was God's promise to him.

At the doctor's office in Detroit, Alois had a presurgery consultation. The doctor warned of all the possible complications. The list went on and on and was difficult to absorb. A stroke could occur at any moment during surgery. Even if the surgery went flawlessly, the brain could swell, and the inflammation could cause death.

Alois interrupted, "Doctor, tell me: how much of a chance do I have to come out of this alive?"

The doctor was positive. "Oh, you have an excellent chance, since you are in good physical shape. Sure, this surgery will take a lot out of you," he said. "We do want you to anticipate the negative things as well. You will lose the hearing on your left side, certainly. Also, your balance on the left side will be affected. The facial nerve could be accidentally cut, and the left side of your face could potentially experience paralyzation. In many cases, patients are unable to completely close the eye on the side of the face where the brain tumor is."

Alois tried not to take everything to heart. He knew the doctor was liable to tell him all the possible consequences. Still, Alois prayed against unnecessary damage to his body. "This surgery will weaken you for a time," the doctor said, "but you are strong. You will make it."

That afternoon, they visited the other doctors at Providence Hospital who would assist in the surgery. Poldie made a particular point to talk to the anesthesiologist. "When you put him to sleep, will you stay by his side throughout the surgery?" she asked. He assured her that he would.

By that evening, Cristie Jo flew in from Kansas City, and Joey joined them, along with some of the grandchildren. In all, more than thirty family members were present to offer support. Alois and Poldie felt bad for Cristie Jo, because for the past couple of years, she struggled with a debilitating panic disorder, and for her to even make the flight alone was a miracle in and of itself. They prayed for her healing and did their best to comfort her. Later, the Huf family went out to dinner. Alois felt like he did the night before he left Czechoslovakia as a young man, quietly studying the faces around the table and listening to each person. He wanted to take in everyone and everything in case it was his last evening with them. Back at the hotel, Alois kissed his children and said good night. Cristie Jo lingered a bit longer, and while her father sat on the side of the bed, she encouraged him to call on the name of Jesus when he woke from the surgery. The children were all concerned that Alois would wake to severe nausea and dizziness, as the doctor anticipated. Cristie Jo shared with her daddy a special time in her life when she was in recovery from surgery and experiencing postsurgery complications. While still in a groggy state, Cristie could not speak or open her eyes but understood that the nurse was running to find the doctor, and at that moment, Cristie Jo began to say the name of Jesus repeatedly. When the doctor arrived, the massive rash covering her body had disappeared, and the nurse was stunned. Cristie Jo hoped her father would cling to that story and do the same when he awoke.

The next morning, Alois took a long shower, and the family headed to Providence Hospital. The surgery began at 7:00 a.m. Poldie and the family sat restlessly in the waiting area and received hourly updates from a nurse. The surgery lasted eight hours. Immediately afterward, Alois was wheeled down a hallway and into the intensive care unit. The family watched as they saw Alois lying on the gurney, lifeless. Once in the room, the attending nurses only allowed two family members at a time to enter and see him. Poldie immediately grabbed Cristie Jo and indicated the two of them would go in first. Poldie knew Cristie Jo's emotions were about spent and wanted her to see her daddy and get back to the hotel to rest before she collapsed. When the two rounded the corner to enter Alois's room, he was waking up. Poldie intuitively rushed to his bed to assist as he was calling out, "Jesus, Jesus, Jesus!" The dizziness and nausea were already impacting him, and he remembered what Cristie Jo suggested, to call on the name of Jesus when it got bad. Cristie Jo consoled her father for a brief moment and then left the room. Poldie remained, and the other family members came in to see their dad.

The dim room appeared blurry, and Alois felt extremely nauseous. On the left side, he had a substantial cone-shaped dressing affixed to his head. He looked like the Conehead aliens from *Saturday Night Live*, but with the cone on the side of his head. Several times throughout the night, Alois felt like he was choking. The nursing staff did not always come quickly to attend to him, and so he cried out to God for help. He was reminded that the darkest night comes before the dawn. "If You'll give me more time, I'll serve You," Alois prayed.

Sweet song lyrics came to his mind: "I will serve Thee because I love Thee. / You have given life to me. / I was nothing before You found me. / You have given life to me. // Heartaches, broken pieces, / Ruined lives are why You died on Calvary. / Your touch is what I longed for. / You have given life to me."

In the darkness of his room, Alois felt tears flowing down his cheeks. He tried to go to sleep but had a hard time because a fellow patient coughed incessantly. The second night was not much better. Jana went to the hospital early in the morning ahead of everyone the day after surgery. She saw her dad lopsided in the bed and his dressing coming loose. She said, "Dad, this is not for you. You need a room where you can rest." A short time later, she was back, and the hospital opened a private room for him.

Later that morning, a physical therapist came to Alois's hospital room. "We are going to help you get up," she announced. This was a lot harder than it seemed. It was an ordeal even to sit up in his bed. Each time Alois tried to stand, he fell on the bed. It felt like the room was spinning. His equilibrium was temporarily affected by the surgery. Finally, with the help of the caregiver and the support of Poldie, Alois stood as straight as he could.

Before he would be able to walk, Alois first needed to practice standing. The medical worker held a small card about twenty inches away from Alois's eyes.

"Try to look from one side of the card to the other," she said. "Now try looking from top to bottom. Okay, look again from left to right."

Alois's eyes struggled to cooperate or synchronize together. One eye looked at the left side of the card and the other eye to the right side. When Alois complained, the therapist said this was a result of the surgery and that his normal vision would come back again. Alois was counting on that. Not having that constant annoying ring in his ear was great, but what a trade-off with all the dizziness and the imbalance. Now he just had to get his eyesight to cooperate. Alois rested for a moment after the eye therapy before the employee told him, "Now we are going for a walk in the hallway."

She might as well have said they were about to walk on the moon! It seemed impossible. Alois stood up again, and the professional tied a medical rope around his chest. When he began to walk and started to lean over to one side, she pulled his torso upward again. It was a good thing the woman was stringent, or else he might have given up. After a few slow treks back and forth in the hallway, Alois was finally able to stand by himself for a while. It was humbling to have to learn how to walk all over again.

In the afternoon, the surgeon came to see Alois and examined his skull and the twenty-one stitches on his head. "Everything looks good," the doctor confirmed. "There is one thing I need to tell you. For the next three weeks, if possible, please force yourself not to sneeze. If you do, this could cause a spinal fluid leak out of your eyes, ears, and nose. At worst, we might have to open your skull again and refill the cavity where the tumor was taken out with body fat. This is why we had to make an incision under your navel. We removed some of your fat and filled the cavity in your skull with extra body fat."

That was the strangest request Alois and Poldie had ever heard. As soon as the doctor left, they prayed together that Alois would not sneeze during the next three weeks. Poldie was always with Alois in his private room and slept in the recliner. The children and grandchildren visited during the day; everyone was pleased with the progress he was making.

After only a week in the hospital, Alois was released and allowed to travel the three-hour trip home. He should have been happy once he was back again in his bed and in the comfort of his home, but instead, he struggled with severe depression. It was uncharacteristic of him to feel so moody and tentative. When the children came to visit, he excused himself to go lie down on the couch alone. He was only able to rest on his right side and never his left.

Along with depression, he had terrible headaches. "How was this a good trade-off?" Alois argued. First, the constant ringing in his ear, then the dizziness and nausea, and now the horrible headaches—what was going on?

Cristie Jo and Jerry called daily to check in, and when they heard of Alois's headaches, they told him of a woman who had gone through the same surgery. Two weeks after Alois came home from the hospital, the woman sent him a packet of literature and newsletters about the operation and patients' stories of recovery. As Alois leafed through one of the newsletters, a story caught his attention, and he began reading.

"Poldie, please come sit by me!" he said. She came in. "You need to read this. Almost all the patients who had the same surgery as I did experienced headaches and depression after. All this time, I thought I was the only one. I wish I could have read this before and known what to expect."

Three weeks after the surgery, Janna drove her parents back to Detroit so the doctor could remove the stitches. A week later, Alois was finally permitted to get his head wet in the shower and wash his hair. Alois soon felt much better and was healing fine. He still woke up with the headaches, but in about half an hour, the pain disappeared.

As Alois's eyesight readjusted, he again read the Bible and studied its pages. God's Word brought renewed meaning and inspiration. He thought about the promise he made to God that he would serve Him if He chose to keep him alive. Alois and Poldie were always sharing their faith through Gospel tracks with whomever they could, but God was speaking to them that He wanted them to do more. Alois was still restricted from operating a vehicle and was not able to expend a lot of energy, but he reminded God that he was available. Jerry and Cristie Jo established a church in 1996, so their global travels for crusade work were minimized, and that meant that Alois was not traveling with Jerry as much and also grounded from the ministry he had learned to love. God must have another plan.

CHAPTER TWENTY-TWO

BRINGING FREEDOM TO INMATES

Abuot a year and a half after the surgery, Alois's hair grew back in all the bald areas, and his energy and stamina returned. If people did not know he had brain surgery, they would not have suspected it. With Alois on the rebound and healing well, he began to look for opportunities to utilize the remaining years of his life for some type of service to God, just as he had committed prior to his surgery.

He and Poldie attended a small Bible church in Jenison, Michigan, and on one particular Sunday, while waiting for the service to begin, an announcement in the church bulletin caught Alois's attention. It read, "Church workers needed for volunteer service at the county jail." Something resonated with Alois when he read it.

"I think this is what I would like to do," Alois said to Poldie as he pointed to the announcement. "I would like to go to the local jail and tell the inmates about Jesus." Alois felt like he could relate in some way to the inmates; they had their freedom taken away just as Alois had—although for entirely different reasons. Alois had lost his when he was a teenager under dictatorial rule, but he knew that loss of freedom could somehow be common ground for them to begin sharing life experiences.

"Call them up and see if that might be something for you," Poldie replied.

Later, Alois called the number and inquired more about the volunteer position. The organization was called Forgotten Man Ministries, and it ministered to inmates in several local jails throughout the state of Michigan. When he called, the representative indicated that they would be excited to have Alois as a volunteer team member. He was invited to attend twenty-four hours of chaplaincy training to be eligible to work with those who were incarcerated. Alois faithfully participated in the preparation and was given an identification badge and permission to minister weekly at the jail.

When he woke on the first morning of his new ministry in 2000, Alois was a bit nervous; he was uncomfortable with going through the heavy metal security doors, which would slam shut behind him with a giant thunder and be followed by the loud click of the mandatory locking system. When he arrived home later that day, Poldie excitedly asked, "How was it?"

"I am not sure this is for me," Alois confided. "I went with the other church worker, and most of the inmates were not at all interested in what we had to say."

Always the consummate encourager, Poldie urged, "Don't get discouraged if they don't want to listen to you the first time. Next time you go, show them a little love, as Jesus would."

"That's it," Alois said. He thought of Jesus's words to his disciples in John 13:35: "By this everyone will know that you are my disciples if you love one another" (NIV). He remembered that it was God's job to draw men to faith in Jesus Christ. He was simply the messenger. Alois wanted to show the inmates love and to make them feel valued. If only they knew of the many previous offenses and addictions he laid before the cross when coming to Jesus all those years ago, perhaps they would realize he was not always the well-manicured Christian person they saw before them.

The next time Alois ministered in the jail, he made more of an effort to show interest in the lives of the men. He invited them to join him for a Bible study. Early on, only a handful showed up. Not long after, the first inmate received Jesus as his Savior. Alois knew he was in the right place at the right time. Service to these forgotten men in the jail ministry became a highlight of his week.

One night, Alois dreamt about the Lamb's Book of Life (Revelation 20:15). When he awoke, he had an idea: How amazing would it be to have a physical book with the signatures of all the inmates who prayed and invited Jesus Christ into their lives? It could be a beautiful visual representation of the real book in heaven the Bible writes about. The dream inspired Alois; he could show the inmates what it looked like to have their names recorded in the eternal Book of Life.

Alois went shopping for just the right journal for this new Book of Life and began utilizing it in jail. The book became unique to every man who received Christ. In the beginning, some of the other volunteers sneered at Alois's unconventional approach and said there was only one Lamb's Book of Life, but that didn't faze Alois. He knew if he could make a visual connection with the inmates who were struggling, the book could have a great impact.

In the coming days and years, Alois's journal documented one name and then another, and before long, many inmates prayed to receive Christ and signed their names and the date of their decision in the book. Long after they signed, some of the men would ask to look at the page where their signature was listed. It appeared to Alois that they wanted to be reminded of that special day in their lives, since freedom seemed to be a lifetime away for many of them, and this was one hope they could hold on to.

By 2002, Alois led at least one man to Jesus Christ nearly every week, sometimes more. Leading them to Jesus Christ gave Alois such tremendous joy!

One day after arriving home, Alois encouraged Poldie, "I think you should consider going to the jail also to share with the women. It is such a blessing."

Poldie dismissed the idea quickly. "This ministry would not be for me," she said.

"Well, why not try it once, and then you could decide how you like it?" Alois suggested.

"Okay, I will try it once then," Poldie said. "But I do not promise anything."

Poldie completed the mandatory paperwork and background check and walked into the women's section of the jail a few weeks later. She was more surprised than Alois at how much she liked it. She began going almost every week to tell the women that only Jesus could change their lives forever (John 14:6). Many of the female inmates were captured by Poldie's German accent and loved hearing her speak in a tender and unsuspecting voice. Several times she was able to lead women to commitments to Christ. Like Alois, she invited the women who professed faith in Christ to enter their names in her Bible. The back pages of

Poldie's brown leather New International Version Bible began to fill with multiple handwritten names. Some wrote in cursive and others penned their names in block letters. One of the inmates, Teresa, recorded her name and took special thought to write that she would be transferring to another jail on Monday or Saturday of that week. She included her address to make sure Poldie would promise to keep encouraging her. Poldie remarked to Alois that she could not get over how the Lord could use two older people with European accents to bring the Good News of the Gospel to those twice bound by sin and imprisonment.

On October 4, 2003, Alois, seventy-two, and Poldie, sixty-nine, celebrated their fiftieth wedding anniversary. It marked the realization of a dream come true for Poldie. Since she had never experienced a formal wedding ceremony, it had always been a wish for her to marry Alois in church, with all their family and beloved friends present. Their six children and seventeen grandchildren put together an unforgettable evening for them. Alois and Poldie even managed to get Maruska and Slavek to attend the celebrated occasion. Earlier, Cristie Jo arranged for a photographer to take special photos of Alois and Poldie during one of their visits to Kansas City. Invitations were designed and mailed out; the church was booked; and the decor, cake, and food were planned for the reception after the ceremony.

The entire family and special friends gathered in the small church. The guests sat expectantly as Alois, dressed in a nice suit, stood at the front of the chapel. The guests stood when Poldie entered.

Poldie wore a delicate white dress and held a bouquet of fragrant flowers; she looked lovely! Joey, Poldie and Alois's only son, walked his mother down the aisle as she held his arm. Beside Alois, Jerry watched with a Bible in hand, waiting to officiate the wedding vow renewal. As Poldie drew closer, Alois could see a gentle tear that flowed from her eyes. As she joined him, he took her arm and then wiped her eyes with his handkerchief.

The couple joined hands, and then Alois whispered, "You look beautiful, Kocicka." She blushed. Alois and Poldie recited their vows, and during the ceremony, some of the grandchildren sang special music. After the ceremony, the joyous family sat down in the pews and watched a video that Cristie Jo produced and Jerry narrated, which included many photos from the last half century of their marriage. What a remarkable and providential journey they had taken by faith together! Poldie and Alois wept multiple times during the video, and when the service came to a close, they did not think they had any tears left; their hearts were so full.

Then all the guests, including their children, grandchildren, and great-grandchildren, drove to a nearby country club for a wedding reception that included dinner, music, and special memorable comments from the guests. The children pooled their money and purchased a large Thomas Kinkade oil painting on canvas called *Sunrise, the Cross*. They presented it to their parents, and it held a special spiritual meaning for the entire family.

Alois and Poldie had not forgotten the days of their youth. At one point, Poldie leaned against Alois's chest and then pulled back for a moment to look into her dear husband's eyes. Alois's eyes twinkled at the sight of her. It seemed to them it was more than a lifetime ago when they had been two young people in Germany, catching each other's glances on a train. When they gazed at one another, it was with the same passion and love as those early days that began their adventure together.

When the couple arrived home, Poldie found a place above the fireplace mantel in their condominium to hang the painting. And on the adjacent wall leading to the upstairs loft, Poldie asked to have their fiftieth-anniversary portrait hung.

Alois and Poldie continued their volunteer work in the jail with such delight. However, in the coming years, Poldie encountered severe and at times imperiling digestive problems and ultimately years of complications after a failed stomach surgery. These problems hindered her from making the weekly visits to the jail with Alois. She developed dumping syndrome postsurgery, which is a condition following gastric surgery in which the person experiences nausea, vomiting, abdominal cramping, diarrhea, dizziness, and flushing. She found it difficult to leave home at times but still mustered the strength to visit the jail when able. Many of the women looked to her for guidance and love. Even though Poldie was hindered from ministering weekly, Alois set aside three and sometimes as many as five days a week for his service to the inmates. Once a month on Sundays, Alois was invited to deliver the sermon for the inmates.

In May 2014, the Huf children anticipated celebrating their mother's eightieth birthday. They had gathered for a party to honor Alois's eightieth in 2011, and now it was time to mark the milestone with their mother. In the months leading up to the birthday party, each child contributed photos of special memories they had experienced with their mother through the years. Cristie Jo collated all the photos into a leather-bound, one-hundred-page memory book that included special messages from each of the six children written to their mother to honor her for years of nurturing, loving, and supporting them. On May 16, the entire family gathered to celebrate Poldie for this monumental occasion.

The day after the party, Cristie Jo's family was preparing to say their good-byes to Poldie and Alois. Poldie stepped outside their condo to hug Cristie Jo's pregnant daughter, Jenilee, one more time as she and her husband, Jeff, stepped into their vehicle to head for home. As Poldie started up the exterior steps of the condo to head back into the house, she felt dizzy, fell, and broke her wrist in several places. She was rushed to the hospital and given meds to relieve the pain until surgery could be performed in the coming days. Poldie was allowed to return home for the intermediate time, and unbeknown to her and Alois, the hospital staff failed to confirm medications with her health history and allergies. In the morning, Alois, thinking she was sleeping far too long, went to wake her, but she was unresponsive. Panicked and weeping, Alois reached for his cell phone. Trembling, he had difficulty dialing 9-1-1 from the smartphone's screen. When he finally connected, the operator dispatched an ambulance and instructed Alois to administer CPR, which the operator guided him through. "Is this how our story will end?" Alois agonized. When the EMTs arrived, they worked on Poldie for several moments and then rushed her off with signals flashing and sirens raging. Left behind, Alois didn't know if he would ever hold his beloved's warm hand again. In a matter of moments, while en route, the EMTs got a pulse back, and Poldie woke to ask, "Where am I, and who are you?" In the coming days, Alois and Poldie rejoiced that the Lord had a plan to keep both of them around for longer.

For seventeen years, Alois continued to visit the jail, ministering to the inmates, and on September 28, 2017, the Forgotten Men Ministries annual fall banquet honored Alois with the Basin and Towel

Servanthood Award. Chaplin Matt Hanson stood before the crowd and reported that more than 220 inmates had accepted Christ during that year alone. He proceeded to share details about Christ and the power displayed as He washed the disciple's feet. As a visual of what Christ did, Matt called Alois forward and presented him with a wooden bowl and towel, honoring him for his years of dedicated volunteer service for Forgotten Men Ministries and the Ottawa County Jail inmates. At the end of nineteen years in jail ministry, Alois had recorded 2,173 inmate names in his Lamb's Book of Life. The signatures fill more than seventy pages, all men who have received Jesus Christ as their personal Savior.

As of 2020, Alois and Poldie Huf still share a home together in Hudsonville, Michigan. Poldie, mostly homebound, has survived many falls and ailments, but her mind is sharp, and her spirit is strong. Alois has committed to be her full-time caregiver, and when able, at age eighty-nine, he still ministers at the jail. Both Poldie and Alois proudly pledge their allegiance to the flag of the United States of America and give their hearts' allegiance to the King of Kings, Jesus Christ.

Five of the Hufs' six children live within a ten-mile radius, and their daughter, Cristie Jo, lives with her husband in Houston, Texas. Alois and Poldie are thankful for the seventeen grandchildren and thirty-four great-grandchildren the Lord has blessed them with. Poldie and Alois give all credit to the Lord for allowing them to lay the foundation to build a Generations Strong culture among their children. Their hopeful prayer is found in 3 John 4, which they paraphrase here: "We have no greater joy than to hear that our children, grandchildren, and great-grandchildren walk in the truth."

A FINAL NOTE BY ALOIS AND LEOPOLDINE HUF

I t is our hearts' desire that you, the reader of our story of two people who were displaced by war from their homes and their countries of birth, will see that it was God's guidance that allowed us to reach the shores of the United States and settle in our new homeland. If our journey has resonated with your life and you have never trusted Christ as Savior, we encourage you to take a step toward Him today and accept His beautiful gift of love and salvation through Jesus Christ, the Savior of the world. Jesus died for all mankind, but only those who believe and receive Christ will be forgiven and given eternal life. In John 1:12, we read, "Yet to all who did receive him, to those who believed in his name, he gave the right to become children of God" (NIV).

As you read our life stories, you no doubt recognized how the Lord repeatedly led and spared us from a terrible fate. God provided us a wonderful and fulfilling life. Most importantly, he sent gentle and loving servants in the form of the Lukeshes to share the Good News of the Gospel. The Gospel has the power to change every person eternally and to set the trajectory of our paths into the places we should go and the people we should become.

Dear reader, if you are at a place in life where you have tried everything else and nothing has delivered you contentment and spiritual assurance, please consider becoming a Christian. Just as we did when we came to that point of commitment, you too can pray a simple prayer, which goes something like this: "I believe that Jesus, the Son of God, died on the cross for me. I ask Jesus to be my Savior and to forgive my sins, for I am sorry for my sins. Thank You, Lord, for giving me eternal life. Help me read Your Word, the Bible, daily, and help me live for You. In Jesus's name, amen." When we first became Christians, we did not understand the importance of praying all prayers in the name of

Jesus. The significance is recorded in John 14:14: "You may ask me for anything in my name, and I will do it" (NIV).

If you prayed that prayer and committed your heart and life to Christ, let us be the first to tenderly welcome you into the family of God. We are delighted for your decision and encourage you to find a Bible-believing church and alert the pastor about your decision. Our prayer is that the pastor will then lead you in the next important steps to follow Christ. We would also appreciate hearing about your decision, so please write to us at Intentional God, Inc., or I.G. Transmedia, LLC, at 1708 Spring Green Blvd., Ste. 120 #25, Katy, TX 77494 or contact us at escapetofreedombook.com. This website will guide you in privately recording your decision so we can support your continued spiritual growth.

If you are interested in hearing us sing the *Glorious Old Hymns* that we recorded years ago, you can also find a link on the escapetofreedombook.com website to listen to or download free of charge. We understand that times have changed and hymns, sung in the traditional manner, are not as popular as the newer, more contemporary worship music, but we request that you print the lyrics of the ten songs we sing directly from the website, and as you listen, take the words to heart as they are all based on strong theological truths from the Bible. And also, you will be able to hear the voices of the two lives you have come to journey with, and that may put a period at the end of our story. However, the narrative continues, since our account is book 1 in the Generations Strong trilogy.

ANGELS

I f you are familiar with the Bible, you might recall that the psalmist reminds us, "For He orders his angels to protect you wherever you go. They will hold you with their hands to keep you from striking your foot on a stone" (Psalm 91:11-12). It is a relief to know that we do not have to conquer the struggles of life alone. God sends us angels in our time of need. They protect, comfort, and strengthen believers. In Bible times, they were utilized as messengers to deliver critical information for very specific instances. The believer in Christ should take great comfort in this knowledge.

There are also certain people who cross our paths at the exact moment we need help. Sometimes we don't even realize we need that extra assistance. We often refer to them as "angels" simply because of the impact they make in our lives during difficult times. In rehearsing the journey, we find it cannot be explained away. It is not happenstance or serendipity. Their involvement in our lives at that exact moment occurs for a reason beyond our understanding. They impact our lives so deeply that we are left changed forever. These angels arrive at the right moment, showing the love we need by lifting us up and reminding us that there are good people serving and working even in the worst of times. Wings might not be part of their physical being like the angels we read about in the Bible, but they bless our lives eternally.

You've read how the Lord led me and my three friends as we attempted to escape communist Czechoslovakia and how He placed people along the way—whom I like to call "Angels of God"—to help us. The first example that comes to mind is at the police station in the city of Cheb, when Jindra, a member of our group, had forgotten his ID at home. The remaining three of us were waiting in the hotel, worrying that the police would come at any moment and arrest us.

The second Angel of God was the former soldier of the Svoboda Army on the outskirts of the city of Cheb who informed me in what direction we needed to go to cross the border to escape.

The third Angels of God were the unknown people in the CIA who blocked my attempts at immigrating to Australia and Canada and joining the US Army. These Angels of God hindered me from leaving Germany so that I would meet the real Angel of God: Leopoldine. She gave me the will and hope to live again.

The fourth Angel of God was the lady at the German transportation office who helped me get my driver's license so that I could start driving for the US Army.

The fifth Angel of God was the anonymous person(s) who sent the missionaries to Poldie and me while we were living in Altach. The Lukeshes brought the Gospel of the Lord Jesus Christ to us, which assured us that if we believe in Jesus and accept Him, He would give us the right to become children of God. This means that when a person becomes a Christian, he or she is a new person. That person is not the same anymore, for his or her old life is gone and a new life has begun. This is the most precious gift that Poldie and I ever received.

The sixth Angel of God was the one who kept Jana from falling overboard as we sailed on the ship somewhere on the Atlantic Ocean between Germany and New York.

The seventh Angel of God was the one who guided me to look back as I was dragging the field on my first job in the US. The tractor wheel caught the drag; the drag would have for sure been a fatal blow if I had not stepped on the brake in a split second and stopped the tractor.

The eighth Angel of God was the one who spared our toddler Jana's life when she opened the car door and rolled out of the car while I was driving through Hudsonville.

The ninth Angel of God was the one who was sent by God to protect Poldie and the children when their car was hit by another car in Germany. The vehicle overturned and landed upside down in the ditch, and incredibly, no one was hurt.

The tenth Angel of God was the one who stayed by my side through the brain surgery in Detroit and long after during the recovery and healing.

You ask, "Do you believe in angels?" Yes, we do! In Hebrews 1:14, we read, "Are they not all ministering spirits [the angels], sent forth to minister for them who shall be heirs of salvation" (KJV). In the New Living Translation, the same verse tells it this way: "But angels are only servants. They are spirits sent from God to care for those who will receive salvation."

These are only samplings of the instances when we encountered angelic spiritual intervention in our lives. Perhaps you can see the same thing as you reflect on your life. Like you, Poldie and I are eternally grateful for the multiple instances during our lives that He sent spiritual and physical angels to help us in our time of need and growth.

Alois Huf

SMALL GROUP STUDY

WEEK ONE

Challenges to Confront and Conquer

- Fear
- Loss
- Death
- Disillusionment
- Captivity

Transformative Truths to Trust In

- Resilience
- Resourcefulness
- Initiative
- Courage
- Bravery
- Freedom

Chapters: 1, 2, and 3

Total pages to read: 57

Alois Huf and Leopoldine Kellner faced terrifying childhoods. At a time in life when they should have been allowed to be innocent, to be free of care and worry, and to experience the essence of play and recreation, their lives were interrupted with unexpected terror and tragedy. During and after World War II, their countries were embroiled in bombings and brutalities, causing each to live through unimaginable circumstances resulting in fear, panic, dread, and disquiet. The constant threat of upheaval was like a monster lurking at the door, begging for entry. Alois and Poldie feared that their parents would not be able to protect them from what appeared in their young minds to be an evil waiting to consume them. Daily dread filled their hearts at the thought of merely surviving. Before reaching the age of eighteen, each mourned the deaths of family members, encountered wartime executions, endured survival drills, lost their homes, suffered from hunger, and experienced disappointment regarding their fates. The challenges facing Alois and Poldie appeared impossible, and yet each of them found a way to not only survive but thrive in spite of all they bore.

Confronting trials in life, resulting from either postwar effects like Alois and Poldie faced or daily struggles we all deal with, can be debilitating. If we fail to confront them, it is the perfect breeding ground for weakness to thrive and eventually paralyze us. We are left with a huge disadvantage. Our chances of moving on and realizing an improved existence are hindered, if not ceased altogether. The hope to endure any situation is often impeded by the fear, panic, and anxiety of the unknown. Fear and uncertainty are tools that can weaken and potentially destroy us if we allow it.

The believer in Christ understands that trusting in biblical truth and seeking God's plan will transform any situation. Prior to even coming to faith in Christ, God's ultimate plan for Alois's and Poldie's lives are hard to overlook. Each exhibits incredible resilience and resourcefulness in the quest for a better life. From an early age, Alois confronted his father's alcohol addiction, a dependency that caused heartache for the entire family. He was sensible enough to realize its impact and had determined to prevent that addictive curse in his own life before it ever took hold. With that promise in place, Alois instilled immense initiative in changing the trajectory of his destiny. He first believed it was possible through promotions in forestry school and did all he could to accomplish that objective. When he was twice rejected and denied the opportunity, he resorted to planning his ultimate freedom: a dangerous escape to what he imagined to be a superior, free country. He had no intention of allowing the communist's control to intimidate him.

His persistence for freedom from oppression is a reminder of the determined resolve William Wallace's character displayed in the epic 1995 movie *Braveheart*. The film was nominated for ten Academy Awards and won five at the sixty-eighth annual award ceremony. Wallace, the thirteenth-century Scottish warrior, became one of the nation's most valiant heroes as he led resistance forces to free Scotland from English rule. In the film, the warrior stands firm and rallies the resistance, saying, "They may take our lives, but they'll never take our freedom."* So committed is Wallace to liberate the land and its people, he ultimately gives his life, never wavering until the last breath. The final climax of the movie gives pause. It invites every viewer to ask if he or she would persist to the end for freedom, no matter the circumstances. As Wallace's character lies on the executioner's table, enduring the brutality of evisceration, the commander says, "The prisoner wishes to say a word." While struggling to conjure a final breath, Wallace ultimately shouts one unforgettable word to the heavens: "Freedom!" Think about your life. Whether it be an addiction or an oppressive situation, do you want freedom as desperately as Wallace?

Alois's longing for an improved future came at a staggering cost, and yet it was a required sacrifice that culminated in joy in the years to come. It took courage and bravery to step out and initiate a plan to leave a life filled with dictatorship and debacle. Escaping from communistic Czechoslovakia as an eighteen-year-old young man required determined effort and unwavering resolve. Risk and danger accompanied Alois's ambition to leave the oppressive state. He could have met his death or been imprisoned in labor camps for the remainder of his life.

Poldie's capacity to press through multiple childhood obstacles allowed her to take one step closer in visualizing a new home and a restored life. She was homeless and lived in a ditch with her eleven family members, and then she transitioned to a horse stable and slept on dirt floors scattered with straw, which she used as her mattress,

---

* Mel Gibson, dir., *Braveheart* (Hollywood: Paramount Pictures, 1995).

but her courageous resiliency was shown. However, her toughness was tested repeatedly. First, at only eleven years of age, a Russian soldier confronted her and tried to rape her, but Poldie fought back with sage-like wisdom. She altered what could have created years of traumatic memories. Again, Poldie's ability to confront desolation and shame while being transported on a cattle car to various refugee camps was tested. Living in peace in the Sudetenland, she and her family, along with millions of Germans, were expelled from their country in 1945. At war's end, the Czech officials accused these nonviolent Germans of prewar hostilities against their country, and they ordered them out of their country. Homeless, Poldie was constantly hungry, and the disgrace from becoming a *flüchtling* (refugee) was draining, but Poldie was determined to persist. Dancing and music in the camps gave Poldie momentary relief and happiness. She was able to ignore the reality of life and laugh while she danced with her father, making memories that gave her uncertain childhood a tiny glimmer of hope for a restored future. Perhaps you can identify with Poldie. Was your childhood traumatic or lacking in some critical way?

People of every race, gender, and ethnicity face challenges in life for various reasons. The Bible refers to challenges as troubles, and as Poldie and Alois experienced, they are sure to come. Job 5:7 says, "But a person is born for trouble as surely as sparks fly up from a fire" (GW). Although difficulties are not easy to accept, God's Word reminds us that "sometimes it takes a painful experience to make us change our ways" (Proverbs 20:30, GNT). Alois and Poldie resolved that the pain of their experiences would be a means to turn things around. The psalmist in Psalm 119:71 follows that thought by revealing, "It was good that I had to suffer in order to learn your laws" (GW). Many times, suffering and uncomfortable situations are the very things God uses to lead us to a fresh start. We may not appreciate the means by which we end up reaching that new beginning, but God is faithful, and His intentions are trustworthy.

Following the Hufs' example, we should be willing to exert initiative and utilize every resource at our disposal to strive for a better life. The Bible provides teachings on initiative and where we go to find it: "I can do all things through Christ who strengthens me" (Philippians 4:13, NKJV). Again, it encourages us to "press toward the goal" (Philippians 3:14, NKJV). Ezra commissions us when confronted with an opportunity or a choice to do right: "Rise up; this matter is in your hands . . . so take courage and do it" (Ezra 10:4, NIV). Will you envision yourself stepping out and rising up to "do it"? Like Alois and Poldie did, dig deep within your own heart, take courage, and do the thing that will set you free. Initiative, when undertaken in the power of the Holy Spirit, will propel us through setbacks and oppositions, threatening our decision to press on. Apply the resources at your disposal to change the course of your life. A transformative truth in God's Word reminds us that "the teachings that come from your mouth are worth more to me than thousands in gold or silver" (Psalm 119:72, GW). Truth that stems from scripture is reliable and worth more to the struggling believer than monetary affluence. The Bible is replete with promises to claim and is authored by a God who cannot lie or negate those promises: "God is not a man, that He should lie" (Numbers 23:19). Look to the Bible for truth and take great comfort in knowing that all His words are true (Psalm 119:160).

Think about a Response

1. In what ways have I responded to fear and anxiety in my life?
2. How have I responded to great losses in my life?
3. Have I demonstrated initiative when attempting to press through each challenge I am confronted with?
4. Is there something or someone enslaving me that I need freedom from?
5. Have I taken biblical steps toward freedom, allowing God to do His best work in me?
6. What are the specific initiatives I need to take at this point in my life?

WEEK TWO

◆

Challenges to Confront and Conquer

- Rejection
- Despondency
- Hopelessness

Transformative Truths to Trust In

- Persistence
- Provision
- Purpose
- Determination
  - Chapters: 4, 5, 6, 7, and 8
  - Total pages to read: 64

In chapters 4 through 8, Alois and Poldie endure living as refugees with thousands of distraught people who either escaped oppressive rule or were simply uprooted from their homes as a result of the war. The European conflict resulted in millions of suffering, homeless people, and Alois and Poldie found themselves included in that number. Each bore the scars of subsisting in an environment clouded with doom and hopelessness. Alois and Poldie experienced a new normal after entering bomb-ravaged Germany. For Alois, once inside the first refugee camp, the freedom he had joyously anticipated was quickly overruled by the shocking, unanticipated reality of his surroundings. After officials dusted him with white delousing insecticide, he was immediately given a distinctive classification: displaced person. The escapee had a roof over his head, but as the days and weeks passed, his thinning physique showed signs of malnutrition.

Chronic hunger was impossible to ignore, and his emotions were raw from despair. Refugees survived varying degrees of physical and emotional hardships, including depression, loneliness, and hopelessness. Alois mourned the loss of one of the men from the camp who resorted to suicide by gassing himself in the basement. The pressures of the life he had naïvely acquired proved intolerable. While his untimely death gave Alois pause, he too contemplated terminating his own life after being rejected multiple times from immigrating to Australia and Canada. Adding to his loneliness was the reality that the three friends he escaped with were given clearance to immigrate. They left Alois behind, alone and unsure of his future. Bitter disappointment and despondency ensued after he continued to appeal for immigration to leave the crippled post–World War II Germany and was repeatedly rejected.

Compounding the isolation was the social alienation from the Germans living nearby, who referred to Alois and his camp inmates as *verfluchte auslanders* (damaged foreigners). Have you ever felt like damaged goods or like you did not belong or fit in? There would be no recourse for Alois, since the certainty of political persecution and imprisonment threatened every hope of returning to his homeland. As you read about Alois's story, are you able to relate to times in your own life when hopelessness and rejection seemed too much to bear?

Poldie and her family dealt with the shock of multiple decrepit refugee camps, which to her signaled an unclear future. While still in her early teens, she and her family, along with other refugees that she embraced as her own, experienced unimaginable hunger. As the oldest daughter, sorrow when hearing the cries of hungry siblings compelled her to join her mother in acquiring food through unconventional means. Stealing potatoes from local farms and apples that fell from trees in nearby orchards became the necessary norm for a time. Watching her mother beg for the family's basic needs triggered Poldie to act in support of her loved ones. Desperate postwar conditions required drastic measures if they were to have any hope of survival.

Prior to graduation from the eighth grade, Poldie was frequently forced to skip school, which she loved. Standing in long bread lines for daily rations for the family and forgoing any social life took priority in order for her younger siblings to survive. At fourteen, Poldie began years of sacrificing her own needs and persevered through multiple hardships while providing for her family. She worked long hours in numerous factories long distances from home. The modest money earned from her jobs helped pay for the basics needs of her family. The young girl's sacrifice was noteworthy, and yet characteristic of people in the struggle to survive, her efforts went unnoticed. Other than fleeting moments of fun with her dog, Tref, eating honey from her father's bee colony, family board games, and dances with her father, Poldie felt robbed of experiencing any enjoyable childhood.

Although assailed with repeated challenges like rejection, hopelessness, hunger, and self-sacrifice, Alois and Poldie made conscious choices to transform their lives. There simply had to be a greater purpose for them.

Alois ultimately began to see fragments of a silver lining pierce through the daunting clouds that seemed to continually surround him. His persistence allowed him to see that every bad situation has an element of good. Once given a chance to prove himself a respectable and responsible driver for the US Army, his tireless determination paved a new course that eventually led to a brighter outcome. Alois resolved to work hard to attain it. Things eventually turned around for the better. Alois learned that his greatest disappointments often turned out to be God's sovereign appointments.

At seventeen, Poldie demonstrated rather unorthodox courage. She intentionally orchestrated plans in chasing a dream for an extraordinary love with Alois. Her audacious spirit sprang into action, allowing a reversal of the status quo and enabling her to reach for a new possibility. Providentially, Poldie's and Alois's paths crossed, and the two would find a love that was destined to last a lifetime. What kind of audacious actions have you intentionally planned to better your life?

As chapter 8 concludes, we see God's provision working in the young newlywed's lives. In every step of their journey, we witness spiritual intervention for a higher purpose. The Lukeshes, a missionary couple, entered the scene, and Alois and Poldie were confronted with new beliefs that would permanently alter their lives and eternal destinies. The newlyweds had no idea that God was drawing them (John 6:44) to Himself and setting them up for a brighter future.

The Bible is replete with truths we can claim while facing any unfamiliar situation. The true Christian understands that there are foes in the unseen world who are working against them. John 10:10 says, "The thief comes only to steal and kill and destroy" (ESV). Imagine if the Christian life is a baseball game. The enemy is on the pitcher's mound preparing to throw. The Christian is up at bat, and John alerts the believer to get in that firm batting stance because the adversary will throw three devastating changeup pitches to get the strikeout. Is it any wonder most humans cannot run the bases of life unhindered with two strikes already against them before even attempting to leave home plate? The remainder of the verse says, "I came that they may have life and have it abundantly." We do not have to experience life alone. Jesus came to give us abundant life regardless of what we are facing. The psalmist reminds us of how we find the truth: "Lead me in your truth and teach me, for you are the God of my salvation; for you I wait all the day long" (Psalm 25:5, ESV).

It took time before Alois and Poldie realized God's purpose for their lives. All along, He was orchestrating something better than what either of them could imagine. God's supernatural provision working in conjunction with human persistence is a win-win situation. Romans 12:12 says, "Rejoice in hope, be patient in tribulation, be constant in prayer" (NIV). While patience may be challenging to employ during the worst of times, the Bible encourages us to pray and rejoice because there is hope. The very God of hope will provide for every need in His appointed time. The apostle Paul reminds us in Romans 15:13, "May the God of hope fill you with all joy and peace in believing, so that by the power of the Holy Spirit you may abound in hope" (ESV).

At times when tears seem to be all you can muster, remember that God promises, "When the righteous cry for help, the LORD hears and delivers them out of all their troubles. The LORD is near to the brokenhearted and saves the crushed in spirit. Many are the afflictions of the righteous, but the LORD delivers him out of them all" (Psalm 34:17-19, ESV).

Alois and Poldie came to understand that every step along their journey was ordered by God. "The steps of a man are established by the LORD, when he delights in his way; though he fall, he shall not be cast headlong, for the LORD upholds his hand" (Psalm 37:23, 24, ESV). God's transformative truths promise to pave the way for every step we take in life.

Think about a Response

1. What rejections have you experienced?
2. How have you responded in times when hopelessness seemed to overwhelm you?
3. Have you adequately responded to rejections in your life, or in the act of self-pity, are you burying them for use at a later time?
4. Do you trust God's Word to provide truths that promise to transform your situation?
5. Can you recollect a time in life when God's divine providence was working on your behalf for a higher purpose?

WEEK THREE

◆

Challenges to Confront and Conquer

- Contemplating biblical truth
- Unfamiliar beliefs
- Encountering unfamiliar territory

Transformative Truths to Trust In

- Hope
- Regeneration
- Mentorship
    Chapters: 9, 10, 11, and 12
    Total pages to read: 67

Alois and Poldie began a new life together. Perseverance had led them through incredible hardships, and their newfound love had bound them together for a hopeful future. With two children and everything set for the much-anticipated travel to a whole new world—the United States of America—the young family prepared for the journey. However, an unexpected interruption left Alois and Poldie searching deep within for answers to troubling eternal questions.

An unsuspecting yet very intentional elderly couple appeared at their doorstep, seeming to proselytize Alois. They conveyed a message containing information neither Alois nor Poldie had ever heard of—the Good News of the Gospel. Alois resisted. Loyalty to the only belief system he had ever known challenged his willingness to receive this new truth. Was it truly possible for a person to have full assurance of his or her eternal destination because of the price

Jesus paid on the cross to redeem sinners? Alois was not indifferent toward spiritual matters, but his mother's overwhelming influence in religious matters during his upbringing gave him pause. Never encouraged to discern spiritual matters with biblical truth during his adolescence, Alois wrestled with comprehending the missionary's message. The religion he pledged his allegiance to expected submission to its ideas and claims while forbidding personal investigation to seek spiritual truth.

The Lukeshes tenderly shared the love of Christ rather than attack faith beliefs. Charles and Edna simply opened the Bible and invited Alois and Poldie to read the truth for themselves and make their own decision regarding the free salvation in Jesus Christ and their eternal destinations. Together, they weighed the evidence presented from the Bible and ultimately committed their lives to Christ. Alois and Poldie expressed that burdens appeared to lift as they turned to God with trusting faith immediately. Peace released pressure, love replaced bitterness, and hope traded for despair. How utterly unusual that for the first time in their lives, Alois and Poldie felt they were given a gift they did not have to work long and hard for; it was free by merely asking. This was a concept that defied everything else they had come to achieve in life.

Alois looked to God often as he faced difficult challenges early in life. In his heart, he genuinely searched for meaning and truth but was never able to find it. The missing person was Jesus Christ. God was patient in extending His grace and love to Alois and Poldie. "The Lord is not slow to fulfill his promise as some count slowness, but is patient toward you, not wishing that any should perish, but that all should reach repentance" (2 Peter 3:9, ESV). Soon after Poldie and Alois trusted Christ for salvation, their decisions began to evidence in transformed lives. In 2 Corinthians 5:17, we read, "Therefore, if anyone is in Christ, he is a new creation. The old has passed away; behold, the new has come." Alois and Poldie sensed God working in their lives to create the new people He had always intended them to be.

The Lukeshes provided primary biblical teaching and spiritual guidance for Alois and Poldie, which laid the groundwork for a stable foundation. As life guaranteed increasing hardships for the young family, the Lukeshes' input proved indispensable. Alois and Poldie needed this support to navigate the spiritual, emotional, physical, and financial challenges about to confront them. The Lukeshes not only initiated the first steps of basic training for the Hufs; they also prayed and utilized their resources and American contacts to change the trajectory of life for Alois and Poldie.

Alois and Poldie quickly realized that not everyone was so eager to accept God's truth and His gift of salvation. Ephesians 2:8–10 went against the grain of everything their respective families had been previously taught: "For by grace you have been saved through faith, and this is not your own doing; it is the gift of God, not a result of works, so that no one may boast" (ESV). How could it be possible for anyone to attain a gift like eternal life without putting in grueling hours in an attempt to work for it? This was antithetical to any beliefs they had been taught. Believing John 3:16 to be true, Alois and Poldie wanted to present the Gospel whenever possible. The passage says, "For God so loved the world, that he gave his only Son, that whosoever believes in him should not perish but have eternal life" (ESV).

As they pursued their dream of immigrating to the United States, Alois and Poldie ventured out for a new beginning far away from the only homes they knew. Clinging to the truth of God's Word proved the best remedy for any situation. Upon saying a sad good-bye to their families and understanding this could be the last time they saw them, they looked to the Lord to provide that hope.

The Lukeshes offered significant help in other areas that troubled Alois and Poldie. If the sea was rough, they recommended the Huf family do what does not come naturally—eat. As other passengers struggled with seasickness while sailing over turbulent waters on the Atlantic Ocean, Alois, Poldie, and the girls did not experience similar sicknesses. As the crew begged passengers to show up to the diner, the Hufs were the only regulars at each meal. Alois and Poldie took to heart the apostle Paul's words in Philippians 4:6–7: "Do not be anxious about anything, but in everything by prayer and supplication with thanksgiving, let your requests be made known to God. And the peace of God, which surpasses all understanding, will guard your hearts and your minds in Christ Jesus" (ESV).

It was vital for them, now more than ever, to lean heavily on the promises of God to guide them. Any harmful or negative thinking could compromise their beliefs for a brighter future. Again, Paul's thoughts were put to the test once the couple arrived in what appeared to be another war-torn city. The community of Hudsonville, Michigan, had just witnessed the most destructive tornado in history for that area, which caused massive fatalities. Alois and Poldie were baffled and unsettled. They had to think good thoughts. Paul said, "Whatever is true, whatever is honorable, whatever is just, whatever is pure, whatever is lovely, whatever is commendable, if there is any excellence, if there is anything worthy of praise, think about these things" (Philippians 4:8, ESV). This truth comforted the young family through many unfamiliar and unsettling situations.

Think about a Response

1. Was it difficult for you to accept the truth and respond to the Gospel when first presented to you?
2. Why is God's Word so important to your spiritual growth?
3. Do you have family members who have rejected true salvation? How have you responded?
4. Were you privileged to have a spiritual mentor? If so, when what was the most significant contribution he or she instilled in you that helped lay a stable foundation?
5. Have you taken on the challenge of mentoring someone spiritually?
6. How have you responded to unsettling environments and unfamiliar territory in your life?

Week Four

Challenges to Confront and Conquer

- Adapting to change
- Discrimination
- Bias
- Unfairness

Transformative Truths to Trust In

- Character
- Integrity
- Honesty
- Steadfastness

Chapters: 13, 14, and 15
Total pages to read: 44

A new environment necessitates flexibility in order to adapt. Making changes in any situation can be difficult, but can you imagine the bending, twisting, and pivoting required by Alois and Poldie as they attempted to fit in with a new culture and community? Life in Michigan proved very dissimilar from European living. From the moment the young family stepped off the train, vicissitudes surrounded them. The shaking of the multicolored Jell-O dessert offered at their first meal was one thing, but terrifying tornados and the fatalities were something else. As the Hufs settled in their new rental home, adjusting to the enormous interior space was overwhelming compared to their one-room dwelling in Germany. Once free from the fear of believing that train robbers and looters lived in the attic, Alois and Poldie relished in restful sleep. Unlike the markets in war-torn Europe, the grocery store in Michigan, with its vast array of items, was filled with plenty. However, Alois and Poldie were offended when the store owner inflated their shopping receipt with a strange thing they did not purchase. It was called "taxes." Alois and Poldie did not care to have any of these taxes and returned directly to the store to alert them of their error.

Many of the adjustments the Hufs came to accept were initially comical. Still, as they began to establish themselves, tensions with suspicious and envious neighbors along with workplace biases would put their characters to the test.

Discrimination rears its ugly head in many forms. Whether bias, racism, misogyny, injustice, or xenophobia, each is a striking example of prejudice. In the workplace, Alois faced multiple instances when employers and employees mistreated him. Mostly jealousy and unfounded insecurity toward the new foreign neighbors were the basis; however, Alois and Poldie committed, in spite of the hurt, that they would respond with honorable character.

Hebrews 1:3, talking about Jesus, says, "He is the radiance of the glory of God and the exact imprint of His nature, and He upholds the universe by the word of His power" (NIV). In Greek, the word *charakter* is used, which is where we get the English word *character*. The greater meaning in this text is an "engraved marking" and implies to inscribe upon or engrave like on a coin. The idea behind this imagery is that the appearance engraved upon the coin represents the exact replica of someone or something. In other words, Jesus is the exact replica or imprint of His Father, God. So the believer in God is called to replicate Christ in all his actions. Taking it a step further, the apostle Paul says in Ephesians 5:1–2, "Therefore be imitators of God as dear children. And walk in love, as Christ also has loved us and given Himself for us, an offering and a sacrifice to God for a sweet-smelling aroma." The word *followers* in this text means to copy, mimic, or imitate Christ in all His attributes and character. Do you get the idea that character is "engraved" in us as children of God? We can choose to respond like Jesus or in vengeance. Each prejudiced remark or action Alois and Poldie faced was an opportunity for them to choose the right character in spite of their broken hearts.

When Alois was confronted with compromising his honor and integrity as a meat inspector, it provided another opportunity to stand firm and demonstrate truth and honesty to his disingenuous employer. The Bible is replete with encouragement for those who keep integrity as the high goal of their life. Proverbs 11:3 states, "The integrity of the upright guides them, but the unfaithful are destroyed by their duplicity" (NIV). Are you able to respond with integrity regardless of the wrongs committed against you? The Lord seeks a blameless heart in every believer. In Proverbs 28:6, we see the advantages of unblemished character: "Better the poor whose walk is blameless than the rich whose ways are perverse" (NIV). Alois and Poldie's overall character simply involved truth-telling and honesty in all they set out to accomplish. A clear conscience facilitates healthy, emotional living. Peter reminds us of the importance of "keeping a clear conscience, so that those who speak maliciously against your good behavior in Christ may be ashamed of their slander" (1 Peter 3:16, NIV). Being honest in every situation is keeping a clear conscience. Dishonesty, underhandedness, and a duplicitous nature kill a good character. The follower of Christ should never be questioned about truth-telling.

Sometimes we will be confronted with taking action in standing for truth, even if it impacts the security of our job, a promotion, or a treasured relationship. There may also be occasions when God invites you to stand against powerful individuals who utilize their influence or position in an attempt to malign or destroy you. It is during these times when resting in the promises and providence of God proves beneficial. Be willing to wait, like Alois, for a good outcome and in God's timing. As he came to understand during various confrontations, mutual concessions and compromises are not necessarily incongruent with integrity and good character. Alois took comfort in knowing that his stand for the truth was essential and provided the way for a joint concession without compromising his integrity.

Think about a Response

1. What sort of adjustments do you remember making as you confronted any new environment or life change?
2. Can you recall a time in your life when someone demonstrated unfounded bias or discrimination toward you?
3. What was your immediate response to the unfairness or injustice?
4. Did you rely on God to master your response and do the right thing?

WEEK FIVE

◆

Challenges to Confront and Conquer

- Hardships
- Trauma
- Death

Transformative Truths to Trust In

- Responsibility
- Trust
    Chapters: 16, 17, and 18
    Total pages to read: 50

The 1982 American musical film *Annie* is a beloved comedy-drama based on the *Little Orphan Annie* comic strip. The movie highlights an orphan, Annie, who finds herself aggressively struggling to tolerate life at a New York City orphanage during the Great Depression in 1933. The film's storyline is packed with fun, fear, loneliness, adventure, and inspiring music. The soundtrack contains many favorites, including "It's a Hard Knock Life." The lyrics for that song state, "Don't it seem like there's never any light? / Once a day, don't you wanna throw the towel in? / It's easier than puttin' up a fight."

Think about your overall life and the instances when challenges you faced were tough to tolerate and seemed, at times, too much to bear. Did you find yourself wanting to throw in the towel and give up the fight? You are not alone. Alois and Poldie overcame many "hard knocks" in life and again entered a significant period of hardship while choosing to trust and believe.

Remarkably, after only three and a half short years of living in the US, Alois and Poldie transitioned surprisingly well in their new surroundings. Poldie was a first-time driver and owned her own car. She and the children learned English while adapting to life and moving to their new twenty-five-acre farm. Alois creatively initiated a plan to save for a deposit on the ideal property for his family by selling the family's piglets. It was an opportunity to see their dream of owning a modest home with acreage for future family businesses to become a reality. Alois and Poldie had to work long, hard hours and sacrifice many family needs in an attempt to reach their goal.

With the recent move and Poldie about to deliver the couple's fifth baby, life seemed complete, but not devoid of challenges. In the blink of an eye, hardships began. Alois was laid off, and jobs, no matter his persistent effort to secure any, were unobtainable. The slight savings Alois and Poldie amassed began to disappear, and the young family faced uncertain times. The kitchen cupboards barely contained enough food for their family of six for two more days.

Alois found himself at the unemployment office, desperate for any work to provide for his family. The responsibility weighed heavily on him to seek out and initiate any possible position. He was given temporary assistance and resorted to picking strawberries for a local farmer. Times were bleak, and the Hufs wrestled to trust the promises of God wholly.

Things began to look up when Alois was called back to work, but the job was only temporary, and again, he struck out in search of employment. Adding to the couple's hardship, their newborn daughter fell extremely ill with pneumonia and was admitted to the hospital. At the end of the infant's ten-day stay, with no employment, savings, groceries, or medical insurance, the Hufs were at their lowest. Seated in the welfare office, Alois and Poldie humbly appealed for money to pay the hospital bill, allowing their baby daughter's release. Upon arriving home, their phone lines were cut because of nonpayment. The knocks intensified as Alois contracted pleurisy, necessitating a week's stay in the hospital. The probability of him losing the new job—which guaranteed him more money than he had ever earned as well as medical insurance for the family—because of his illness was inevitable. Alone at home with their children, Poldie anguished. There had to be a solution. Respectfully and facing humiliation, she drove to the factory where Alois had a job waiting and pleaded with the leadership to have mercy on their family and secure his position. They understood the predicament but offered no promise. All of the Hufs' provisions, in a matter of days, were gone. Desperation continued, and it hovered over their household. When released from the hospital, Alois stooped to cleaning barns for a meager wage to feed the family.

The Hufs appealed to God for His provision and care. He sent compassionate friends from church who benevolently offered assistance. The struggles intensified as Poldie faced surgery to remove a large lump in her breast. Alois and Poldie worried that she may have cancer and struggled with the what-ifs in their future. Five children were in her care at home, and they sorely needed their mother. The hurting couple prayed, "God, do You see us? Are You turning Your back on us and not able to hear our pleas for help?" Alois and Poldie wept before God and asked, "How much more can we handle, God?"

Initially, their prayers for mercy and help seemed to go unanswered, but even so, the Hufs held tightly to the assurance, through scripture, of God's provision. Trust in God had to be unwavering. Proverbs 3:5-6 says to "trust in the LORD with all your heart, and lean not on your own understanding; in all your ways acknowledge Him, and He will direct your paths." Alois's and Poldie's hearts were heavy from the hurt and pain of unanticipated hardships. With the uncertainty of their future, they understood that looking to God and trusting Him during each bleak situation must take incredible faith. True reliance on and trust in God alone would see them through these difficulties.

The couple learned they could not realize change on their own merit. John 15:5 says, "I am the vine; you are the branches. Whoever abides in me and I in him, he it is that bears much fruit, for apart from Me you can do nothing" (NIV). The world's approach to success emboldens people to rely on themselves and strong people in their sphere of influence who can intervene and help bring about change. While this may be good advice, there are no guarantees. The best counsel comes from the Bible, offered by John in the previous passage. The believer's source is always Jesus. When He is not consulted, the follower of Christ can accomplish nothing of lasting value. Jesus provides everything we need in both good and hard times. Trusting God means accepting that He knows what is best, even if the outcome is not what we desire or when help arrives in His timing and not ours.

Alois and Poldie had every right to give up, but they kept their focus on God. In spite of incredible hardships, they demonstrated responsibility, and it paid off. God sees our efforts in working together with Him for a change. He observes when we are responsible and do all within our own strength to set ourselves up for His favor. Hebrews 11:6 reminds us, "And without faith it is impossible to please Him, for whoever would draw near to God must believe that He exists and that He rewards those who seek Him" (NIV). Yes, we can believe the Word of God to be true and faith will reap the rewards. Psalm 18:30 says, "This God—His way is perfect; the word of the LORD proves true; He is a shield for all those who take refuge in Him" (ESV). Are you waiting for God to act on your behalf? Psalm 37:5 says, "Commit your way to the LORD: trust in Him, and He will act" (ESV). Turn your trust toward the One who will never forsake you. Psalm 9:9–10 declares (ESV), "The LORD is a stronghold for the oppressed, a stronghold in times of trouble. And those who know Your name put their trust in You, for You, O LORD, have not forsaken those who seek You." How beautiful to fully understand that God is a refuge—a sanctuary, retreat, or haven. Run to Him. Seek rest and renewal in His presence.

The brief moments of reprieve for Alois and Poldie were heaven-sent amid the excitement of the Hufs' achievement of citizenship in the United States and the joy of the arrival of their youngest child. These blessings were short-lived, as within a space of four months, Poldie and Alois suffered the sudden deaths of two family members as well as a beloved friend. Poldie's father died unexpectedly after complications from surgery. The missionary who shared the Gospel with them, Mr. Lukesh, passed, and tragically, Poldie's twenty-three-year-old brother was murdered. The burden appeared too much to bear for Poldie, the thirty-one-year-old wife and mother of six children. The shock and trauma she experienced when suddenly losing family who she and Alois anticipated welcoming to America and building a new life with was crushing.

Poldie struggled with the uncertainty of her father and brother's eternal destinations. Not knowing if they had placed their faith in Christ and committed their lives to Jesus before their passing was heartbreaking. This single burden recurrently troubled the Hufs. Can you relate to Poldie's distress over unbelieving family members? Only God knows the heart, and we are instructed not to judge, but this does not negate the command to share the Gospel to compel family and friends to receive Christ.

Alois and Poldie understood the importance of pushing through quickly and moving forward from difficult times. Allowing any ongoing self-pity or defeatism in their home would make matters worse. They needed to rise above the fog that temporarily hung over them in order to gain a greater vision of what was to come. The Hufs learned that every hardship, challenge, and concern was an opportunity to go deeper with God. Will you allow for trying times in your own life to be occasions when you search for the greater spiritual meaning and understand in your own life?

Think about a Response

1. How have you handled the hard knocks in your life?
2. Is it easier for you to trust God for slight stresses and inconveniences rather than significant life traumas in your life?
3. Do you see yourself as a responsible person working with God to develop plans for a better outcome?

4. If you mourn the death of someone you dearly loved, how are you coping?

5. Have you memorized critical Bible passages to utilize when praying and asking God for His intervention during tough times?

WEEK SIX

Challenges to Confront and Conquer

- Risk
- Uncertainty
- Anxiety about illness

Transformative Truths to Trust In

- Faith
- Leadership
- Self-discipline
- Entrepreneurship
- Personal witness
- Generations Strong foundation
    Chapters: 19, 20, 21, and 22
    Total pages to read: 64

Life was good for Alois and Poldie. The Lord was faithful in providing. Emerging from the meager and uncertain beginnings they withstood in Europe, their modest but thriving lifestyle in Michigan appeared to rival the American Dream. The family had come so far by faith. God graciously led them through many challenging circumstances. Alois and Poldie's faith was continually tested, but they regarded each life interruption and uncertainty as an opportunity to draw closer to the Lord they had come to trust.

Within Alois's DNA was a relentless leadership drive to reach new levels of security and stability for his family. Discontent to settle or rest on his laurels, Alois chased new dreams and undertook risky ventures. Skeptical, Poldie relied on her God-given discernment to help guide Alois when making significant decisions. She was more cautious, fearing the possibility of loss and harm to their family. Content with what they had achieved, she asked, why risk it all now? However, Alois could not shake certain burnings in his heart.

One ever-present longing was the desire to see his siblings after eighteen long years of separation. Traveling beyond the border into his former homeland, communist Czechoslovakia would be the most considerable risk he ever attempted, even more dangerous than escaping almost two decades earlier. Was this gamble worth the price of potential imprisonment and the possibility of losing everything? This weighed heavily on Poldie's heart. She and three of their younger children made the precarious first journey with Alois, hoping to travel with God's presence going ahead of them.

The Hufs understood, from scripture, that there is a season for everything in life, as conveyed in Ecclesiastes 3:1–8. Alois felt confident that this was the time to cross over into dangerous territory to reconnect with family. He took to heart the biblical passage in Exodus 33:1–15, where God, for understandable reasons, initially withdraws His presence as His children make plans to cross over the border. They would need to go it alone. Thankfully, Moses mediates on their behalf when God promises, "My Presence will go with you, and I will give you rest" (14).

Can you remember a time in your life when you took an enormous risk to see a better end? Alois and Poldie believed God for the promise of His presence while heading into adversarial terrain. Alois and Poldie echoed Moses's plea when praying, "If Your Presence does not go with us, do not bring us up from here. For how then will it be known that Your people and I have found grace in Your sight, except You go with us?" (15). Fearful but hopeful, Alois encouraged Poldie to see the grace of God unfold as He went ahead of them.

Poldie and the children waited for hours while communist officials interrogated Alois. She worried about the uncertainty of her husband's safety and future in secret, not wanting the children to fret. Imagine her anxiety. Place yourself in the vehicle with Poldie and the young girls. Can you picture their fear, stress, doubt, and anxiety extant as they waited for God to return Alois to them unharmed? As their prayers continued, Alois finally emerged. The grace of God is displayed in unending ways as they were finally allowed to enter the communist country without detainment. A happy reunion ensued, and the two-week visit ended as good-byes were said. Try to envision leaving your loved ones behind to face the oppression and poverty of a totalitarian system of hopelessness. What sacrifices would you make to see their lives changed financially and spiritually?

Once Poldie and Alois arrived back in the United States, Alois was compelled to launch a new business venture, this time in Germany. The move allowed them time to personally share Christ with their families while also building a new company. Poldie was on board with the plan but struggled to leave the country and home she had come to love. They were on a spiritual mission to see family members experience the Gospel message, and little would detour them. Can you imagine risking everything you painstakingly built and leaving the comfort of an established lifestyle to make significant sacrifices on behalf of others less fortunate than you?

With their possessions sold at the slam of the auctioneer's gavel and their brand-new home on the market, the Hufs were Europe bound. For the Hufs, the flight overseas was a mix of physical fatigue and emotional unrest, and they contemplated whether or not they made the right decision to move. Poldie trusted Alois to do right by their family but proceeded carefully as their stay in Germany commenced. She knew readjusting to European culture would add a new dimension for the entire family.

The sixteen months in Europe had its benefits and proved to be an incredible experience for the entire family. Within six weeks, the kids were engaging with the neighborhood children and learning the German language. Alois took the time to build the business while Poldie worked forty hours a week and socialized whenever possible with her European family. Alois planned for several family members to cross from Czechoslovakia over the border into Germany for lengthy stays. His father especially enjoyed the visits and accompanied Alois on many business trips driving throughout Germany. God had indeed given Alois time to reconnect with his father after years of absence. It was satisfying to visualize multiple generations making connections and to witness God's gracious hand in unsuspecting ways.

During the first summer in Europe, Alois and Poldie gathered the children in the Microbus and again headed across the border into Russian-occupied Czechoslovakia. Alois understood that he put the family's safety in jeopardy each time they traversed to see family, but he depended upon God's continual presence. Poldie approached the visits cautiously, realizing the children had the most to lose if their father was apprehended and sent to prison for escaping years earlier. The trip was fun and uneventful until the echoes of bombings boomed in the distance. Alois and his family returned to Germany. They later realized that the five countries representing the Warsaw Pact had invaded Czechoslovakia the day after they crossed back over into Germany.

The business continued to grow as Alois's entrepreneurial approach and the ability to act quickly on opportunities paid off. His notion of efficiently connecting with people and discerning situational awareness allowed him to sell the company. Utilizing his practical negotiating skills, Alois sealed the deal, and the Hufs headed back to America.

Once settled back in the US, plenty of prospects surfaced for Alois and Poldie to grow the new business while the children engaged in typical teenage life. Then seemingly in a split second, dating, courtships, engagements, and marriages became a part of the next season of life for the Hufs. A bittersweet time followed as one strong wartime generation passed and Alois and Poldie witnessed the rising of a new generation through their children and grandchildren. The Hufs were now at a turning point in life as they embarked on retirement while also focused on being present for their grandchildren. Alois and Poldie claimed the scripture 3 John 1:4: "I have no greater joy than to hear that my children walk in truth."

As if the Hufs had not encountered more than their share of hardships, the retirement years proved a mix of joy and anxious uncertainty. At sixty-eight years of age, Alois faced the ultimate test of his faith—a brain tumor. Many who have tasted a teaspoon of trials compared to Alois's cupful might be tempted to confront God and ask, "Really, God?" Yet the tumor and the anxiety it caused allowed Alois to demonstrate how radical faith and trust in God can do the impossible. While awaiting surgery to remove the golf-ball-sized tumor, Alois bespoke the Lord. A time of refining and heart cleansing prompted him to right any wrongs or possible misperceptions by family. It was a time to redress possible wrongs. Compassion and forgiveness followed, and the family showed a strong, confident, and united front walking with Alois through the monumental battle and uncertain outcome.

Alois rested in the peace of God. Jesus said, "Peace I leave with you; my peace I give to you. Not as the world gives do I give to you. Let not your hearts be troubled, neither let them be afraid" (John 14:27). Anxiety would not thwart God's promise. Through the many toils and trials Alois endured, he was assured that God's love and care for him were ever-present. In 1 Peter 5:7, we read, "Casting all your anxieties on Him, because He cares for you" (ESV). As Alois continued to trust the Lord for special grace and mercy, the prayers and encouragement from friends and family were significant. Proverbs 12:25 says, "Anxiety in a man's heart weighs him down, but a good word makes him glad" (ESV). Alois treasured every inspiring word spoken in faith for a good outcome and realized that day was a gift.

With the health issue behind him, Alois wanted to make good on his promise to God for service in His work. Alois prayed and considered prospects. When an opportunity presented itself for ministry to inmates in the local jail, Alois's interest peaked. Some believe God has a sense of humor in responding to His children. Alois realized that the imprisoned life he sought desperately to leave behind to gain freedom was, in later years, his opportunity to find common ground with the inmates. Commissioned as a minister, Alois shared Christ with those who were imprisoned and bound where freedom was lost. Only a creative and compassionate God could mix the one set free with the one bound for His higher purpose. In scripture, Jesus used human commonality in John chapter 4. The Bible states that Jesus needed to go through Samaria. The reason is that He intentionally intersected with a Samaritan woman who needed the Gospel message. And how was the message delivered? Jesus reached out through a mutual need for water to gain an entrance into her heart. Jesus asks, "Give Me a drink" (John 4:7). The conversation starts with water from the well because He is thirsty and transitions to living water. Jesus promises, "Everyone who drinks of this water will be thirsty again, but whoever drinks of the water that I will give him will never be thirsty again. The water that I give him will become in him a spring of water welling up to eternal life" (John 4:13, 14, ESV). How satisfied the servant of God is when he or she transparently shares the hurt and heartaches of his or her journey to find common ground in sharing Christ.

As Poldie and Alois navigate the inevitable bumps resulting from the aging process, their joy in witnessing and knowing that the subsequent generations of their offspring have chosen to follow God is unending. The Hufs cherish multiple Bible passages that speak to God's faithfulness from generation to generation. Psalm 145:4 says, "One generation shall commend your works to another, and shall declare your mighty acts" (ESV). Psalm 100:5 states, "For the LORD is good; His steadfast love endures forever, and His faithfulness to all generations" (ESV). When reflecting on their lives, Alois and Poldie realize that God's favor is connected to obedience. Genesis 22:18 says, "And in your offspring shall all the nations of the earth be blessed, because you have obeyed my voice" (ESV). The strength of character within generations is passed on from the one(s) who fear God and seek His truth. "And His mercy is for those who fear Him from generation to generation" (Luke 1:50, ESV).

Think about a Response

1. When taking inventory of your life, prompted by the Lord, have you risked certain things for a better outcome?
2. On a scale of one to ten, with ten being the highest, how would you rate your current faith amid uncertainty?
3. What do you perceive to be the best option at your attempt to navigate health issues or an uncertain future?
4. Regardless of your age, are you setting up healthy habits and spiritual disciplines to model for the upcoming generations within your family?

ABOUT THE AUTHOR

Cristie Jo Huf Johnston is a popular speaker, author, and content creator of *This Is Christian Strong*™, a multilayer, global endeavor that includes a transmedia experience across multiple traditional and digital platforms through drama and docuseries as well as trade, scholarly, educational, and children's books. She is passionate about entertaining, engaging, and educating children through her five-part picture book series Lil Cristie Chronicles™. The set includes true tales of Cristie Jo's childhood experiences, featuring herself as Teetee along with her puppy, Tref. Together they introduce children to curious and charming stories: life on the farm, living with immigrant parents, a rich family history, international travel, educational and emotive journeys behind the communist border to visit cousins, adjusting to foreign customs while living abroad as a child, responding to bullying, finding a special place among siblings, and God and faith. The chronicles introduce children to strong values and help them learn valuable lessons, experience God, and personalize their faith. Cristie Jo has a doctorate in ministry from Acadia University-Acadia Divinity College, Nova Scotia, Canada, and a master of divinity degree from Midwestern Theological Seminary. She lives in Houston, Texas, with her husband, Jerry, and they have three married children and nine grandchildren.

Connect with Cristie Jo!

Connect with Cristie Jo to learn about future books, projects, speaking schedules, blogs, and podcasts **@CristieJoJohnston.com**.

f CristieJoJohnston　　**◻** cristiejohnston　　**▶** @CristieJoJohn

Like book 1 of the nonfiction trilogy
GENERATIONS STRONG?
Books 2 and 3 are coming soon!

SHARE ON SOCIAL MEDIA PLATFORMS: Use the hashtags #EscapeToFreedom #GenerationsStrongBook1.

 Share on FACEBOOK: "Must Read #EscapeToFreedom #GenerationsStrongBook1 by @cristiejojohnston"

 Tweet on TWITTER: "Must Read #EscapeToFreedom #GenerationsStrongBook1 by @CristieJoJohn"

 Share on INSTAGRAM: "Must Read #EscapeToFreedom #GenerationsStrongBook1 by @CristieJohnston"

- Write a book review on Amazon.com or on your blog.

- Go to Amazon.com and deliver a copy to friends and family or someone who might be impacted by our story.

- Utilize the six small group studies in the back of this book as a curriculum for your book club, bible study, or small group.

- Follow Cristie Jo Johnston on all social media platforms (listed above) and spread the word about *Escape to Freedom*, book 1 of the Generations Strong trilogy.

Coming Soon!
Books 2 and 3

If you love *ESCAPE TO FREEDOM*, book 1
of our family's **Generations Strong**
trilogy, the story continues.
Look for upcoming announcements
for the release of books 2 and 3 via
our social media platforms.